"The

normal school

was,

from the beginning,

a

peoples college."

striving

The title "Striving" was inspired by the sculpture entitled "Reaching"
by David Lee Brown which stands in front of the Wallace E. Mason
Library on the Keene State campus.

striving

KEENE STATE COLLEGE 1909/ 1984

the history of a small public institution

by
James G. Smart

PHOENIX PUBLISHING
Canaan, New Hampshire

PERMISSIONS

The extract on page 148 from "In Such an Age" which appeared in
The Hour Has Struck by Angela Morgan, was published by Dodd,
Mead & Company, Inc. and is reproduced with the kind permis-
sion of the publisher.

The cartoon on page 24, "Do the Slope People Want a Normal
School?" which originally appeared in *The Leader* is reprinted with
permission from Osbourne T. Belsheim's *The Story of Dickinson
State: A History of Dickinson State College 1918-1968*, published
by Dickinson State College in 1968.

Smart, James G., 1929-
   Striving: Keene State College, 1909-1984.

   Bibliography: p. 317.
   Includes Index.
   1. Keene State College — History — 20th century. I. Title.
LD2750.K44S63   1984   378.742'9   84-5906
ISBN 0-914659-04-9

Printed in the United States of America
by Courier Printing Company
Binding by New Hampshire Bindery
Design by A. L. Morris

This book

is dedicated to all those people

who have endeavored to make the College

a meaningful experience

for its students

Editorial Committee

Dr. Richard A. Gustafson
Vice President: Academic Affairs, Keene State College

Dr. Wilfred J. Bisson
Associate Professor of History, Keene State College

David R. Leinster
Assistant Professor of History, Keene State College

Clair Wyman, '39
Educator and Businessman

Dr. Jacqueline A. Abbott, '58
Professor of Education, Eastern Connecticut State University

Ernest Hebert, '69
Author and Journalist, Keene, New Hampshire

CONTENTS

ACKNOWLEDGMENTS

Many people and two organizations, the Alumni Association and Keene State College, helped get this history into print. Etta Merrill, class of 1925, and Marion T. Wood, class of 1926, promoted and supported the idea throughout the decade of the 1970s. They and some of their classmates and friends were among the most committed to the idea of a written history for the college's 75th anniversary. Wood originally agreed to write a chapter on the activities of the Alumni Association, but one chapter soon turned into three, and those three chapters are now Part IV of this book! Many thanks to her for the work and information she provided.

A history is not an encyclopedia; it cannot tell everything. It must confine itself to only meaningful and demonstrative stories. By its very nature it is exclusive and denies recognition of many events and activities of many committed individuals. In an effort to maintain some sort of justice to committed individuals who received either insufficient or no attention in the text, one writes, "acknowledgments."

Even acknowledgments work some injustice, particularly when written by a forgetful professor. Nonetheless, some names do stick in his memory as especially deserving recognition. Those who most readily come to mind are Fred L. Barry, dean and director of the Alumni Association; his successor, Donald Carle, who assisted in innumerable ways in the book's development; Trustee Margaret Ramsay, class of 1956, Representative to the New Hampshire General Court, Alumni Association president and friend of President Redfern; Eleanor Betz, registrar, and her successor in that post, David Porter; Newell J. Paire, class of 1936, Commissioner of Education and Alumni Association board member; Richard and

Jeanne Clason and Carlton E. Brett, class of 1933; Dr. and Mrs. Gilbert LeVine Mellion of the Parents Association; Arthur Giovannangeli, class of 1937 and Professor of Science; former Professors Frank Tisdale and Dorothy Kingsbury and current Professors Harold Nugent and Fred Fosher, who helped the project along through many informal chats. Claire Smith, Director of Financial Aid; Lydia Pellerin Tolman, Phyllis Hall Curtiss, Carol Jeffery, Charles Eaton and Paul Davidson were encouraging supporters, as were David Proper and many members of the Cheshire County Historical Society. Lillian O'Reilly and Reba Filiault of Student Services were patient and understanding with the author's inability to remember account numbers and accounting procedures. Many other people should be recognized but either space limitations or lapses of the human memory preclude their mention. The author asks indulgence for all oversights. He realizes that not only many people but also many stories still need to be recorded as do the activities of many disciplines and organizations which attained noteworthy achievement. While aware of the injustices of selectivity, the author was still unable to accomplish all that even he had hoped. He simply ran out of time. Assuredly no intentional oversight to people, events, or to entire programs was intended.

The Alumni Boards since 1980, when the proposal was first made to them, have given full support. Each year the Alumni Board has granted money for research expenses and has wished the project Godspeed. Without this hearty encouragement, the work would never have gotten beyond the planning stage. Alumni in general have taken time from their reunions to give interviews, answer querries, and make suggestions. In many ways this is literally their book. Certainly they have contributed substantively to it and to a larger extent than other institutional histories; and they should, therefore, have propriety rights to it.

Leo Redfern was always supportive. Between the time of the original proposal in 1975 which called for work during the author's free time only and the time of final agreement, September 8, 1978, several valuable summers had gone by. Acting President William E. Whybrew (1979-80) then agreed to new terms proposed by the author by which he taught only two classes (1980-83) to provide time for research and writing. It was also agreed that he maintain an average of 40 students in each class and work full-time during the summers on the project. Thus a happy arrangement was made whereby the author had time for his work and yet need not feel to be under any obligation for special privileges from his sponsor in as much as he maintained the college's student faculty ratio of 20-1 for four classes, the average full-time load.

Vice President Richard A. Gustafson has aided the project in many ways. He has provided information, extra student assistance when needed, and additional writing time in 1983 when it was required. He has insisted on accountability but still allowed the author a free framework in which to operate. Both he and President Barbara J. Seelye have fully honored the provision on academic freedom set forth in the original proposal and have acted as colleagues rather than as monitors in the book's development. Richard E. Cunningham, Acting Dean of Arts and Humanities, kindly arranged for a course reduction in the Spring of 1984 to give the author time for picture selection, preparation of the index, proof reading, and other details involved in last stages of publication. Robert L. Mallat Jr. gave the book a most needful assist in its crucial last stages of development.

Many students have been involved in this project. Nancy Ericsson, Stacey Milbouer, Colgate Gilbert, and especially Crista Price helped during the 1970s in gathering background information and in conducting good oral interviews. Students and former students should also be mentioned who gave valuable aid: Mary Mason, Rinske Hayes, Tom Sidebotham, Randall Gates, Lynn Duffy, Dawn Fuller, and especially Leslie VanAlstyne and Christine L. Hobart, both of whom were particularly valuable research assistants. Terrilee Mongeon, James White, Laura Hall, and Abigail Atwood deserve recognition for preparing most of the index.

The whole library staff but particularly Christopher Z. Barnes, the former librarian and Edwart Scott the present librarian, Clifford Mead, curator of the Preston Room, Robert Madden, Christopher Pratt, Margarett A. Barrett, and Madelaine Sica have all bent a few rules on room use, the lending of materials, and the use of the xerox machine which has inconvenienced them but helped to expedite the project.

Giving valuable help in picture selection were Hope McMahon, John Greene, Medora Hebert, John E. Mullin, Dean Hartwell and Al Morris of Phoenix Publishing. On the text itself the whole editorial committee, Leo Redfern, and Adrian A. Paradis of Phoenix gave thoughtful analysis to the text and valuable advice. Frank Kirk as copy editor made special exertions to reduce grammatical errors and stylistic inconsistencies. The editorial committee's role was advisory only, but certainly most helpful. Had there only been time to carry through on all suggestions!

Two people were particularly helpful in supplying information on Henry Clinton Morrison. One was his son, John A. Morrison, who provided written information and valuable memories. The other was Dr. Richard A. Martin of New England College who lent materials he had collected on Morrison.

College is similar to family, but an exceedingly complex family, in which many members strive for the good of the whole, but often choose different means to attain that end. Conflicts and differences occur. Family feuds develop. Some good members have left the college convinced that their efforts were not appreciated. They left in disappointment, frustration, and bitterness. They were, however, appreciated more than they knew. Acknowledgment is due to many of them for their noble efforts and kind dispositions.

I wish to acknowledge Mr. Herbert Block of Herblock Cartoons, for permission to use one of his cartoons from *Staight Herblock* (Simon & Schuster, 1964) and Mr. Jonathan Dodd for permission to quote from Angela Morgan's poem, "In Such an Age" from Dodd, Mead and Company's *The Hour Has Struck* (1927).

Recognition is due to Terrilee Mongeon, the secretary who deciphered all my interlineations, returned the chapters rapidly, and kept track of a host of other details.

Lastly, the author's wife, Eleanore Smart, his daughter, Angela, and sons, Michael and Christopher, should be acknowledged for their tolerance and patience in dealing with a husband and father who seemed to have his college family mixed up with his natural family.

J.G.S.

Preface

T HIS is an excellent history of Keene Normal School, Keene Teachers College, and Keene State College. It is the result of a great deal of research and study. It relates many of the situations and actions at the time of the main events in the history of the college.

In addition to describing these events, it discusses the great interest in public education in New Hampshire and some of the actions taken to expand and improve the state's educational programs. In the early 1900s the main concern was to provide more and better education for children attending the elementary schools. This required more and better-prepared teachers. New Hampshire educators and legislators felt that a second normal school was needed to supply these teachers. This led to the establishment of Keene Normal School in 1909. The curriculum was developed to prepare elementary school teachers, grades 1-8.

Within a few years the demand increased for more secondary schools, grades 9-12, which required more qualified teachers for these schools. The normal schools broadened their curricula to prepare teachers in such fields as English, mathematics, the sciences, and some foreign languages. This resulted, in 1939, in changing the normal schools to state teachers colleges.

As more students enrolled in the teachers colleges, some wanted to be qualified to work in other fields than teaching. This led to offering courses in the teachers colleges in fields of general education, industrial education, the arts, and music. This broadening of the scope of the teachers colleges caused them to become state colleges, which allowed students to specialize in some fields other than teaching.

By 1960 almost all colleges and universities offered several fields of specialization. Some students wanted to take courses at different colleges but to transfer such credits to one of the colleges in order to obtain an advanced degree or certificate. This led in 1963 to the consolidation of New Hampshire state colleges as divisions of the New Hampshire University System.

In our democratic form of government the citizens are involved, in various ways , in the operation of the government. Some are elected or appointed state officials or are members of committees. All state citizens have the opportunity to participate in citizenship. This same principle applies to students at state colleges.

As described in this book, faculty and students have become involved in the operation and administration of the colleges. In order to get action, some groups hold rallies or meetings or put on demonstrations. Sometimes these activities are run by minority groups which are not willing to abide by the action of the majority. Continual efforts are being made to stress that the opportunity to participate in government also carries equal responsibility to abide by, and to support, the decisions of the majority.

I am proud to have been a part of Keene State College for many years. Many changes have been made, and will continue to be made, in order for the college to meet the educational needs of New Hampshire and the country.

—Lloyd P. Young
President Emeritus
Keene State College

Dublin, New Hampshire
December 1, 1983

Foreword

EDUCATION for all who desire to learn has been a dream pursued in the United States since its founding to the present. Distortions caused by disparate pressures diverted and thwarted the progress of education for the population but, with the resilience of all well-guarded dreams, after a time of economic or social upheaval, the pursuit of education begins ever again.

In this country we have turned to education for solutions to most of our problems and for encouragement of that which is best in areas such as human services, environmental preservation, rural and urban planning, and the fine and performing arts. We have, on the other hand, been quick to turn away from education when financial appropriations were meagre, solutions not quickly forthcoming, or more exciting possibilities were in vogue. Like the prodigal, however, our concern, as with that of the nation, has eventually returned to that great dream which has motivated, frustrated, captivated and enriched us from our beginnings: the dream of an educated and caring people capable of developing the best which resides in each of us. It was in this context that the small state college has played an important role.

Small state colleges have been overlooked by the major chroniclers of higher education, and their role is generally not recorded in the annals of the development of the post-secondary outreach. Yet all institutions of higher education are dependent upon the graduates of our public schools; and the public schools themselves would be pressed for teachers if the evolution from normal school to state teachers college to state college had not taken place. The warp upon which superior teachers created the patterns of liberal, career, and professional education has been responsible for our creative, conscientious, and dedicated citizens. Many of these same citizens have expanded our knowledge of the universe, discovered cures for centuries-old illnesses, established small and large businesses and industries to stimulate our economy, and developed a food production system that makes us the envy of most of the world. We now place our hopes for an inspiriting future in a new generation of teachers, the majority of whom are still educated at these same state colleges.

In *Striving* Professor Smart has achieved more than a record of the events, philosophies, activities, and people involved in conceptualizing Keene Normal School and those who shaped the institution through its evolution into the liberal arts and sciences-based institution known as Keene State College. He has noted and interpreted the influences of time and the multiple constituencies upon the developing institution and upon those who kept the dream steadfast, though at times shaken. This is the story of those faculty and staff who created and continue to enhance an environment to challenge the mind, explore the questionable, release the spirit, and give life to the "Great Dream." Just as important it is the record of the students who, as alumni, give meaning to the dream in their daily lives; of a community with a continuing interest in and a tradition of aiding education; and finally of the governors and legislators who initiated and continue to believe in and support the state post-secondary schools. The story is, in fact, one of most small state colleges.

Barbara J. Seelye
President
Keene State College

March 1, 1984

Introduction

THIS HISTORY had several origins and has several purposes. As to its origins Leo Redfern, Keene State College president from 1969 to 1979, took the first definite step. Leo, as everyone called him, liked to socialize and believed that much could be accomplished by getting people together over a drink or in a friendly atmosphere. In such situations he heard many interesting stories about the college which he was sure (and he was right) were not written down; he thought that many of these stories ought to be preserved. He asked Howard Wheelock of the Department of History to preserve on tape the memories of alumni and others for a historian of 2009, when Keene State College would mark its one hundredth anniversary.

Wheelock started the KSC Oral History Project. He and several groups of his students interviewed about fifty people closely connected with the college. When Wheelock retired in 1975, Redfern asked if anyone else in the history department wished to continue the project. I was interested — nobody else was — and so I accepted the offer to carry on the work begun by Wheelock. Actually, I had ulterior motives. I was not really interested in oral history. I was interested in a written history for 1984, the seventy-fifth anniversary — not because of any belief in an Orwellian rendezvous the college might have with destiny, but because I thought a history earlier than one in 2009 would be of benefit to the college. In fact, when I first came to Keene in 1966, I thought even then of writing a history for the sixtieth anniversary.

There were alive in the late 1960s — and luckily, there still are — several members of the class of 1911, the first full graduating class. It would be good, I thought, to have a history written while memories of the very first days of the institution could be tapped. Should there be any deficiencies in this history (hard as that may be to imagine), the Keene State College historian of 2009 will nonetheless have a model to build on, rectify, or disassemble. I should add at this point that this is history with a personal flavor, not only because of the oral history sources, but also because the author is part of it and has written it in a personal style. Nonetheless, I have tried to keep myself out of it as much as possible, but no work can (nor should) escape the personality of its author. Whatever criticisms I have made are intended to be constructive and are motivated by a high regard for the truth of the situation. I have been guided by Cromwell's response to his portraitist: "Paint me as I am, warts and all."

As to the purposes of the history, I thought that the college community needed an identifiable past. The college's past, as I believed it to be, was largely forgotten or handed down haphazardly at Alumni reunions. I agreed with Redfern: some of the memories repeated at these occasions gave meaning to the present and ought to be preserved.

I also thought that it would be good for the college community to be more aware of that exciting part of the democratic process which enabled the youth of New Hampshire, usually for the first time in their families' history, to get a college education. I knew it was an exciting part of history — and an ongoing history that is generally overlooked or forgotten.

John Brubacker and Willis Rudy in their grand study, *Higher Education in Transition: A History of American College and Universities, 1636-1968*, sum up that, after 300 years, higher education assumed a variety of forms — the New England hilltop college, the state university, schools of technology, complex municipal colleges or universities, and the community or junior colleges. They forgot to mention the small state colleges, so many of which had their roots in teachers colleges and normal schools. Brickman and Leher, in *A Century of Higher Education*, also forgot to mention them, as did I. L. Kandle in an excellent article in the *American Scholar*.[1] Until fairly recently one simply did not write histories of state colleges. Yet, about 50 percent of all the nations' teachers come from small state colleges, and about 15 percent of all college youth attend this type of institution.

Not much is overlooked, however, in the world of higher education. In 1968 the Carnegie Commission of Higher Education hired E. Alden

Dunham to prepare a work focusing on the nation's state colleges. That work, the only one of its kind, Dunham entitled (appropriately enough) *Colleges of Forgotten Americans.* Thus, I thought it would also be useful to write about some of the "forgotten" Americans in one state college.

What have I learned from this project that may be of value to my colleagues and also fit in with the purpose of the history? I have learned, first of all, that the whole field of the "Colleges of Forgotten Americans," which is primarily that of normal school development, is a tremendously exciting one. Scholarship in this field has been neglected because of the apparent lockstep sameness to it all — 150 institutions marching from normal schools to teachers colleges to state colleges to state universities. The appearance is that of simplicity and uniformity, and there is, of course, some truth in that view. On the other hand, there was tremendous diversity in normal school development which has not been chronicled. While it is much beyond the scope of this book, the few following examples are in order to make a point that is rarely if ever made, in fact, to make a point that is usually denied.

One normal school, for instance, was founded by an ex-slave. Another was the first opportunity for women to get a chance at higher education in a state that was otherwise full of colleges — but for men only. A number were founded by carpetbaggers who were seeking to give both women and blacks a chance at equal opportunity. John Langston, a black congressman of the late nineteenth century, was instrumental in the founding of two normal schools. A number were founded by groups of "dedicated citizens," both black and white. The normal school was, in fact, the first chance at equal opportunity for many forgotten Americans.[2]

Sarah Josepha Hale, one of New Hampshire's most distinguished public citizens, through her magazine, *Godey's Lady's Book*, promoted the idea of teachers being women when most teachers were men. She saw it as an opportunity to improve both the quality of common school education and the lot of women. She rejoiced that Lexington, the first state-supported normal school, was for women only (a tradition it kept up till 1964). Long before the Morrill Act, which established the state agricultural and mechanical colleges and the state universities, Hale petitioned Congress to set aside millions of acres so that at least one normal school could be maintained *in each state* "for the gratuitous education of female teachers." She promoted the idea in her magazine for decades. The idea came to fruition partly, and in only one instance, when in 1893 Congress set aside 100,000 acres of the public domain to establish a state normal school in western Montana.[3]

Most normal schools were created by the state legislature, but there is much interesting variety on that, too. One was created by an act of Congress as a condition of statehood! Another was established by Congress in a territory even before it became a state, and still another by a state constitutional convention![4] States made normal schools out of academies or colleges created for other purposes such as the education of blacks or women, and in one case the education of Indians. Sometimes the purpose was religious, and normal schools grew out of academies started by the Methodist, African Methodist, Congregational, and Disciples of Christ churches. One normal school was a publicly supported institution attached to a privately supported university for black citizens. Many grew out of select private academies and seminaries for whites only.[5]

Some normal schools were attached to high schools; some were united with agricultural, mechanical, or industrial colleges or institutes (sometimes, with all three). Some were united with colleges, some with universities.[6] The most ambitious efforts were the establishment in 1857 of Illinois Normal University and in 1893 of New Mexico Normal University. These few examples, which could be extended still further, suggest both a most varied background and that normal schools had their own unusual and distinctive pasts and cannot be characterized as having had a bland uniform development. Only very recently have a few scholars begun to study this most interesting field.

At this point one might well ask, then, if there is anything distinctive about Keene State College compared with other institutions which had their beginnings as state normal schools and have remained relatively small (under 5,000), that is, those colleges of "forgotten Americans." There are about 200 of these institutions, over 60 of which began as normal schools. I have made a brief study of the historical backgrounds of these institutions. This study is more up to date but also more limited in depth and scope than Dunham's, which was made in 1968. Nonetheless, my investigation indicates that Keene State has, indeed, special distinction both in its founder and in its campus.

Other than those founded by Horace Mann in Massachusetts and Rhode Island College founded by Henry Barnard, no other small state college and one-time normal school can claim (or does claim) a founder of such distinction as Henry Clinton Morrison. As founder Morrison ranks with Charles Hovey of Illinois Normal University and Francis Parker of the Cooke County Normal School. As theorist he ranks with no less a person than John Dewey. Ronald D. Szoke of the University of Illinois wrote in one sketch of Morrison, that he was "one of the very few educational thinkers to set forth a rival systematic theory comparable in scope and power to the Deweyean viewpoint."[7]

It should also be pointed out that founding an institution of higher learning through state auspices can be much more difficult than founding a private college. With his talents Morrison could more easily have become a millionaire and bequeathed a large endowment for a new institution than to move the whole educational and political apparatus of the state for overall education and social reform.

Keene can claim, however, not only a particularly distinguished founder, but also a particularly distinguished campus. Other than Mary Washington College in Viriginia, no other small state college can claim (or does claim) as many historic homes. Three of Keene State's — Elliot Hall, Hale Building, and the President's House — are already on the National Register of Historic Places. Blake House may yet be put on the register. Joslin House and Rhodes Hall are distinctive. Proctor House won the 1875 architectural award for frame construction. It is not unlikely that the college will in time purchase Governor Hale's older house, which is next to the campus.

Keene has also made some noteworthy contributions in education, particularly in the development of the junior high school idea and the whole Morrison curriculum of 1916. On first glance, however, it is the founder himself and the historic homes combined with an attractively laid out campus still beautifully maintained that one finds as being most noteworthy.

Other than learning something about normal schools in general as well as our own in particular, one sees that the liberal arts faculty and the professional faculty at Keene get along, and have gotten along, with each other much better than many of us ever suspected. The debate between the two faculties essentially goes back 2400 years to that between Plato and Sophists, if not further back, to that between priest and businessman on the banks of the Tigris and the Euphrates. It has really raged on other campuses. The debate has been mild on this campus because each faculty generously concedes the value of what the other is doing, and on a personal level there are many close friendships. What difference there are lie primarily in the concept of the role of a state college. The professional faculty often see the role of a college as fulfilling the desires of people of the state, as expressed through the legislature; thus, the professional faculty often talk about fulfilling "mandates," "charges," and "missions." The liberal arts faculty, on the other hand, are suspicious of all legislatures; they are aware of the democratic component in public education but are as dubious about any popular mandates as they are about the "wisdom of the legislature" (a term often used — and often in seriousness). Their models are Plato, the medieval universities, and the German universities of the nineteenth century, all of which taught apart from (or counter to) popular wishes but whose achievements are the glory of the entire world. There is, of course, validity to both views.

The normal school, and later the teachers college, found itself in the middle of the Plato-Sophist debate. In fact, this debate was exacerbated by the development of the normal school. When Horace Mann and his friends first proposed the idea of a normal school, neither existing colleges nor academies wanted to be associated with them. The normal school was, therefore, established, *sui generis*, as a new type of institution, to be devoted solely to pedagogy, that is, the art of teaching. But, as soon as it was established, both the students and the parents of students wanted to learn more than how to teach. They wanted, as Charles Hovey said, "Not only to know how to teach but what to teach and why such a thing is taught in a particular way."[8] As the normal school moved south, it was often united with agricultural, mechanical, and industrial "colleges." There they served often enough as the first college experience for blacks and for women. As they moved west, there was a greater emphasis on content, and they served as "people's colleges."

Professor Jurgen Herbst of the University of Wisconsin, who is currently studying normal school development, has written that in the Midwest the state universities were generally "developed at a central location or state capital, whereas the normal schools were scattered to the small country-towns across the prairie. We should look to them," Herbst writes, "not to the land-grant universities, when we speak of the 'democratization of higher education.' "[9]

Thus, on one hand, the normal school was expected to be a people's college; on the other hand, the very reason for its existence was that it was not a college but a "trade" school. It was often damned if it went one way and damned if it went the other — or damned if it did not go one way or the other fast enough.

These conflicting expectations gave the old Plato-Sophist dispute new vigor and, as far as many faculties were concerned, deeper division. Here at Keene we have moved a good distance from the ancient debate and survived remarkably well the pressures of more recent ones. Further, we have done so with better grace and understanding then many well-known colleges. Hopefully, this history will further aid in definition and understanding of different roles.

I, like Professor Herbst, have found in the normal school something more than generally presumed, namely, a college-type environment and often enough college level inquiry and intellectual excitement. Therefore, I sometimes refer to the normal school as a college. Other terms need to be explained. Students who attended Keene in the early years were often only sixteen years old. They seldom, if ever, referred to themselves as young women but always as girls. Because of modern sensitivity on this point, I often refer to them as young women or as students. Where the text seemed to demand it, however, I used the term "girls," and there should be no pejorative connotation attached to that. If women graduates have been long active in alumni affairs, I refer to them by their married name, by which they are most widely known; otherwise I have used the name by which they were known as students, usually their maiden name.

This study has made me realize how impermanent a segment of higher education we are in. The original purpose of the normal school was clearly defined, but because the normal school was also a "people's college," no one knew where the growth would stop, or when it should stop. The teachers college era turned out to be a very brief one. For many institutions the state college era was equally brief, and they zipped on to being state universities. "Some day we will play in the Rose Bowl," one state college official told Alden Dunham. Don't laugh, student editors Rolly Stoodly and Gordon Bean wrote in 1954, "KTC is on the move! . . . Time will tell, but one can see visions of Keene Teachers College in the future — the greatest in the U.S.A.!"[10] Penn State became larger than the University of Pennsylvania; Michigan State exceeded in size the University of Michigan. Millersville and Slippery Rock, so often cited as representatives of the small state colleges, have stepped well over the 5,000 mark. The bigger the better is standard American fare. Even the community colleges, Dunham claimed, have sharper definition of focus and thus more intellectual and emotional stability than the state colleges. If we here at Keene have had our debates over purposes and programs — as we have and no doubt will continue to have — it is helpful to know under what pressures we have been operating.

One can see in this history the difficult role a small state college must play, trying to be answerable and responsible to its various constituents. It must strive for quality, yet at the same time keep its doors fairly wide open; it must strive to be responsible to parents and legislators, yet make sure that students have their rights; and it must strive to be sensitive to its students and its alumni — ever, it seems, it must be striving to satisfy one constituency or another.

One will be able to see also, I believe, that each administration brought to the college certain characteristics that contributed to its overall development. Hopefully some of these can be remembered and taken advantage of.

There was as much, possibly more, dedication at our college as there was at other fine institutions. Faculty and administrators — janitors and grounds crew people, too — have unselfishly given of their lives to an ideal of service; their pay was meagre, their work load heavy. There were saints even in the public school system. They all deserve to be remembered.

Last, this history ought to be written, for as Redfern said in his last commencement address, "this piece of real estate," has been "made into something special because it has been dedicated to learning and the uplift of the human mind and spirit . . . and because it is where you and I have spent so many golden days."[11]

James G. Smart

January 15, 1984

"I believe Normal Schools to be a new instrumentality in the advancement of the race. I believe that, without them, Free Schools themselves would be shorn of their strength and healing power and would at length become more charity schools, and thus die out in fact and form."

Horace Mann

"I do not see why college graduates, then, or now, would naturally flock into a profession which paid less than a minor clerk in business, and hemmed in by social taboos which prevented an individual from considering his life his own. In other words, I should guess that the normal schools . . . were an inevitable growth in a certain historical situation, and that father's efforts, at Keene and Plymouth, to make the normal schools as good as they could be made, were the best and only course that could be followed."

Hugh Morrison to Richard Martin

"We wanted an education. It was the place that we could afford."

Mariam Roby Carpenter, Class of 1936

"I just loved my days at Keene. The campus was so beautiful."

Mary Perkins Wood, Class of 1931

"The college was a wonderful thing to us."

Randy Gregory, Class of 1942

striving

I

KEENE
NORMAL SCHOOL

1909 / 1939

The Hale Mansion, from an early print

1

Cheshire County's Commitment
to Teacher Training

K EENE BECAME the home of a new normal school in 1909 primarily because it already had in operation a good public school system. Unlike many other cities in the state, all Keene's schools were equally well supported — or relatively so. This was unusual because New Hampshire had had a pernicious system of education, called the "district system." Under that system each single grammar school, or high school, was supported solely by the taxpayers in that school's area, or district. The district system resulted in extraordinarily uneven education. Keene also, of course, was under the district system but in spite of that fact, it had escaped the worst influences of the district system and had even established a fairly standard and equal education in all schools.[1]

The good status of Keene's school system in 1909 was no accident or fluke in history. It was due to the area's longtime commitment to quality education. Cheshire County had had an impressive number of excellent academies, which had an influence on the area. Chesterfield Academy for boys was established in 1791. The Walpole Academy also had an excellent reputation, and in 1843 the Universalists established the Mount Caesar Academy in Swanzey Center. There were still others, but these three were particularly good and drew talent in both teachers and students from a large area.

Most famous and influential was Catherine Fiske's Young Ladies' Seminary in Keene, the main building of which is now the President's

President's House

House. This school, established in 1811, was the second oldest of its kind in the United States. Fiske and her staff educated for a quarter of a century over 2,500 young women, and eventually some young men, too. Sarah Josepha Hale studied under Fiske and thought that her seminary was the best such institution in the country. She sent both her daughters to the school. Helen L. Thoreau and Harriet Noyes were among other well-known women that attended. Isabelle Webb Entrikin, who wrote a doctoral dissertation on Sarah Hale, rated Fiske on a par with Emma Willard, the founder of Troy (N.Y.) Female Seminary; Catherine Maria Sedgwick, author and educator; Almira H. L. Phelps (Willard's sister); and Jesse Clement — all people with national reputations at that time.

Hale wrote:

Miss Catherine Fiske may truly be styled the Benefactress of Keene. No individual did so much as she during the twenty-six years of her sojourn there for the material prosperity of that pleasant town, combined with the intellectual and moral improvement of the people; and the elevated and refined tone of social life which now distinguishes it, inducing many intellectual and rich denizens of Boston and other cities to make it their chosen place of retreat, is, in a great measure, traceable to the influence of her school and her beautiful exhibition of the character of an educated Christian lady.

The second progressive influence on Cheshire County's educational system was the influence of the Cheshire County Common Schools Association, founded in 1835. Keene resident Salma Hale, brother-in-law of Sarah Josepha Hale, was particularly influential in it. Hale was a trustee of Dartmouth and the University of Vermont; he was also a noted lawyer, author of a national history textbook, a state politician, and a United States congressman.

Salma Hale's devotion to public education is interesting, when compared with his sister-in-law's high regard for private education, because it reflects a growing national shift away from the more select private academies toward widespread education. Because of this trend, more than anything else, Eliza Withington was able to carry on the Fiske School for only six years after Catherine's death in 1837. Also because of this trend Keene Academy, founded the same year in which Fiske died, never had a vigorous life. It gave way in 1853 to the publicly supported Keene High School.

Salma Hale was aware not only of these shifts but also of Horace Mann's pioneering work in education. Mann had established the first state normal schools in Massachusetts. Hale knew of the difficulties as well as the successes of these schools. By the early 1840s it was demonstrated that teachers especially prepared for their work performed better in the classroom than under the old "hit-or-miss" method of hiring teachers. The trouble was that maintaining normal schools was expensive.

In Horace Mann's *Eighth Annual Report,* which Hale must have read as it came off the press, Mann suggested that teacher institutes be held in the spring and fall of the year for about a fortnight. Teachers could learn some new methods of instruction and discipline at these gatherings at much less time and expense than by regular attendance at a normal school.

By March 15, 1845, someone who signed himself, in a letter to the *Sentinel,* as "A Friend to Common Schools" (no doubt, Hale himself), suggested, organized, and made a monetary contribution to an "Institute for Teachers of Cheshire County" to be held on April 8, 1845, and to last for one month. Seventy young female teachers attended, "and about 50 went through the course." The institute was considered a huge success. "We hope to see other Counties and States adopt the same idea of elevating the standards of Teachers," commented the *Sentinel,* "and we are happy to learn that Hillsboro County is already proposing to go and do likewise!"³

The *Sentinel* believed that this was the first such institute in New England. It may well have been the first in the United States. Certainly Horace Mann, who proposed the idea, and Governor George Briggs of Massachusetts, who officially launched the teacher institutes, did not do so until July-August 1845, three months after the Cheshire County Institute! The *Sentinel* accurately stated: "Our Schools in Cheshire County are ahead of those in other parts of the State."

The Cheshire Institutes continued, usually meeting in Keene, but often in other towns in the county. All the ministers in Keene were at one time or another members of the local Committee of Education; and they were the ones who usually inspected the institutes. The Dublin Institute, on October 5, 1846, was the first to accept both male and female teachers.⁴

The institutes were, at first, unquestionably successful. "No movement to improve common schools has equalled this," claimed the *Sentinel*. Yet the institutes were voluntary. The first one had been free. Tuition, room, and board had to be paid in subsequent ones, but still the institutes always depended on too much donated labor. When public interest was high, the quality of that labor was exceptionally good. When the institutes ceased to be exciting news, the quality of the donated labor declined.

John Prentiss of Keene, J. K. Smith of Dublin, and others realized that much more than institutes was needed. In a meeting of the Cheshire County Common Schools Association, Prentiss spoke effectively on the poor training most teachers received; Smith then moved "that a committee of five be appointed by the chair [Prentiss] to inquire into and report upon . . . the expediency of petitioning the legislature for the establishment of a state normal school, for the better preparation of teachers." The resolution was quickly adopted. Thus the Cheshire County Association proposed serious consideration of a state-supported normal school in 1845 when there were only three other such institutions in the country! Quite possibly Keene, given its leadership at the time, would have had a normal school in 1845 had not the institutes been so spectacularly successful. But the institutes were, at first, successful. County after county adopted them as the method for training teachers, and it became abundantly clear that tax money for a more expensive normal school would not be forthcoming. Even so, S. H. McChollister, a prominent minister and school commissioner, continued throughout the next decade in efforts to establish a normal school in Cheshire County.⁵

After the Civil War interest revived when it appeared that a normal school might be established in Grafton County. Horatio Colony, Edward Joslin, George A. Wheelock, and others met in Keene "to see what can be done about securing the location of the [Normal] School in Keene." They acted too late. The state normal school was established in 1871 in Plymouth in Grafton County.[6] For a short period after the establishment of Plymouth Normal, the Cheshire County teachers institutes were abolished. When it became apparent that Plymouth could not supply all the state's needs for qualified teachers, the institutes were revived.

Portsmouth, Manchester, and Nashua established municipal normal schools, and in 1887 Louis J. Rundlett, the superintendent of schools for Concord, established a small but successful private Training School for Teachers which continued in the Capital City until 1935. By the turn of the century these four schools graduated only about twenty students a year. The majority of trained teachers still came from Plymouth or the teachers institutes, but the vast majority of all teachers was untrained.

Such was the situation when Channing Folsom was state superintendent of public instruction at the turn of the century. Folsom was a scholar and a dedicated educator. He had attended Dartmouth for two years but had to leave for financial reasons. Eventually he earned his baccalaureate and was also awarded an honorary master's degree. He was a cultured, but informal, man and looked older than his fifty years. Temperamentally he still belonged to the Nineteenth Century. He was prepared to accept the situation as it was and to work with it. Realizing that Plymouth was not supplying nearly enough qualified teachers, he wrote, "we should look first of all to the quality of the graduate rather than to the quantity. 'A little leaven leaveneth the whole lump'."[7]

That was 1900, and Folsom's attitudes may be taken as being representative of the best of the nineteenth century. Cheshire County's attitude, as evidenced by its well-known academies, its highly successful institutes, and its early proposals for a normal school, shows that the people in the area were hospitable to the idea of teacher training institutions. For the twentieth century, however, there was a new spirit in the land, and some of the old solutions were no longer workable.

2

Henry C. Morrison: The Founder

HENRY CLINTON MORRISON may properly be considered as the founder of Keene State College. This will, no doubt, come as a surprise to many who have often recited the fact that in 1909 the New Hampshire Legislature established Keene Normal School. Of course it did, but somebody had to move the legislature. Plymouth once trusted "the good judgment of the legislature to do what was needed," and that year, 1877, the legislature did not bother to vote a single penny for the institution. As a result, it nearly died![1] In Keene's case, Morrison was unquestionably the person who moved the legislature. Morrison moved not only the legislature but the whole educational apparatus of the state as well.

Morrison once wrote that he did not go much for social planning, yet he probably did more effective social planning in New Hampshire than any other single human being either before or since his time. The first question that arises is why is this fact so little known. Why has the institution not more properly recognized its own founder? The answer is simple. Morrison was not popular. He was respected, he was able, he was effective; but he was not popular, and he made many enemies. Why was this? Let us take a closer look at Morrison. Most people have seen the photograph of him in Morrison Hall. Actually, that portrait is of a kind, almost soft man. It was taken when he was older, after he had been teaching for a number of years, and when he was, no doubt, kinder and softer. Imagine him, however, in his youth. He was over six feet tall at a time when the average American male was five feet five inches tall. His mouth, with firm teeth behind it, protruded more in a profile view than in frontal views. Thus, with a protruding mouth, serious mien, and penetrating, piercing eyes, he seemed to be physically threatening. In argument or debate he was absolutely devastating. He worked harder than anybody else; he knew more than anybody else; and his gift for analysis was deadly accurate and extraordinarily rapid. He could undo an opponent in seconds — not that he often did, generally he did not — but when he did, the word got around. Generally, he relied on persuasion, persuasion based on accumulations of facts which only he had at his command, and generally that was enough to convince most people. Generally, he was right and they were wrong. "I recall no instance where in the end Morrison failed to have his way. Nor any important one where he was wrong," wrote A. B. Rotch, who served on the Milford School Board. Ernest L. Silver of Plymouth could barely say anything good about Morrison and wrote Richard Martin that, if he wanted "an enthusiastic appraisal" of Morrison, he should contact someone else.[2] Most alumnae say simply and without affection, "He was a man who got what he wanted." For these reasons Morrison was not well beloved. What can be favorably said about him, however, is hardly exaggerated. He ranks well, indeed, with earlier and more well known founders such as Horace Mann, Henry Barnard, Francis Parker, and Charles Hovey. After his spectacular performance in New Hampshire, he became Director of the laboratory schools and professor of school administration at the University of Chicago, from which he published some of the most important books on education, particularly on curriculum development, in the twentieth century.

Morrison was the son of John Alexander Morrison, of Scotch ancestry, and Mary Louise Ham, of an old colonial family of English derivation. He was christened Henry Clinton Morrison after his birth, October 7, 1871, in Old Town, Maine. He was a bright and sturdy child and acquired a muscular physique during high school, when he was a log-scaler for several lumber camps along the Penobscot River.

"His father kept a general store, trading largely with the Penobscot Indians who lived on an island reservation in the river above Old Town and for whom he at one time was the U.S. Indian Agent. He suffered financial reverses and could not afford to send his son to college." In high school Morrison came under the influence of an unusual teacher, a Dartmouth alumnus, Alexander B. Crawford. "I recall his saying, that whatever he attained he owed mainly to Crawford," Morrison's son has written. Upon graduation Morrison began teaching. After two years a still unidentified citizen of Old Town decided to lend Morrison, the town's brightest young scholar, $1,000 to attend Dartmouth. So he entered Dartmouth in 1891 with two years of teaching behind him.

Intellectually, Morrison took Dartmouth by storm. Socially, he didn't make a dent. Dr. Richard A. Martin of New England College, who wrote a doctoral dissertation on Morrison, collected letters about Morrison from some of his classmates, which are enlightening on both his college life and his character. William Foster Rice wrote, "He read widely in History . . . His major interests were languages and philosophy, but he was also a fine mathematician. We took a course in Advanced Astronomy under the later famous Edwin B. Frost. It was mostly math . . . and the text book was in German, but it didn't bother him." Edward Watson wrote, "I recall he read Pindar [in Greek] for recreation . . . [he] was in a class by himself." "He seemed to be unusually strong," wrote still another, "in all subjects. . . . He reflected a maturity and ability beyond his contemporaries." Morrison was particularly influenced at Dartmouth by James Fairbanks Colby, a professor of constitutional law. In his class Morrison came to realize that moral and intellectual achievement made the good American, not racial inheritance,[3] an idea that certainly was not in general vogue in the 1890s.

Socially he was, by choice, isolated. "While in the same class with him and in the same fraternity delegation, yet I never felt at all close to Morrison, and I am not at all sure that anyone else in the class did. He was very exclusive, flocked by himself, spent most of his time in study, and seemed not to welcome any interruptions," wrote another. President Ernest Martin Hopkins of Dartmouth said the same: "Dr. Morrison was not a man it was possible to know well . . . at least not unless one of his intimates."

As far as courage is concerned, Morrison had plenty of it. One really delightful letter that Martin collected was one of 1917 in which the author writing to a friend in Connecticut said of Morrison, "he is coy and bashful in love and a flaming sword in battle. . . . His back bone was born first and he had grown round it."[4]

Such, then, is the man who graduated — valedictorian, of course — from Dartmouth in 1895. In his first teaching job in Milford he had a school of rowdies shaped up in weeks. "While Morrison was head master in Milford, I visited his school, and I have never seen any better administered," wrote Edward Watson of Pittsfield. "The spirit there was excellent and everything was running like clockwork." A. B. Rotch of Milford, who knew him quite well, gives an excellent description:

H. C. M. quickly made himself boss. Not only with his Daniel Webster type of scowl, but by strong-arm methods that even the Russians would understand. Though not overly muscular he had the troublesome lads who outweighed him flying through the air in short order. I know, I had one Morrison-impelled flight myself, and saw many more. . . . He sure dominated that school (and I guess the school board too) for the four or five years he ran it. . . . I'd say his control of the pupils was the result of wholesome fear, with only a modicum of affection, but with complete respect. No headmaster here has ever left such a reputation for efficient management and control.

Morrison's methods may seem a little rough, but one must remember that some of the students hung (but did not hang) the previous headmaster from a classroom window![5] After four years in Milford, Morrison became superintendent at Portsmouth.

As principal and superintendent, Morrison continued to educate himself by reading philosophies of education, particularly Johann Herbart, who had succeeded Immanuel Kant in philosophy at Königsberg. The whole purpose of education, said Herbart, was to make people good and thereby happy. The term "virtue," he said, "expressed the whole purpose of education." Herbart was the one who got education accepted seriously as a discipline on the university level, and he was the one who established the model schools to test educational theories. Herbart's ideas were being promoted by the state normal school at Normal, Illinios, from which his doctrine radiated. That may explain why so many of Keene's faculty (and half its presidents) have come from the Midwest. Francis W. Parker (for whom Parker Hall was named) was also an influence on Morrison, as was Friedrich Froebel. Morrison gave himself a good education. "He was," concluded Hopkins, "liberal in his philosophy, progressive in all his attitudes, and completely independent so far as deriving and working operating polices were concerned."[6]

It is no wonder, then, that when Folsom got into trouble with the state commission of education he called upon the brightest person he knew for help, Morrison. The exact nature of the trouble can be only a matter of conjecture. "Incidentally," recalled John Morrison in 1983, "father was fond of his predecessor and always referred to him affectionately. I have a vague recollection that mother thought him a shade informal in appearance. I recall that the day he called on us at the house — it was in summer and a warm day — he had his coat under his arm and his galluses were very conspicuous. Perhaps the Commission considered his appearance and manner a bit too informal for the position." More likely the commission realized that New Hampshire was behind in many areas of public education and wanted a more dynamic person. At any rate, Morrison appeared before

the commission and spoke on Folsom's behalf. Perhaps he spoke too eloquently, for after hearing him the commission dismissed Folsom and hired
Morrison. On October 25, 1904, Governor Nahum J. Batchelder formally appointed Morrison state superintendent of public instruction.

No superintendent or commissioner of education ever had the influence
on state education that Morrison had. To do all that he did, he had to
convince the people and the legislature of the state that it needed to be
done. He bombarded them with facts. The days of a "little leven leaven-
ing the whole lump" were over.

Morrison fits very well into a model of a "typical" Progressive. He was
Protestant, white, male (although there were some notable women like
Jane Addams), with a better-than-average education, better-than-average
income, and fairly young. The Progressive was tired of the corruption
of the Gilded Age and wanted to reestablish equality for all Americans
and to do it with the force of the government. He wanted to use the principles of massive business organization that the great businessmen had
used and to apply them to the democratic process. He was sincere,
dedicated, confident, and extraordinarily hardworking. Teddy Roosevelt
and Robert La Follette were the best representatives of progressivism on
the national level. In New Hampshire the best representatives were Morrison; Robert Bass; the novelist Winston Churchill; and one old-timer,
Senator William E. Chandler.

Morrison believed that the professional school superintendent was the
result of the work of Francis Parker and Charles Francis Adams, Jr. They
started a movement, he claimed, which was seldom noted but one "which
has been one of the most satisfying developments in our American political
institutions."

As a professional, Morrison called the shots as he saw them. No
superintendent ever exposed so many weaknesses in his own school system.
Nor did the political system escape his pen. "It is politically unjust," he
wrote, "that one town should tax itself twice or three times as much as
another town in its effort to do its part of the state's work." He added:
*there can be no permanent abolishment of special privileges, except we
begin at the bottom by providing equal opportunity in the education of
the child,"* (italics in original).[7]

What was the purpose of the public school system? Morrison claimed
that it was the "general training in the elements of learning which would
. . . enable the future voter and citizen to act intelligently in the common
affairs of life." Some of this knowledge was so valuable for the state that
is must be taught to its citizenry whether they liked it or not. Those who

taught otherwise belonged to the "lunatic fringe" of the Progressive movement.[8]

Morrison's work schedule was staggering. He sometimes visited as many as 200 schools a year — in an era before the automobile and when school terms were short and irregular. The whole state office consisted of himself and two secretaries. In his first report to the legislature he gave 117 pages of his "Doings" and 130 pages on the "Conditions and Progress of Education" in the state. In his next report he said, "I have been continuously in the discharge of the duties of the office, save one week in September, 1905 and a few days in December of the same year." He did this himself because he could not rely on his superintendents. Only six of the thirty-nine superintendents had any formal training. They were, he said, "in the nature of things prejudiced, and unrestrained by submission of their facts to a competent and impartial tribunal, their prejudice sometimes runs wild and sometimes comes almost to amount to insanity."[9] Obviously, he was stepping on toes.

Morrison often found the worst possible examples of teaching being carried out. Some teachers possessed "little education beyond the point of mere literacy." Many of these were "stupid and too frequently worthless." Some of the small schools kept by these teachers were "little if any better than no schools at all." Occasionally he found an excellent example. On a visit to Pinkerton Academy in Derry, he stepped into an English class in which a young man was teaching poetry. He immediately realized that "this was great teaching and within a very short time, Morrison was parading [Robert] Frost all over the state to demonstrate the teaching of poetry to secondary school students." Soon he had him teaching at Plymouth. Frost spoke highly of Morrison and always referred to him as "the great, great boss." "When Frost was Resident Poet at Dartmouth, he made a point of looking up my brother Hugh," recalls John Morrison, "and telling him that he owed much to HCM."[10]

Morrison visited schools in the daytime, talked with superintendents, principals, and teachers in the evening, and wrote up his reports in his hotel rooms or at home at night. On the trains he read educational philosophy, but generally he worked at collecting data. In 1909 he reported that there were 2,113 public schools with 2,795 rooms, and by this time he had visited them all.

After establishing Keene Normal School, Morrison continued his duties as superintendent for eight more years. During that time he worked (successfully) to get a tougher child labor law passed. "I vaguely recall his coming home one evening, embracing mother and saying, 'Marion, we won!' "

Henry Clinton Morrison in 1909

recalled John Morrison. "It was the passage of the N.H. Child Labor Law." Legally, the large companies in the center of the state, particularly the textile mills, could no longer employ cheap, young, immigrant labor. Morrison estimated that 2,000 more children were in school because of the act. Not everyone agreed, however. Some businessmen were opposed, as were some of the immigrants themselves and the churches representing them. "I am quite sure," Morrison wrote Winston Churchill, that "no school matter has stirred the state as this has within the memory of the present generation. Governor Batchelder quite agrees with me. Pretty nearly every paper in the state has vigorously expressed its ideas in the matter."[11] What caused the uproar was the fact that Morrison enforced the law.

In other duties Morrison often had to take people to court for child abuse or child neglect. He instituted health inspections and nutrition investigations of all the students in the state and got increased funds under the mother's aid law; and he can be given much of the credit for getting a fourfold increase in state aid to public schools during his years as superintendent. He laid the basis also for the state's secondary schools, and then its junior high schools. He kept track of the curricula in the normal schools and made some unusual innovations there. He took some of the earliest steps to make the agricultural college in Durham a state university.

Morrison did much more which cannot be traced here but should be the subject of further research. Much of what he did will never be known. "I wish now," writes his son John, "I had asked him more about his N.H. days — modest as he was about his achievements and contributions, I am sure he would have answered all questions."[12]

In 1917 he took what appeared to be an attractive offer as coadjutor-secretary of the Connecticut state board of education. The position had more authority than the name indicates. There were some elements in Connecticut who wanted reform, and they were able to attract Morrison there. Other forces, particularly the Catholic church and the Democratic party, however, were not interested in thorough reform, and Morrison was in a deadlock with them. By this time, however, he was one of the most highly respected state education administrators in the country. He was getting offers to write books from publishers and to take positions in other states. He was considered for the presidency at both the University of New Hampshire and Dartmouth. After refusing the presidency of the former institution, Morrison wrote Ernest Butterfield, his successor in Concord, "I do not feel any enthusiasm at all for ever undertaking executive work again . . . . As an executive I break too many eggs in making omlettes, and since trustees and other such folk do not have to eat the omlettes, they prefer that they should be made without breaking the eggs."[13]

The opportunity Morrison chose was professor of education at the University of Chicago, and the possibility of holding a chair once held by Francis Parker and, for a brief time, by John Dewey. He taught and wrote at Chicago until his retirement in 1937. Morrison wrote six books on education. The most famous was his first one, *The Practice of Teaching in the Secondary Schools* (1926). Of this work Hugo Beck stated that "Any child who has ever studied a unit of work from any textbook during the past 30 years has felt the influence of Henry Clinton Morrison. He was not the first man to ever organize subject matter and knowledge into significant and comprehensive units, but his clear exposition of this method of organization set the pattern for many textbook writers in almost every subject of the elementary and secondary school curriculum."

"Father once laughingly said," recalled John Morrison, "that it was too bad that he could not have had it [the unit system] copyrighted!" The idea of the unit system caught on quickly. By 1930 the National Survey of Secondary Education revealed that 737 schools in 46 states attempted Morrisons methods. Richard Martin commented, "Textbooks were quick to adopt his unit plan of organization. . . . So wide-spread was the use of the word 'unit' that certain publishers of elementary and secondary school textbooks jumped quickly on the bandwagon by changing the word 'Chapter' to 'Unit,' with little or no revision of the content." Even as it was, John Morrison wrote, "the royalties from that book put us three boys through college."

Unit meant much more than chapter, or a group of chapters. The unit was, according to Henry Morrison, "a comprehensive and significant aspect of the environment, of an organized science, of an art, or of conduct, which being learned results in an adaptation of personality." That is a significant, and even a controversial, idea in itself. What made the Morrison Unit plan so immensely popular, however, was the fact that by the 1920s, the American high school was just becoming a part of universal education. The growth of the public high school began to pick up speed only in the 1890s. Thereafter, the growth was phenomenal. In the 1920s with a much different clientele, public high schools could no longer slavishly copy the old academy curricula. They had to establish new curricula; but what? and how? Morrison's *Teaching in the Secondary Schools* provided the intellectual framework for developing curricula in the public high schools just when demand was greatest for some guidance on how to develop courses of studies for new and heretofore uneducated groups from society. But his particular idea of the unit caused revamping of most traditional studies as well.

As Professor of Education at the University of Chicago Morrison developed the Unit idea even further. Eventually he divided all formal education into "School" and "University." In school, which could run anywhere from grammar school to junior college, one learned certain basic skills and study habits. Completing school did not mean one could enter university, which was for only educationally mature students. University was devoted to pursuit of knowledge for its own sake and to professional study. It had no curriculum and no credits. Students graduated only on the basis of competency. This grand idea was never adopted by anyone. With its emphasis on competency and its non concern with socialization, it stood in marked contrast to John Dewey's Philosophy. Like Dewey, however, Morrison also hoped to produce a better citizen for the state; but the route was certainly different.

The Practice of Teaching in the Secondary Schools," wrote Charles Judd of the University of Chicago, gave Morrison "a national reputation and [was] the most influential book he ever published." "I am sure," Judd added, that "his philosophy had its roots in his New Hampshire experience." Ernest Butterfield reported that the book was even being read in New Hampshire — "from Pittsburg to Pelham, and from Westmoreland to Newcastle!"[14]

Morrison also authored *School Revenue* (1930), *The Management of School Money* (1932), *Basic Principles of Education* (1934), *School and Commonwealth* (1937), *The Curriculum of the Common School* (1940), and *American Schools: A Critical Study of our School System* (1943). He was also known for his speeches and articles such as "The Recruitment of the Teaching Force," "The Battle for Competent Supervision," and the "Social Consequence of Bad Administration."

This, then, is the man whom we can legitimately claim as our founder. His accomplishments in the public realm and in educational thought place him in a category with such other noted founders as Horace Mann, Francis Parker, Henry Barnard, and Charles Hovey. Four men, Richard A. Martin, Hugo Beck, Eugene A. Bishop, and Harry A. Brown — all wrote doctoral dissertations on Morrison's ideas and/or his work. Brown's and Bishop's works were published by Columbia University Press.

Morrison is certainly more lovable now than he was in the past. Viewing him now, we see mostly his labor, his brilliant mind, his acute sense of justice, his compassion, and his honesty. In the past one saw more quickly his scowl, his impatience, and his aloofness. It is good, however, on this occasion, the college's seventy-fifth anniversary, to recall his many positive virtues.

3

*City and The State Endorse
Morrison's Proposals*

DUNHAM IN *The Colleges of Forgotten Americans* tells a story of a state legislater who lobbied hard to get the state university in his hometown. It would have been a matter of great prestige. He failed but was soon lobbying for the state prison as a consolation prize. That, at least, would bring in some handsome construction contracts. He failed in this effort also. By this time some of his colleagues, feeling sorry for him, offered him one of the new normal schools. He replied, "I don't know what it is, but I'll take it." Leaders in most communities knew what normal schools were even if they might not know how the term originated. The name applied to institutions which established norms, or normal standards, for the teaching profession.

Enough evidence is now available to indicate not only that towns knew what normal schools were but also that they were quite anxious to have them. In fact, since Horace Mann's day, it had become a tradition for towns to contribute money, a site, or both, to secure the normal school. In this regard, Keene's response was similar to that of most other communities throughout the nation.

Since the creation of Keene Normal School was a public act, it is worthwhile to trace the idea of the new normal school through the political processes. Morrison was barely in office before he began agitating for state action to provide for more qualified teachers. "The state and the state alone," he reminded the political hierarchy, "can in the last analysis guarantee the character of any profession or calling." Matrimony, better salaries in other states, and more attractive callings drew off most of the good teachers. "About one teacher in three was properly trained for his or her work. Eighteen percent must be taken as utterly incompetent from the academic as well as the professional standpoint," he told the legislature.

Through his contacts in southeastern New Hampshire, Morrison persuaded Representative James Tufts of Exeter to sponsor in 1905 "An Act to establish a Second Normal School and to Provide for its Maintenance." The bill fared well until it got to the Appropriations Committee, chaired by Betram Ellis of Keene, an accomplished legislator and since 1890 editor of the *Sentinel*. The *Journals* of the Senate and the House simply recorded that Mr. Ellis "reported the bill out with the following resolution: Resolved, that it is inexpedient to legislate."[1]

Undoubtedly Ellis's views can be better ascertained through the words of the *Sentinel's* legislative correspondent in Concord, H. C. Pearson. Pearson wrote that the House passed thirteen bills and killed fifteen. "This does not sound as though much was accomplished, but as a matter of fact some troublesome measures were put out of the way." First on Pearson's list of troublesome measures was "the act to establish a new state normal school at an expense of construction of $80,000 and for maintenance of $25,000 a year." It appears as if one of Keene's most distinguished citizens and legislators had a role in killing Morrison's first effort to establish a new normal school.

Morrison's effort in 1907 to get a normal school out of the legislature was better organized. In his public reports he bluntly entitled one section, "The Need of More Normal Schools." To demonstrate the need, it was not necessary, Morrison wrote, "to do more than cite again the facts that were reported last year . . . as teaching for the first time, three hundred and seventy-six persons, while our normal school graduates for this year were fifty-four." His report to the governor was a voluminous 490 pages, and he recommended "that the legislature authorize the immediate erection of at least two normal schools."

In yet another report for the 1907 legislature he had another long section, again bluntly entitled "More Normal Schools Needed." Last, he got the State Teachers Association to adopt a strongly worded "Declaration of Principles" and forwarded it to the legislature. "We . . . reaffirm our belief

Charles Gale Shedd, public-minded citizen and businessman, steered the Keene Normal School bill through the State Senate in 1909.

in the need of more normal schools in this state and urgently ask the next legislature to provide for their establishment," the teachers stated. The whole rationale behind the teachers' statement was so like Morrison's that it is difficult to believe he did not write it himself. The final statement, "We pledge to Superintendent Morrison our hearty support and cooperation," was undoubtedly a sentiment of the Teachers Association at the time. By these methods Morrison generated a popular mandate.[2]

This time Morrison did his work too well. Now everybody wanted a normal school. Shortly after the 1907 legislature convened, Oliver H. Toothaker of Berlin, chairman of the Normal School Committee entered a bill "to establish a State Normal School." Five days later Nathan Goldsmith of Chester proposed a normal school for Rockingham County. Six days later Henry Greeley of Nashua proposed one for that city, and the next day Orrin Hussey of Farmington proposed another one for Stratford County. The person to come up with the idea, and a bill, for Keene, was Joseph Madden, a Ward Five Democrat. He was quickly and ably supported by another distinguished Democrat of Keene, Senator Gale Shedd (of Bullard and Shedd), whom the *Granite Monthly* described as being liberal in all his ways.[3]

Bertram Ellis, who up to this time had thought normal school bills good things to dispose of, now that Keene had a chance to get one of them, became an enthusiastic supporter. Indeed, Keene stood an unusually good chance of getting the normal school in 1907, for Ellis himself was speaker of the House and Shedd was president protempore of the Senate, both powerful positions.

Joseph Madden, Representative from Ward Five, steered the Keene Normal School bill through the State House of Representatives the same year.

About three weeks after Ellis introduced his bill, Madden, Shedd, and Leslie Cleveland, former principal of the high school, appeared before the city council and the board of aldermen of Keene and proposed the idea to them.

Senator Shedd opened the discussion before the councils . . . by stating in substance that there are five normal school bills pending before the House Committee on Education, the one introduced by Representative Madden, provides for such a school in Keene. Nashua, Dover, Portsmouth, Farmington and other towns are desirous of getting such a school, and if Keene wants a chance . . . its wishes must be known speedily.

Madden "thought Keene would be very favorably considered by those in authority and by the legislative committees." He believed that the Hale or Thayer estates on Main Street would be good locations for the beginning of a school.

It was, admitted the *Sentinel*, "A question new to nearly everyone." Mayor Martin Clark and the city councils called for a citywide meeting to discuss the issue.

On a Saturday evening, February 10, 1907, residents met en masse to hear arguments for and against having a normal school in Keene and to make their decision. Shedd, Madden, and other county representatives were in attendance. Bertram Ellis was chairman of the meeting.

Reasons for having a normal school in Keene ranged from the practical to the sublime. School costs might decline, since the practice teachers would be teaching for free. Some cited the low cost of education in

Plymouth. Others cited cases in which a normal school raised the general level of education. "Twenty years or so ago," said Superintendent of Education George A. Keith, Massachusetts asked the town of Bridgewater "to turn over 250 scholars to be taught by the normal school pupils. The town did so and after two years found them so far ahead of their other pupils, that they wished to turn over more." Other advocates thought a normal school would give the town an intellectual spark.

There was no real opposition, but Rev. Josiah L. Seward offered a few words of caution. "There are always two sides to a contract," he said, "and the city ought to thoroughly understand what it is expected to do." He questioned if student teachers would be as good as full-time teachers. In an obvious reference to the quality of the normal school, he said, "we must remember that there are schools and schools and that all would depend on having a first class normal school."

Finally, when everyone had his say, Representative Madden introduced the following resolution:

That the Board of Education delegate a committee to meet the committee which is to visit Keene to inspect the lots and advantages of the city as a site of a normal school and to cooperate with the city councils or any committee appointed by them for that purpose.

"Mr. Madden's resolution was adopted without a dissenting vote," the *Sentinel* noted.[4] The actual wording of the resolution, especially the last three important words, "for that purpose," is vague. The words in the resolution which pick up the spirit of the entire meeting, however, are those stressing cooperation with the city council and the advantage to Keene as a site for a normal school.

The Normal School Committee of the legislature shortly toured Keene on open sleighs in the winter of 1906-7, visiting all the sites and the elementary schools and were wined and dined by Madden, Shedd, and others.

It turned out that Keene had several distinct advantages in the eyes of the committee. First, it had no taverns — or "nuisances" — as they were referred to in the reports. Keene had a nuisance of another sort. The workmen from several factories along the Ashuelot took "swim breaks" in the river during the summer. There was usually consternation on both sides when canoeing parties of ladies came upon these bathers who were, most often, naked. Several efforts to pass a city ordinance to prohibit nude bathing in the Ashuelot ended by postponements until September, when everyone forgot about them. Of course, when the committee members were bundled up in their open sleighs in February 1907, no one, not even the Nashua politicians, thought of naked male bathers in the Ashuelot in the summertime. But the Nashua taverns were still visible in February.

Another advantage that Keene had was in the Hale and Pearson properties. One city resolution stated that Keene could present "as fine a site as can be offered by any city in the state." Most important was the area's past educational performance and its current advantages. Even Toothaker, chairman of the committee, who favored Nashua over Keene, stated "that Cheshire County furnished more teachers in proportion to its population than any similar section in the state." Finally, the normal school would be within walking distance of most of the city schools, and the quality of those schools impressed the legislators.

As the bill worked its way through the legislature, the *Sentinel* headlined, "Cheshire County Delegation Working for Keene" and "Committee Appointed to talk up the Merits of this City." But, alas! too many other cities were talking up their merits, too, and there was at the time simply not enough money to establish five normal schools. Politically there was no way to decide to which city to award only one normal school. The 1907 legislature ended with an "indefinite postponement" on the normal school question.[5]

The year 1907 was, however, an important one. The city of Keene decided to do all it could to attract a normal school, and the legislature had agreed to establish more normal schools. The only real questions for the 1909 legislature to decide was where.

The political situation in 1909 in New Hampshire was extraordinarily interesting. Henry B. Quinby of Lakeport held the governor's chair by the slimmest of margins. But that was better than the previous governor, who was never able to obtain a majority and had to be elected by the General Court. Behind this unsettling situation was not "politics as usual" but the arrival of the Progressive revolt in New Hampshire.

This revolt began when the novelist Winston Churchill casually and without much forethought threw his hat into the 1906 gubernatorial race. Churchill ran on a reform platform of curbing the Boston & Maine Railroad, fairer taxation, a direct primary, better education, and other issues. To his and everyone else's surprise, although he expended little effort on his own campaign, Churchill did very well at the polls. He so divided the vote that that General Court had to elect the next governor.

To prevent another 1906 imbroglio, the Republicans nominated Quinby, a man who was eminently fair and moderately Progressive. He was also wealthy, a successful businessman, dignified, and courteous. At his elec-

Do the Slope People Want a Normal School?

This cartoon published by a non-partisan league in North Dakota reflected attitudes held throughout the country.

—Courtesy Nonpartisan Leader.

By Heck, We'll Help Them Get It!

Vote the Amendment Ballot "Yes".

tion he knew he faced a turbulent legislature, but he determined to maintain an even course and to play no favorites.

The legislature was full of Progressives seeking an end to two generations of business domination of the state. The new legislature, said the *Cheshire Republican,* "is expected to be one of more than ordinary interest." Indeed it was. It considered 781 measures, of which 304 became law. The major laws passed in 1909 were the direct primary, the registration of lobbyists, and the anti-free-pass law. The General Court had a standing committee for normal schools, and the Senate had a well-informed Committee on Education. While not major legislation, the normal school bill received adequate attention from the state's newspapers and was occasionally mentioned as part of the major legislation of 1909.[6]

Keene did not have the advantages in 1909 that it had in 1907. Ellis was no longer speaker of the House. Henry Swan of Ward Two, however, organized the education committee "so that its members and not its chairman decided what the committee would or would not recommend." Members were particularly well chosen with only one, Daniel Goodnow, from Cheshire County. Even though the 1909 legislature seemed more committed to action than previous legislatures, Morrison presented a still more specific plan. He asked for four new normal schools. "The greatest, most evident need . . . is undoubtedly in the counties of Cheshire, Sullivan,

Hillsboro and Rockingham . . . and the greatest of all in the first two." He then made a priority listing under big Roman numerals. Number I was "Keene, the only community in that part of the state which has an average attendance sufficient to furnish training facilities." Not only did Keene and Cheshire County have good records of support for education, but Keene was also the right-sized city. Morrison was opposed to building a normal school in Manchester, the state's largest city. "No school should be established in a locality where there will be temptation of the upbuilding of a very large school," he said. "A large enrollment of students is fatal to efficiency in any higher institution." Number II on his priority list was the lower Merrimack Valley region; number III was the southeastern part of the state; and number IV was "the extreme northern part of the state." "It would probably be unwise to undertake the building of this full program at once," Morrison said; "it ought to be entered upon, however, at once by the erection of at least two of the four schools."[7] With this report the 1909 legislature had a more definite plan to work with than had the 1907 legislature.

Madden again entered a bill for a normal school in Keene. Representative Edward Wason entered one for Nashua. The Normal School Committee reported both bills out favorably. Governor Quinby, however, notified the legislature that there was sufficient money for only one normal school and that he would veto any bill to establish two normal schools. The governor's decision did not give Madden much time. The bill had passed its second reading in the House and had already come up for its third and final reading. Madden had to move quickly to suspend the rules and send the bill back to the second reading. That carried, but he lost on his motion to send it back to the Appropriations Committee. There followed some exceedingly complicated legislative maneuvers in which Madden and Wason traded setbacks and successes. A real setback for Madden came, many believed, when the chairman of the Normal School Committee, Toothaker, proposed an amendment to let the superintendent of education make the decision, hoping that he would select Nashua. To make a still stronger case, Nashua offered $100,000 in property values for the normal school site — about six times as much as Keene was planning to offer. Francis Buffum of Winchester reminded the legislature that "Nashua was a licensed city," implying that the ways to sin were more abundant there. The *Nashua Telegraph* was quick to respond, alleging that Buffum was "making his characteristic attack upon the good faith of the city of Nashua." Indeed, the *Telegraph* headlined, "Rushing Keene Normal School Bill Through Legislature," and claimed that the Cheshire County delegation wanted "to railroad the bill through."[8] Fortunately, no one in Nashua knew about naked workmen swimming in the Ashuelot in the summertime.

There continued in the last stages of the bill a good bit of horse trading, or politics as usual. Bertram Ellis was "not without influence," the *Granite Monthly* politely said. Stephen Bullock of Richmond later said that "he 'traded' his vote for the first and last time [in his life] in order to meet the competition of Manchester for locating the school there." He told of agreeing "to vote a state road in the north country in return for a fellow legislator's vote to build the Normal School at Keene."

On the night of the passage of the bill through the House, the Keene School Board held a special meeting to celebrate the occasion. The board passed a special vote of thanks to Joseph Madden for his legislative success.[9]

On April 1, 1909, shortly after opening for the morning session, the clerk of the House announced to the Senate: "Mr. President: The House of Representatives has passed a bill with the following title, in the passage of which it asks the concurrence of the Honorable Senate: House Bill 579, An Act to establish a Normal School, to appropriate money for the same and to provide for its maintenance."

No trouble had been expected in the Senate, but suddenly Senate passage appeared doubtful. Manchester and Nashua had not given up the fight to have the school in the south-central part of the state. At this point, Gale Shedd "went to Concord and got busy as did other members of the Cheshire County delegation." It was still a close call. The vote on the first call was only 13-10 in favor of the Keene Normal School bill. But it was enough. For the final vote four more senators changed. So the bill finally passed the Senate by a vote of 17-6; the senators from the center of the state held out to the very end, but after April 8, when the Senate voted, there was no more opposition.[10] The city of Keene decided to have a normal school in 1907. The state decided in 1909.

4

The Hale and Pearson Properties

A LMOST AS IMPORTANT as the idea of a university was the site of a university wrote the good cardinal, John Henry Newman. The site "should be a liberal and noble one; who will deny it? . . . What has a better claim to the purest and fairest possessions of nature, than the seat of wisdom?" As soon as the idea of Keene Normal School gestated, the site of the school had to be-selected.

In 1984 when, according to George Orwell, we should be organized down to the last detail, it stretches the limits of credibility to believe how much was done in such a short period of time in 1909. The normal school bill was debated in the legislature, passed through three committees, two houses, three readings, a subcommittee of the trustees, the joint board of normal trustees, and then went through four more legislative bodies on the local level all in a matter of four months. In 1909 Keene had a two-house city government composed of a common council and a board of alderman. The normal school legislation had to pass both these bodies and have the signature of the mayor. After that, the Keene School Board and the Keene School District had to vote. These bodies voted on three different issues: the contract with the state and the purchase of two separate pieces of property. Further, excellent sites were acquired, repaired, and altered; students were advertised for, received, and lodged, and only in state-approved housing; a highly qualified principal and faculty were hired; and a curriculum was developed all in another four month's time. We will now focus, however, primarily on acquiring the sites of the normal school.

Representative Madden appeared before the city councils at a special meeting, Saturday evening, March 20, 1909, and stated that if the city agreed to buy the Hale Mansion, the normal school could begin in 1909 because there was need of only minor alterations in the residence and adjoining buildings. In addition, the first classes would be relatively small.

The Hale Building was not only a particularly attractive building — it is the best example of Italianate architecture in Keene — but it was also associated with three governors of the state — Samual Dinsmoor, who built it in 1861, and the two William Hales, father and son, who were governors of the state, 1840-42 and 1882-84, respectively. The younger Hale bought the property in 1869. He was a very successful businessman. His chief business was the manufacturing of wooden pegs for shoes, although he had many other investments. His practice of politics, while successful, was not considered to be particularly exemplary. A contemporary of his was not wide of the mark when he wrote in 1910, "As a matter of local pride, Cheshire County went the limit for Gov. Hale and has not since accumulated a reserve stock for another favorite son to draw upon."[1] Nonetheless, the house that bears his name was a most attractive one. Several buildings behind the main residence went with the property, and behind them, running parallel with Winchester Street, was one of the two largest greenhouses in the state, 25 feet wide and a full 125 feet long. Madden formally put the purchase of this property before the city councils.

The following resolution then passed the common council by unanimous vote and the alderman concurred, in like manner, without debate:

That the city of Keene hereby pledges itself, if the legislature shall make provision for the establishment of a normal school in said city and shall grant to said city the power to do so, to purchase and present to the State of New Hampshire of the W. S. Hale property as a site for said school, together with the building now standing thereon, satisfactory to the board of officials having in charge the establishment of said school.[2]

On May 4 Governor Quinby, Morrison, Charles Corning, the Governor's Council, the principal of Plymouth, and others toured the Hale property with Keene city councilmen. They also looked at the neighboring Pearson property. Governor Quinby was the first to suggest that it also be purchased for the normal school. It would, he thought, make a suitable residence for the chief officer of the new school.

Morrison headed a subcommittee consisting of Councilor Albert Annette and Judge Corning of the joint board of trustees and through this agency took care of all the property details. The day after the governor's visit, Morrison again inspected the Hale property, this time with George Gordon, a Keene building contractor, and planned renovations and alterations.[3]

In late May the voters of the Keene Union School District met and unanimously passed the following resolution:

That the board of education of Union School district be, and it hereby is, authorized and instructed to make a contract with duly authorized officials on the part of the state for the purpose of cooperating with the proposed normal school to be established in Keene in the maintenance of model and practice schools for a term of years, in accordance with an act passed by the legislature of 1909 establishing said normal school.

Shortly thereafter the city council voted to raise $12,000 to purchase the Hale property from its owner, Mrs. Mary E. Woodbury. This vote passed, as the *Sentinel* noted, "without division or debate."[4]

So all was set. The normal school could now be established. But Governor Quinby, for all his identification with men of wealth and its connotation of standpatism, was also a man of vision. He took a special interest in the establishment of a new normal school, and he still wanted it to have the Pearson property. Pearson had just bought the old Catherine Fiske residence as part of the settlement of the John Thayer estate. Pearson had paid $8,000 for it and had spent over $3,000 on it for repairs. Perhaps it was too expensive for him. At any rate, he was willing to sell it for $12,000, the same price as the Hale property and nearly as big. The great attraction of the Hale property was the mansion itself. The attraction of the Pearson property was that even in 1909 it was one of Cheshire County's famous homes. Built in 1805, a fine example of the Federal style of architecture, it reached its most lasting fame as Catherine Fiske's Young Ladies' Seminary. Like the Hale property, it too had connecting buildings behind it. Next to them was a beautiful sunken garden, which was a landmark of the campus until Morrison Hall preempted the spot when it was built in 1960. West of the garden were two tennis courts. Beyond the tennis courts was a simple but attractive two-story frame house located where Huntress Hall now is. This house was purchased in 1912 for the home economics classes. It was a familiar landmark for more than a dozen years, when it was moved to Hyde Street and resold as a private residence. It was named Penelope House — after Ulysses' faithful and frugal wife.

All this property bordered Appian Way — another classical name! For the first few years our *via Appia* was not to be so much the center of life as it is today, but as faculty began to move into houses on the south side of it, it began to take on the characteristics of a popular concourse. It was named by John Elliot, a distinguished and public-minded citizen of Keene. Looking out from the top of his wonderful mansion on Main Street (now Elliot Hall), he saw seven major hills — Beech Hill to the east and Bald Hill somewhat north of it, to the south Mount Cresson and Mount Huggins to the southeast, West Hill and Highland Hill to the west, and Surry Mountain to the north. They recalled to him the Seven Hills of Rome, and for this reason he named the road that bordered his property Appian Way.

Thus far everything had gone well. The people of Keene had voted several times, as had their authorized representatives — unanimously — to have a normal school. They had also voted unanimously for taxing themselves for the Hale Mansion, but the Pearson property was a different matter. Was it really necessary for the normal school? Nobody up to this point had said so. But the governor himself was the one behind it. Morrison, of course, had to resolve the issue. He and Judge Charles Corning of the normal school board agreed with the governor and took their case before the city councils. Specifically, their case was that the state government currently had $5,000 which it could contribute toward the purchase price if the city of Keene was willing to raise another $7,000 and that such an opportunity was not likely to present itself again because the state rarely had a surplus.

The city councils then called a public meeting to decide the issue by popular vote. Morrison, Corning, Madden, and Shedd all spoke in favor of purchasing the Pearson property. Morrison voiced the hope that one of the best normal schools in New England would be established here and that it would have a suitable home. There was, however, some opposition to the extra expense, and the final vote showed 257 voting in favor and 85 voting against purchase of the Pearson property. The matter went back to the councils where it was tied up again, particularly in the upper chamber, with the aldermen. They did not give approval until July 22, and then only by a 3-2 vote. Thus, Keene residents raised a total of $19,000 to help get a normal school in their city, far less than the $100,000 offered by Nashua and about the same as the $18,000 raised by the residents of Plymouth in 1871.[5] By comparison, the price was not expensive for Keene. On the other hand, Keene had certainly given some of its fairest possessions for the site of the normal school.

5

The Rhodes Administration

MANY ALUMNI remember when the college advertised itself as a "Class A Institution as judged by the American Teachers Association," and everyone undoubtedly took a measure of pride in that. On the other hand, many faculty and others positively insist that Keene State College must rid itself of the normal school association as if the past were some dead weight on today's progress. Must it really? Can we be proud of the college's beginnings, or is there good reason to cover them up? Before considering the Rhodes administration by itself, a few facts about normal schools in general will help put the college's beginning in perspective.

In 1910 there were in the United States 264 normal schools enrolling 132,000 students. Of these, 151 were state-operated; the rest were city, county, or private institutions. The largest number established in any one decade was 31 in the 1890s. The second-largest number was 27 in the same decade that Keene was founded. That meant there was extensive experience in the founding and operation of normal schools by 1909.

Much (but certainly not all) of the previous and some of the subsequent experience was not good. Too many schools had been founded too quickly by people who barely knew what they were doing. Some normal schools reported that their teachers had less education than their students. Normal school instructors often had no high school diploma, and of course one was not required for entrance to those normal schools. In some cases instructors did not even have an eighth-grade education. As late as 1926, 56 of our normal schools had faculties whose average preparation was less than the bachelor's degree.[1] It is not surprising, therefore, that many people held normal schools in general in low esteem.

Keene's first faculty and administration of six people far exceeded the qualifications of most normal school faculties. Indeed, they compared favorably with contemporary liberal arts colleges. Three either had their Ph.D.'s or would have them soon, and two of the others were unusual and distinguished teachers. The assurance by Morrison, Quinby, and such local people as Madden, Ellis, Shedd, and the Reverend Mr. Seward about establishing an institution of quality had real substance.

It would be interesting to have now the correspondence between Morrison and Jeremiah Rhodes, the first principal. (Presidents of normal schools were then called principals.) How Morrison first contacted Rhodes we do not know. Thus, we will have to make some assumptions as to how the first faculty developed.

In a recent telephone conversation, Jeremiah Rhodes, Jr., said that his father, Jeremiah, Sr., always sought to attract highly qualified faculty. Since half of the first faculty came from Kansas with Rhodes, it would be fairly safe to assume that, once Morrison was satisfied with Rhodes's qualifications, he told him to recruit qualified faculty from his area. Very likely Morrison stressed the attractive site of Keene Normal School and its future growth potential as further incentives for midwesterners to come east. It must be remembered also that neither Rhodes nor Morrison had much time to search for faculty. Both men had many other things to attend to. At any rate, let us look at what could be considered as the Rhodes faculty.

First of all, there was Rhodes himself, forty-seven years old, a history/political science professor at Kansas State Normal School, who had done undergraduate work at Stanford and then transferred to Indiana University where he received his B.A. He earned his master's degree from Harvard and was working toward his doctorate, which he received in 1913. With him came his wife, Cora Ingels Rhodes of Bentonville, Indiana.

Second came Harry Llewllen Kent, also an instructor at Kansas State Normal. Kent had attended Kansas State College and the University of Chicago. His primary interest was agriculture, and he was an unusually good teacher. Eventually he got his doctorate and became president (1921-35) of New Mexico's agricultural and mechanical college. Also from Kansas was Chester Haveland-Crane Dudley. He was the first faculty member to live on Appian Way, which in time would be known as "Professor's Row." He was a graduate of the college at Emporia, Kansas, and had done some graduate work in Kansas and at Princeton Theological

Seminary. He was particularly gifted and an excellent teacher, who had a broad range of specialties — history, music, and manual training — and performed quite well and enthusiastically in each area.

Those recruited in the East may be considered as Morrison's faculty. First of them was Kate Fairbanks Puffer, in psychology. She had an A.B. from Smith and had just received her Ph.D. from Radcliffe. She was a good scholar and a popular teacher. Next was Clayton Eugene Hotchkiss, in music. Not much is known about him, but two of the living alumni remember him as a "fine" teacher. Last was Sarah Jane Rogers, in pedagogy. The *Sentinel* described her as a "lady of large experience as a public and normal school teacher." She stayed only one year, and little is known about her.

Aiding these faculty members were six supervising practice teachers. Two were in a model school, behind the Hale property, the Winchester Street School, and four were in Wheelock School (called the Elliot Street School until 1915).

It was an impressive faculty indeed. It was certainly a more auspicious beginning than that of the University of New Hampshire in 1869 when one man, Professor Ezekiel Dimmond, was president, admissions officer, teacher, clerk, secretary, recruiter, professor, housefather, and lobbyist in the legislature. He literally killed himself trying to do everything. And it was a better beginning then Plymouth's, when Amos Hadly had to open the school by himself and teach, feed, administer, and be a housefather to eighty girls! Keene's beginning was what Morrison planned for it — the foundation for the best normal school in New England.

Mrs. A. Lizzie Sargent of the New Hampshire Grange visited Keene in 1910 and was much impressed with Rhodes and his faculty — a Ph.D. from Harvard and two others with extensive graduate work at first-rate institutions, she exclaimed. "We believe the school cannot fail to meet the demands of a normal school under such able instruction."[2]

The Grange at that time was no insignificant organization. One of its many ideas was an insurance company which opened up an office in Keene, now National Grange Mutual. Particularly interested in rural New Hampshire, the Grange at that time was influential in getting legislators to vote for funds not only for the agricultural college at Durham but also for Plymouth and Keene Normal schools so that the rural youth of the state could have an education equal to that of city or town youth.

John Colony, editor of the *Cheshire Republican*, also noticed the outstanding qualities of Keene's first faculty, about whom he wrote a beautiful little editorial entitled "One Reason Why You Should Attend the

Keene Normal School." The reason, said Colony, was to have acquaintance with the "strong, vigorous, and enthusiastic men and women faculty as well as with books."

On July 6, 1909, Morrison announced through flyers, press releases, and advertisements throughout the state the opening of the new school in Keene. The courses "will be in all essential particulars, the same as those at Plymouth school, notably the regular course of two years for graduates of approved high schools and academies, and the teachers course of one year for experienced teachers."[3]

The program was remarkably flexible. The courses were about 50 percent method and 50 percent content. Those taking the one-year course, for instance, could concentrate on the methods courses or the content courses according to need. Subjects offered during the first year were psychology, pedagogy, school management, school law, history and philosophy of education, English, history, nature studies, school gardening, elementary argriculture, music, drawing, manual training, and library science.

There were no dormitories and would not be any for five years. The first students either commuted from home or rented rooms in Keene homes that had been inspected and approved by Harriet Lane Huntress, a member of Morrison's office.

To make certain that the school was off to a good start, some 100 prominent people from Keene and other parts of the state gathered for the opening exercises on September 28, 1909. Mayor Martin Clark of Keene spoke, as did Rhodes and the principal of Plymouth. Edward A. Renouf, the first pastor of St. James Episcopal Church, offered the invocation and benediction. The main speakers were Morrison and Bertram Ellis of the *Sentinel*. "Quality, excellence and not the size should be the goal," said Ellis. "Our city has given material aid. It will also expect much in return. We may ask the normal school to aid us in improving our public schools, already good, until they are recognized as the best in New Hampshire, and through cooperation may we succeed in attaining our desire for one of the best normal schools and the best of public schools."[4]

The occasion was certainly an emotional event for Morrison. "If I were to take the time to express my own personal feeling ... at this culmination of our thought and work, it should take the rest of the forenoon," he said. Of course, he desisted and spoke instead of the future. "I want to speak with special force of the rare opportunity which is offered to these young ladies....We hope to build up the best school for training teachers that can possibly be made."

The ceremonies concluded with the remarks of Principal Rhodes, who thanked the people of Keene for their hospitality and pledged that he would "always be found on the side of progress and of those things that are to build up your community and your state."[5]

It soon became obvious that, of the six faculty members, four were excellent teachers, an unusually high percentage! First in popularity was Kent. Young and good-looking, his classes in nature and agriculture, conducted in the spectacular 125-foot-long greenhouse behind the Hale Mansion, offered a welcome relief to the bookwork classes conducted on the second floor of Hale. He was married, but the girls fell in love with him anyhow — that is, all except Millicent Washburn, who, when interviewed, swore she didn't.

Second in popularity was Kate Puffer, who not only worked hard with the girls on their student plays but was remembered mostly as the one who made them think in the classroom. "With Kate Puffer, we studied 'Miss Shim's Baby.' I'll never forget that!" said Margaret Gallagher over seventy years later. "We studied that baby from the time it was born to — I don't known how old she was."

"Another especially interesting class," wrote Alice May Lord, the historian of the class of 1911, was "the course in Pedagogy taught by Mr. Rhodes. Ask any Senior what she considered the value of those hours spent in the front office with our prinicpal and she will tell you how we became so interested one day that we stayed there until chapel was over; how we looked forward to the meeting of that class, and also the hours we spent preparing for lessons."

Last but not least of the good teachers was Dudley. Of the Rhodes faculty, he remained the longest, until 1924. He allowed the girls to talk in his manual training course as they worked on their baskets and bookcases, so much so that the class was "commonly known as the Sewing Society, because of the never ceasing chatter of tongues."

The first faculty and administration was exceptionally strong and impressive. Even the state college at Durham began talking about adding a normal department.[6] Keene was much more fortunate than its sister institutions in its beginnings. It was not yet officially classified as a "Class A Institution," but it already was one in fact.

6

Student Life Before the Dorms

MOST ALUMNI are likely to regale the listener with stories of dorm regulations, but Fiske Hall, the first dormitory, was not a part of college life until September 1914. Before that time the students of the Rhodes administration set up their own pattern, much of which applied later to dormitory life. It is worthwhile, therefore, to take a look at student life in the very early years.

Most girls arrived the day before opening exercises, either by horse and buggy or by train. The train station was located where the present Cheshire County Transportation Center is. From there the students engaged porters to carry their trunks to their assigned rooms in Keene. The landlords generally acted more as host families than as landlords. The $1.75 to $3.00 per week room-and-board fee had already been negotiated.

On the day of opening exercises, September 28, 1909, twenty-seven students met together for the first time. They were very much aware of the historical significance of the event. The first classes appointed historians who kept a record of the major events of the class year. Luckily, the first two class histories are still preserved. The writing of these histories is somewhat stilted, but they give a good idea of the cyclical kinds of activities students engaged in then and for years to come.

"I am sure," wrote Josephine Howes, the class historian of 1909-10, "we all made the best of those first few hours in carefully examining each other as to our possibilities as future companions. Doubtless," she continued, "few realized what joyous friendships would exist by the close of the year."[1]

*For years nature study classes were held in the spectacular greenhouse
that was a part of the original Hale property.*

The students climbed to the third floor of the Hale Building, which
served as the first assembly hall and chapel. Here, after more introductions, they were assigned to their classes. Subjects offered the first term
were psychology, pedagogy, history, elementary agriculture, nature study,
English, and drawing. For a couple of months the young women settled
down to serious study.

After the initial excitement wore off, the students prepared for a Halloween party, which "became an annual event." "Miss Linquist, the fortune
teller, revealed many horrible futures and was a success as a palm reader,"
wrote Howes. "The [main] feature of the evening was a ghost story told
in absolute darkness by Miss Marietta Willoughby of Bedford. Her story
was about her deceased brother in India and was ghastly in itself, while
during the telling, she passed around uncanny remains which caused much
laughter and fun."

The first party was a tremendous success, not only with the students,
but also with the neighbors. "Residents in the neighborhood," commented
the *Sentinel*, "were glad to see the mansion again brightly lighted, after
being closed for so long, and to hear the music, the chatter of tongues and

the shouts of laughter of the young people coming from its long silent walls." The next year another Halloween party was held, and by this time the class historian pronounced that "No normal party is ever a failure and this one did not prove contrary to custom."[2] So the Halloween party became an annual event, at least for a while.

As the [class] work went on, need was felt for developing the physical as well as the mental side of our natures and accordingly an athletic association was formed and officers elected who served as school officers throughout the year. As an outcome of this interest in athletics, a basketball team was formed and almost every pleasant afternoon the girls might be seen practicing on the campus.

By the following spring the girls had three teams and some lively games were played. That same first spring "The Athletic Association invested the money received from dues in a tennis net and balls, so that another form of athletics was introduced." The tennis courts behind the old Fiske School were included with the Pearson property. Thus, Keene students have played tennis on the same location for seventy-five years.

Valentine's Day was another time to be celebrated. The committee in charge "provided a very clever entertainment, and the rest of the evening was spent in games and dancing," according to the class historian. The second year the girls persuaded Principal Rhodes to allow them to invite boyfriends; thus originated the longest-standing social tradition at Keene. Although formal dress has now been abandoned, one special collegewide dance, held in late January or early February, still carries on this tradition, which for almost sixty years was known officially as the Mid-Year Ball.

Through late winter and early spring "the theatrical fever seized the school," according to the historian, and the next year Kate Puffer drilled the senior class for "Robin and Marion."

"Another fever seized the school as warm weather approached. That was the picnic fever. So on Fast Day practically all the students departed for Harris Grove." Thus began another tradition — the Spring Picnic, which was at Harris Grove (i.e., Wilson Pond in North Swanzey). During the first week in June was Mountain Day, a climb up Mount Monadnock, later moved to Memorial Day.[3]

There were other social events, such as play readings or going to the silent movies (except for piano accompaniment). There were at the time three such movie houses in Keene. Rhodes and his wife often had the girls in for teas and receptions. Often Dudley played the piano at these events, and often they ended in a game of charades. On New Year's Eve the faculty held receptions for the students, "so the party took the form of a progressive reception until the latter part of the evening when the faculty and students gathered at the home of the principal to play games, sing and have refreshments."

Generally, however, once on campus the students lived a strict, cloisterlike life. Chapel exercises were conducted daily. There was a demanding class load, and all actions were closely observed. Morrison and Rhodes (and Mason, later) believed that the teaching was not just any kind of profession. It *was* different. The well-being of society depended on it more than on other professions. Teachers and student teachers had to live by a stricter moral code. Before Fiske Hall was built, however, the girls were able to escape the regimen at the end of the day. "We were on our own pretty much," recalled one alumna; "we had plenty of dates." But, whether they were aware of it or not, the school was keeping an eye on them.

At one time it was brought to Kent's attention that several girls living on Washington Street assembled late every afternoon and walked downtown giggling. Surely there was some mischief afoot there. So Kent did his duty. He followed the students, trying to remain undetected. In this he was unsuccessful. He succeeded, however, in finding what they were up to. They were making their daily visit to the post office.

Probably the most enjoyable affair of the whole year [Howe wrote] was the reception which Mr. and Mrs. Rhodes gave to the seniors just before graduation. Not a single junior would give a definite answer when asked whether the juniors were invited to the reception. This looked rather suspicious, but when some time had gone by and none of them apeared at the reception they were promptly forgotten. Therefore, there was a general exclamation of surprise from the guests when, upon being led to the dining room, they found behind each chair a junior dressed as a dainty little waitress. Never were people more skillfully served than those guests.[4]

Dr. Charles Jefferson of the Broadway Tabernacle, New York City, offered a brilliant baccalaureat sermon, and President E. Buritt Bryan of Colgate University delivered the commencement address to the first graduating class on June 28, 1910. Graduating were Josephine Holt Howes; Nina May Ball; Bertha Sara Merriam; and two sisters, Catherine Matilda and Marietta Isabelle Willoughby. Today they would be called non-traditional students, since they were already teachers but needed further academic preparation. "As the five graduates went out into the world," wrote Josephine Howes, "I think that they could not but feel that they were better teachers and stronger women, not only on account of the actual book knowledge they had gained but also from their contact with other students and above all from their contact with the strong men and women of which our faculty is composed."[5]

So ended the first school year: it had been obviously successful from the student's perspective, and very likely also from Rhodes' point of view, although perhaps less so from the faculty viewpoint. Rogers resigned, and although Hotchkiss as music instructor remained another year, it must have been rather difficult for him to work with the effervescent Dudley who, aside from his history and manual training classes, was singing solos, playing the piano at various public functions, and more pertinently forming his own music groups.

Alice Lord opened her history of the class of 1911, the first traditional class, with an account that is not that unfamiliar today:

Girls of every description were walking down the Main Street in Keene, some going, some coming, but their destination was the Keene Normal School. On the coming day the school was to open for its second year of work, and already girls were beginning to arrive from all over the state. The new pupils watched longingly when they saw some seniors who had already arrived, greet a sister classmate. It was enough to make even the bravest heart homesick, to see those girls greet each other after the summer's separation. Surely it was a proof of the friendships formed the preceding year.

Leita Dodge, a student, "had charge of assigning boarding places for all new comers, but while she hunted lodging houses, she kept one eye on the driveway and the minute she saw a senior coming, she would drop everything, give one glad cry, and rush into the other girl's outstretched arms. But who is this uttering that joyful cry, 'Oh, Mr. Kent.' None other than Catherine Bowles, who had just caught a glimpse of our science teacher across the hall."

Student teaching became a major experience for the students in the second year. Jane Blair of Emporia, Kansas, replaced Rogers, but instead of pedagogy, she began teaching home economics in January 1911. The home economics courses, wrote Alice Lord, "will prove more useful to some girls than others," but she noted that it was "very interesting to some members of the faculty who always knew when the cooking class was in session." She was thinking primarily, it turns out, of Dudley.

The seniors elected Agnes Barrett as president of their class. She helped organize many of the extracurricular activities, and at one of their meetings the class chose red and white for the school's colors. Rhodes chose the word "Service" as the college motto. Under the direction of Mr. Hotchkiss the glee club put on an operetta, *The Jap Girl*, which was such a success that it was repeated several times in subsequent years.

Morrison knew well enough from his studies that matrimony was a major reason for high turnover among teachers. Lord noted it even in student teaching. "Let me give this note of warning," she wrote. "Beware of soldier boys on your teaching experience. They sometimes prove dangerous to the heart."

Despite this danger, Keene's first class of traditional students remained very much intact. Morrison and Rhodes planned a particularly special commencement for the first twenty-one graduates of the two-year curriculum. Dr. William W. Fenn, Dean of the Harvard Divinity School, gave the baccalaureat sermon in the Unitarian church, and Dr. Paul Monroe of Columbia delivered the commencement address. Morrison himself presented the diplomas, but the celebration did not end there. The home economics juniors served a dinner for the first graduating class, after which each of the commencement speakers, guests, and faculty offered a toast to the class. Then, wrote Lord,

> came the hardest part of the day — saying goodbye. Some slipped out without a word of farewell, feeling that the ordeal would be too much; others started in bravely but broke down before the goodbyes were over; and those whose hearts were fullest, could only hold out their hands in mute farewell. So the end came as we parted. Then we began to realize that whereas our Normal School days were over, twenty-one teachers, however, had been started out into the world to show what the Keene Normal School has prepared them to do. With willing hands did we set out that day, knowing that even as the past history of the school had been in our hands, so in some degree would its future history be as we should make it ... and to this our school, we would most willingly dedicate our best endeavors, and strive to make them worthy of her.

The graduates of 1910 and 1911 kept in touch with each other throughout their lives. When being interviewed in 1976, the six survivors generally said they had not been active in alumni affairs, although they held their own reunions and still kept in touch with each other. They said, pretty soon the faculty they knew left and it became a different school, and so it did.[6] Kent left with Rhodes in 1911. Three of the four practice teachers resigned. By next year Puffer went to Cambridge, Massachusetts, Hotchkiss left, Blair left. Of the original Morrison-Rhodes faculty only Dudley remained.

The students from the Rhodes adminstration set a pattern of student life that carried on into the Mason years. They never associated much with later graduates, even though they chose the school colors and established an excellent tradition of teacher dedication.

7

Rhodes' Resignation

IN 1911 RHODES RESIGNED as principal to become superintendent of schools in Pasadena, California. Was that a step down, a step up, or a step out? For all the austere look of his official photograph, there is a hint that Rhodes was too progressive in his educational theories. Morrison reported:

> the criticism was made that while the schooling which the [Keene] children received tended to make them mentally alert, it left them far from capable in any of the specific arts of the school room. No course of study was followed and nobody could tell at any given time whether the schools were making good their expectations or not.

Marietta Willoughby Derby, class of 1910, and Blanche Chandler, class of 1911, recalled that Rhodes "was noted here for his outstanding theories of pedagogy, one of which was his unique idea of 'no rules,' " to which these old-timers added, "we respected his principle and carried out his theory to the letter."[1] Rhodes was, apparently, much more liberal than the average normal school principal at the turn of the century. Circumstantial evidence indicates, however, that his liberalism was not a source of real disagreement, but disappointment was. He stepped out of the New Hampshire system.

From 1910 to 1912 New Hampshire had in Robert Bass its most Progressives governor up to that time — and quite possibly for the entire twentieth century. He had been a part of the Progressive revolt started by Winston Churchill in 1906, and his governorship signaled success for the Progressive in the state house. What Morrison was doing for state education, Bass now did for state politics; he set about abolishing abuses and favoritism, establishing the direct primary, demanding rigorous civil service performance, and promoting other democratic principles. Keene was established during an excellent political climate.

Mrs. Sargeant, an officer of the New Hampshire Grange, visited the college and publicized its needs: a new school building and a dormitory. Very likely Morrison assured Rhodes that the normal school could expect the full backing of the state and that appropriations for expansion would soon be forthcoming. Certainly, if the state were to take another educational step forward it would be in Bass's term — or so it seemed. Bass encouraged his supporters to work for a bill to expand the educational facilities at both Durham and Keene. His bill passed by 225-47 votes in the House and by 22-1 votes in the Senate. Keene was to receive $44,000 for two new buildings.

One can only imagine Rhodes' shock when in April 1911 Bass vetoed the bill for educational expansion. The veto was doubly bitter because the legislature had just approved the appropriation of $40,000 to Dartmouth — which it later received. That came on heels of news that Dartmouth had just received a large sum from private sources.

A storm of protest arose after the veto of the bill, which included a $50,000 appropriation for Durham. Professor Charles Parsons, head of the chemistry department at Durham for twenty years, a man who had established a national reputation, resigned in protest.

The *Cheshire Republican* printed a letter from John Neal of Portsmouth to Bass, which began, "I am the son of a farmer and know what a struggle for an education without assistance means." He then compared with bitterness the facilities at Dartmouth with the needs of Durham and Keene.[2] Letters poured into the governor's office. One correspondent wrote simply, "Mr. Bass, why did you do this?" Another wrote, "In regard to the Keene Normal School you said, 'there does not seem to be an immediate necessity for an enlargement of its capacity.' What is Dartmouth College's immediate necessity?" It was a real shock. Three years later at the laying of the cornerstone of Fiske Hall, Charles O'Neill said he still could not "quite see why the governor encouraged all its supporters to work for it until the last minute and then threw a bucket of cold water on them." Wallace Mason later reported that "the failure to secure an appropriation for new buildings in 1911 was a great disappointment to the school and its friends and set back its advancement very materially."[3]

Bass had been caught in a difficult political game. The legislature had approved spending more money than was available. Someone had to act responsibly, and it fell to the governor. The legislators had put the Dartmouth appropriation into the state budget, and Bass could not alter individual items in the budget without vetoing the entire bill. The only place left to cut expenses was in special appropriations bills like the one for Keene and Durham. It was certainly a tough situation. Mayor Herbert E. Fay of Keene said in 1914, "Gov. Bass vetoed this normal school appropriation, but down deep in my heart I know that if ever there was an honest man it was Ex Gov. Bass. He may have been right to veto the bill if the condition of the treasury did not warrant spending the money. If the situation demanded it, I might have done the same."[4]

Given these circumstances, Rhodes may very well have thought that, if this were an example of New Hampshire's most progressive stage, perhaps he should seek professional advancement elsewhere.

The 1911 catalog suggests the general chaos that took place after the Bass veto. The first thirty pages were a well-planned, traditional-looking catalog, but it appeared that after his resignation Rhodes turned the completion of the catalog over to Kent, who was interested in succeeding Rhodes. Rhodes did not think Kent sufficiently qualified to be principal, because of his lack of advanced degrees. As a result, Kent also resigned before the end of the school year. Rather than finishing the catalog in a reasonable way, Kent apparently ran out of time and just threw in his nature study notes to give the catalog a little body. Or, perhaps in his haste he stuck the catalog notes in the Kansas envelope and the nature study notes in the New Hampshire printer's envelope instead of vice versa.

Kent certainly provided enough material to produce a nice sized catalog for 1911, but it also made for some of the oddest reading in catalog history. For instance, the reader is instructed on how to make a seed tester, and how to prune, bud, and graft apple trees. The prospective student was faced with a whole series of questions which had never occurred to her before, such as, "What is the color of the gills of a toadstool?" and "How deep shall we plant our radish seeds?" In another place the reader is advised to place some yeast into two bottles of sweetened water. "Cork one...tightly, and put both of them away in a warm place, yet where children can see them...thrust a match into the bottle [see what happens?]" After talking about a whole range of substances and experiments, the catalog concludes: "Sum up all you have learned about the substance and their uses. Ask all the practical questions possible, such as those connected with cooking above, and could you keep acids in tin cans?" The catalog ends with this puzzler: "Would vinegar do as well in a tin can as in a jug, etc.?"

While both Kent and Rhodes left in a hurry, neither left with animosity. Rhodes was always fond of Keene and Keene Normal School, and he kept in touch with people at the college and in the town for the rest of his life. In 1926 he wrote to Mason from Mexico City, where he was superintendent of the American School Foundation, saying what a wonderful person and wonderful graduate Frances Cram, Keene Normal School class of 1924, was. He visited the school twice, in September and December 1932, when his son was a student at Dartmouth and he was professor of education at Indiana University. He died at age seventy-five following an operation in Houston, Texas, where he had made his home and where his son still lives. The *Sentinel* noted that he was a nationally known educator and that he had "made many friends here."[5]

8

"Daddy" Mason

"ONE WORD for Daddy Mason — RESPONSIBILITY!!! — Whenever I see that Rolaid sign on television, I read responsibility! That was Daddy's word." So said Ray Harwood, class of 1931, basking in Florida sunshine and far, far removed from Keene Normal School; but obviously his experiences at the college and with its president, Wallace E. Mason, were still, after half a century, very much on his mind.

After Morrison, Mason was the man who was most responsible for Keene's reputation as an excellent normal school. He was the one who made his influence felt on nearly every single student during his long tenure of twenty-eight years.

The year 1911 was the beginning of a new era in teacher training in New Hampshire. Morrison had discovered that the principal at Plymouth had dipped his hands into the school's finances and had to dismiss him. Morrison then appointed Ernest L. Silver, who remained at Plymouth until 1946. The year 1911 was not only one of new principals for the normal schools but also one of unification of both schools under one board of trustees and of further standardization of the curriculum and of business practices.

Mason looked like a "daddy" when in 1911 he became principal of Keene Normal School. Born on June 24, 1861, in North Conway, New Hampshire, the son of John Edward and Lizzie Randall Mason, he attended Bowdoin College, from which he received by 1881 both his B.A. and M.A. degrees. After Bowdoin he had a brief teaching experience and then decided

Bertha McKenna "crossing the bar" in 1917 during a contest between the classes of 1917 and 1918. From left are Bertha Bryant, Laura Bradley, Miriam Nichols, Grace Fitzgerald, Caroline Marston, Doris Potter, Helen Rand, Ann Drenan, an unknown, Mary Riddle, Harriet Powers, and the last two also unknown. All were from the class of 1918 except the scorekeeper. Miriam Nichols and Bertha McKenna who were from the class of 1917. "I hope from noting Miriam's smile that 1917 won!" Madrienne McDonough wrote the author in 1983.

to study law. The years 1887 and 1888 were big ones for Mason. He concluded his high school teaching experience; married Nettie Robinson of Thomaston, Maine; passed the Colorado bar exam; and set up a law practice in Cardiff, Tennessee, which he maintained from 1888 to 1890. He then returned to the field of education in New England. Before coming to Keene he had been superintendent of schools in North Andover, Massachusetts, for five years.

After returning to the Northeast, Mason attended summer sessions at both Harvard and Clark universities. Professor Paul Hanus, head of the Department of Education at Harvard, said of Mason, "he is a fine man, possessing excellent personal qualities and scholarship, and excellent insight into, and skill in dealing with, educational and administrative questions. He is in my opinion one of the ablest of the younger superintendents."[1]

Mason was young only in the experience he had spent as superintendent. At age fifty he was hardly young in years. He was, however, full of confidence, and he always spoke and wrote directly and personally on all issues. His hair had long since thinned out to almost complete baldness. To the student he immediately became "Daddy" Mason. It was an honored tradition in those years to make one's principal into a legend of lovable eccentricity if he allowed the opportunity; and Mason afforded many opportunities.

In some ways Mason's career paralleled Morrison's. Mason was bright, well educated, a self-made man for whom the promise of American life had come true. He was confident of himself, of his country, and of the steady march of progress. He was, like Morrison and John Dewey, one of the early group of educators who had a strong classical background, but who then devoted their lives to education and considered themselves professional educators. Like Morrison, he had also climbed the educational ladder as teacher, principal, superintendent, and now principal of the Keene Normal School. There the similarity ends. Morrison was basically an intellectual. Morrison went on to become professor of education at the University of Chicago as already noted. He soon became identified with "the Chicago school," and with the president of the University of Chicago, Robert Hutchins, a man who, in many ways, was very similar to Morrison. Mason was essentially a doer. He enjoyed the doing of education rather than thinking about it. It is not surprising, therefore, that he, and the whole college in time, fell under Dewey's more popular influence rather than under Morrison's.

Mason had little more than a month to prepare for his new task. Rhodes had left by the time Mason arrived, but Rhodes had met with Morrison and Trustee Corning "to go over school matters," and they in turn introduced Mason to the work ahead of him. Morale was the major problem. Most of the Rhodes faculty had left, and student enrollment was only three more than in 1910.

Mason had no trouble in reestablishing morale. He infused the spirit of confidence in others. He was an expert in public relations. Enrollment for 1912, after Mason's first year in office, took a jump upward, as it would continue to do until 1929, except for one year during World War I. Given his natural proclivities, Mason's task was not difficult. He did not have to make any significant curriculum changes. He acknowledged Rhodes "and his able assistants for their organizational work. . . . So much has been accomplished in the two short years of the school's history," Mason wrote, "that the work of his successor was comparatively easy."[2]

More important for the future of the college were Mason's attitudes toward the nature of work in the classroom and on hiring faculty. "Our teaching," Mason once said, "differs greatly from that of the ordinary cultural college work. The college teaches the subject matter. We teach the subject matter also, but with this added idea constantly in mind, 'How are you going to teach these facts and these ideas to your pupils in elementary and high schools?' " There was a strong moral emphasis on the work. "We stress also the idea that as teachers they are not only teaching children Reading, History, French, Latin, *etc.*, but more important that they are so to teach these subjects as to develop character in their pupils. We are somewhat old-fashioned, holding daily simple devotional exercises consisting of scripture reading, the Lord's prayer, and the singing of a hymn."

Equally revealing was a speech Mason made in 1931 on faculty hiring. He said:

Scan with thoughtful mind the character of the faculty you employ. As the teacher, so the school. In the long list of instructors of the past, the men who stand out above all others are those who are men of strong Christian character. Forty years of educational experience convince me that teachers who have strong Christian character, who are intimately connected with the church of their choice and who participate in the work of the church in their communities, are the ones who are best fitted to train our boys and girls for the highest type of life work. Before employing teachers for my institution, I ask them, "What is your relation to the church life of your community and how do you spend your Sabbath?" in the firm belief that those who can answer those questions satisfactorily will make the finest leaders of youth.[3]

The trouble with Mason's philosophy was not that he went too far with his emphasis on moral development but that he neglected the intellectual life that should take place in a normal school. After Puffer left in 1912, Mason's faculty included only three Ph.D.'s for the next thirty years; and each of them stayed only a short period of time. Morrison complained about this, but only indirectly, and when discussing finances. He wrote, "As pointed out in my last report," the teachers at Keene Normal School "were in some cases paid much more for their services than their training, ability or attainments would warrant." "We learned to teach, but we were not challenged intellectually," recalled Marion Tebbetts Wood. Too many teachers taught from the book. Ruth Seaver Kirk recalled that "the male teachers, in particular, were glued to what was on the printed page." Mason himself remained intellectually alert, surprisingly so. Early in his administration he invited the well-known social reformer Margaret Sanger

*The old assembly hall, now Drenan Auditorium, where daily chapel exercises were held.
On the west wall was the school motto, "Enter to learn... Go forth to serve."
On the east was Mason's favorite, "If you do this, you can't do that."*

to talk to the students. In her speech Sanger said that it was now the time for women to "enter to learn and go forth to serve." Mason liked the phrase. He talked about it with his faculty, and with their approval it became the school motto and Mason had it painted on the wall in the new auditorium in Parker Hall. Sanger's phrase fitted Mason's philosophy and the theme of "Service" that Rhodes had established.

The very strictness of the moral code made the Keene Normal School experience a memorable one. Usually the first things that alumni of 1911 to 1939 relate about the college were the dress codes and the curfew hours. Mason himself lived by these strict codes. After retirement, for instance, he refused to run for the school board because his son Harold had already submitted bids for proposed school buildings in Keene, and Mason "did not wish to be tainted with a conflict of interest."[4]

"Daddy," as Harwood recalled, was a real demon on responsibility. Once a member of a janitor's family, who were college camp tenants, failed to build a fire there for some female students visiting it. "If another slip-up like this occurs," Mason warned, "I shall have to change tenants as we must have somebody there who will do the work." Sometimes, of course, he got enmeshed in his own code. One widely circulated story was that one of his children stole a cannonball from Central Square in Keene. After all his preaching, Mason was too embarrassed to have his son take it back so he buried it in the basement of his home and said, "If anyone ever finds this, he will think it a relic of some past war." Another instance was when the old gym (i.e., the old, old gym, the barn behind Hale Building) was being remodeled, he took from it fine black cherry wood—it had to come out, anyhow—and used it as wainscoting in the dining room of his newly constructed house on Appian Way. That was a sore point for both faculty and students. But these two examples are the exceptions. By and large, he was as strict with himself as he was with others. He was kind, forgiving, even loving; and by and large, the students and faculty appreciated and loved him. When superintendents needed teachers, they contacted Mason. Mason then contacted the student. He was usually the contact for the student's first job, and that association alone created strong loyalty. The dedication of the first yearbook was to Wallace E. Mason, "Our Director who starts us on our journey with solicitous care, who champions our struggle for the coveted goal; who steers us to our haven in triumph, this book is most affectionately dedicated." In 1925 Evelyn Fuller wrote in her diary what many other students experienced. "Tonight," she recorded, "Daddy Mason was just the best ever!"[5]

The First Construction: Fiske, Parker, and the Heating Plant

New Hampshire was more committed to its second normal school than Rhodes believed. Morrison knew that he had wide support in the legislature for major construction in Keene, and Mason was politician enough to realize that all was not lost because of Bass's veto. In late 1912 the board of trustees contacted the architectural firm of Brainerd and Leeds in Boston to draw up plans for a classroom building with an assembly hall, a dormitory building with dining facilities, and a central heating plant that could be used for both buildings as well as for additional ones that might be added. Brainerd himself presented the plans to the board. The legislative campaign got under way immediately, and Governor Samuel Felker gave it his endorsement. By May 5, 1913, the bill had passed all legislative hurdles.

On a cold but snowless Thursday afternoon, January 22, 1914, about 400 people gathered around the footings of what is now Fiske Hall for cornerstone ceremonies. There were brief remarks outside by Mason,

Governor Felker, and Mayor Herbert Fay of Keene. Felker, with the assistance of the mason foreman, who of course did all the work, laid the cornerstone. In it was placed a copper box with the issues of the *Sentinel,* the *Cheshire Republican,* and other memorabilia. The party then hurried into Hale Building where longer speeches were made. Frank H. Whitcomb, city clerk and member of the state board of education, spoke eloquently, as did Charles J. O'Neill, a late convert to the normal school idea, and the Reverend Josiah H. Seward, the main speaker for the occasion.

Morrison was unable to attend the ceremonies, but almost certainly he selected the names for the two major buildings. The dormitory was to be named for Catherine Fiske, whom we all know as the founder and proprietor of the Young Ladies Seminary in Keene, and the classroom building was named for Francis Wayland Parker. Parker, whom most of us do not know, was a native of New Hampshire who had served with distinction in the embattled New Hampshire Fourth Regiment during the Civil War. After the war he went into teaching and then into teacher training at Quincy, Massachusetts. With ideas too radical for Massachusetts, he headed for the Midwest, where he became head of the Cook County Normal School, outside Chicago. There he assembled one of the ablest bodies of teachers ever gathered under one roof. He struck out at the mechanized, assembly-line tactics of teaching made popular and easy by textbook publishers and insisted that a child should study things before reading about them. He made the Chicago area a think tank for educational philosophy. "The glory of Colonel Parker's influence," wrote an informed admirer, was "that it elevated the teacher from a day laborer to a worker for life and eternity, from a lesson-assigner and reciting post to the co-operator with God in the education of children, from a taskmaster to a friend of children." Parker had made his own path in higher education, although he himself claimed to be a follower of Froebel and Johann Pestalozzi. His place in Chicago as professional educator was taken by John Dewey (1894-1904) and later by Morrison himself. Those conscientious people who have to serve on committees can appreciate Parker, who once prayed, "O Lord, preserve thou me from the foregone conclusion."[6]

In 1914 only the central hall and the west wing of Fiske were completed. "In the building," Morrison reported, "is a large living room and a beautiful dining room [the Central Hall]. Kitchen space has been provided to take care of 250." The three new buildings, Fiske, Parker, and the heating plant, were barely ready for operation when school opened in September 1914.

Fiske "was so new that the stain on the doors and in the closets had not dried. Many of us had clothes that got stained. Later the matron came around to make a list of those things that were spoiled. We told her and later we were reimbursed. I remember," said Elinor Gibney Paine, "I had one blouse which I valued at fifty cents!"

Parker Hall had a capacity for 200 students in the classrooms. The heating plant housed two large coal-fed boilers, and heated Parker; Fiske; Hale; and two buildings long since gone, the greenhouse and the barn, then used as a gymnasium.

"The main building and the dormitory are both of Colonial style of architecture, closely resembling the old college halls at Dartmouth and Harvard," noted the public announcement. "The principal contractor was the Nashua Building Company which provided some sub-contracting in Keene for electricians and plumbers."

"The rooms on the first floor [of Parker]. . .comprise a laboratory. . .a psychology room, a supervisory room, an English room, a history room, and a sewing room." A manual training room in the basement housed twenty workbenches, an electric motor, a lathe, and other equipment.

"The assembly hall on the second floor occupies two stories," the announcement read. "The hall will seat 200 and the stage 100. A special ventilation system was installed for the hall. A domestic science room complete with sinks, cookstoves, and 'sani-steel individual cooking tables' " was also housed in Parker.[7] After September 1914 dorm life became a dominant part of student life at the school.

Student Life after the Building of Fiske

For the first ten years of its existence Keene Normal School was similar to a nineteenth-century female academy. The only difference was its emphasis on the education curriculum and practicum and in its legal openness to men. One young man, Harlon Goodwin, enrolled in 1915, but being alone with 150 young women proved too much; and he did not return after the Christmas holiday. Beyond that, school rigor, including even dress styles, was not much different from that of Miss Fiske's seminary.

The social status was, of course, different. It was Morrison's goal to draw upon "the best native stock" of New Hampshire, refine, educate, and use it.[8] The school was an avenue, an opportunity for young women disposed to better themselves through the process of helping still younger people better themselves. Elinor Paine recalled:

Most of us had come from smaller places, although a few came from Manchester and Nashua. It was a 'big deal' to be living in a large town [like Keene]. It was a wonderful experience living with other girls. There might sometimes be differences of opinion, [but] there was never anything really very serious. And as we look back over the friendships that we made, it was really a wonderful time that we lived through.

These reminiscences hark back to one of Horace Mann's statements that "coiled up in this institution, as in a spring, there is a vigor whose un-coiling may wheel the spheres." Unfortunately, high academic standards were not upheld. Had they been, the normal school perhaps would have been the truly revolutionary institution Mann saw as possible. Even so, the concept was revolutionary in that it gave to many the opportunity for a college-type experience, which had a profound effect on their lives. Indeed, at Keene the academic demands were more rigorous than they were at most normal schools.

Morrison did everything he could to support the students. In 1914 he hired Dr. Sue L. Koons, "a graduate physician," a woman of education and refinement, "to act as dorm mother for the students." It was hard to keep a woman physician in that role for long, but that was always the ideal, and Morrison was able to hire several, each staying only a year. The young women had plenty of opportunity for physical exercise and plenty of good food at low cost. Most of them realized and appreciated what was being offered and took advantage of it.

For the years that Keene was a girls' school a rhythmic, almost ritualistic pattern developed in student life. When new students first arrived on open-ing day, they always arrived scared and apprehensive. Then their hearts sank when they watched the seniors greet each other. They then became wretchedly homesick for exactly one week. But just before they died of homesickness a welcoming event, usually a corn roast, restored their spirits, and they "decided that life was worth living after all."[9]

The leading downtown Protestant churches always had receptions for the girls which were always very popular. No wonder! They could go to church unchaperoned! Church receptions also provided one of the few occasions to meet young men or, second best, a Keene girl who had some brothers. The West Hill Climb, the Harris Grove picnic, the Halloween party, Christmas recital, Mid-Year Ball, the Spring Hop, Mountain Day, and various sports events continued very much in the same pattern in the teens, the 1920s, and the 1930s as that established by the classes of 1910 and 1911. The pattern became so ritualistic that one student wrote of the opening day experience, "As usual, we arrived rather tired and nervous."[10]

The girls viewed themselves as being very modern, of course, and when they talked about giving a "tiger" to the "swells" and "peaches" at a "corking," everyone knew that they were going to give a "cheer" to the "young men" and "women" at a "party."

Some classes have always been more dynamic than others. At Keene the first dynamic classes were those of 1914 and 1915. Undoubtedly, Fiske Hall provided a good place for an exchange of ideas as well as good housing. Students organized a current events club, and members read papers on the "Causes of the European War," the "Effects of the War in America," "New Trends in Education," "Probable Results of the Mexican War," the "Origins and History of Wall Street," and "New Hampshire Industries." This was quite a performance on a wide range of topics! They were making a college out of their normal school. A glee club with thirty-four members also organized and was particularly active.

Two of the sparks from these classes were Alice ("Stub") Stebbins and Ruth McQuestin. They organized the first regular student publication, a quarterly, which they named the *Kronicle*. Stub was the editor, but she always worked closely with McQuestin. Together they produced a vigorous and surprisingly frank publication. Perhaps they had heard Sanger speak, for there was latent feminism in much of their writing. Although there was a lot of discussion about engagements and marriages, there were also references to "the holy bands of padlock" and to a dropout "who *thought* she preferred married life to teaching."

One written composition, "A Mid-Spring Day Dream," is about two Keene Normal School girls, about whom one "the Fairy Queen predicts will go on to 'teach in the art school in Boston and the other in a new college in Mexico.' " Stub never taught art in Boston, but she did adopt a child in addition to one of her own, and she became very active in public affairs in Granville, Massachusetts.[11]

McQuestin wrote the first school song, and Maude Howes wrote the music:

> Girls, up and fight, fight for old Keene Normal
> Our loyalty proclaim!!!
> In every contest we must strive to conquer,
> For there must be no limit to her fame....
> So kindle bright the fires upon her altar,
> To burn while time shall last,

In future years its flame may be the emblem
Of courage, strength and vigor unsurpassed.
She reigns supreme, the loved and honored sovereign,
That through our lives shall rule.
Unfurl the red and white, the only colors in sight,
As we hail our dear Keene Normal School.

Not great poetry, but compare it, for instance, with a few lines from Vassar's "Alma Mater":

Hark, Alma Mater, through the world is ringing
The praise thy grateful daughters bring to thee!
Oh, thou, who dost hold the torch of truth before us
Across the lawns we hear the magic song:
    'Tis Vassar, our beloved Alma Mater, that stands
For ever fair and high and strong!

Or compare it with Smith's, written at about the same time (1910):

To you, O Alma Mater,
    O mother great and true
From all your loyal children
    Comes up the song anew.
Where swings the red sun upward,
    Where sinks he down to rest,
Are hearts that backward turning
    Still find you first and best.

McQuestin's work certainly compares favorably!

Very few students complained openly to Daddy Mason. He ruled with a firm hand, as all alumni know, but Stub and McQuestin did. At one point they complained, "life at Keene Normal is just one fee after another." In December 1913 Mason changed the Christmas holidays, and, said Stub, "A lot of the girls did not like it a bit." Even their humor was frank. Under "Personals" one could read, "Helen Peabody in Psychology discussion on Emotions: 'Mr. Leonard, what would I mean if I should say, I loved you with all my heart?' "[12]

The only way to stop this trend, Mason knew, was to get "safer" editors for succeeding years, and by and large he was able to do this. The editor following Stub annunced that, among other things, the school needed "a few young men," "two nights out a week," and "concrete side walks on campus." After that blast the *Kronicle* became a meaningless and uninteresting publication. Not surprisingly, many alumnae of the late teens could not remember it at all.

Subsequent classes were quite spirited even if their publications were not. The class of 1916 put on *A Midsummer Night's Dream,* which was so successful that it was talked about for years — even in the college catalogue! The class of 1917 had a lot of live wires in it and has been most active in alumni participation.

Elinor Gibney Paine recalled:

We had some tennis. We also played cricket. That probably was our most vigorous sport.... The chief recreation for my group of friends was to take long walks on Sunday afternoons and sometimes on weekdays after school.... One time we were out for a walk. One of our group was a little older than the rest of us. We thought she was very old. I think she was twenty-five! On this particular occasion some boys came along, and started acting rather fresh, so we began calling this girl mother so the boys would think we had our mother with us.

And the trick worked! Hiking continued to be a popular form of recreation until the late 1930s.

One of the highlights in our social life...was when one or the other of us would receive a box from home. And there was a grand celebration that night. But of course, our lights had to be out by ten o'clock so it didn't last very long after study hours. Everyone shared what they had.

Another memorable occasion was the short free time between the end of supper and the seven o'clock bell for study hours. "Then we could play games. One such game was Pit — and we made plenty of noise playing it."

"Sometimes the eggs tasted like rubber," Elinor G. Paine continued, and "if they weren't eaten at breakfast they reappeared in the hash at lunchtime." One meal that was always popular was "Corridor Breakfast." "Sunday mornings we didn't have to go down to the dining room, and we could have corridor breakfast up in our room area," recalled Bertha Davis. Paine remembered it was

one of the meals we did enjoy.... Most of us stayed on weekends. There was no way of getting out.... On Sunday morning our breakfast consisted of coffee, toast and jelly." The toast, "was put into big pans, like milk pans — if anybody knows what a milk pan is — and heaped up high for however many people happened to be eating breakfast together.... We could just relax and take our time eating our toast. We had plenty.... That would be our Sunday morning breakfast which we really enjoyed.

Before radio and record players, students sang and danced more readily than now. Florence Wheeler, class of 1917, remembered:

They had a fireplace down in the large living room. We used to go down and have fireplace chats; sometimes we'd sing. Many times we'd have dances. I used to love to dance with Ellen Record because she had long legs and we could swing around. We'd just dance together and have fun....Sometimes we'd do other things. We had a gym teacher and she'd show us how to do a massage, rub your neck and get rid of headaches.

"We formed very close friendships. Perhaps because the school was so small and we knew everybody. A group of us kept a round robin letter going for more than sixty years," Elinor Gibney Paine and Carrie Burr Paine, both of class 1916, recalled, "and those of us who are still able to write continue that letter to this day."

Q.* "Could you describe it?"

"We have a regular numbered list. It goes from one to the other. We have people in New Hampshire and Massachusetts only now. We are supposed to keep it two weeks. Sometimes it's longer than that. But we have kept in very close touch by means of doing this."[13]

Closer, more meaningful friendships could hardly have been formed. One is indeed touched by these lasting associations. Visiting some of the older alumnae who have little left but a few clothes and a few pieces of furniture, since space in retirement homes is at a premium, one notices that their last few prized possessions is always a scrapbook or a collection of pictures and clippings from the days when they were at Keene Normal. It is obvious that the ragged clippings and the cracked pictures have been looked at often. The alumna will point out who her favorite teachers were and who her best friends were and what they did with their lives. "We shall keep in touch with each other," said Elinor Gibney Paine, "as long as any of us are able to hold a pencil or pen."

*In this and subsequent chapters the interrogator is designated as "Q."

9

Town-Gown Relationship Under Mason

GENERALLY TOWN-GOWN relationships under Mason were excellent. Mason knew how to communicate with groups of people as well as with individuals in simple yet meaningful ways. This effectiveness was apparent whether he was dealing with the public on a municipal, regional, or state level. Mason's development of the tomato club is an example of how he used a very simple project to build strong, meaningful external relations.

In his faculty position as director of nature studies, Mason took advantage of the great greenhouse behind Hale Building. He decided in 1912 to establish a seed nursery for the boys and girls of Cheshire and Hillsboro counties. Some places have corn and potato clubs, he said, but "I suggest a tomato club." "What we wish," he wrote to the youth of southwestern New Hampshire (and later the entire state), "is that you may have the pleasure of watching a seed sprout, grow into a plant and bear its fruit." It made no difference if the youth had an acre or only a flower pot; the seeds would still be sent. The youth signed a pledge card which read: "I wish to become a member of the Keene Normal Tomato Club and agree to plant the seeds sent me, to take care of at least one plant as directed and keep a written diary describing my work." Mason was assisted by Nahum Leonard, who was hired in 1912, and by students in nature studies classes, who were growing their own plants and doing their own experiments. It was new, novel, and popular. The tomato was an ideal plant to work with because the growing period was long and required much regular attention. In September came Tomato Day, during which prizes were awarded on the basis of the diary, the experiment, and the end product, the tomato. There were prizes for tomatoes of all kinds — the earliest tomato, the biggest tomato, the best plate of five, and others. Before they began winning all the prizes girls were, in the early years of the club, encouraged to join as well as boys. Soon there was no trouble in getting them to join. In the first year alone over 1,000 students enrolled in Mason's tomato club.[1] The club increased in popularity until the early 1920s. Thousands of parents were interested in their children's tomato growing. It was a simple, popular, and effective way of reaching the communities and establishing good town-gown relationships.

For the statewide community Mason developed a new and significantly different type of curriculum. He planned to train teachers for rural schools. Usually, he wrote to the board of trustees, a normal graduate goes to a rural school for "experience," and after she gets that "she flies to the city" as soon as she can. "Unless State Normal Schools help the schools that most need their help, they do not fulfill their mission."

Many students, he said, were trained in city conditions, were successful under these conditions, but were complete failures in the country. Mason therefore directed that one hour each week be devoted to the study of rural sociology. By September of his second year Mason had established a model rural school (then referred to as the Model District School) a short trolley ride down Marlboro Street. The building still stands, now a private residence. Essentially it was an old-fashioned red-brick schoolhouse comprising grades 1-7. It was, however, a model — "to make here a demonstration of how the new school activities of cooking, sewing, manual arts and nature study can add to the efficiency of the ordinary district school."

This was a real service to the state, in that over 50 percent of its students lived in rural areas and most often had poorly trained teachers. Morrison had already taken a big step toward assisting rural education by persuading the legislature to pass a compensatory funding law. The law provided that rural districts hiring qualified teachers would receive some financial aid.

Both Mason and Morrison were very much aware of services the college could perform for teachers outside the regular school sessions. As early as 1912 Mason started a series of Saturday afternoon sessions for area teachers who wanted more pedagogical training. By 1914 he had planned for the first full summer session, but it had to be canceled because of "serious miscalculations." The first full summer school was established the following year and has continued on a regular basis since then. After 1925 Keene and Plymouth rotated the holding of the summer school session.[2]

Scarcely a half-dozen years after its founding, Keene Normal's impact on the larger community was definitely felt. Cheshire and Carroll counties, for instance, far outstripped other counties in the rate of gain in trained teachers. Admittedly both, exclusive of Keene proper, had more room for improvement than the others, but, regardless, Keene Normal was largely responsible for these gains. There was still a lot of work to do. Seventy-five towns in New Hampshire had absolutely no trained teachers in their schools and 161 other towns "boasted" that they had at least one! For 1913 and 1914, 70 percent of the Keene Normal School students came from southwestern New Hampshire, including Manchester and Nashua, and about the same percentage of graduates returned to the same area to teach.[3] Thus, the college had an almost immediate beneficial impact on the southwestern third of the state.

The Morrison Curriculum of 1916

Mason's insistence on hiring only morally good instructors and graduating only morally good students helped establish Keene's reputation as an excellent teacher training institution. What focused national attention on Keene, however, was Morrison's curriculum of 1916. The two notable aspects of this curriculum were the new development of a junior high school course of studies and the unique practice/theory curriculum.

Significant change in public institutions of higher learning always takes place in response to society's needs or demands. Very likely this is another reason that so few histories of normal schools/state colleges have been written. All seem the same. What makes each distinct is how quickly, how slowly, and more important, how intelligently it responded to the demands of the times.

The greatest impact on education in the early twentieth century was the Progressive movement to abolish child labor. Morrison himself was particularly active in getting a stronger New Hampshire bill passed. After its passage, he had the job of seeing to it that the children, newly freed from labor, attended school.

Child labor laws, both state and national, meant much larger student populations which required significant curriculum changes. The parents of this new student population did not want their working children to be frittering away time learning French and Latin. If their children were going to school, as the new laws said they must, then they should learn something practical. This new school population brought to an end the singularness of the old classical curriculum, formerly the mainstay of the academies and the seminaries.

Two school systems in the United States — Los Angeles and New

Hampshire — broke away early from the traditional grammar school-high school system and set up an intermediate school, called the junior high school. Most educators watched. As soon as Morrison had enough evidence that the junior high school concept was sound, he established a teaching curriculum for it at both Keene and Plymouth. In the meantime, Rhodes, who was now in Texas, was keeping his eyes on the junior high movement and became a pioneer in that field in Texas. In the East, however, Keene would soon be the largest training ground.[4]

To meet the new development, in 1916 the board of trustees, under Morrison's direction, added a third year of instruction for students wishing to teach junior high school students. As the junior high school movement caught on rapidly in the late teens and throughout the decade of the 1920s, Keene was one of very few schools with a curriculum to prepare teachers in this new educational field.

Still more significant was the total revision of the curriculum in 1916. Just what prompted Morrison to do this we cannot know for certain. He was radical, wrote his son Hugh, in that he liked to go to the root of things. The junior high movement had already forced his attention on the curriculum. Also, Mason had by this time gobbled up the entire Keene School District and had it under the supervision of the normal school. Morrison was somewhat skeptical of that, but Mason had gone ahead anyhow. Mason's aggrandizement provided Keene with one of the largest practice areas in the nation. This also may have been an incentive for Morrison to work on the curriculum.

Perhaps his motivation was simply what he wrote in one of his reports, that "in this day of rapid development, the programs of most educational institutions need organizing about once in five years." At least one of Morrison's reasons was to raise standards in the high schools.

First of all, Morrison raised admission standards to both Keene and Plymouth. Now one had to be not only a high school graduate but a graduate of an approved high school. To make sure there was no doubt about it, he published a list of approved high schools in the catalogue! An applicant from a high school that was not approved would have to demonstrate proficiency by special testing in all academic areas.[5]

Second, the one-year program for those who were already teachers was dropped. This had been essentially a liberal arts year for those who had learned how to teach by on-the-job experience but needed academic course work. This action appeared to be politically motivated. (It is hard to justify educationally.) Morrison had written forcefully about the inequities of the state's tax system, saying that it was deliberate political injustice. The trouble, of course, was that the poor towns agreed to the tradition of local tax support as much as the rich towns. Therefore, those towns would have to realize the consequences of their decisions. Morrison still believed that teachers should receive a classical education in the high schools. If the local high schools did not do the job of educating, they could not expect the normal schools to take up the slack. For this reason Morrison abolished the "liberal arts" year.

As for the curriculum itself, Morrison interwove theories of education with the practice of it to a greater extent than was done in any other state in the nation. For three semesters a student did her "professional" study — that is, one education course, which met three times a week, plus two hours of observation. At the same time, there were ten to twelve hours of "methodological" study, which meant learning, often in the practice rooms, how to teach language, geography, arithmetic, history, and so forth. Last, she took "academic" studies, which was somewhat of a misnomer. Actually, this was a collection of the leftovers that did not fit into the "methodological" category. "Academic," therefore, not only included such courses as nature study, music, and drawing but also manual arts, sewing, and gardening! Following two or three semesters of this program was a full semester of practice teaching. Sometimes this program was divided into a half day of practice teaching and a half day of study. Some students in their senior year were put on a nine-week sequence in the classroom, and then nine weeks in the practice school, or vice versa, repeating the sequence for the second semester. "Theory and practice were made as nearly simultaneous as possible," Harry A. Brown wrote. Furthermore, Brown declared that he "searched through catalogs of teachers colleges of the early period in an effort to discover another and as complete and early an example of the union of theory and experience in the education of teachers extending throughout an entire curriculum," and his "search failed to reveal an earlier example of such a practice in such complete operation in an entire state." The welding together of teaching experience and educational theory had been done before but never on a statewide basis. Therein lay the uniqueness of Morrison's program.[6] Brown was one of the bright young superintendents whom Morrison had attracted to his office, and soon had him in charge of educational research. As a doctoral student at Columbia, in the 1930s, Brown realized more fully the uniqueness of his experience under Morrison in New Hampshire and based his doctoral dissertation on that experience.

In 1915 John Dewey published his famous *Schools of Tomorrow* and, in 1916, the book that established him as foremost of American philosophers, *Democracy and Education.* Dewey was often misquoted and greatly misunderstood, but one of the catch phrases that came from his works was "to learn by doing." As soon as Dewey's ideas got to be understood, even if incompletely, it appeared that Keene already had in full operation exactly the kind of program that Dewey and his followers were expounding. Keene (and Plymouth) already had the "schools of tomorrow." That is how Keene got its high reputation in teacher education. That is why Florence Wheeler could say in fully accurate recollection, "Oh, a Keene girl could get a job anyplace." Indeed, she could! Keene's first years under Mason and Morrison were spectacularly successful.

Student Teaching Experiences

"Teaching," said Jacques Barzun, "is extremely hard work; it is the original and literal brain-drain, being the continual readjustment of one's thought to another's . . . to strengthen and enlarge [another's thought]." The graduates of Keene Normal not only had the hard intellectual challenge of teaching but many other difficulties and situations of which Barzun had not the slightest experience. Teaching in rural New Hampshire provided situations undreamed of by Barzun or education textbook writers.

Ruth Seaver Kirk described her first job at Newington. "It wasn't a school at all. It was the downstairs of the town hall, and the town hall was divided into two rooms. And there was an older woman who had the first four grades, and I had the four upper grades." She, like so many others, worked from 8:00 A.M. to 6:00 P.M. for thirteen dollars per week.

"My first day . . . with grades 5, 6, 7, 8 was something which I shall not forget," Kirk recalled. "The three members of the school board came in and stood at the front of the room because they wanted to see this new teacher in action!" Certainly this situation was not in the lesson plan. Nonetheless, she began with the Pledge of Allegiance, Psalm 100 ("Old Hundred"), and the Lord's Prayer. She convinced them of her orthodoxy, and they left. "I relaxed and was glad to see them go."

Practice teaching often meant "learning by doing" in the most basic sense. Students were sent out to practice-teach without a supervising teacher, and sometimes they were expected to open the school term. After they had done their stint, the school would be closed until the assignment of the next "free" practice teacher. Mason went along with this system. Eventually it got him in trouble, as we shall see. It appears that it became fairly common after Morrison left the state.

Kirk found student teaching "one great horror. I was so scared that if

I did know anything about the subject when I went into the class...whatever I knew went right out of my head. It was a nightmare, dreadful. I don't remember one day that was really pleasant. It was that bad." Elinor Gibney Paine liked second grade at Lincoln School, but "advanced eighth at the old junior high school were my worst times...those were pure horror."

Florence Wheeler related experiences that pointed to the missionarylike work of teaching in rural New Hampshire — and even in Keene! Her first practice-teaching experience was at the junior high in Keene. The students there, she said,

> were from the north end of Keene, tough, oh boy were they tough. They had put out three or four teachers. They couldn't take it, they couldn't stand it. So finally they put me in... I walked in, and they started to cut up, and I started in laying the law down. You couldn't do it now, but I did then. They were great big boys — as big as you are — so they started to act up, so I got right after them, and I walked up and down the aisles — "Just fold your hands on your desks right now." They weren't going to do it, so I walked around with a book, and anyone who didn't have his hands folded, I whanged 'im....So I got 'em quieted down. They weren't going to learn arithmetic. I decided they were, so I taught them. Pretty soon the principal came in — his name was Davis....He opened the door in great amazement.

But at that time Wheeler was really an experienced practice teacher. Handling the north end boys was not as challenging as her very first practice-teaching experience:

> I was sent to East _____ville to practice teach, and when I got there all that was there was a red schoolhouse, your typical red schoolhouse. The hedgehogs had been out and had eaten the seats out of the toilet, and if the children went to sit on the toilet, they'd go down through there because the hedgehogs had eaten them all out. I went in and there was a rat hole over here and a rat hole over there and a pile of hay over here and there was a stove here....There was no blackboard. I had to use a piece of paper. There was practically nothing to do with. There were some books. So that's what I managed with....I started teaching, and along comes a mouse, and now if there's anything I'm afraid of it's a mouse. It came out of one hole over there and ran right across my foot. Oh, I was just sick! But I didn't say anything. I just said to one of the boys, "Can't you get that mouse?" He said, "Sure I can." So he got up and took a board, and whang, whang, whang all around. He killed the mouse and dropped it in the stove.
>
> Then I went to open the bottom drawer [of the desk]...and there was a rat's nest. So I said, "Somebody want to take care of these mice?"
>
> "Oh, sure!"

So he came up and dumped them in the stove.

They were just lits bits of things, you know, no hair or anything on them, but it just made me sick to think about them.

And the place I lived [in] was unthinkable; you just can't believe it. I was supposed to go to Spendle's, but Mrs. Spendle was in the hospital having a baby. So I had to go to the Whites. When I arrived, it was a big rambly old farmhouse, not painted or anything, just a big gray farmhouse. And I was ushered into my bedroom, which was pretty near as big as this whole house. Over in this corner was a bed, and it consisted of four boxes with a cornhusk mattress on top of it. That was where I slept, and that's where I suppose Grandma died. Because they announced to me I couldn't hang in the closet. There was nothing but shelves, but there was no place for me to put anything, because those were all Grandma's. Grandma had just died. So I couldn't put anything in there. So over here there was a stove; and over here was a commode with the door all broken off and the pot inside. Over here was this pile of hay under the window; and then there was one of those highboys and on that were nails and hammers and screws and those kinds of things. Well, anyhow, that's where I was, and I had just come out of a dormitory. I went to bed there, and the wind came up at night, and Grandma had just died there, and you know when you're nineteen . . . and all the windows began to rattle. I could see Grandma coming in every one of those windows. Then in the morning, in comes Mr. White and puts a little fire in the stove — this is in March so I'll have something without freezing to death.

So then I went to breakfast, and little Billie would sit at the table, and little brother sitting on the floor, and anything he didn't like he'd throw in his mother's face. And if I had coffee, the kids'd line up behind me waiting for me to finish my coffee and then they'd grab the cup and get their coffee. The sheep and everything came in the kitchen and peed all around on the floor and the little boy would sit on the floor in big puddles of pee.

She apparently didn't have a big dish, so she took the top part of a tureen — the knob was knocked off — and she braced it up on some dishes. She was serving for dinner. And you know how slippery lamb can be sometimes. It was all slippery and slimy, and it turned my stomach even to look at it, and with it she had frozen white potatoes. Oh, it was the most awful thing, but I can do anything anybody else can, so I ate it. I stayed there for a week.

Then I moved from there over to the Spendle's when she came home from the hospital; and that was a little old flat house. It wasn't safe to walk in. The man didn't dare step in the sink room, because he'd go through the floor. And out in the barn. He had cows, and he was so darn lazy the cow manure was so high behind them the cows had to stand — with their hind end up and their front end down. Oh, it was just terrible. And when I went to bed, I had to sleep in a room there hadn't been anybody in for months, I guess; and it was cold and the icicles were hanging on the window. So I had just barely space enough to get into the bed, between the bed and the wall. Well, anyway, I got in and I nearly froze to death, so I got up and put on my heavy sweater; but that wasn't enough, because my bottom was cold. Those were the days when you wore two petticoats and large pants, so I got up and wrapped the pants around one foot and the two petticoats around the other foot, and I went back to bed and pulled the sweater way down, and that's how I spent the night.

Then the next day she asked if I slept comfortably, and I said, well, I was cold, and she said, well, you take a hot-water bottle tonight. So she gave me a hot-water bottle that night and that wasn't quite so bad, but it [still] wasn't comfortable.... I stayed there for the rest of the time. I had eight weeks to put in there.[7]

Equally remarkable with Wheeler's experiences was the fact that people like the Spendles and the Whites, who obviously had very little, thought highly enough of education to take in a practice teacher. In this case, it was not just helping out; rather, it was a case of providing education for the town's children. Otherwise, there would have been no teacher at all in the town. When Wheeler went there in March, she in fact opened a school that should have been in operation since the previous September!

In the meantime, Mason had been adding, year by year, first this grammar school then that one, until by the mid-teens all the grammar schools and the three junior high schools in Keene and adjacent rural areas were acting as practice schools for the normal school. This gave the normal school one of the two largest practice-teaching areas in the United States, as already noted. "This makes the problem of efficient organization of teaching difficult," said Morrison. "The effective administration of the school system in a metropolitan area of 10,000 is not a small matter." It seemed, however, to be an unbeatable combination in the mid-teens. Each student had to do a full eighteen-week semester of practice teaching. Before that she had had lessons on how to teach and had observed professional teachers in the classroom. It was expected that she would be able to handle a class by herself. And she in fact did. But what happened to the regularly hired teacher for that class? She would have time, and it was so planned, to supervise another cadet teacher. The board instructed Mason in 1912 to "use every endeavor during the present school year to reduce the model school teaching force to a basis of not more than one regular teacher to every two school rooms." That meant that the city of Keene could rely on the student cadets for part of its teaching program if the program were well organized — and Mason was a superior organizer. The Keene School Board report of 1915-16 noted the advantage. The average cost of educating students at the eleven largest cities in New Hampshire was $30.49, but in Keene it was only $24.28. That means, the report said, "that Keene is getting its elementary pupils educated at a per capita cost of $6.21 less than the average of the other cities of the state, an approximate total savings of $8,000." Before long Mason outdid his instructions from the board and had in some instances one regular teacher supervising four practice teachers. Plymouth had difficulty with so many student teachers and only one small model school.[8] Keene's problems were just the reverse — too many practice classrooms.

By the end of the decade of the teens Mason had put in an impressive performance. He had restored the spirit and energy that was sapped after the Bass veto. He had increased enrollments dramatically, supervised the building of the school's first educationally designed buildings, provided a meaningful life for the student body, maintained a good public relations stance, and given the college a meaningful role in the war effort (discussed in the next chapter). By his incorporating the entire Keene Union School District under the jurisdiction of the college, he had given Keene Normal one of the two largest practice areas in the country. By using practice teachers as part of the Keene School District teaching load, he was able to reduce the per pupil cost of education for the local district. He lost no time in advertising his advantage. Keene had the equipment for practice school experience "unexcelled by any Normal School in the United States," he wrote in the catalogue. "The entire elementary school system of Keene, comprising thirteen hundred pupils is under the direction and control of the Normal School. . . . This means that we have over forty rooms including Junior High, rural and special grades to which students may be sent for training and it is never necessary to place two girls in the same room."[9] Mason had, it seemed, an unbeatable system.

10

World War I

MASON responded quickly and intelligently to the special demands created by World War I. He realized that most high school principals urged their graduates into fields other than teaching during the war. Careers in nursing, the Red Cross, and war industries beckoned successfully to many young women. Mason, assisted by Silver at Plymouth and Ernest Butterfield, who replaced Morrison in 1917, urged New Hampshire principals to impress upon their graduates the importance of a teaching career despite the war.

Mason published a circular which headlined "WE MUST WIN THE WAR," and proclaimed, we "must do not only our bit, but our all." "I am writing," he explained, " to urge you not to yield to the impulse to forsake your work as a teacher....There is no more patriotic work anywhere....It is not spectacular. You do not wear a uniform, but you are exerting an influence which cannot be measured." He assured readers that there were many others who could do defense work and other war tasks, but there were just not enough teachers.

To meet the increased demand for teachers Mason ran special summer sessions in 1917 and 1918, patterned after some of the U.S. Army's famous "ninety-day-wonder" projects. These sessions accepted about sixty high school graduates and prepared them for teaching in six weeks. Toward the end of the crisis one such session was conducted during the regular school year.

Throughout the United States attendance at normal schools fell off precipitously. Not so in Keene. Mason's efforts had the desired effect. Enrollments held, and the special sessions produced even more teachers.

Thus, after the war, and to some extent, during it, Keene graduates were able to "flood the whole Northeast," whose teacher supply had pretty well dried up.

Hoke Smith announced to the U.S. Senate in 1916, "in case of war, more men and women would be required at home to prepare . . . food and clothing [as well as the instruments of war] for the soldier than those who would be required at the front."[1]

Even before dealing with the enrollment problem, Mason, through his horticultural interest, moved to increase the food supply, which was particularly important during World War I. A large portion of the population in northern France and in nearly all Belgium was close to starvation. The Allied Powers looked to the United States for relief. But the United States was hit with a combination of bad harvests, abnormally severe winters, and a railroad system broken down by overuse and bad weather. What Keene Normal itself did, of course, did not change the main course of events. But Herbert Hoover's appeals to "forgotten Americans" to save and to produce more resulted in some of the most spectacular food production figures in world history. In spite of the adverse conditions, the United States was able to feed not only itself and its armies but nearly all Belgium and northern France as well.

With the declaration of war, Mason made an immediate survey of garden space that would be available to an army of youthful gardeners. He directed all teachers in the school districts to ask students how much land they could get for a war garden. He then made a direct appeal to the youth: "All boys and girls should 'do their bit' to help the country at this time. You can help by planting such things as your folks can use on their table for food." Since by this time the entire school district was under the jurisdiction of the college, Mason was able to get over 500 home and school gardens started by the pupils of the practice schools. From its own greenhouse, Keene Normal School gave over 5,000 cabbage plants, 4,000 tomato plants, and 3,000 beet plants to the pupils. When federal agents arrived to inspect all this activity, Commissioner Butterfield reported, "they found our plan in so satisfactory a condition that no changes were needed and the Army of Junior Goods Producers became at once a unit in the United States School Garden Army."

In 1912 Keene Normal had acquired Penelope House where many home economics exercises were conducted, and there were also modern kitchens in Parker Hall. Mason offered these facilities to the local canning and conservation commission. The commission then announced in a big broadside: "COME TO THE OPENING OF THE COMMUNITY KITCHENS AT KEENE NOR-

MAL SCHOOL, August 15, 1917." "LET NO FOOD GO TO WASTE." "Come," one poster read, and "learn how to can and dry fruits and vegetables in your own home." The community was expected not only to come and learn but also to use the school's facilities as needed. Irene Weed Landis and Mildred Blanch Murphy, the domestic science teachers, gave canning and preservation demonstrations off campus. They were assisted by Marion Butters, a particularly effective teacher and demonstrator. The local home economics department was further aided by Miss Bertha Titsworth from the Durham campus. Titsworth was assistant to Federal Food Administrator Huntley Spaulding.

The school engaged in a number of other patriotic activities. Misses Vaughn, Brown, and Hooper and Mr. Leonard put together a pageant, *The Triumph of Democracy,* which featured such characters as Civilization, Literature, Autocracy, Red Cross, and Belgium, who paraded across the stage and said their parts. Over eighty people were involved in the play. Less learned but more interesting was a play directed by Mildred Murphy, starring a group of eighth-grade girls. Her play opened with the girls knitting and talking about the war victims in Belgium. They then decided to make a dress and divide the labor between them. On stage then, each began her work. Cutting took ten minutes longer than expected, but they still completely finished the dress in seventy-two minutes, after which it was modeled by Helen Fairbanks for the audience to see.[2]

Two other events were more incidental to the war effort but just as memorable. One was "lightless night." This was a citywide project to save electricity. Although no electricity was used, the students celebrated the evening with "a thousand candles dance." More money was spent on candles that night than would normally have been spent on electricity. How this was defeating the enemy was not quite clear, but everyone had a lot of fun being patriotic. The second event, in the spring of 1917, involved an epidemic of chicken pox, and also a number of cases of measles and mumps, which quickly spread throughout the dormitory. The epidemic replaced the Mid-Year Ball as a topic of conversation.

Eventually, a two-star service flag was flown in front of Hale Building when John F. Kane of the junior high faculty and Raymond Pinkham, the junior high principal, joined the armed services. Finally, on armistice night, there was a big party and celebration which students remembered for generations.[3] In these ways Keene Normal "did its bit" for victory in World War I.

11

School District Revolt

NEARLY EVERYONE who knew him, whether closely associated with the college or not, spoke highly of Mason. As noted at the beginning of Chapter 8, responsibility was his byword. From all that was said about him both before 1921 and after one would hardly believe that nearly the whole citizenry of Keene would rise up against his system and tell him in humiliating terms that the normal school's management of the school district was a disaster and that they wanted the normal school out of the school system and they wanted it out quickly. Such, however, was the case.

The temper of the whole country after World War I was reactionary. The United States had just elected Warren G. Harding president by the largest majority ever accorded a presidential candidate. The election is generally regarded not as a rejection of James M. Cox, Harding's opponent, but as a rejection of the whole Progressive philosophy. Progressive education came under attack as much as Progressive economics, politicis, and social legislation.

One poor ill-prepared school superintendent in New Hampshire struggled mightily with his annual report. He couldn't get the verbs to agree with the subjects; the decimal point kept slipping around in his expense account; and, to top it all off, he was having trouble with "the left side of the school." "There are too many 'left' sides of schools nowadays, say the legislators." Keene Normal School's left side was soon to come under attack.

Mason had a few early warning signals, but he paid no attention to them. He was too wrapped up in plans for the future. He and Butterfield were courting the legislature for another dormitory building; he was working on ways to qualify for funds under the Smith-Hughes Act and through it to bring male students on campus; and he had his fingers in everything else. The whole operation had gotten too big for one-man control.

In the spring of 1920 the citizens of Claremont mounted an attack on their school system. They urged the "persistent teaching of oral reading, spelling, grammar, arithmetic and penmanship" and that more geography be taught. "We deplore," they said, "the teaching of drawing, domestic science, manual training, general science, algebra, geometry or foreign languages to such an extent as to interfere with continuous drill in reading, spelling, grammar, arithmetic and writing; and we disapprove of any plan to complete in grade schools any course of study heretofore usually begun in the high school."

Very nearly the same charges would be made in Keene the next year. In reporting the Claremont reaction, the *Sentinel* took the very unusual step of making a local report, based largely on rumor. "So far as is known," the paper said, "there has been no organized complaint [in Keene]...although at times — and perhaps it might be said, frequently — there have been individual cases where parents believed some of the old standbys of schooling were not given sufficient emphasis."[1] For that day, and for that editor, that was a most unusual comment.

As a Progressive educator, Mason undoubtedly was familiar with the constant "back-to-basics" cry and the alarmism over new teaching methods, but the action of the Claremont citizenry should have alerted him as well as the comments by the *Sentinel*.

Soon a number of concerned parents met with a lawyer, Roy M. Pickard, to formalize their complaints against the management of the public schools. There were three major areas of complaint. The first dealt with the very heart of Mason's system, which was to provide cheaper education and at the same time train teachers. The weaknesses of the system were now apparent. It was all right as long as Mason had exceptional people like Ruth Seaver and Florence Wheeler to send out to practice-teach, and he was lucky he had as many of that caliber as he had.

Second, the system of filling half the schoolrooms in Keene with practice teachers did in fact provide for cheaper education. But, of course, it did not provide uniform quality education, and that was what the parents were concerned about. The catch phrase of complaint was the "three weeks' teacher," meaning the student teacher who spent only three weeks in one class and then moved on to another. The situation was further aggravated by some schools having a much higher number of student teachers than others — making the overall educational system even more chaotic.

The third complaint was against Progressive or "visionary" education, which meant teaching Latin and French in the grade schools before English grammar was learned or teaching percentages or trigonometry before the multiplication tables had been mastered. Lumped with this complaint was the opinion that there was the teaching of too many extraneous subjects, usually cited as "cutting paper dolls" and "playing" in the classroom.

Parents apprised the board of education of their concern, and a special meeting was called for February 7, 1921, in the high school (now the junior high on Washington Street). Everything was still fairly calm, and the board expected to meet with only a few concerned parents. All of a sudden, however, over 200 people showed up at the meeting; it was then obvious that a major revolution was in the making.

At the center of it all was an able public-minded citizen and, at the time, chairman of the school board, Robert T. Kingsbury. Kingsbury frankly admitted his surprise at the size of the audience but welcomed the parents. He tried to head off some of the criticism, which was obviously going to come, by referring to reports which showed that Keene ranked highly among the cities of the state in education. But the inevitable came. After Kingsbury's remarks, R. C. Carrick got the floor and voiced the major areas of complaint, giving specific incidences in each category. He ended by saying that he was tired of "seeing children used as raw material for manufacturing purposes," and he emphasized that the system ought to be changed. His comments brought thunderous applause from the audience; thereafter, parent after parent spoke reinforcing what Carrick said. "Good constructive criticism was offered by the speakers," noted the *Sentinel*, "and there was not a single attempt to spare anybody's sensibilities when it came to placing blame for the methods of instruction practiced in the graded schools in the city." The meeting ended with a resolution presented to the board by attorney Pickard, expressing dissatisfaction with the conduct of the school system by the normal school and demanding that "practice teaching shall be abolished in the said grade schools, and that such schools shall be placed under the immediate control of the Board of Education for the Union School district." Soon this resolution became two, placed by petition, on the school warrant.

The town was so excited about the whole affair that it caused the *Sentinel* to take the unusual step of highlighting it on the front page, a page normally devoted to ads and national or foreign news.[2] There had not been so much interest in a school matter, said the *Sentinel*, since the decision to abolish the old Main Street School in the early 1890s.

Mason, Butterfield, Kingsbury, Pickard, and others held several meetings to work out a solution with the concerned citizens. It was not an easy task, and the solution was worked out only a few hours before the annual district meeting.

On the night of March 24, 1921, over 1,200 people packed into the high school to vote on the issue. At a crucial time in the meeting the lights went out (owing to regulator failure), but the crowd stayed on to enact its business using candles, lanterns, and flashlights.

The main points in reestablishing the formal relationship between the normal school and the town were, after July 1, 1921: (1) that the normal school would have the jurisdiction of not more than two practice schools in the district and (2) that a competent superintendent of education be hired by the school board to administer most of Keene's schools. This arrangement was a compromise in that the concerned parents preferred that Keene Normal School's jurisdiction be limited to one school, the Wheelock School.

Mason usually gave a glowing annual report to the school board, but in 1921 he said only, "The past year has been one of stress and strain in all departments of life. Education has had its share....In my opinion the peak of our difficulties has been reached....I anticipate more satisfactory results in our schools the coming year."[3]

There was one more bitter pill for Mason. William C. T. Adams, the man hired to reorganize or, as some would put it, to "straighten out the mess," was superintendent of the Plymouth schools. The only consolation, if such it was, was that the Keene School District now faced "unusual expenses." That showed, at any rate, that the former arrangement had at least been financially beneficial to the city.

For all those connected with the college, it was certainly a difficult time. "Oh, that was a terrible time," recalled Ruth Kirk. "Oh, it was dreadful. People went out from the normal school who were not equipped to teach. And it was a broil all the livelong time. It was really terrible." Gertrude Merriam recalled the root of the problem being Mason's desire for inexpensive education.[4] The college certainly suffered in prestige. Soon it would have only Wheelock and the Central Junior High School as practice schools. It could no longer boast one of the two largest practice-teaching areas in the nation.

What were the causes of the school district revolt? Certainly the drive for cheaper education as the long-range goal was a cause. A century before, Pennsylvania was thought to have found the answer with the Lancaster system, a system by which students taught each other after having learned their first lesson from the principal; but that system soon developed short-comings. Mason's system went a step or two beyond the Lancaster method, since the practice teachers were better prepared than grammar school students, and at the beginning at least, when the operation was small, it worked well. Mason, in his effort to please the community, exceeded his instructions to have one qualified teacher for two rooms. In Symonds School, for instance, eight grades had only two teachers and one assistant. The bulk of the work was done by practice teachers.

Another reason for the eruption was the high turnover in the supervisory staff. Eugene Tuttle, who had been supervisor of practice teaching since 1914, left in 1919 and was replaced by Nahum Leonard. Leonard had been with the normal school since 1912 as a teacher of psychology and his educational background was as good as Tuttle's, but apparently he was not as good an organizer. Not only was he new to the job, but in 1920 Mason hired eight new faculty members. Leonard had to work with these unknown quantities, plus others who worked with district teachers and assistants, who worked with student cadets who taught the pupils. It is no wonder that this house of cards came crashing down. Ultimately, however, one must conclude that Mason had expanded too rapidly and had tried to do too much too cheaply.

12

The Smith-Hughes and Bartlett Acts

WHILE MASON was struggling with the school district revolt of 1920-21, significant and unprecedented events were occurring in the world of education; and these events had major effects on Keene Normal School. Most significant were the New Hampshire education bill of 1919 and the national Smith-Hughes Act of 1917.

The education bill of 1919 began in 1915 as opposition to Morrison. Just what the cause of opposition was is hard to say and impossible to find out. We may, of course, be fairly safe with the general rule that anyone who calls a spade a spade and emphasizes quality performance brings about a lot of opposition. This is certainly what Morrison had done. We can grasp the situation in a letter from C. W. Bickford, superintendent of schools in Manchester, to Frank B. Preston, chairman of the House Committee on Education:

> In regard to the proposed measure for establishing a State Board of Education, the bill is unquestionably designed to displace an able officer. The animus of some of those supporting it plainly indicates this. I have come into contact with the head of the educational department in every New England state. I believe that New Hampshire has the leader among all these men. The educational advances in recent years in New Hampshire is due to his initiative, energy and vision. He holds the secondary schools to a high standard of efficiency. He embodies power and responsibility. Efficiency can be secured only by union of these.

Soon other superintendents and educators came to Morrison's support. On March 2, 1915, Edward Miller of Keene reported for the House Committee on Education that the bill was "inexpedient to legislate."[1]

No bill came up in the next legislative session because interest in the war was predominant and possibly also because Morrison had taken a position in the Connecticut State Office of Education.

When a bill was introduced in 1919, it was under a completely different context from that of the 1915 bill. Governor John H. Bartlett was trying to modernize state government to the extent that a governor would be held more responsible for the performance of state agencies. "Boards of trustees," he once thundered, are "the supreme court of state expenditures, from which there is no appeal." Up to this point, the normal schools, the state college, the prison, the orphanage, and other institutions each had its own board of trustees. All these boards spent over $700,000 per year, and the governor had almost no control over them.

Governor Bartlett railed against boards of trustees for another good reason, which he never mentioned publicly. Under the Smith-Hughes Act, just recently passed, the state qualified for funds for improving the salaries and working conditions of teachers of agriculture, trade, home economics, and industrial subjects as well as the training of teachers in these fields. He felt it would be much better that this money be expended by some responsible state agency rather than by separate boards of trustees.

"Hearings on the new education [Bartlett] bill, the most important measure of the legislative session, begun yesterday, were continued to to-day," noted the *Sentinel* of February 12, 1919. "General Frank S. Streeter, who is chairman of the committee which framed the bill at the request of Governor Bartlett, is in charge of its interest at hearings and is putting up a very strong case in its favor. Votes against it will be based upon the high expense and the loss of local home rule which it entails."[2]

The Education Act of 1919, more commonly known as the Bartlett Act, had also the great force of patriotism behind it. Many Americans were shocked during World War I to learn that 200 infantry divisions could not be mobilized into the U.S. Army because that many men could not speak, write, or understand English. New Hampshire's rate, one out of ten, of those who could not understand English was the same as the national average. Most people agreed that a common tongue was necessary for rapid communication of ideas and good citizenship. Americanization committees were formed for this purpose. Later in the 1920s the idea of "100 percent American" went too far. Its beginnings, however, were sensible enough. The Americanization Committee of New Hampshire decided that the teaching of the common language should be done through the public school system.

After Bartlett won the governorship in 1918, he set up a special committee to investigate the condition of education in the state. The committee did not read Morrison's old reports. It did not see the 75 percent of the work he had done under severe handicaps. It saw only the 25 percent that was left undone. It was shocked when it learned that 40,000 adults in New Hampshire could not communicate in English. It recommended that a board of education be set up and, in a fit of patriotism, recommended that it be given all the powers of a modern business corporation.

Under the new education bill the commissioner of education was to be appointed by the governor and would be directly responsible to him. Also under the new bill the two normal schools would come under the supervision of the commissioner.[3]

The duties of the new commissioner were very similar to those which Morrison had established for his office and which Butterfield was now performing. By virtue of his character, Morrison had established a strong office, and the state merely legalized many of his practices. In 1915 Vermont had passed a progressive education act which was often cited as the model for the New Hampshire law. Nonetheless, Morrison would have been very comfortable with the new law. It was the department as he in fact ran it.

Evidence indicated to Eugene A. Bishop, who made a study of it, "that no state in the Union has . . . a higher degree of centralization of authority and power in the organization, administration, and support of the public schools than has New Hampshire. In no state does the law, in general, give greater power to a state-wide authority to initiate, direct, and decide the educational policy and practice which is to affect each of the small local communities." Bishop readily saw the irony, for on the same page he noted that in no other place in New England was local self-government "more deeply rooted than it has been from the beginning of New Hampshire."

The education bill of 1919 caused some consternation in Keene's fight with the normal school in 1921 because some citizens believed that their best redress was to the new state board of education rather than to the local school board. During that crisis the new commissioner of education, Ernest Butterfield, came to Keene and explained to the citizenry, jam-packed in the Unitarian church, the legal status of the new board of education.[4]

After the passage of the Bartlett Act, the difference between the administrations of Morrison and Butterfield was striking. Morrison had operated under a weak law and had built up the school systems by intelligent investigation, able presentation of facts, and finally by the strength of his own personality. Butterfield, on the other hand, who had the force of a strong department and the strongest state law in the nation to support him, could afford to be gracious and patient with school districts which begged for more time to comply with higher standards.

The new state board of education was to "outline the general policy of teacher training in the state." The commissioner was to "recommend to the state board the program of studies for the normal schools." The directors of the normal schools were given broad executive powers.[5]

While New Hampshire was passing a major new piece of educational legislation, the United States government had already passed a major piece. Few educators or historians realize what an educational watershed the Smith-Hughes Act was. The Smith-Hughes Act of 1917 necessitates a brief discussion of the trends and realities of massive popular education. As noted earlier, the academies of the nineteenth century were held in high regard in that they were somewhat exclusive, taught the liberal arts, and were of no expense to the taxpayer. The public high school copied the curriculum of the academies, but public educators soon found out that liberal arts subjects (at least as then taught) were not a suitable educational base for absolutely everyone. Further, the parents of working children wanted their children taught more practical subjects. Shortly after the public high school movement was under way, a demand for vocational education arose. As early as 1910 Rhodes endorsed the development of a vocational educational program for Keene.

The many needs for vocational education were nowhere better stated than in a committee report to Congress by the Vocational Education Commission. Vocational training would, first of all, "democratize the education of the country" by recognizing different desires and abilities of students and "by giving an equal opportunity to all to prepare for their life's work." The important word in all this is "democratize," because it was an attempt to give to professional learning status equal to that heretofore enjoyed by the students of the liberal arts. Second, there was a very significant social aspect to it. Many saw vocational education as a means of eradicating juvenile delinquency, and it was to do this by a new teaching method; in the words of the committee: "by developing a better teaching method by which the children who do not respond to book instruction alone may be reached and educated through learning by doing." Another factor was of economic betterment, which has always been an aspect of vocational education. This applied also to home economics where it was demonstrated that by good home management a family could, in effect, increase its income by as much as 25 percent. Last, there was the element of social control, as there was in the Vocational Amendments Act of 1968. "Industrial and social unrest," said the committee, "is due to a lack of a system of practical education fitting workers for their callings." All told, it was a highly significant piece of legislation designed to redress the educational imbalance of the society and to offer opportunity to those who otherwise would never have it, as well as to rid society of juvenile delinquency and social agitation.[6]

Much aid went directly to the high schools, but some was allocated to the preparation of teachers of industrial subjects and of home economics. It is, of course, somewhat ironic that those departments which were so significantly aided are usually the most politically conservative on campus. The sponsors of the acts were all liberal Democrats, either populists like Dudley Hughes and Hoke Smith (and later Lyndon Johnson) or intellectuals like Woodrow Wilson and John F. Kennedy. Be that as it may, in the next few years a thoroughly liberal Democratic measure became the keystone to the development of significant educational departments at Keene.

13

A College but Not a College (1926)

ONE REASON for studying normal school history, as mentioned in the Introduction, is that normal schools became, as soon as established, poor people's colleges. This was in itself its own social revolution. It was not supposed to happen. Neither Horace Mann, Salma Hale, nor anyone else involved in the foundings thought of this as an eventuality. John Colony seems to have grasped the possibility in his editorial, "Why You Should Attend the Normal School"—Colony's main reason being the association with ideas, books, and people. The Ivy League colleges, both large and small, did not approve. If society were to expect an expansion of the role of higher education, then the Ivies would assume that role. They had no intention of allowing state-supported institutions to intrude on their educational prerogatives. The select private colleges had an enviable record even in the nineteenth century of accepting poor but talented youth. One need go no further than Daniel Webster, Channing Folsom, or Henry Morrison to cite representative cases. Ivy League colleges justifiably saw themselves as the only educational font for the best brains and talent, both wealthy and poor, in the land. They would provide the leadership for the welfare of all.

The accomplishment of these colleges was magnificent, but it was on a limited scale. They should not be criticized for their resistance to state-supported higher education. Nevertheless, democracy is still a most interesting phenomenon, and some "dumb" people never did know their "place" in society, and they continued to search out various ladders of success regardless of impoverished and sometimes embarrassing backgrounds. When democracy decreed that everyone had an equal chance to succeed, the sheer number of those striving (and succeeding) was overwhelming. Even if the select private colleges had made the effort, they had neither the physical facilities nor the mental framework to meet the demand. This upsurge of humanity, facing closed doors at private colleges and later closed doors at their own state colleges and universities, eventually turned to normal schools as their own road to success — and that road was not necessarily to successful teaching careers. While we can cite many examples on our own campus of those who chose this route, the best national example is Lyndon B. Johnson. Destitute of funds, Johnson had no other path to an education and opportunity in the mid-1920s but that afforded by Southwest Texas State Normal School, which was just then in the process of becoming a teachers college. So it was that Keene in the 1920s and 1930s afforded an opportunity for advancement, and often other than in teaching. It became, in effect, a college for those who could afford nothing else. It did not say so; in fact, it insisted it was not a college but rather a teacher training institution. It did not want to offend Dartmouth or even the University of New Hampshire, which as recently as 1923 had become a university, at least in name. The university itself was enough offense to Dartmouth's long-standing position as *the* institution of higher education in the state, and Keene did not intend to further rub Dartmouth the wrong way; yet Keene Normal School gradually offered more and more to its student body. The key year was 1926. For the first time, Keene Normal offered enrollees a four-year degree and organized itself into academic departments, "like a real college."

If one had ability but a poor secondary education (a local prerogative), had won no scholarships, had no money, and particularly if one was female, she or he could attend Keene, using it as a stepping-stone to something greater, something better.

For nearly thirty years, from the 1920s to the 1950s, it cost the state about $600 per year to educate a normal school student, a tuition that was waived if the student agreed to teach in the state after graduation. Board-and-room costs of five or six dollars a week could be halved if the student waited on tables. Thus, Keene Normal School/Teachers College/State College offered an avenue of opportunity that was never envisioned in its founding. "We wanted an education," said Marion Roby Carpenter. "It was the place that we could afford."[1]

Most often that something greater, something better that Keene Normal students sought was teaching. Very often it was not. A study ought to be made of students who used normal schools or teachers colleges as fully established colleges. Discussions with alumni over the last eight years indicate that it might run as high as 33 percent. It was that "33 percent" which used the teacher training facilities as a college that eventually brought about the establishment of a full college. But until the time of Keene State College a number of more tentative steps had to be taken.

This 33 percent was one significant cause for growth in the 1920s. Even more significant was Keene's reputation as an excellent training school for teachers and as having excellent cultural and practice facilities in Keene and nearby communities. Keene exceeded Plymouth in enrollment in 1915 and was always a bigger school until the 1960s. By 1916 Keene had brought an increase of 117 percent of trained teachers in the state, most of whom stayed in the Monadnock region, at least for their first few years. As early as 1924 Ernest Butterfield reported that Keene was one of the fastest-growing normal schools in the nation and "one of the largest teacher training institutions in the east." By 1930 five out of every six teachers in the state were fully trained — thus almost exactly reversing the situation Morrison found before 1909. Of those five, four were normal school graduates; and of the four, an average of nearly three were from Keene.[2]

External reasons helped account for Keene's rapid growth, such as the automobile and better rail transportation. With eventually four practice schools during the 1920s, Keene, even after the district revolt, had a much larger training area than Plymouth. Further, Butterfield decided to build no more normal schools but rather to have Keene and Durham share the southern half of the state and to have Plymouth serve the northern half. Last and most important was Butterfield's decision, possibly on Mason's recommendation, to adopt an open admissions policy. He was doing it, he said, "on the ground that the normal schools are public schools and pupils have the right in a well-organized system to pass freely from any grade which they have completed to the one which follows."

Butterfield's decision was counter to all that Morrison, Parker, and Horace Mann had stood for in their idea of the role of the normal school — something that, as Mann said, "could whirl the spheres"; or such schools could become "holding places" and mere "charity schools." His decision represented a perennial problem not only of Keene but of all state colleges — the effort to have high standards (or at least some standards) and the tremendous pressure to be "democratic," that is, to open the doors to all. The pendulum would swing back in a few years, and Keene would again become selective; but, then, the pendulum keeps swinging and can be expected periodically to garner scoops of raw democracy.

The most important reasons for Keene's growth were internal ones. The spirit of the school was excellent, and the school was as well run as any institution at any time or place could be. Normal school graduates did make better teachers. Usually one of every five untrained teachers failed, with personal distress and great disruption to the classroom. Less than one in twenty-five normal school graduates failed, and Keene had a very high success rate.[3]

Student population at Keene Normal tripled in the 1920s from about 200 at the beginning of the decade to 600 at the end. It would be most interesting to have Mason's thoughts about the role of the school in the mid-1920s. We do not have them, however. We can only conjecture that it was because of the various pressures on him that in 1926 he took steps to move the school to near-college status.

The first step could be interpreted not only as logical but also as very shrewd, a type of decision that was certainly not inconsistent with Mason. Many alumni remember him as being a shrewd politician as well as an alert educator. At any rate, he decided to offer a four-year program in industrial arts, or mechanic arts, as it was then called. The proposal had been discussed for years by the board of education, but the board's minutes do not reveal who said what about what. The program, however, was a unique entering wedge. Funding could be obtained through the Smith-Hughes Act. Further, it was a program that could not possibly offend either Dartmouth or the University of New Hampshire. In 1924 Mason made a strenuous effort to increase the male population on campus, and he probably did so by methods that today would be clearly considered as sex discrimination—in this case, more in favor of men rather than against women. He made a special point of welcoming the first 50 boys in 1927 and the first 100 in 1929.[4]

Many states had already embarked on the teachers college designation for their four-year programs for teacher training. Keene's four-year program made the normal school in effect a teachers college, although it would not officially be recognized as such for another thirteen years.

Mason's second move, in 1926, was to reorganize the normal school along college lines. Up until this time there was little specialization. Dudley, as already mentioned, taught manual arts, music, and other subjects as needed. Mason still taught. Mabel Brown was a secretary. She also taught history and was, in addition, in charge of "manners and customs."

Mason now differentiated for the first time between faculty and administration. Further, he established two deans and eleven different academic departments. In the next few years he found the department

Isabelle U. Esten, Dean of Women
1919 to 1950

H. Dwight Carle, Dean of Men,
1925 to 1955

chairpersons who would be familiar characters on campus for the next thirty to forty years.

The first full-time dean of the college, appointed in 1923, was Isabelle U. Esten. Esten had an A.B. degree from Middlebury College, from which she graduated in 1914 at age twenty. Her concentrations at Middlebury were in home economics, chemistry, and French—all exact subjects or sciences. She expected social science to be equally exact. Before coming to Keene in 1919 she taught home economics at Colby Academy (New Hampshire) and had done educational and religious work at the West Side YWCA Branch in New York City.

Most graduates remember Esten as dean, although she was first employed as a teacher of home economics in 1919. "We have down here, in the South, the Mason-Dixon line," commented Ray Harwood. "Up there was had the Mason-Esten line." On campus she was remembered as a tyrant, but professionally she was well respected. She was elected president of the New Hampshire Deans Association in the 1930s and was awarded an honorary doctorate of pedagogy by Middlebury College in 1943.

Esten normally wore long black dresses which, except for a slight —
very slight — opening in the front, kept her covered to her neck, to her
wrists, and down to her high black shoes. This attire changed but mildly
over the years. Daddy Mason approved. She had a game leg, and went
limping around on campus ever concerned about the possibility that the
Dean Carle's boys and her girls might succumb to the ways of the flesh,
either in the rose arbor at the end of Fiske lawn, or over in the sunken
garden behind the President's House. Some students believed that she had
a pair of binoculars with which she surveyed the arbor and the gardens
from behind her drapes in her Fiske (and later Huntress) apartment, her
line of vision blurred only by errant tennis balls.

A few recollections from different time periods give a good view of
Esten. Marion Tebbetts Wood recalled:

> Now, Dean Esten was a formidable character. She called me in one morn-
> ing...and she accused me of going around campus and saying they put saltpeter
> in the food — and that saltpeter in the food was supposed to keep you calm, and
> not interested in the other sex, and so forth. There was a lot of scuttlebutt about
> this [as in all other boarding colleges, also]. I didn't even know what she was talk-
> ing about till I got back out with the other girls, and they told me.

Another recalled:

> I'm walking in and she's locking the door. She said, "Oh, you're that kind of
> girl." You got to realize, this was two after ten! And I worked in the office for
> her. I had to be on her good list, or I wouldn't have been allowed to work for
> her. She kept a file; and afterwards, I took my file out and there it was, what
> I had done. I had been two minutes late. You had to be up to no good if you
> were out late!

One time in the late 1940s Sherman Lovering took her to a dance as
chaperon. Afterward he insisted on driving her from the gym back to her
apartment. They could, of course, have easily walked the one-block
distance from the present Mabel Brown Room to her apartment. Lovering was sporting one of his classy "new" cars and wanted Esten to be
generous to any possible latecomers to the dorm. They had motored only
half a block when Lovering ran out of gas. Esten was actually alone with
a man in a car that was out of gas! All she said was that from now on
she would give more credence to those running-out-of-gas stories.

The college was her whole life. She had a stroke in her apartment in
October 1949 and died three months later. If she was overly strict, it was
because she wanted her children and her faculty to be the better for it.

*Francis Molloy (left) and Anna Hedman laying the pavement
in front of Parker Hall with the help of a classmate in 1924.*

As dean she was aided for years by her assistant and prototype, Ida E.
Fernald.[5]

Esten was dean until 1932, when the office was divided. She then became
dean of women; H. Dwight Carle became dean of men, a position he occupied until 1955. Carle also had a degree from Middlebury and had joined
the faculty in 1924. He is often remembered for his role as dean and also
for his forgetfulness and his moral preachings. Carle was supposed to have
said (typically) in chapel: "There are four things necessary for a full life:
a happy domestic life, an active church life, a vital civic life, and — uh —
and — now, let me see. Never mind. We'll do well if we get those three."[6]
Despite his increasingly heavy duties as dean, he never gave up teaching
or conducting experiments in many fields of science.

Ruth Kirk, who had no use for the men teachers in 1917, said of Carle,

I don't think I ever took a course that was more interesting than Mr. Carle's
geology. . . . He took us everywhere. We had to go to Gilsum and go down that
bank that was as steep as a side of a house, into that river, you know, by the
bridge, and go down by the river looking for things. . . . We went to Alstead and
went down into the mine. We went down ladders. I don't know how I ever dared
to do it.

In 1926 Mason designated department heads and the academic department very much as they remained up until 1978. There is still some discipline pride and controversy as to which was the first department on campus. Education can, of course, claim that the whole school was an education department from 1909 offering a full range of subjects. Art also has a shaky claim to being the first department. In 1916 one Pauline Patch arrived here to teach art. For the four years that she was here, she insisted on being listed as "Head of the Art Department." No one else at that time could boast such a title, even though there were then two people each in manual training and domestic arts and three in nature study, including Mason himself. When Patch left, the "art department" vanished. Her successor was merely an "art teacher."

Home economics became in 1918 the first enduring department. Marion Butters was the first chair. She and Mildred Murphy, both excellent teachers and organizers, had used their facilities exceptionally well, not only for teacher education, but also for Keene Normal School's World War I contributions. Esten succeeded Butters in 1919 as head of the department.

A Department of Education was formally established in 1920 with Almon W. Bushnell as head. He stayed only a few years and was succeeded by a number of others, no one staying a long time. The most dominating character in education, aside from Mason himself, was Inez Vaughn, supervisor of practice teaching. She first came to Keene Normal in 1913 as an instructor in history and English. She then taught in Wisconsin for two years before returning to Keene in 1920. As supervisor of practice teaching, she was as awesome as Esten because her appraisal of one's teaching ability meant the difference between a job or no job; or between a more desirable and a less desirable position. Many students thought she made her judgments too quickly and too whimsically. She was, at any rate, another of the department characters appointed in the 1920s that generations of students had to deal with.

It is interesting to note the number of women involved in college life before the major reorganization of 1926. Not only was the student body predominantly female, but often the faculty was as well. In the mid-1920s Mason achieved about a 50-50 ratio on the faculty which continued until the late 1950s, when men became a majority.

Throughout the teens and most of the 1920s women were the majority participants in sports and even in manual training. Thus, when one talked about the cricket, hockey, basketball, and baseball clubs or teams, he or she was talking about women's clubs or teams. During the entire normal

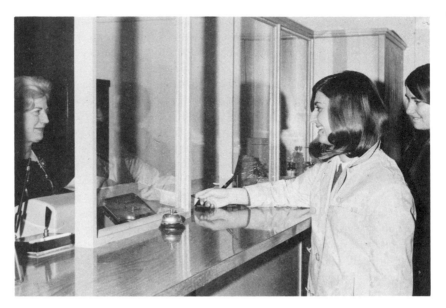

Clara Giovannangeli, (left), college bursar from 1940 to 1973
and dedicated staff member for forty-five years

school period girls took some type of manual training. This was meant to be practical. When Mason hired Spencer Eaton, he told him, "Teach 'em to fix the locks on the doors, how to make the window blinds work, and how to repair the rope on the flagpole." Like boys afterward, girls found themselves called upon to fix up the campus. In 1924 it was both girls and boys who poured and finished the sidewalks in front of Parker Hall. Women were also hired to teach manual training. Louise Roberts, Kathryn Smith, and Olive Butler assisted Dudley and Kane from 1916 on. After 1924 Shirley Pollard was an assistant to Conrad Adams in industrial education.

Besides home economics and education, the departments formed in 1926 were English, headed by Martha Randall and after 1929 by Sprague Drenan; social science, headed by Mabel R. Brown and, for a longer time, by Frederick Simmons; health and physical education, whose head changed rapidly until Sumner Joyce joined in 1942; mathematics, later headed by Merton T. Goodrich; science, with Dwight Carle; languages, with Frank Blackington; music, with Harry W. Davis; and mechanic arts, with Conrad Adams. To all this a twelfth department, economics and geography, was added in 1929. It is obvious from this list of names, many of which are still familiar, that Mason had chosen his people well. They were, by and large, both scholars and able administrators. To avoid duplication with Plymouth, the New Hampshire Department of Education decided that Keene would have majors in home economics, mechanic arts, English, French, and science; Plymouth, in commerce, history, Latin, and mathematics.[7]

One other important appointment was made in the 1920s, and that was a stenographer, Clara Giovannangeli. She was then only seventeen years old. Her total service to the college would be forty-five years, thirty-three of them as bursar. She was one of the most pleasing and able administrators on campus.

Having looked at the school organization, it would now be profitable to know the intellectual tenor of the college at this point, but with the absence of manuscripts and formal statements it is nearly impossible to do so. Nonetheless, a few tentative and hopefully reasonably accurate statements can be made.

As early as 1916 Mason had stated his belief in "learning by doing." Whether the influence of that comment was Dewey, William James, or just plain American pragmatism is difficult to say. Mason seems to have been a bit more conservative in his educational philosophy after the 1921 blowup — as well he might be — but there is not much of Dewey's influence evident in any of the college catalogs. The 1926-27 catalog does mention "socialized recitations" as part of an elementary education course. The same description mentions, however, the "project method," which is closer to Morrison's ideas. Morrison and Dewey, as educators with significantly different approaches, were not, it should be pointed out, in ideological conflict. Morrison and Dewey as popularized were.

Indications are that after the 1921 revolt Mason stayed fairly close to basics and common sense and did not become too much swayed by any particular philosophy. His own background was in nature studies, and he continued to emphasize that, physical health, and moral health. He often quoted L. H. Bailey of Cornell, who wrote, "Nature Study gives the child a sense of companionship with life out-of-doors and an abiding love of nature." To this Mason added, "This is the keynote of our work at Keene." It was Mason who bought an abandoned schoolhouse on Beech Hill for the "outing club" and later a house on Wilson Pond where students would enjoy the out-of-doors. He devised the "Health Chore Card" by which "each student is required to keep [the] amount of open air exercise taken, the number of baths taken, attention given to the teeth, windows open at night, and other health habits."[8]

The heads of the education department and Miss Vaughn either had degrees from, or had taken courses at, Columbia. Very likely they came under the influence of the highly popular and dramatic lecturer, William Kilpatrick, who was even more popular than our own Henry Freedman and who won converts to Dewey "by the hundreds." He was, said one educator, "an irresistible John the Baptist."

For hard evidence of what the faculty was thinking, we must at this point rely upon a student. Pauline Reed prepared a paper for Marion Frost Hudson's class and published it in the school newspaper. Pauline wrote:

> I have learned that education means living today, not preparation for higher institutions or preparing to live. Therefore, I must teach life situations, not mere fact.... If education is growth I must realize this and give my pupils a chance to grow as slowly or as quickly as they are able. Since I believe that education is a social process I will teach more than the three R's in order to make my pupils good citizens.

Young Miss Reed wrote the first clear evidence of the Dewey philosophy extant at Keene. "It was already here when I got here in 1939," said Lloyd Young. Just exactly when and how it arrived is still somewhat of a mystery.

Identifying intellectual changes is much harder than identifying structural ones. Since 1926 was a year of significant structural change, perhaps we may use that year also as the year of significant intellectual change. It was the year of Morrison's influential *Teaching in the Secondary Schools.* By that year John Dewey was clearly established as America's foremost philosopher. By that year Butterfield had adopted the open admissions policy. Because of Mason's and Butterfield's close association with Morrison, it is hard to believe that even in 1926 they did not know what he was saying. Butterfield had written Morrison that his book was being read in New Hampshire, "from Pittsburg to Pelham, and from Westmoreland to Newcastle."

It is possible, of course, that Mason and Butterfield got only a hasty notion of Morrison's unit plan and then subsumed it under Dewey's general philosophy. It is also possible that society's pressures were so great that Mason and Butterfield (and Silver at Plymouth) had to adopt Dewey's philosophy whether they wanted to or not. Here is a great irony. Dewey's philosophy, generally considered "liberal," was actually more in tune with the American situation than Morrison's. Morrison's philosophy with its primary emphasis on performance was, overall, more conservative. Putting it into practice, however, would have been daring and radical. It would have wreaked havoc, for instance, in the state legislature, which would have had to face a number of social maladjustment problems and other social issues instead of foisting them off on the public school system. Most other states by this time were adopting Dewey's "easier" philosophy. Mason and Butterfield should not be criticized too harshly for adopting the popular trend. Morrison's philosophy was, however, in 1926 possible of adoption. Unlike most other similar institutions, Keene Normal School had in that year a clear choice of two distinct paths in the forest of educational ideas. One cannot help but speculate, for a brief time at least, on the institution's impact on state and nation had it embarked on "the road not taken."

In June 1927 nine students received a bachelor's degree for completing the four-year program. The degrees were clearly proclaimed to be degrees in mechanic arts education so as not to offend the University of New Hampshire and the older liberal arts institutions. Dean Craven Laycock of Dartmouth was even persuaded to come to commencement to bring that institution's best wishes for the new program.[9] The next year Mason, possibly with Drenan's urging, decided to offer a four-year program for teachers of English. That was getting awfully close to a liberal arts program and to college status.

For the moment, Keene Normal School remained a college that technically was not a college. On grounds already purchased and some newly acquired property, a small but beautiful campus would soon be constructed. Students lived a life that was similar to college life anywhere and everywhere, and it is to these aspects of college life that we now turn.

14

Student Life — The 1920s

EVERY NORMAL SCHOOL had its Dean Esten, Dean Carle, and Daddy Mason who supervised the general morality of the campus. Thus, there is a sameness to it all. Yet, the mold varied interestingly from person to person and from campus to campus. Each group of students on every campus had its own special characteristics. It would be well now to record in this chapter activities and college life from the students' point of view. The things that hold a school together, that give it its distinctive difference are not only the campus characters among faculty and administration but also the experiences of its students, who are so often overlooked in college histories. To prevent topical repetition, some events in this chapter are taken from the 1930s. For the same reason the chapters on the 1930s include some events of the 1920s, both decades spanning Mason's presidency.

No exercise held the school together more than daily chapel. Each midmorning the entire student body filed into what is now Drenan Auditorium for chapel. On the west wall they read the words from Mrs. Sanger, "Enter to learn. Go forth to serve." Later Mason added a bit of his own homespun wisdom on the east wall. "If you do this, you can't do that." Some students wondered if the second motto applied to the first motto, but obviously Mason did not think so. As far as he was concerned, his motto was about priorities and time management, in today's parlance. Mason's saying was interesting in that he did not apply it to himself. He had his hands in everything.

A possible conflict in mottoes, however, was the least concern of the students. Their greatest concern was: "Am I going to be called on today for recitation?" As Dorothy LaPointe recalled, in chapel "We were responsible for coming up with the invocation, and you never knew when it was going to be your turn." Mason "gave you a proverb and then you had to give him one to match it, or another one. And then that proverb would be printed, put up, and the next day there would be another one." Sometimes the proverb-matching took place in speech class and sometimes in chapel. When in chapel, it was assigned to the juniors. The seniors had a stiffer ordeal. They had to give a talk of a minimum two minutes' duration on a current-events topic. Getting up in chapel in front of faculty, administration, and fellow students was a terrifying experience for most. To this day, most alumni remember exactly their answer to a Mason proverb, and they remember well the topic of their senior speech.

While chapel may have been an ordeal for individual students, it was also the most unifying exercise of the school. It was the daily meeting place for faculty and administration, and it was here that problems common to all were discussed. Here the goals and expectations of the college were stated and restated. General announcements of all kinds were made. Individuals gave reports on special experiences they had that related to the college. At chapel students were inspired to do their best, not only for themselves, but for their college.

The college had no apparent problem on the issue of tolerance during the 1920s. It is very much to Keene's credit that during the period of intense "Americanization" after World War I there was no racial discrimination and very little on the basis of sex. When Harlan Goodwin applied in 1915, he was accepted as an equal. (As mentioned earlier, Harlan did not remain long.) Sheldon Barker and Albert Brooks did not shy away so easily. "Are you kidding?" said Barker; those were "very happy" days. "You can imagine, two boys and all those girls." In 1921 they became the first two male graduates, and in 1984 Barker was the oldest living male graduate.

By 1923 three mulattoes, who did not fit into the "100 percent American" stereotype of the 1920s, completed the normal school program. Margaret Reid, class of 1916, was one of these. "But no one thought a thing of it," said Elinor Paine. Gladys Young, class of 1923, had no trouble at Keene Normal, although she did have difficulty getting a job after graduating. Another girl of the teen years came from a wealthy family. "The family gave her all that she needed. But after normal school she had to go to camp. The family was ashamed of her," recalled one classmate. It is certainly to Keene's credit that it was not ashamed. Common strictures

Debate coach Franklin Roberts takes his medicine en route to the big debate with Plymouth State. "Mr. Roberts got out of a sick bed to go with us in his car," wrote a member of the class of 1926. "We stopped on the road, picknicked, and took pictures of him taking his medicine."

prevailed against pregnant women, both as students and as teachers; but the school accepted married women in either category. One of the first, if not the first, to graduate was Mrs. Ruth Connor of Keene in 1925.[1]

Clubs and Sports

"We formed a club at the drop of a hat," recalled Marion Tebbetts Wood. Indeed! There were more student organizations in the 1920s than there are in the 1980s, and nearly as large a percentage of students worked then as now. There was a Vermont club, a Keene club, and a Manchester club, a camera club, and a radio club with twenty-one members. The Catholic girls in 1922 formed the De La Salle Club, which in 1945 became the Newman Club. A French club, La Petit Salon, was formed in 1919. There was a banjo-mandolin club with eighteen members; unfortunately, they made no recordings.

A club of unusual vitality was the debating club with sixty members! Even Bagley in his history of Plymouth comments on the annual exchange of debates with Keene. This was due to the dedication of its advisor, Franklin Roberts. "I remember when it was my turn to go to Plymouth," wrote one alumna. "Mr. Roberts got out of a sickbed to go with us in his car. He had cough medicine with him. We stopped on the road and picnicked and took pictures of him taking his medicine." The debating club eventually developed into "The Forum," complete with Greek letters, Kappa Pi Omicron.

"We [nineteen] girls decided we needed to have a rifle club," said Wood, "and the school bought some rifles. I had a twenty-two. My father taught me how to shoot, and I was a pretty good marksman." The club lost most of its matches, but it seldom took on anyone of less than university status, and it gave everyone good competition. In 1928 contesting the Universities of West Virginia, Maryland, Maine, Nevada, Nebraska, and Cornell, the club lost all six matches; but the total points were 2,886 to 2,811.

The constitution of the outing club stated that it was for the "promotion in the school of tramping, snow-shoeing, skating, sliding, and similar outdoor activities." Mason, as noted, took great interest in this because of his belief in encouraging healthful activities. At one time he had negotiated with the school district for three abandoned one-room schools, on the outskirts of Keene, as camps or destination points for hikes. One, located on Wilson Pond, was the beginning of the college camp there. "I know it sounds dumb today," said Sheldon Barker, "but we were interested in hiking." "One day Alice Collins and I hiked to Winchendon, Mass. and took the train home."

In the winter of 1927 under the direction of Austin Keyes, who also taught mathematics, the Latin department staged *Andromeda*, with all dialogue and songs in Latin. "All the parts were well taken, the Latin was clearly spoken, the emphasis well placed, and the drift of the play could be followed from the action as well as the spoken word," commented the *Sentinel*.

Male students had scarcely been established on campus when they formed a fraternity. "The first year there were two [men], and the next year there were five and we established Kappa Delta Phi," recalled Barker. The charter members were the seniors Barker and Brooks, and juniors Henry C. Dumont, Edgar E. Howe, and Harold F. Mayette. Formal initiation ceremonies were held on a Saturday morning, April 9, 1921. A social fraternity, it was established, nonetheless, "to be an inducement for young men to enter the normal school," and to maintain "an interest in teaching and professional spirit in educational work." The fraternity's first year was a good one. After its advisor, Nahum Leonard, left, it became less active but revived again in 1925 and has left its various marks on campus ever since.

In June 1925 as soon as more men came to campus another fraternity, Alpha Pi Tau, was founded with the help of Blackington and Mason. Alpha was a local fraternity, whereas Kappa was then regional with other chapters in the Bridgewater and Salem Normal schools in Massachusetts.[2]

Mason was anxious to get men on campus. He not only involved them with fraternities, but in 1921 he ran a picture of all five boys as the basketball team.

Great spirit was involved in any game with Plymouth, but in the 1920s and 1930s they were more gentlemenlike and ladylike competitions than they later became. The real competition with Plymouth was with the debating club. In athletics the real competition was to the south — Fitchburg Normal.

The highlight of these competitions undoubtedly took place in Spaulding Gymnasium in the winter of 1931 in a men's basketball game. That was a game of real guts. Keene's previous year with only two wins in ten games was not exactly a coach's dream. But 1931 was different. That year the team won nine out of ten games. Only two members of the old team were left — Captain "Jingle" Peavey and Charles Beaudette, both sophomores and both good players. All the rest were highly talented freshmen. Keene defeated Fitchburg in December by five points. It was obvious that in January Fitchburg would be out for blood.

The fates seemed to be sitting on the Fitchburg bench. Sickness laid low two Keene men, including Peavey. The home squad was now down to eight players. Nonetheless, adversity would be overcome! From the opening whistle on January 10 the teams went at each other on the field of honor. Both teams fouled, dribbled, passed, and shot courageously, but at the end of the first quarter their valiant efforts had resulted in a complete standoff, and the score tied at 0-0.

The stalemate called for special help. The KNS cheerleaders came to the rescue with their special cheer:

> Rickity rickity russ
> We're not allowed to cuss!!!
> But, nevertheless, we must confess:
> There's nothing the matter with KNS!!!

Thus inspired, the team went all out to score eight points in the next quarter, but, alas, Fitchburg also did well. Keene managed a one-point advantage in the third quarter, and the cheerleaders gave their "With a vevo, vevo, vum, *bum*!!!" yell. The team then pulled ahead six points late in the fourth period, and it looked as if the fates had been licked or switched benches and that the Keene five would roll to another stunning victory. But then disaster struck. Another Keene man fouled out, the fourth one to do so. Thirty-seven personal fouls and two technicals had been called thus far. (The *Sentinel*, ever loyal to the home team, said that despite the number of fouls it was a clean game.) Keene was now down to four players against Fitchburg's full team, and there were still three minutes to play. The team just had to hold on. Then the cheerleaders brought out a very special formula:

OS-KI-WOW-WOW!
WISK-KI-WEE-WEE!
OLI-MI-KI-IA!!
OLI-KEENE-EI!
KEENE-WOW!!!

What a daring yell for the home court! "It is no wonder," the reporter for the *Alpha* actually wrote, "that the faculty does not appreciate our 'owski-Wow-Wow,' when one of its members understood 'Oli-Keene-Ei, Oli-Mi-Ki-Ia' to be 'Holy Peter, Holy Mother.' "

The gamble paid off. The Keene four held off the threatening Fitchburg five until the very end and wound up with a 24-22 victory. There were tears and cheers in the old gym that night! On a similar occasion the school newspaper commented: "Found: Keene Normal School Spirit! Is it any wonder that Coach Caldwell has a winning basketball team? Those hearty cheers and songs are a big help. Build up your own school; don't tear it down!"

A few years later, in 1935, the girls played an equally exciting game with Plymouth. By the end of the first quarter Plymouth had doubled the tally on Keene with a score of 4-2. In the next quarter Keene zipped ahead of the opponent to an amazing 11-8 score. The game seesawed back and forth the rest of the evening, building up to an exciting finish. It will be well at this point to take up the narrative as the school newspaper reported it:

About two minutes before the finish of the game, the score stood 18-17 in Plymouth's favor, when Miss Georgia Day made a beautiful long shot and the whistle sounded — leaving a score of 19-18 in favor of Keene.

Following the game, Keene was royally entertained by the Plymouth squad at a banquet and dance. We left Sunday morning on the return trip and arrived safely, but half frozen amid a delightful snow storm.

Marion Butters (home economics) and Martha E. Randall (English, and no relation to Dorothy Randall) supervised the editing of the *Kronicle* in 1922. On the editorial page they ran a picture of themselves and their six-

*The owl first became identified with the college through
this representation in the 1922 Kronicle.*

teen student assistants. Over the picture they placed an owl clutching a
pencil and quill. Succeeding editors in the 1920s liked that symbol and
used it also for their yearbooks. That was the beginning of the use of the
owl as a college mascot, which has been made most popular by the athletic
teams.

In the early 1930s the Women's Athletic Association (WAA) was formed
to encourage physical activity and sport. The WAA sponsored "Sport
Days" in the fall and spring of each year. Red and White teams competed
with each other in baseball, archery, hockey, bowling, badminton, basketball, volleyball, and swimming. For years their slogan was, "A sport for
every girl, and every girl in a sport."[3]

Regulating Morals

It is now pretty well agreed that the 1920s as the era of the flapper, the
flivver, and the flask was an exaggerated stereotype. Women had,
however, gained some new freedom and were insistent on gaining more.
On campus Mason resisted the trend as much as he could, but at times
even he had to give in.

Cassie Haven Sweet recalled:

Oh, you can't imagine the regimentation. You could not go uptown without
an escort. You couldn't go to the movies without an escort, you know, another
teacher. If anyone bobbed her hair, she was immediately expelled. We once got
reprimanded for having an onion sandwich party. Mason was very stern. And
when somebody was being expelled, we always knew, because he would read from
the Bible the verse which says "some seeds fall by the wayside." We would always
look at each other and say, "Who now?"

Stacy Milbouer: "So people got expelled for bobbing their hair?"

"Yes, for bobbing their hair! That's it, *out!*"

"Oh, wow! permanently expelled! I didn't know that."

"Well, that was the 1920s."

Marion Wood recalled that one woman was interviewed and hired while still wearing her hat. When she began to teach, it was discovered that she had short hair. Thereafter all women were interviewed with their hats off! "Daddy Mason liked long hair! And we began to cut our hair. He stood up in assembly one time and gave a long dissertation on the evils of short hair and the beauty of long hair. Girls were cutting their hair right and left." Mason eventually had to give way. Before the end of the decade short hair had won out, and so had short dresses. By 1929 women's knees were showing even in the *Kronicle.*

Wood continued:

I come from the day of the midi-blouses and black bloomers. Now, the black stockings that Leo used to talk about, I don't seem to remember. I remember we thought it was real risqué to take those bloomers — oh, they were voluminous — and we would pull them up as high as we could and they'd blouse down over the leg — and the higher we could pull them the better we thought it was.

Mrs. Frank Blackington recalled:

Daddy Mason insisted that the girls wear black stockings when they were taking gym, and they had to be entirely covered. And when they were having a dance, and a saxophone happened to be in the orchestra, Daddy Mason would come to Frank and say, "Do you think that's a little too peppy for them?" Those were the two things that I remember.

Elese Wright Tarris remembered the "gray bathing suit, [the] long black stockings that came with our gymsuit. Those I really hated as they didn't stay up well."

Wood commented again: "I remember Marge Masters; she was more sophisticated than most of us, and she liked to smoke. I can remember crawling out the window with her so she could take a smoke. I was sick about this because if she got caught and I got caught...that was it for both of us."

Christa Price: "She fit more into the idea of the flapper?"

"Yes. Smoking was beginning to be a feature on campus."

Traditions flourished. Whist became *the* card game on campus, and it stayed so till the 1960s. The Mid-Year Ball that had begun in Rhodes's time continued. "Frank and I," recalled Mrs. Blackington, "always led the group in the grand march, and then when they played 'Let me call you

Mason conducting chapel exercises outside in June, 1925.

sweetheart,' we danced around the floor. We were supposed to dance the whole dance; but we'd go round the floor at least a couple of times."

Another popular tradition was Rose Night. "The junior class gave the senior class a rose," Mrs. Blackington continued. "And they all gathered out there in the quadrangle, and somebody sang from up in Parker Hall. We made a big circle and the junior class made an inner circle, and as the singing was going on the juniors would give us a rose. It was a very beautiful occasion." It was often modified. Sometimes a K or a KNS was made instead of a circle.

Ruth Wilson Keddy recalled a later version of it:

Commencement really started with Rose Night. It was the night on which the undergraduates honored those who were graduating. With a background of special music, seniors filed through a white trellis arch placed in front of Fiske Hall. As they continued through a double column of juniors, each senior was handed a single red rose while the traditional Rose Night song was sung:
"Take this rose, this lovely rose,
And wear it for a day.
Take the love that with it goes,
To keep or throw away.
Just a tea rose, kissed by dew
Kissed by tender tear drops, too
May it bring our love to you,
So take this rose."

Girls baseball game during Field Day in 1924

The words were attributed to Merton Goodrich of the mathematics faculty. After this the seniors responded with specially composed words from a melody of the day. "Our class response," recalled Keddy, "was sung to the tune of 'Mexicali Rose' ":

> Graduation Rose we take you
> With the love and friendship that you show.
> You're a Symbol of our happy days here...
> Underclassmen, now we leave you—
> Thank you for this rose; goodnight.

The Riot of 1925

"In these restive years, student outbreaks and proclaimed dissatisfaction are common at other institutions," wrote Commissioner Butterfield, "but our normal schools know only harmonious and happy cooperation." He had either forgotten about or glossed over the "Riot of '25." Although somewhat incomplete, the best account comes from Etta Merrill:

I was awakened by a loud noise.... I looked at the clock and it was four o'clock in the morning. I put on Marion Tebbett's dress, that I had been wearing the day before. Here was this gang on campus. I looked over in this direction [Appian Way] where there was an old boiler. They heated the tar for the road with it.... I saw these four or five men tied to that. The gang was just out of control all over

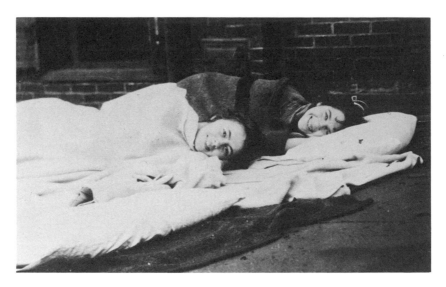

Evelyn Fuller (left) and Gerry Hanson sleeping out on a warm spring night in 1925 on the south porch roof of the Brick House, now Peter Christian's restaurant.

campus. I enquired as to what it was all about and learned . . . that some boys had attempted to put a banner on top of Fiske. It was the custom for them to have a banner on the highest place on campus. And they wanted to put a banner on the cupola of Fiske Hall, which they did. It happened to be a warm night. The girls were sleeping in the nude—and when they saw two men going through the dormitory—with the standards that we had in those days, they were very much distressed. I think the boys did get up there, but the girls got their clothes on and went out to fight them—to get them out of the dormitory.

Well, we got outdoors. I had also put on a pair of shoes that my mother had bought me which were very expensive for graduation week. It was just a mob scene. The first thing I knew Roy Terrill had a can of paint and a brush. Anyhow, it wasn't very long till he had splashed red paint on Marion's dress and my shoes! Well, it irritated me beyond words, and so I was out to get Roy Terrill. In due time we got him into Hale Building. . . . We'd come to tie him up with a rope. So we got the rope, and we tied Roy Terrill between the upstairs and the downstairs. We had him stretched out there [on the staircase]. Of course, he'd sprayed other people with paint besides me. I remember he had just one hand free, and I grabbed that hand and I jumped on it. I worked with him years afterwards teaching here. We even taught in the third floor of Hale at the same time, and I also worked with him at the junior high. He once said he had trouble in the area where I jumped, and I told him. He said, "Oh, Etta, that couldn't have been you!" and I said, "I'm sorry but it was.

Stacey: "Did you get in trouble with Daddy Mason?"

Well, Daddy Mason slept through the first part of it. When he did wake up, I don't think he wanted to come out and get into the crowd. I don't remember, but someone turned water on the group and sprayed them down. That took care of the group.

Then I learned that these people on the boiler — there had been only about half a dozen men here and they were the seniors. This other gang, the underclassmen — Daddy Mason had gone out and gotten a gang of men to come in. He had gotten almost anyone he could get in here. They had caused trouble throughout the whole year. This was just the climax of the whole thing. But they had gone to the different houses where the 'men' seniors lived and told them of some terrible thing on campus, whatever they could think up, and got them to come on campus. And when they did, this gang of thirty men overpowered them and tied them to the boiler. It started after midnight. And here it was five or six in the morning before they were released. There were placecards on them, I think. The alumni association has my pictures — the pictures I brought of this sort of thing. They will verify my story. Daddy Mason finally came out, and that was the end.

Other accounts vary in detail, but all confirm in broad outline Merrill's story.

On another occasion, evidently some of the same "gang" pretended to have a breakdown with their car. When Dean Carle and another teacher came out to help them, they "held up their rescuers." That, too, was meant to be a joke, but since one of the boys had a real gun in the "play" holdup, it was not funny and was dangerous.

Butterfield by his open admissions decision had made it possible to accept "almost anybody." Nearly sixty years after the event older, valuable alumni who were pained and humiliated by the riot of 1925 were still pained and humiliated by it. The event makes one wonder how much emphasis should be placed on coaxing into college those who really do not qualify for it — or how much value there is in being able to say that in a certain category enrollments are up — or how the public good is being served by making some of the most decent people pay a frightful price in self respect in order to entertain a few rowdies. Why did mature, adult educators such as Mason and Butterfield make such an effort to have warm male bodies on campus? Billy Whitehead commented, "I honestly think they accepted men to get the Smith-Hughes [funds] because the school needed money." It was the age old question of monetary value *vs.* moral value; and for the moment, despite all protestations to the contrary, moral values were not faring well.

After the riot Mason tried to regain moral losses by preaching and example. In 1927 when the fiftieth boy arrived he announced in chapel the enrollment of the "noble half-hundred," and in 1929 he proudly proclaimed the total of 100 boys admitted. In the meantime Mason and several faculty were working hard with the fraternities. "Bear in mind the fact that by our fruits we shall be known," wrote one Alpha brother, who had picked up the new gospel, so "let us cooperate and assume the responsibility of giving only our best to our school."

In the next years the situation again stabilized, and life on campus could even be boring! Evelyn Fuller Lamond copied in her notebook the Keene fire alarm code: "2 — Call to Quarters, 3 — All Out. . ., 5 — City Hospital;" after which she noted, "The only excitement — attending fires!"

The 1920s was a special decade throughout the United States, and it was also for the students at Keene Normal School, who by and large profited from their few years here. Only two need to speak; first Marion T. Wood and then James Whitehead:

I've been fortunate, Jim. The background I got here was a marvelous springboard, and I used it. You know, I've had a fabulous life and it started right here. I got maturity here. I got sociability here. I got a feeling of importance here. And I guess I got courage here.

Believe me, I learned how to teach at Keene. . . . Now I get. . .[appeals] from the University of Connecticut, from the University of New Hampshire, and from William and Mary. I get appeals as a degree holder from those schools, but the only one that I accept is Keene. Keene is my school.[4]

Both these statements of former students are representative and are eloquent testimony to the meaning and to the special experiences that Keene Normal School gave to their lives.

15

The Second Building Program

THE RAPID GROWTH to near-college status in the 1920s brought about another spurt of building between 1925 and 1929, after which the college remained basically the same for the next thirty-six years. Mason had been lobbying legislatures since 1919 trying to get a new dormitory but with little success. Finally, a miraculous event touched off a four-year building boom. On Christmas Day, 1925, a "heaven-sent" fire devoured the old stable and coach house, which had been the manual training department, and wreaked havoc with the old barn, which had been the gymnasium. Many stories circulated about the fire. Dean Carle was the last one seen leaving the building, and jokes traveled around that the "heaven-sent" fire came from the godlike Carle. Everyone knew, of course, of Carle's consistent integrity and dedication. No one may be above suspicion to today's generation. Then, however, one could be the butt of such jokes and not be suspect.

The legislature, undoubtedly inspired by this providential blaze, appropriated money for Butterfield Building with up-to-date equipment in it for the "T&I" (trades and industry) boys. It was erected on the site of the recent fire. Two and a half stories high, it was built in a classical style in keeping with Fiske and Parker. Under incentive from the Smith-Hughes Act the legislature provided money also for the "home-ecers." Mason purchased the historic Blake House and site on the corner of Winchester and Main streets. The size of the house was tripled by building westward a central core and wing, and was so designed as to preserve the architectural integrity of the original house. The final structure had a central unit

Huntress Hall

of wood construction with identical brick wings, a fitting remodeling of the house built for Abel Blake in 1833. The old greenhouse was removed to a location immediately west of the Blake House, and it, too, was renovated.

Governor Winant was the friend of the college at this time. He not only supported construction of the Butterfield and Blake Houses but also the building of Huntress Dormitory at $250,000, which was designed to house 157 female students. The building was named for Harriet Lane Huntress, who had devoted all her life to work for the state office of education. As various superintendents came and went, she gave the office continuity for nearly thirty-five years. She was a public-minded woman who entertained graciously and ably served many organizations. She left $10,000 of her estate as a memorial fund for needy students. So popular was she that at her death teachers throughout the state took up an additional subscription to add to the Huntress Fund in memory of her. Although she lived in Concord, she was well known in Keene through her visits here and through her brother, Frank, a local businessman, politician, and resident of Keene.

Mason knew that it would be impossible to get any more out of the legislature, but he needed a gymnasium, so he made the request anyhow. After the purchase of the land west of Hyde Street (now roughly the gym parking lot) for an athletic field, it seemed that that was all that athletics could expect. Then another miracle happened — a miracle, that is, in the history of normal schools. Governor Huntley Spaulding was independently wealthy. He liked Mason and Keene Normal School. He believed that "the boy and girl with a fine mind, an active brain, is greatly handicapped without a healthy body and strong physique with which to sustain the mental efforts and carry them into effect."[1] He contributed his own money for the new gym. As he put it:

and so the thought came to me that while I could not, as governor, conscientiously recommend to the legislature the making of an appropriation for a gymnasium at the Keene Normal School, I could as a private citizen, give myself the pleasure of presenting such a building to the school, as a token of my sincere and continued interest in its educational system.

It was to be built on a historic site, the south corner of Appian Way and Main Street. That was the site of Keene's first public grammar school, built in 1776; and what a fight it was when it was torn down and replaced by the larger Wheelock School.

Besides the utilitarian gym floor and stage (now the Mable Brown Room), the gym also had bowling alleys and a social room with a nice large fireplace; but it was fake, which Lloyd Young found out the hard way. Spaulding was also thinking about giving a large inside swimming pool, a rare thing in those days, to either Plymouth or Durham. One weekend Mason, Silver, and Lewis (of Durham) were meeting the governor in Concord. That Sunday morning Spaulding asked Lewis to play golf, but Lewis had plans for church. He then tried Silver, who also decided to stick to his church plans. He then asked Mason. Mason, of course, was a regular churchgoer himself, but he hadn't been in Tennessee politics for nothing. He accepted the governor's invitation, and while out on the golf course, the governor thought, "well, here I wanted to play golf this morning, and Mason was the only one who accepted my invitation, and he's such a nice chap, I believe I'll give the gym *and* the swimming pool to Keene." By the early 1950s the pool, only four lanes wide, looked terribly antiquated, but for the first twenty years it was a modern wonder, the only indoor pool in the area and enjoyed by the college and the town.

"It is needless to say," said one of the Alpha brothers, "how much the present Keene Normalites appreciate the gift." Not only did the students appreciate it, but the city did too. Mayor Kingsbury thanked Spaulding "for the greatest gift which has ever been placed within Keene's borders." Student Louise N. Barnum recalled,

they dug a trench across the campus for the steam pipes and electric wires. Of course, we all know what a high water level is to be found in Keene. Soon

The old Spaulding Gymnasium is now part of the Lloyd P. Young Student Union.

if one of us brushed against another in going to chapel..., we got a spark and a belt. If one tried to turn off the radiator, the same thing occurred. Our science teacher, Dean Carle, laughed at us when we said there must be a short circuit some place in the line. Soon they began to dig up the pipeline, and when we asked about it, they said there must be a short circuit somewhere in the line.[2]

Despite some building quirks like that, the good luck continued. The state department of education in 1929 had an unallocated cash surplus and used the money to build a large reading room onto Ball House, which had heretofore been used as a dormitory. It was dedicated as the Wallace E. Mason Library. It is now Rhodes Hall. After construction of the library there would be no more construction on campus for a full generation.

16

The Campus in the Early 1930s

OFTEN IT APPEARS at first glance that one can write about life in a single decade such as the 1920s or 1930s, but on closer examination one finds that there are too many disparate elements and that the decade does not hold together at all. The decade of the 1930s at Keene was a much tighter decade than the 1920s and, therefore, is easier to write about as a unit. There were common concerns about jobs, about quality, about performance. The time was static, the growth recessive. Intellectually (and socially, as one might expect) the campus was alive. Enough happened that it will be necessary to break this time unit up into two chapters, roughly, "the early 1930s" and "the latter 1930s." After all these years, former students deserve some relief from a long-winded historian.

During the depression decade, Keene's administrative staff dropped from 15 to 11; the faculty, from 44 to 30; the student body, from a record high of 628 in 1931 to 333 in 1939. The decline in numbers of the 1930s was almost as steep as the rise had been in the 1920s. There were plenty of students at Keene with scarcely two dimes to rub together, but as the college had never drawn from a wealthy clientele, the situation was not unusual. It was only a little worse than usual. What was unusual for the 1930s was the high percentage of graduates that did get jobs. Most members of the 1931 graduating class got positions "in spite of the very general oversupply of teachers," noted the *Kronicle*. The worst years were 1932 and 1933. The graduating class of 1932 was one of the largest, 174, and of those only 78 got jobs. It is noteworthy that this class left an unusually nice gift for the college—the outside clock in the Huntress Hall front pediment. Only thirty-three percent of the 1933 graduating class got positions, about the same percentage as Plymouth's. Thereafter the percentage of placement was appreciably higher—of course, the graduating classes were at the same time getting smaller. Almost 60 percent of the class of 1935 got jobs; 128 members, 80 percent, of the class of 1936 got teaching positions; and in 1937, 90 percent of its high school majors received positions, and "practically all of the elementary graduates were placed before the beginning of the school year." "The placement of so many," noted the *Kronicle* with pride, "puts Keene out in the lead over many of the Teachers Colleges."

At one time in the 1920s Keene and Plymouth were to limit themselves to preparing elementary and junior high school teachers, and the University of New Hampshire was to prepare high school teachers. The university, however, produced very few such graduates; and Mason since the teens had been claiming that Keene could prepare teachers for high school. Gradually he gave the claim substance. By the late 1930s Keene produced a majority of the high school teachers hired annually in the state and also sent a great number into other New England states and to the rest of the nation.

While the students at Keene had a much better chance of getting a position after graduation than students at most other colleges, they were, while here, hard pressed. "One thing I do remember was the bank holiday when my roommate and I had 32 cents between us," recalled Mariam Roby Carpenter. "My roommate, who was majoring in home ec., had to have a yard of material to make an apron. We scrounged around town until we found a yard of material that we could buy with our combined 32 cents so she could make her apron."

"Went to the movies upstreet on dime day (Tuesdays) — got a big charge out of slapping down a nickel at the ticket booth and saying, 'Balcony, please!' " recalled another. A favorite hangout, for boys only, was the Donkas Café at 87 Main Street. With a fig bar topped with ice cream for 10 cents and a cup of coffee for a nickel, a boy had enough to last the whole evening.

Some of the ways in which students financed themselves were ingenious. "One fellow put a chair under the window [in the basement of the dormitory] so the girls [who broke curfew] could get in without breaking a leg. They could step on the chair and get in. We found the guy who did it," recalled Ray Harwood and Dorothy LaPointe. "I was going to mention this when I stood up at the alumni dinner to speak for our class president, who didn't show up," Harwood said. "So they hurriedly told me to get up. I was going to tell this story, but when I got that alumni recognition award [the next day] — thank God, I didn't tell that story."

Q: "Who was it?"

LaPointe: "No, we're not going to tell."

Harwood: "It wouldn't be fair." "Come on outside, I'll tell you."

LaPointe: "Don't you dare! We laughed so — to think — we never knew. He loved to beat the crowds. The girls put their quarters in a bowl for him. He got three bucks a week to put the chair there, so the girls wouldn't break a leg. He's the last person in the world you would have ever expected. That paid half his tuition."[1]

Student Publications

The first student publication, the *Kronicle*, began in 1914 as a quarterly. In 1921 it became a yearbook and has remained so. In 1929 Mason envisioned the yearbook staff as producing a monthly edition, to be called the *Keene Kronicle*, "to keep our students and the alumni fully informed" about campus events. Harry B. Preston was the first advisor. Preston was assisted by Robert Tinkham, who did the photography work, and by Roy A. Sullivan of the *Sentinel*. Sullivan had lived on campus for a number of years and was the link between Mason and the *Sentinel*. The *Keene Kronicle* quickly became in effect the campus newspaper. Preston and, later, Blackington got the students motivated each year. In the fall of 1936 the students decided to run the paper themselves, and it nearly died. Only four issues came out that year and two the next, and for the next twelve years the college newspaper was an occasional occurrence.

The Alpha brothers may very well have been the ones who inspired Mason. On April 7, 1926, appeared the first edition of the *Alpha*, which the brothers clearly intended to be a regular campus publication. It announced that it had to sell a minimum of 500 copies at 5 cents a copy to be a financial success. Its policy was "Service and Responsibility," and it stated that it would print only the truth and would accept just criticism. James Connell was the force behind the effort, and it was a setback when he had to leave school the next year. Leonard Dewyea took over as editor, hoping "that Jim will be back next fall." However Jim did not return, and after five publications in the spring of 1926 and six in the spring semester of 1927, the *Alpha* practically expired. After that the *Alpha* was published only sporadically.

The first three years of the *Keene Kronicle* were marked by an intellectual vigor and toughness that would not characterize the college newspaper for another twenty years. Sara McKinney, class of 1931, was editor for the first two years. She was ably assisted by her comrade from Berlin, Nella Morin, class of 1930, as news editor. Contributing to the intellectual vigor of the paper were Rosamond Parker Jerauld, who went on to Simmons College, and Genevieve Jaastad, class of 1932, who was an outstanding League of Nations worker in Dublin, New Hampshire, and also secretary to Robert Sagendroff of *Yankee* Magazine Inc. Both Jerauld and Jaastad wrote poetry and perceptive articles for the *Kronicle.* Their early issues with articles on various philosophies of education, including Dewey's, and on the merits of a liberal education versus the merits of a professional education are still enjoyable reading.

As with the first issues of the quarterly *Kronicle* in the mid-teens, one can pick up a trace of feminism in the paper. It appears often enough so that it cannot be readily dismissed. There were frequent articles on the activities of Smith and Mount Holyoke colleges.

Humor often ran:

M. Perkins: "What's wrong with this school?"

B. Macy: "The masucline population."

Instructor: "I maintain that men and women are equal."

Coed: "Oh, sir, you're braggin' again."

Definitions:

Boy — "An easily trained pet; obeys very well when correctly educated. Very useful thing when the Prom comes around."

Brother — "General informer on sister's conduct."

Comment:

"It is not easy to classify the girls, but the boys all come under one class beginning with D."

One time some girls complained that they were being discriminated against because they had to be in by ten and the boys could stay out till eleven. Mason fixed that. The boys had to be in by ten!

It was not a strong theme but is nonetheless detectable. Even at the end of the decade one newspaper complained, "The class [1940] has suffered from the usual casualty, marriage, and has decreased through the years."

Much more space, however, was given to marriage and engagement announcements. "I remember well," writes one alumnus, "the usual early evening strolls with my little blonde, a kiss or two. Then back to the books. But, who could study after those strolls. No wonder I couldn't make any honor society." One freshman commented that "about this campus" a young man's fancy turning to love was "a year round disease rather than a seasonal one."[2] This disease occurred not only in flivvers but also in trucks.

Truckin' at KNS

Paul Nordman, class of 1938, wrote:

There was a student who lived in town. His father owned a Model A truck...which looked like a Conestoga wagon with 4 ft. side rails and a canvas top that rounded up over on steel supports. From time to time the student could "borrow" the truck evenings and the guys would go out and load it with hay before picking up the gals. The back would hold ten to fourteen rather cosy like—all out of sight and bothering no one.... Various places were used to park for an enjoyable evening, in fact, one time the gang parked on Main Street right in front of the Old Colonial theatre. (Being quiet was most important.)

One evening it was decided we would use the mattresses at the school camp as hay was rather messy. Upon arrival at the camp it was found that the Dean was making a presentation to a rather large group of students. Nevertheless, we got the attention of one and told him what was cooking, whereupon he casually went upstairs and unlocked a window allowing the truck to be backed up against the wall. By one fellow standing on another's shoulders he was able to raise the window and boost up a couple other guys who assisted as quickly as possible in tossing the mattresses out. Well, the fellow who unlocked the window couldn't keep it to himself and in no time everyone in the audience knew what was up and began snickering....Here the dean thought he was going over in great style, never dreaming what was going on three feet over his head.

Mason and his deans, however, were quite well aware of the weaknesses of the flesh. Most accounts indicate overconcern about sexual morality.

All set for the Mid-Year Ball, 1939

Barbara Jefferey Stimson, class of 1941, recalled:

I was a "townie," and remember well the time that Miss Esten called me into the inner sanctum to tell me what a wonderful mother I had to allow so many Keene students to be entertained in our home—I chuckled silently and failed to tell her that I had two eligible brothers. One was a real Casanova. She had just called a friend "townie" in to tell her no more girls could visit her as she had three brothers and it might create too much temptation.

In the 1930s Sonja Henie was a popular figure skater. One can imagine the guffaws as Mason announced one winter day there would be ice skating after supper, "and I hope to see a lot of little 'Heines' out on the ice."
Another alumna recalled:

When it came to the proms, you could import anybody you wanted to take. But of course they were very, very critical of any of the town people inviting anybody. They put 'em through the tenth degree. So I never bothered to go to any school stuff. I just went other places. . . . They used to have a dance hall down at Wilson Pond and it was called "The Rec," and you were not supposed to go to any Saturday night dances because that was against the rules of the school. I thought it was a nice place to go. . . . So every Saturday night my father and mother would take me down. The college always sent a spotter down who always wanted to be sure that they saw you so that you would get reported. In fact, [one time] there were quite a few . . . boys [there], and they weren't supposed to be there. One of them happened to be a cousin of mine. I happened to spy one of these spotters, and I told them that they were coming in. I can see him now. He jumped over the side rail [to the ground ten feet below]. There was no other way out of the place. The following Monday morning you'd always be called into Daddy Mason's office. . . . And he'd ask me where I'd been . . . but I told him when I left campus Friday afternoon, and until I returned Monday morning, my parents were responsible for me.

Saturday nights on campus were nearly as strict as other nights. Frank Knox recalled:

As long as we could get a program for a half an hour on a Saturday night, we could have a dance in the gym, from seven to nine. A great many times I was digging around Saturday trying to get the entertainment to have the dance. The girls had to be back in the dorms by 9:15, and I can remember Dean Esten many times rapping on the window, signaling the girls they had better get inside.

Each year there were four major "formals" (tux, black tie, and evening gowns) when dancing could continue until midnight. Kappa and Alpha each sponsored one, and there was an old-fashioned junior-senior prom. The greatest of all, however, was the Mid-Year Ball. The Masons, the Carles, Dean Esten, Dean Fernald, Mable Brown, and many faculty came as guests. Important townspeople, such as Mr. and Mrs. Robert Kingsbury and the current mayor and his wife, were often invited. Ruth Wilson Keddy recalled preparing herself for one of these:

My date that night was very important to me. I really needed the afternoon off to do up my hair . . . and to press a long evening gown with layers and layers of material. So I made the decision not to go to Maynard Waltz's psychology class. . . . I was sure no one would miss me. No problem. We had a very fine weekend. I enjoyed the ball very, very much.

But Monday she discovered that most of the other girls in class had made the same decision. They were all sent to Miss Brown to receive their blue slips — unexcused absences! One could not collect very many blue slips.

To recoup psychologically from the Mid-Year Ball, a tea, and then later an informal Tea Dance, was held the following afternoon. This was put on by the Alpha brothers and Nu Beta Upsilon (home economics) Sorority. Under Vivian Rockwood the sorority really blossomed, having at times

The Grand March began the formal dance.

as many as forty members. With this enthusiasm and all the tea and goodies that Nu Beta U could produce, the Tea Dance became as big and as highly decorative an event as the Mid-Year Ball itself. Many enjoyed it more, since the decorations were still fresh; the music was by a smaller, more intimate orchestra; there were fewer attending; and the chaperon line was much, much shorter.

Both smoking and drinking, although limited, arrived permanently on the campus in the 1930s. "The third floor of Huntress became known as 'Firefly Dorm,' " LaPointe recalled. "What would happen, they'd wait till lights were out, and they'd hang out the window. You couldn't do it certain nights. You had to wait till bed check was over because if you didn't the smoke would drift by and they could tell." At the beginning of the decade Prohibition was still on, but uptown you could buy "Padres, a tonic for the blood." It was 5 percent alcohol, and "it was good!"

Another problem of manners and morals was the way students crowded into the downstairs commons in Fiske. That was a problem as long as the dining room remained in the basement of Fiske. Wally Tripp, a generation later, drew one of his first cartoons about it, which the *Monadnock* reprinted several times. The *Kronicle* imagined Emily Post visiting campus and saying, "But why are they crowding around the door so?" and a Keene student replying, "We go to meals that way."

Inflexible dining hours and family-style serving practices created a near mob scene outside the entrance on the descending staircase when the dinner bell rang. If one could not make it to the first serving, he or she had to wait until a whole table was dismissed and reset. The crush was created not only by hunger but also by fear that there would be no food or that it would be cold.[3]

Generally, however, the student body was well behaved. Good character was a requirement for entrance, and the catalog clearly and prominently stated that "Anything that affects unfavorably a student's character during the normal school term is sufficient cause for dismissal." Most students realized that and acted accordingly.

Clubs continued to be formed. The Keene club, the Orpheus club, and the rural club made their appearance in the 1930s. More important was the formation of the first student council in 1936, an organization that appeared threatening at the time. The concern stemmed from an incident of dining commons food.

Clair Wyman wrote:

In the winter of 1935-36, Mason was vacationing in Florida. The students had been complaining in progressively louder tones about the food being served. . . . Eventually a dinner was served that brought the matter to a climactic boil. The meal consisted of hard boiled eggs, which had been boiled too long, coloring the yolks a handsome green. To camouflage this, either by accident or design, the chef added creamed asparagus, resulting in a concoction of indescribable odor and color. Even if you were blindfolded, you could smell the mess uptown. Nevertheless, this was dinner and it was served.

Those in the dining room rose *en masse* and walked out, describing the delicacy in ever more lurid terms to the late arrivals, who decided they needed no firsthand experience and joined the retreating throng.

It was a relatively calm action, but effective. Mason was informed, quick changes were made in the professional dining room personnel and the quality of the food improved, at least for a while.

Mason assigned as advisors to the council the campus "heavies," Deans Carle, Esten, and Fernald, to make sure the council limited itself to reforms and that there would be no more demonstrations.

Most important, the council was the beginning of student government, another extracurricular activity. One editor thought there were too many clubs and too much activity. "The result of this craze for DOING

SOMETHING," he wrote, "is an increase in insanity. The Asylums are full of patients. The next one may be YOU!" And he advised his readers to take it easy.

While there was a lot of nonsense among the student body, and returning alumni like to recall the most extreme examples, one cannot help but notice an unmistakable reverence for education. The depression, despite Butterfield's open-door policy, actually raised standards. Mason and the state board believed, as did nearly everyone else, that the way to better the situation was to reduce expenses and to limit admissions, since not as many teachers were needed. By the end of the decade no more than twelve people each year were accepted into the high school English program, for instance. The same was true of several other programs. These students had to be good to be accepted!

As already noted, a student's tuition was waived if he or she agreed to teach in New Hampshire for as long a time as he or she attended normal school. It was education "on loan" for those who had no money but were striving to better their lives. Their situation was made easier after the passage of the Federal National Youth Administration Act, whereby money was available for on-campus student jobs. It was the forerunner of today's "work/study" money. This economic "bonus" further increased the competition for admittance as a student to Keene.

Students speculated on who would win the debate with Plymouth each year; and the topics debated are still challenging, such as the desirability of chain stores and the necessity for mechanical progress to civilization. The Academy of Science became one of the most popular of the new clubs. Jerauld was its first president. She and Jaastad also formed the English club in 1931 with Drenan as faculty advisor. The League of Nations club was active throughout the decade. Both were more intellectual than "clubby."

Scholarship Day, "more commonly known as the Battle of the Brains," where several hundred high school students competed for scholarship money, always generated an active interest. Part of the excitement lay in the competitive atmosphere, since other students were taking the exams at Plymouth, and the final scores were tallied by the relatively modern "phone hook-up." Tremendous respect and courtesy was shown to guest speakers, who ranged from Edwin Markham to United States Senator Styles Bridges. Markham, the Dean of American Poetry, had graduated from a "people's" college, San Jose Normal School. It was, said the *Kronicle*, a "red-letter day" on campus when he spoke.

In 1937 the Latin club compared Will Rogers with Horace in honor of the bimillennial birth of the poet. Articles and books, such as Stephan Lorant's *I Was Hitler's Prisoner*, were recommended by the student newspaper for general reading. Concerning an article by Robert Hutchins, the editors announced, "Here, without fanfare and without flourishes, is stated the purpose of college and of all education. Here is the broad vista, of which we gain an occasional glimpse when we have a good day in our classwork or teaching, but which is rarely possible to see in its entirety."[4]

Under Harry Davis's able direction students provided a sophisticated musical program. In reviewing it all, it is hard to understand how Davis accomplished so much. If there was a musical group, usually he directed it, and there were plenty of musical groups. In some years the college's string orchestra had over forty members! The Orpheus club had in some years over fifty-five members. There was always the Campus Choir, a men's glee club and a woman's glee club, a school band, cantatas, and quartets. Besides these, Davis directed the choir for the United Church for a number of years. He supervised the music programs at the Wheelock, junior high, and high schools and was active in town-gown musical enterprises. There was a music department; but, at the end of the 1930s, it consisted of Davis and one student assistant! Most of Davis's work was with the nonmusic majors, just as most of the sports activity was done by non-physical-education majors.

Sometimes Davis was assisted by talented students or faculty. In 1939 a group of students, mostly Kappa brothers, calling themselves the Kampus Kids under the direction of Roland A. Nault, organized into a swing band for Saturday night socials. William Wolffer and Arthur Cram were the vocalists. The next year Laverne Bushnell helped by directing it.

Davis, of course, also taught, and apparently he taught well. Dr. Vanda Sanguinette Steele wrote:

I benefitted greatly from Davis's teaching, and I owe the success of my teaching of music to what I received from him. I have studied in many universities throughout the world: Adelphi University in Salzburg...Portland State in Oregon, Western Illinois University, the International University in Missouri...and the Universidad Internacional de Alcapulco. Yet in all that studying I never found the type of music appreciation training with the use of rhythm band instruments that Harry Davis gave me.

Steele taught Davis's methods to her granddaughter, who told her, "Through you I feel that I too have studied with him."

The intellectual impress was made by other notable faculty: Martha Randall and Sprague Drenan in English, Frank Blackington in French,

Frederick Simmons in philosophy, Harry Preston in history and New Hampshire resources, and Leonard Morrison in secondary education. T&I was especially strong with Conrad Adams, Spencer Eaton, Clarence DeMar, and Laverne Bushnell.

In a small college individual faculty members stand out as unusual personalities. Keene had its full share of them.

Frederick Simmons had difficulty accepting women as serious scholars. He, himself, was very masculine, impressive in his angular face and in athletic physique. Peering through his *pince-nez*, with tight neck and downward-turned mouth, he was formidable. Ruth Keddy recalled "He stood in front of the [new] class for what seemed to us at least ten minutes." Then he boomed out at the class, "Who are you?" And his pince-nez never slipped a bit. He had complete control, recalled another. "We didn't know," Keddy said, "if he meant each of us individually or all of us collectively, or who was going to be called upon to answer, and we were all scared stiff." The intellectuals on campus, however, would miss him when he left.

Isabel Blake had an A.B. from Middlebury and an M.A. from Columbia, had taught in Turkey, and had done relief work in Palestine after World War I. Legend had it that she knew Lawrence of Arabia. After she gave a particularly unorganized lecture in her history class (a not unusual occurrence), her students declared she was still "heady" or "dizzy" from something, such as her past experiences, and she became known as "Bugsy."

One alumnus wrote:

She had an Airedale, "Mac," who was as old as she was, give or take a year or two. He came to class with her. . . . He used to sleep in the air shaft, and often his snores [and other disturbing noises] would drown out the recitations. Every so often, he would stagger out into the classroom, turn around two or three times to orient himself, and then amble back into the air shaft, plop down and go back to sleep.

Marion Frost Hudson "used to regale her classes with descriptions of her courtship and her wedding night with her husband, Percy Hudson, a most proper and loveable Englishman." Hudson herself was actually quite proper and remembered for her favorite quote, "What you are speaks so loudly, I cannot hear what you say."

By far the most famous of the faculty members was Clarence DeMar, the winner of marathons. Stories about him were legion. He always thought he grew up in a penal institution on an island (it was an orphanage on Thompson's Island) not far from Boston, recalled Laverne Bushnell. He practiced running around the island. "He was planning on swimming ashore and then running away." He and his friends did plan such an escape but were caught. His inspiration to run, however, came from a coach at the University of Vermont, not from his orphanage experience, nice as that story is. He had won six Boston Marathons when hired in 1929, and he won one more in 1930. At Keene Normal he still trained and competed. When he came in seventh in 1938 at age fifty, he won more applause than the winner.

As a faculty member, he began work on his master's degree at Boston University. Every Thursday he ran toward Boston and at someplace along the way would accept a ride from a friendly motorist, and he returned the same way. He always ran in his business suit, usually with jacket and tie thrown over one arm. By the time he arrived his dress clothes were stinky and wrinkled. The situation worsened when he took up goat keeping and attended them in the same clothes. Sweat or goat manure became familiar odors in the printshop. This disturbed Mason. But DeMar was religious. He taught Sunday school at the First Baptist Church. Mason liked that, and it far outweighed his flaws in personal grooming. DeMar was also conscientious. Bushnell remembered that in the 1936 flood he offered to take DeMar to class in a boat, but DeMar was so anxious to be to work on time that he splashed into three feet of water on Appian Way and headed for Butterfield. He was on time. Of course, no students were there.

Mason wanted Demar on the faculty to help give the normal school a male image. To induce him to come Mason promised a suitable press and type for his printing class. (Heretofore DeMar had worked in newspaper typography.) Mason, however, succumbed to a "bargain" — an old press and worn-out type. Mason was still wheeling and dealing; and his Yankee heart told him that if he did enough of it he could always double the value of his money. DeMar became so exasperated with his materials that he printed a whole edition of the school newspaper with every conceivable kind of type — roman, gothic, italic, Old English, most of it worn out, but with enough new pieces to make his point. "It was a masterpiece of horrors," wrote Clair Wyman.[5] But alas! it served no purpose — except to infuriate Sprague Drenan, the advisor to the paper. Mason was still quite pleased with his "bargain."

17

The Campus in the Latter 1930s

Two Floods, A Hurricane, and Typhoid Fever

INTELLECTUAL CONCERNS and concerns about faculty were interrupted by two great natural disasters and an epidemic in the latter 1930s. Students had fun in accusing Dean Carle of coining a new phrase when he once talked about a "bunch of water." Students of the 1930s actually saw a bunch of water — in fact, two bunches of water.

From March 18 to March 20, 1936, Keene had one of the worst floods on the entire East Coast. Water was three feet deep on some parts of the campus. Faculty got out their canoes and rowboats and hauled students from one building to another, but generally the water was not deep enough to do much damage to the buildings or to stop classes for long. After the flood all students were inoculated against communicable diseases. The rains and melting snow continued. By mid-April, Keene had had almost twelve inches of rain in six weeks, but the flooding in April was not as severe as that of March. Men students from campus helped in rescue work for some 250 people in town who were stranded.

Two years later students had barely gotten settled into the fall routine when the second great storm of the 1930s hit. As Frances Day Bolles waited on tables at suppertime she looked through the dining room windows and saw the roofing of Hale Building sailing across Winchester Street. She commented to James Burrill, "That looks just like a *real* hurricane." Indeed, it was a real hurricane! The great New England hurricane of 1938 wreaked

The Hale Building after the hurricane of 1938

havoc on the campus as it did on the town. The campus was again inundated with water. Giant elms, maples, and oaks were uprooted and fell like so many dominoes, carrying power and communication lines down with them. Buildings were damaged by both wind and water. Students huddled with friends in their rooms and in the hallways, seeking protection against nature's wrath.

There were no handy power saws in that day. Students spent over a week with axes and crosscut saws cleaning up the campus and part of the city. Damage to the campus was estimated of $7,000. The city's total damage estimate was $1 million.

There was another natural disaster in 1938 — typhoid fever. No one knew about it at the time. Several people got sick, some terribly so; and the campus atmosphere beame tense. Who would be sick next, and what was it? Tension was relieved when Dean Carle came through with another malapropism. One doctor, he reported, said it was only "Unguentine fever." Unguentine was a popular cure-all-type salve of the day. Carle's remark broke the tension. Unfortunately, the situation was more serious than "Unguentine fever." It was later identified as typhoid fever, and one student, Myrtle Straw, died of it.[1]

Town-Gown Relations, 1921-40

During the 1920s and 1930s Keene and the campus were good neighbors. Mason and the college survived the 1921 revolt extraordinarily well. During the whole time of that incident, Dudley was the one faculty member who, by his numerous recitals, music lectures, and demonstrations, was able to demonstrate to the town the cultural advantage of the college. It was sad in many respects when he had to leave abruptly in 1924. He was the last direct link to the Rhodes administration and the founding of the college.

In 1924 the *Sentinel* headlined, *Faculty Follies Furnish Fun for Friendly Frolic*, a play which clearly delighted the town as much as it did the campus. The setting was a railroad station in a small town, like Keene, with various characters who had nothing else in common except meeting a train. The audience went wild with applause when Dudley, "dressed as a little boy in pink and white, with short stockings, made his appearance," and again when Enid Straw, Marge Masters and Mrs. Remington did some "shocking" dances. Mabel Brown (who directed the play) scolded them and then demonstrated "proper" entertainment and promptly put all those in the station to sleep.

In 1935 Sprague Drenan took his first plunge into musical drama with the Alpha Opera. The first production was such a success that he was soon the advisor for a drama club. The Alpha Opera became an annual event with the faculty being afforded front-row seats. They all dressed up in proper opera attire. Their timed appearance became as much an event to the students as the opera itself.

La Vie de Napoleon (or Cast Away on a Desert Island), undoubtedly Drenan's masterpiece, was performed in 1938. As soon as the faculty had been seated, the orchestra introduced the theme. In the orchestra were Ernest Fiske at the piano and "Eager Dave" Appleton with the cymbals, who made several attempts to get in his clang but, of course, missed *the* moment. They were complemented by a one-note organ and a few bass and percussion instruments of dubious quality.

The opera opened with Napoleon (James McKeon) at Waterloo surrounded by his generals, played by James Leh, Christopher Anastosopoulous, and Harold Graeme. From there the plot progressed, either forward or backward, until Napoleon finally landed at St. Helena. Josephine was played by Dick Hopwood, several inches taller than Napoleon. They nontheless managed a talented and memorable duet.

Eventually the curtain fell after a long-winded demise by Napoleon. Everyone loved it.

Kappa, of course, was not to be outdone. The Kappa Kapers also became an annual event. Some of their plays, particularly those produced by Dean Corrigan, were of professional quality, Ruth Keddy recalled.

By 1924 more Keene High graduates were going to "college" at Keene Normal School than to any other institution, which is another indication of town approval of the school, but there were still other indications. The *Kronicle* told its readers in clear and unmistakable terms: "PATRONIZE OUR ADVERTISERS." The Cheshire National Bank boldly asked the campus: "CAN WE BE OF SERVICE TO YOU?" Summer's Sport Shop offered discounts to students (it still does!). Bullard and Shedd sponsored jingle contests, and the winner(s) always got free sundaes and greatly reduced prices on the biggest ice-cream dishes available.

After the Keene chorus club disbanded, Mason and Davis felt that such a group would be missed by the town, so they formed a college community choral group. Davis was able to generate so much enthusiasm that he soon had a large group. Beginning in 1933 there was a series of annual musical festivals combining college groups with Ludwig Werniger's Maennerchor and Carl Beedle's Orchestral Society, several church choirs, and the Mac-Dowell Male Chorus. In one grand effort in 1936, 150 people from these and other groups produced a rendition of Gounod's *Faust*. The next year almost as many people were involved in a spectacular production of *Pinafore*.

For several years the college hosted a Community Concert Series, which brought the finest talent (not just big names) available to Keene. These events were cosponsored by the Keene Women's and the Fortnightly clubs. By opening the school's facilities to the public Mason accomplished several things. He enhanced the college's public image. He afforded the opportunity for participants, students, and faculty to "rub elbows" with members of the community. Many of these events were free to the students. Most important, he got students who normally avoided such culture as if it were a plague to attend these events.

Sheldon Barker recalled not only the hurricanes but also numerous forest fires to which college volunteers offered help as another aspect of good town-gown-relations. "There was always a lot of manpower there for different civic projects."

In light of all this, it seems odd that the college would still feel that it had to justify its existence and to do so primarily on economic grounds.

IN ITS SECOND BIG SEASON

THE ALPHA OPERA COMPANY

presents

MURDERO A MUSICI

(Murder To Music)

THE PLOT

The distinguished author and composer have combined the best traditions of grand opera (Wagner and Verdi and all those fellows) with the popular detective story in an irresistible way. The story deals with a certain Lord Piltdown, who does not live long enough to become a very engaging character to the audience. In fact he should have been killed long before. Detectives of great skill (vocal) fail to find a single useful clue. How is the murderer found, you ask? Ah, that is revealed in a manner both dramatic and laughable.

THE CAST

LORD PILTDOWN, noble in name only, the old crook .... Harold Graeme
BOGGINS, a butler, the sly rascal .... James Noucas
AUNT HELIOTROPE MISGIVINGS, sister to the lord, and an old frump, if you ask me,
.... Paul Perkins
LADY CECILE, niece of the above, but pretty sweet .... Ira Stopford
HERBERT FUMBLY, one of those things found about in old country houses ...... Larry Goss
HON. FREDDIE, a bird-brained young man about town .... James McKeon
SHERLOCK HOLMES, yes, really .... Richard Hopwood
PHILO VANCE, ditto, and he knows all the answers .... James Leh
CONSTABLE BLEAKMOOR, the kind of rural cop rarely fooled by criminals under six
years old .... Wesley Brett
EUSTACE MALTRAVERS, caught skulking about the place .... Ha!-David Greenlaw
SIR HERKIMER MISGIVINGS, the long-lost heir; is he villain or hero? .... Gordon Tate
TIME—Wild
  PLACE—Misgivings Castle, Lowerteeth-on-Washstand, Eng.
  Act 1, Library in the castle
  Act 2, The castle library, somewhat later

Sprague Drenan's program notes were as entertaining as his plays.
Murdero A Musici made its debut in 1937.

Such, however, was the case. In 1926 Dean Carle conducted the first survey asking students to estimate how much money they spent uptown, how much their parents spent when they came, and the like. In 1936 Mason published another survey showing how the faculty rendered "various services to civic, church and fraternal groups" in the city.[2]

All colleges go through this. In 1983 Harvard had to again "prove" to Cambridge that the university was valuable to the city on economic grounds if for nothing else. In the same year the University of New Hampshire system also justified its existence by like methods for the state of New Hampshire.

Several people in Keene formed vital links between the campus and the community. First of these was Charles Gale Shedd. He had been with Morrison at the founding of the college, and he was always a true friend. He helped furnish dorm space when needed. For a while one of the "minidorms" on Marlboro Street was known as the Shedd House. At his death in 1930 under the heading "We Lose a Friend," the student newspaper said of him, "He talked to us at school, presided over our debates, welcomed us in his store, greeted us on the street. He represented for us the best feeling of Keene toward the Normal School. We knew him as a splendid man and our friend." What a wonderful epitaph!

Another such person was Robert T. Kingsbury. Kingsbury had served on the Keene Board of Education, as mayor of the city, and on the state board of education. Like Shedd, he attended many college functions, sometimes as participant and sometimes for enjoyment. He was instrumental in acquiring the college camp, and he served the college in innumerable ways.

When comparing Mason with Morrison and Rhodes in Chapter 8, Mason appears not to have been sufficiently concerned about the academic quality of his faculty. That was particularly true for the early years. In the 1920s after the school district revolt he became at least more aware of the necessity for having well-qualified faculty. Moral rigor as applied to faculty still came first; intellectual rigor, a clear and distinct second.

In his long tenure, he had, as previously noted, only three Ph.D.'s on the faculty: Kate Puffer, whom Morrison hired; Austin Keyes in mathematics in the late 1920s; and Edna McGlynn in history in the mid-1930s. Nevertheless, his faculty was impressive. Out of thirty faculty members in 1939, twenty-three held a master's degree (fifteen M.A.'s and eight M.Ed.'s), five held the bachelor's degree only, and two had normal school certificates. Three of those holding the bachelor's degree were stellar faculty members. They included Davis, a miracle man in the

As this ad from the Kronicle *indicates, a special relationship existed between the campus and Mr. Shedd's drug store during the Normal School era.*

music world; Harry Preston, the best-informed historian on New Hampshire anywhere; and Leonard Morrison (no relation to Henry Morrison), who produced four successful textbooks on education and provided real leadership on the Keene School Board! Because of the quality of its faculty, in large part, Keene Normal was still rated as a Class A Institution for teacher preparation.

Not only did this faculty teach fifteen to eighteen hours a week and supervise extracurricular activities, but many of them who lived on campus served also as houseparents, available to students during evening hours. It certainly required total commitment and for very little money. Even those faculty living off campus were available to students in the evening. This was especially true of Dean Carle, Bushnell, Blackington, and Charles Cutts (not yet introduced), a professor of economics and sociology. This was true even of Simmons, the "Who are you?" man. Simmons, in fact, on his own time and with his own resources took students, serious students (i.e., the men students, in his view) to concerts, theaters, arts shows, and baseball games. He invited them to teas, where they had to learn some etiquette and some social graces, which they and their local culture generally regarded as trivia and a waste of time.

Butterfield once reported that only one teacher at either Keene or Plymouth made more money that the average headmaster of a rural high school with only five to seven teachers. What Butterfield wrote in 1922 could as truly be said in 1939 (and for many years afterward): "The faculties of our normal schools have been composed of a small number of devoted men and women who have remained at inadequate salaries because they have loved these schools and have believed in the service they were rendering."[3]

That Keene had such a fine faculty was due in no small measure to the leadership and inspiration that Mason provided. Mason commanded almost universal respect even in his own time. As a student Evelyn Fuller Lamond wrote in her scrapbook, "Tonight Daddy Mason was just the best ever!" The class of 1929 decided to have a portrait of him as their class gift. (It now hangs in the library.) In his last year Mason became ever more forgetful. His dear wife, Nettie, feared in his many crossings of Main and Winchester streets that he would forget to look out for traffic and be struck. The fear was needless. He survived Keene traffic well enough. Many were the testimonials to him from campus, city, and state on his retirement in 1939. He was seventy-eight years old. He then decided to give still further service for the public good. He ran for, and was elected to, the New Hampshire General Court, which he served until his death in 1944.

On the larger scene, the peace following World War I ended in the late 1930s, and the depression ended. On campus Keene Normal School ended, and Daddy Mason ended his long tenure as head of the institution.

Students of the 1930s experienced the Great Depression but had better-than-average job opportunities. They experienced intellectual and cultural vigor and engaged in some enriching social events as well as, of course, quite a few pranks. They published a steady newspaper, enjoyed a talented and devoted faculty, lived through a hurricane, two floods, a typhoid epidemic, and were the end of an era.

II

KEENE
TEACHERS COLLEGE

1939 / 1963

Parker Hall, the main classroom building of Keene Teachers College.

18

Keene Teachers College, Lloyd Young, and World War II

D ESPITE THE TITLE of this chapter, there was no causal relationship between Lloyd Young's coming to Keene Teachers College and World War II. The three topics are related only in the closeness of their association with each other in one time frame and the noteworthy changes each brought about in the institution that was now thirty years old. The official recognition of college status was the first change to take place.

On May 31, 1939, Keene Normal School officially became Keene Teachers College. Many faculty and administrators were so anxious for the change that they had stationery printed with the new name long before it was a legally entity. They undoubtedly felt some national pressure on the issue. Most normal schools changed to teachers colleges in the decade of 1920s. "A closer cooperation and a more friendly feeling [among] students and faculty has been an outstanding feature" of the new status, claimed the student newspaper.

Most of the change was psychological. It was the satisfaction of being recognized as a college for doing college work, a satisfaction that normal school did not offer. In the late 1920s Boston University began to accept normal school courses as college credits, but most other universities did not do so. Now there would be a wider recognition for the credits taken and the diplomas issued.

The only real change that took place was the institution of a four-year program for elementary teachers. This program was built on the three-year program, which in 1933 had replaced the old two-year program. Otherwise things stayed about the same. Keene (and Plymouth) had been offering four-year courses since 1926. The term "teachers college" merely recognized what had been taking place in several major curricula for the past thirteen years. There would be a somewhat greater effort to provide content courses on the collegiate level, but the institution was still, according to the college catalogue, "specifically vocational in attitudes and motivated to scholarship as a means of inspiring cultural ambition and higher types of citizenship in the youth of America. . . . It was created by law to perform this function and has no other aim." Thus, the message to Dartmouth, the University of New Hampshire, and to nearby liberal arts colleges was: "Don't worry, we are still not treading on your ground."

On one hand, a secondary education major did have a minimum of 25 percent of his college work in education, including practice teaching. At the time, that made the degree a professional one. On the other hand — and in retrospect — one can now receive a liberal arts degree in a field of his choice and use his 25 percent electives in education, including practice teaching, and thus also be certified to teach.

Senator Stanley James of Nashua is considered the father of the bill for the name change. A similar bill had been introduced earlier in the House, but it "got lost," so James introduced his own in the Senate. Robert Kingsbury was one of the strongest supporters from Keene behind James's bill. Kingsbury told the legislature that Keene had the largest normal school in New England and that it was "the most efficiently run institution in the state."[1]

The new president, Lloyd Percy Young, was much different in temperament from Daddy Mason. He did not convey the immediate excitement and the dynamic energy that Mason did. Young was more reflective, more intellectual. He enjoyed listening; he absorbed ideas rapidly and liked to entertain them. Young developed a speech pattern in which he used phrases, clauses, even sentences as nouns in his major sentences, such as, "Why can't we get together on this was my approach to that problem." His speech, although the words he used and the manner in which he delivered them were simple, was not as direct and unmistakable as Mason's. If one liked ideas, he found Young interesting; if not, he found him boring and wordy.

Young brought three great assets to the college. The first and most exciting was his ability to handle difficult problems easily, that is, he was superb in the hot seat. He once said, after reading an article critical of teachers colleges, that it made his blood pressure go up. Undoubtedly it did in private. But, when Young appeared in public, he had the problems analyzed on the basis of cold facts. He clearly presented the fallacies of charges made on one side of an issue and dispassionately presented evidence on the other side. His appearance of having complete control of the essential facts, and his seeming ability to shed all emotion, made him in such instances devastatingly effective.

His second ability was to make the democratic process work with faculty and students. There was not much democracy under Mason. According to Arthur Giovananngelli, Mason thought democracy was "all right," but in running a college, there was not time enough for it. Young certainly did not consult his "constituents" at every turn or at every major event. He still liked the consultation process, however. An early issue of the *Monadnock* stated that Young often concluded a meeting thus: "After your thinking through the problem, I would rather trust the judgment of several of you than trust my judgment alone."[2] One can see in this last statement a note of genuine humility in Young. Further, there is no evidence to suggest, at least on major issues, that Young's sole judgment could not be trusted.

The third asset that Young brought to the institution was his close affiliation with educational associations and his ability to keep abreast of the latest developments in education.

Young attended Kansas State Teachers College (nine years after Rhodes had left it to become the principal at Keene) after having served in the infantry in World War I. He and his wife, Dorothy, decided to delay having a family and to devote their early years to intellectual pursuits and professional advancement. They started their graduate work at Wisconsin, but their professors kept referring to Dewey and his colleagues at Columbia. They decided to hear Dewey at first hand and moved to New York City. Young received his M.A. in 1929 and his Ph.D. in 1931 from Columbia University. When he arrived in New Hampshire the next year as superintendent of the Berlin school system, he was the best-educated superintendent in the state. He was therefore almost naturally in line to succeed Mason. He taught, however, a summer session at Keene to allow both candidate and college to get a good look at each other, and essentially each liked the other.

Young quickly used one of his talents shortly after he was established as president. In the early 1940s the New England Crediting Association was interested primarily in accrediting liberal arts institutions rather than teachers colleges. But Young realized the importance of recognition from such national associations. He invited a team, composed of all liberal arts people, to investigate Keene Teachers College. The college passed all tests on its first try. It was remarkable and a tribute to the administration and faculty that Mason had attracted. Keene had held on to normal school status longer than most similar institutions, yet it was the second teachers college in New England (after New Britain, Connecticut) to be fully accredited as a four-year institution of higher learning.

The First Panty Raids

S tudents grew more restive on the approach of Mason's retirement. Even in the 1938 *Kronicle* one student appeared with her shorts rolled up to expose part of her thigh, the first thigh to appear in thirty years. It couldn't be delayed much longer. The girls' basketball team had gotten some new uniforms and ran around all over the court barelegged. The 1939 *Kronicle* had even more eyes on the thighs after it was certain that Mason would not be back in September. It was natural that there would be some exuberant expressions after he left. The first of these, however, was a sensible request. Several young women approached Young after he took office and asked him to drop the regulation requiring them to wear the long black stockings for outdoor sports activities, and to allow them to wear short white gym socks. In fact, this was Young's first executive decision. His affirmative answer was highly popular and got him off to a good start with the students.

With the disappearance of the long black stockings other expressions were tried that would not have been tried in Mason's time. One was at a "masquerade" party in Spaulding Gymnasium in which four seminude male slaves bore their sheikh reclining on a divan. Another representation of the new atmosphere was an attractive art teacher, Juanita Vietre, recently hired, whom everyone remembered for her "extremely high heels."

Most surprising of all was when someone in 1941 "raided Huntress and stole all the panties [those with] holes and all." The event still remains a mystery. It is not known if the raiders were boys or girls. The college newspaper regretted all the publicity the newly recognized college was getting about the event. Many of the women did not like the extra expense involved in purchasing new underwear. Students expressed the same complaints of the panty raiders of the 1950s. An alert fraternity at the University of New Hampshire, however, learned the lesson. The raid was conducted at suppertime when the dorm was left vacant and unguarded. That was a project for the pleb class of 1943. Accordingly, in 1943 a University of New Hampshire fraternity lifted all the panties out of Huntress Hall again, slick as a whistle. They had, however, learned their lesson from the Keene Teachers College mystery raiders of 1941.[3]

Keene Teachers College and World War II

Time for levity, however, was brief because the new president and the new college were soon caught up in World War II. Young was not aware of Mason's quick-mindedness in developing home front activities during World War I. He had, however, a good historical sense, and he saw political events clearly. As a result, he made a number of forward-looking decisions of his own.

The first of Young's wartime decisions was to involve the college in the Civil Aeronautics program. This would be described today as a federal "outreach" program to train civilian pilots. With World War II already under way in Europe and Asia, Young saw the program as an early wartime measure. The benefit for the student was that he could learn to fly for practically nothing. Uncle Sam paid for all the expenses except for a six-dollar medical examination, seven dollars for insurance, and three dollars for the license. Young got Lee Bowman from Hanover to head the program and a Mr. Delany as flight instructor.

"One of the most popular and worthwhile activities on campus," exclaimed the student newspaper, was the new Civil Aeronautics program. "It is a stiff course taking long hours of study and practice — which means the girl friend doesn't get down town for a Coke any Tuesday or Thursday evening from 7 to 10 — unless she is a traitor to the budding civilian pilot." Girl friend? What about Patricia Thompson, the first and only woman to join the program? Thompson passed her flight training here with high marks, only to learn that the armed services were not yet ready to accept women as pilots. She then said "phooey" to the armed services, married her college boyfriend, Arthur Shedd, and eventually got a Ph.D. in English. Keene Teachers College knew her talents even if the navy did not!

"One can't turn a corner," the campus newspaper continued, "without running into a detailed...account [with gestures] of 'My three-point, motor-stalled, forced-landing in a harvest cornfield.' " The maneuvers taught are "straight and level flights, landings and take-offs, steep and shallow turns, figure eights — here we pause to take a deep breath and hang on to our hats — spins, and finally a cross-country flight!" Roughly seventy-two hours were spent in ground school and thirty-five to forty-five hours

Andrew Moynihan was one of the many students who received pilot training on campus during the early years of World War II.

in actual flying. Many local Keene men also took advantage of the program.

Then one Sunday in 1941 as Lloyd Young was celebrating his birthday and student Ruth Wilson Keddy and her roommate were listening to a symphony on the radio, news came that the Japanese had bombed Pearl Harbor. After the declaration of war, Young moved quickly. He offered the college's civil air training facilities to the government. Soon a government official was on the campus inspecting the program and all its facilities. The official said that a bigger airstrip was needed than the pasture field on Barrett's farm currently being used. Young negotiated with Mayor Richard Holbrook of Keene and with the selectmen of Swanzey to establish an airstrip in North Swanzey that would serve Keene, Swanzey, and the entire Monadnock region.[4]

Second, the government official said, if the government were to use the college's facilities, the air cadets sent here needed proper housing. The program was nearly lost on this issue. The college thought that what was good enough for its boys was good enough for military men. The government, however, wanted to keep strict control over its own men and did not want them scattered all over campus and town as the teachers college men were. The problem was solved by kicking the women out of Huntress and putting them in the college's resident houses. The women occupied all the boys' houses—Alpha, Kappa, Wilcox, and Cheshire—but there was still a surplus of women. There was no alternative. They were assigned to live with the air cadets in Huntress. Thus, the first "coeducational living" took place under the exigencies of World War II. Such were the sacrifices made in wartime. The young cadets, however, were kept busy and strictly supervised. There may have been some lovemaking at the 9:30 P.M. break outside the dorms—for twenty minutes!—but today's "intervisitation" was unknown.

When the government's two conditions were met, Secretary of War Knox approved Keene Teachers College as a training school for navy pilots. Every three months 50 to 100 cadets arrived for the program and spent about eight weeks on campus. The course of study was similar to the Civil Aeronautics program, with so many hours of classroom instruction on campus and so many flight hours at the new North Swanzey airstrip. When finished the cadets went on to other naval air stations. In all, over 1,000 cadets trained at the college.

The third military program that Young got the college involved with was the V-5 program. This was primarily a stepped-up academic program in which men were encouraged to take extra credit during the regular semesters, go to summer school, and finish their education early so that they would qualify for OCS (officer candidate school). To their credit, nearly every man on campus, if he did not join the service outright, joined the V-5 program.

Bill Wollfer, key vocalist for the Kampus Kids swing band, was the first to join the military for World War II. He left in the 1940 call-up of the National Guard. At one time in 1943 there were only two male students on campus, and one of those was a disabled veteran! Except for the naval cadets in part of Huntress, the college was again a women's college. "The most striking changes on campus," noted the 1944 *Kronicle*, were "the absence of men students—excepting Chris [Sakelarios, the disabled vet] who is known to all—and the presence of the many Naval Air Cadets and the transferring of men's dormitories to women and a woman's dormitory to men."[5]

The students, mostly women, who remained on campus during World War II were active on the home front. Like their World War I counterparts, most felt it was their duty to keep the public schools going; they were begging for teachers. The students went to school overtime and in speeded-up sessions so that they could take care of this newly created teacher shortage. Each year a number of seniors delayed their education in order to take classrooms during the emergency. Many others served either in the Red Cross or in defense industries. Edith Hansen, Class of

1943, was, apparently, the first of twenty-one women to join the military, the WAC (Women's Army Corps), rising in rank to sergeant before the end of the war.

The navy program added color to the campus. Each morning and evening at 7:15 the flag was raised and lowered with the accompaniment of color guards and bugle calls. "One of the most marvelous times I ever went through," recalled Mrs. Blackington, "was when the navy was there on campus. . . and the navy tea the faculty wives put on — we had uniforms all over — and it was beautiful."

As mentioned earlier, the cadets' time here was strictly supervised and was usually of two months' duration. Young recalls only two or three marriages between cadets and the college's women. During the Alumni Weekend of 1981, one of these interesting couples reminisced and answered questions.

Q. Are you the only one to marry a Keene Teachers College girl?

He: "As far as I know. There may have been some others."

She: "I've heard various stories. I've heard there really wasn't much time for dating. Others say no, there was more going on."

He: "Oh, there was always stuff going on. Every once in awhile someone would find a stepladder at the first-floor window of the girls' dorm and stuff like that. Weekends were free, but during the week there wasn't much time. They'd lock us up in Huntress Hall for study right after dinner; 9:30 you'd get a twenty-minute break to run outside and get some fresh air. There were some dates then [ha-ha]!

Q. That's how you met your wife?

He: "Yes, and from here I went on to more navy training and got my wings. We corresponded for two years. She graduated. We took off and have been traveling ever since."

Q. "You were one of the girls who married a navy man, weren't you?"

She: "There weren't too many of us who did. I looked them all over for a couple of years before I finally decided, but he was the one."

Q: "Before you came here was there any scuttlebutt about KTC?"

He: "No, we weren't aware of where it was, or what it was."

She: "I waited on tables, and they were bringing in, well, first it was college guys, but near the end it wasn't. It was people from the fleet. And I waited on tables one morning, and these guys had been out at sea in a submarine. They brought them into Boston Harbor, put them on a train at night, and in the night they marched them down from the Keene railroad station. In the morning they got up and went to the college amidst all these girls. They said, Aaaahh, *we're in heaven!!*"

"What a time I had with — — —."

"They couldn't believe they were in a college with all these girls! They thought 'we're going to like this duty.' "

By 1943 the teachers college women had established several traditions by which they could meet cadets. In October there was a reception for new cadets and several "break-dances," "in which the girls cut in to help get acquainted and to allow all the girls to dance." A Halloween party and a Christmas party with the cadets were also held.[6]

The only lasting impression that the cadets left, so far as is known, was the ghost of Huntress Hall, which has since become famous. It has, needless to say, always been shrouded in mystery. Steve Gordon and Stacy Milbouer, who researched it in the 1970s for the school newspaper, claimed that the wheelchair in the attic belonged to Mr. Butterfield but that Miss Huntress rode it when she got angry with the misbehavior of women students in her dorm. Others believe that Miss Huntress first started the noises when the women were kicked out and the first men students were allowed to "overnight it" in her dorm during World War II.[7]

All students had an hour of physical fitness each day, supervised by Sumner Joyce and Marjorie Bateman. The idea behind this was that they might be called upon to work in heavy war industries and therefore had to be physically strong. They, in turn, ran physical fitness institutes in the secondary and primary schools throughout the state.

Shortly after the declaration of war, several students took an air-raid warden course. On January 28, 1942, they conducted a blackout on campus, which they reported as "successful beyond our best expectations, not a vestige of light shone."

The theory for the necessity of blackouts in small towns was that enemy planes would target the larger cities, such as Boston or the naval base at Portsmouth. If they could not make their bomb run as planned because of coastal defense, they would then seek any target visible, which very well might be a small town. Just where these planes were to come from was always vague, but during the early years of the war it was commonly believed that the Germans could do anything.

Students participated with townspeople not only in blackouts but in emergency operations after a bombing. These operations were called "incidents." In March 1943 students participated in one of the largest "incidents" the state ever had. In Keene "a factory was supposed to have been hit by high-explosive bombs, the result of which summoned a large number of emergency services to the scene," which was Spaulding Gymnasium. Students participated also in a statewide bomb alert when Young was the chief umpire.[8]

Women students earned money to buy war stamps and war bonds by

*During World War II, students dug potatoes at the Dodd Farm in Westmoreland.
This was 1944.*

shinning shoes and carrying mail to the post office for people. Nearly
everyone took first-aid and lifesaving courses or folded bandages for the
Red Cross two nights a week. Many donated blood, and in those days
that involved an all-day drive to and from Concord.

Edith Dexter remembered: "The freshman class all went picking
potatoes. There was a shortage of help that year [1943]. We had more
fun on that day. It was better than an organized outing."

Q. "Did you get paid for that?"

"Yes...I think we did."

They did — 5 cents for every bushel! Women students picked at three
farms in Cheshire County. The favorite one was the Dodd farm in
Westmoreland, which they picked for three years in a row. In one year
eighty-five girls put in a full week's work at this farm.[9]

By 1943 Young had gotten commando training equipment placed on
the athletic field. Judging from contemporary accounts, one must say that
most of the girls were proud of the equipment. They often went down
to look at it, but they preferred to work in more traditional home front
activities.

On the fighting front, Bill Wollfer, Steve Valla, and Newell Paire served
in the South Pacific; Alson Clark and Malcolm Keddy, in Sicily; John

Dufour, with a torpedo squadron. Clair Wyman and Jim McKeon met in Japan. Airman Walter ("Waxey") Lucien was credited with sinking a Japanese warship in the Pacific. Elson Herrick flew many missions over Germany. George Zoulias served in North Africa. Art Giovananngeli "is stationed near Manila," reported the school newspaper, and he "has been distributing Jap invasion money among our Faculty, apparently unaware of the dangers of inflation." The college's men and women kept in touch with each other through the extraordinary efforts of Sprague Drenan, who kept up a personal correspondence with nearly all of them.

Two of the highest-ranking graduates were Col. Raymond Curtice, class of 1936, stationed in Sweden, and Comdr. Neale W. Curtin, class of 1933, who "was rescued after a long ordeal in the sinking of the *Gambier Bay*. In all, 263 (241 men and 21 women) served in the Armed Forces in World War II. Many others served in the Red Cross and similar organizations.[10]

Nine gave their lives. The first death was particularly hard to take, Thomas D. Dillant's. A Keene native, he had been in many school musicals, had been catcher for the baseball team, and had been president of his class. He had civilian pilot training here and was killed in a forced landing off Myrtle Beach, South Carolina. The last words to his class (1941) were: "Let education be every man's lantern, common sense his path, and success will be his destiny." It is often said that war draws off from a country its best blood and brains. It seemed to be true. His memorial was the airport in North Swanzey dedicated to him and to Edwin Hopkins, the first Swanzey youth to die in uniform. Others who paid the supreme sacrifice were Frederick Clayton, class of 1942; Francis Driscoll, class of 1933; Thomas Essie, class of 1946; Hollis Furbush, class of 1943; Edwin Hill, class of 1934; Lloyd Marin, class of 1943; Lewis Montrone, class of 1936; and Bruce Sullivan, class of 1934. The nine lilac bushes planted at the head of Fiske lawn commemorate their lives.

19

The Postwar Years of Optimism

EDUCATION WAS in the driver's seat for a short time after World War II. It was generally believed that education would end future world wars and would make the world a safe place to live in. Former Governor Lane Dwinnell recalled:

In 1947 the legislature had some various surpluses [for education]...the large sum for that day of two million dollars. We had a very gung ho, dynamic type of commissioner, Edgar Fuller....He was, I might say, even though I'm being recorded, it's fair to call him one of those hit-and-run types. He came in, the money was there, the time was right, and he expanded state aid for education. Then, whether he saw the handwriting on the wall or whether since he'd increased New Hampshire's state aid by a few thousand percent, some other states probably wanted him. But he left and Buhle came in. And Buhle, of course, got the shock of his life because he thought everything was on the up and up. He found that New Hampshire didn't believe in taxation and New Hampshire believed in frugality in appropriations. So one of the first areas to feel the ax was sort of like a life boat, last in, first out. State aid for education was the last in and the first out. So in the '49 session it was greatly reduced from $2 million to $700,000 or something like that.

But from 1945 to 1949 there was cause for optimism.

In the postwar era Young not only devised programs to accommodate the returning veterans on campus but offered to Keene, to veterans, and to teachers the most attractive evening programs ever. A list of courses to be offered in the spring of 1946 included "Great Characters of the Bible," "The Fine Arts and Their Social Significance," "Music for the Listener,"

The first Bushnell Apartments, 1946-1964

"Children's Literature for Mothers," "Child Psychology," "World Relations," "The Geology of Cheshire County," "Cabinet Making," "Principles of Photography," "School Lunchroom Management," "Weaving," "Botany," and "Aeronautics."

Nationally both Harvard and Columbia made powerful recommendations for the necessity of general education requirements (the ones that were abolished in the late 1960s and early 1970s). The theory was that a citizenry that had a well-rounded education would be able to avoid the steps to war. Young had faculty members studying such requirements for Keene Teachers College. Because of the demands of teacher preparation, Keene really did not have to change much. It already required of its students a good general education.

Jacqueline Paquette (Rayno), class of 1947, recorded the new atmosphere the veterans made on campus. "Have you noticed a change on the campus?" she wrote for the *Kronicle* in 1946.

I'll say. Three years ago a man in class was an oddity — now he's a regular[ly] accepted member. . . . We have welcomed back about forty veterans. Twenty-two are old members of our campus and are taking up where they left off. It seems like old times seeing and hearing these men in the dining room, in the classroom and just around the college. The Trades and Industry course seems to be the apple of their eye. Twenty-one are enrolled in this course, sixteen in the secondary, and four are taking the elementary course. There is a great demand for these men teachers, and the positions that have been offered our senior men are excellent.

The vets are more serious, responsible and conscientious than those men students coming directly from high school. They really afford some competition and will make the girls work harder. They are bringing back from all corners of the globe diversified ideas and aims of college education. They are happy to be back and are getting into the swing of things. They don't ask for special privileges; they want to be just plain students.

For the first few years after the war a disproportionately large number of veterans resumed their college careers in the January term. Paquette reported that twenty-four men and one woman veteran registered for the January 1947 term.[1]

As early as 1942 Young had voiced the concern about establishing machinery and attitudes for a lasting peace settlement. Hester Perkins, class of 1944, addressed the same question to her classmates: "After the war, what?" Thelma Partridge, class of 1946, offered an answer: "We must dedicate our lives to the advancement of finer human relationships and follow the thought of a recent poet, Angela Morgan:

> To be alive in such an age!
> With every year a lightening page
> Turned in the world's great wonder-book
> Whereon the leaning nations look
> Where men speak strong for brotherhood
> For peace and universal good;
> Breathe the world-thought, do the world-deed
> Think highly of thy brother's need.

The obvious answer on ways to keep peace was support of the United Nations and United Nations-type activities. Eleanor Roosevelt popularized the idea at her highly successful visit to the campus in early 1945, shortly before she won her stunning victory for human rights in the United Nations charter. For a few years the largest and most active club on campus was the international relations club, with Bugsy Blake as the most appropriate advisor and with Charles Perkins and gregarious Sherm Lovering as two of its presidents.

The club spent its efforts in sending teaching materials to needy schools in France and in the Philippines. For a few years all was hard work, good fun, and optimism.

One of the landmarks of the early postwar years was the first Bushnell apartments. Laverne Bushnell taught shop and physics and directed a college swing band. He had in 1935 established a driver training course that

Ceremonial applause for seniors after graduation is a long-standing tradition.

drew wide attention. But his lasting fame is due to the fact that he owned some property on South Marlboro Street.

When the opportunity arose to acquire free some army barracks from Windsor Locks, Connecticut, the legislature was not in session. Bushnell then offered his property as the site for two large barracks, twelve apartments in each. The government paid for transferring the housing to Keene and for the preparation of the site. So began family housing as part of campus life. The idea was to accommodate veterans and their families. No one at the time thought that this was the beginning of family housing as a permanent aspect of college life.

Those who lived in the old apartments had by and large a nice life. The only distraction was the 3:00 A.M. train, which gave a good blast each morning as it passed by. Babies started crying and parents got up and wandered around. Every time another pregnancy occurred, students wondered if the B&M freight train was the real beginning of it all.

Additional dorm space was needed for single postwar students. Number 16-18 Blake Street was leased from Miss Celia Finkelstein and "The Brick House," now Peter Christians Restaurant, again became a residence, as it had been in the 1920s, but the largest single unit was the old Eagle Hotel, which was used to house women students until Randall Hall was built.[2]

Dancing styles 1940 to 1980.

The Campaign for the Social Room

At 6:00 A.M. one Thursday in March 1947 students Gloria Mara, Marge Hunter, Charles Eaton, Eleanor Smith, and Richard Mills piled into Dean Carle's Buick and drove to New York City for a Conference of Students of Professional Teachers Colleges. The purpose of the conference was in keeping with the times — discussion of educational and world problems. The students, however, began comparing notes with students from other colleges about rules and regulations and came home convinced that they were overregulated.

Before chapel hour on March 24, 1947 was over, commented the student newspaper,

> the placidity of Parker Hall received a jar that fairly loosened the foundations....Dick Mills stepped once more to the podium and with just a slight hesitance summed up the assembly with a comparison of Keene to other colleges at the conference. The comparison dealt with such matters as late permissions, class cuts, girls smoking, girls and joint social rooms, student council duties and powers and student-faculty relationships in general. On the whole the comparison was not in Keene's favor; in certain cases we seemed to be unique in a distinctly unfavorable sense.

The reaction of the student body was of a nature that this reporter [Charles Perkins] had not before seen during his time at KTC. Mr. Mills must have certainly felt well rewarded for his courage in presenting the subject in so straightforward a manner.[3]

As already noted, in such situations Young reacted well. He merely stated that reforms were possible. He listed, however, three conditions: they must come through the student council; they must be enforceable; and they must be to the best interests of the college. Thus began a two-year campaign for liberalizing regulations on smoking, curfews, and other conditions of campus life. The focus of all these reforms came to be symbolized in the movement for a social room.

There already was a social room in the basement of Spaulding, but it was for men only. What was desired was a place where both men and women students could congregate, smoke if they liked, and enjoy coffee, Cokes, and a few snacks. It does not seem like much of a request, but when a faculty questionnaire proposed that the men's social room in Spaulding be made coed just for weekends, only 50 percent of the faculty agreed, 33 percent said no, and 17 percent were neutral. The student council labored long on many of the problems brought up by Mills at the March

Retirement party in 1948 for Isabelle Blake, Inez Vaughn, and Idella Farnum,
each of whom had served the college for more than a full generation.

chapel period. Marilyn Goldstein wrote several tough editorials. In one
strongly worded blast entitled "Alka-Seltzer or Action," she wrote, "We
can have a front door or a back door approach [to our problems]. Right
now its the back door." She charged that there was no coed recreational
room where students could "meet under unsuspicious conditions and enjoy the freedom of healthy, normal relationships." Realistically, the law
was "Smoking is permitted as long as you don't get caught!" She wrote
candidly on curfew: "We could do just as much damage before 9:45 as
we could until 1:00 a.m.!" She concluded her editorials by saying that her
comments were also "aimed at the feminine portion of the student body
whose lack of interest and indifference to these prevailing conditions have
failed to remedy them in any way."

On April 3, 1947, the student council, after a long, hard session, finally
sent to President Young the following resolution: "A blanket late permission at 12 o'clock for the men and women for Friday and Saturday nights;
smoking be allowed for girls in the men's social room on nights when social
functions are being held in the gym for both men and women."[4]

Further procedures were required. Young accepted the demands after
determining the propriety of the student council action and obtaining
assurance that the students were willing to assume regulatory respon-

sibilities.

After everything cleared the student government and Young, Alpha Phi Omega, a service fraternity, did the work in converting a small shower room in the basement of Huntress into the campus club. The next year it was moved to the barn behind Proctor House and named "The Owl's Nest." Upstairs were a dance floor, a jukebox, and tables; downstairs were a sitting room, a store, and offices. "Hurray," wrote Charles Mitchell, "the Owl's Nest is open and doing a great job. We have all enjoyed and look forward to the social room upstairs." It came about because "A FEW hard working individuals. . . recognized the need for a co-ed social room, and expended the physical energy necessary, instead of sitting around griping." The next year even better facilities were established in an old building behind Huntress. "One would have to go a long way," wrote Francis L. Sorger, "to find a student project that has echoed greater success and more concrete value to the college than the Campus Club." Liberalization of the rules had been achieved.

The whole social club reform and all that it symbolized began with student government and was realized through student government. That organization seemed to be the students' best hope for airing their concerns in the future. Ronnie Banner worked particularly hard on this premise and was the prime force in organizing a Student Government Clinic on the campus. On Saturday, October 14, 1950, fifty-five delegates from fifteen New England colleges came to the clinic. Key speakers were Dean Charles Camp of Dartmouth and Lloyd Young and students Claude Leavitt and Charles Mitchell. Delegates each attended one of four different discussion/study groups meeting that afternoon. The Nu Beta Epsilon, the honorary organization of the home economics department, furnished refreshment to the delegates after the meeting. The Kappa brothers held their annual barn dance that weekend "for the enjoyment of the visitors." The clinic was judged by all to be a tremendous success. Patricia Bonardi, Nina Krochmal, Lorraine Fournier, Mildred Turner, and John Nay also contributed significantly to it.[5]

During the clinic, the college's students got a chance to see how their student government "stacked up" with others and to see what its weaknesses were. They learned that their primary weakness was their own failure to voice their own concerns. It seemed, therefore, that all they needed to do was to voice these concerns and the future would continue to be bright. They had a president who listened well. Disillusionment among the student body, however, arising from sources outside the walls of the college, had already set in.

20

Tension and Disillusionment
of the 1950s

THE 1950s ARE OFTEN pictured as a rerun of the 1920s. Republicans had a majority in Congress and a president in the White House. Businessmen and bankers were forgiven their excesses of the 1920s and were again directing society's tastes and mores. Although dress styles changed, college youth still "dressed like it should." Business enterprise developed the consumer market further than ever thought possible. Detroit offered tail fins for automobiles; television, the *I Love Lucy* and *I Remember Mama* shows; and Hollywood, *The Ten Commandments* and *Pollyanna*, all highly unreal portrayals of life.

There was an air of unreality in the 1950s, a feeling of nonmotion. Governor Lane Dwinell (1955-60) recalled:

I look back on those [teachers] colleges, during my years as governor, as the ideal type of institution. They posed no problems. . . . The teachers colleges were just there, and they were nice, quiet, no-trouble-type institutions. They had good leadership. Young was a conservative guy; maybe he'd been beaten down, I don't know, but he didn't make any waves.

Actually some waves were made, even in Dwinell's time, but by 1982 memory of them had faded away.

In the spring of 1983 Lawrence Benaquist and William Sullivan, both of the English department, offered a seminar and film series on the 1950s. In their study of the period they concluded that instead of finding a period of gay abandon, such as the 1920s were *supposed* to be, they found a period full of tension. An examination of the writings of the students at Keene Teachers College supports their findings.

One might assume that the social room and liberalization of other student regulations brought about student contentment. By the 1950s, however, the nationalization of events through radio, television, and advertisements so overwhelmed the individual that it affected his attitudes on the local level also. Some of the world events were indeed overwhelming: Russia getting the atom bomb, China falling to communism, spies in the United States arrested and convicted, the outbreak of war in Korea. *Monadnock* editor Donald Johnson wrote in 1952: "Unfortunately. . .Korea is still with us with its Old Baldy, Heartbreak Ridge, and the bloody rest." Also disheartening was Russia's use of the veto eighty-nine out of the first ninety times in the UN. That meant the one-world idea promoted by the international relations club at the college, and similar clubs throughout the country, had to be diminished in light of the facts.

With a worsening world situation some looked for the fault at home. This situation made Bernard Iddings Bell's book, *Crisis in Education* (1949), exceedingly popular. Bell was a very proper-looking and pedigreed Anglican canon who hated the shams of society and who thought independently. He touched on the very heart of the problem of teachers colleges. "Democratic education," he said, "must be not only democratic, but also education." No one would disagree. The problem of quality versus equality has remained, nonetheless, a constant one since the days of Andrew Jackson. Bell, however, drove his point home with tremendous force. Henry Aldrich, not Tom Sawyer, he said, was now the representative American youth. Aldrich, like his sister Mary and his parents, were "not free men and women but base mechanicals. . .the products and patrons of mass management. . .of a standardized press and radio, of slick magazines and book clubs, of an overly vocationalized education, of pressure salesmanship." Worse still, even though they conformed to cultural stereotypes promoted by the great business corporations was the fact that they were basically unhappy. Then Isaiah Berlin, popular British foreign secretary during World War II and lecturer at Oxford, attacked American higher education in similar fashion. Soon these attacks were picked up by magazines that were read by "forgotten Americans" — *Look, Life, Saturday Evening Post, Time, U.S. News and World Report, Reader's Digest.* Articles appeared on "Academic Truncation," "Academic Elephantiasis," the "Chaotic University," the "Crisis of the University." *Reader's Digest* advised, "Don't send your son to college," and the *Rotarian*, "So, You're Sending Bill to College!" (a-ha). *Time* featured "The Search for Cam-

Before the Butterfield addition in 1958, auto mechanics were trained in nature's classroom.

pus Subversives." "You have today," said Henry Wriston of Brown, "a bullying of intellectuals of the United States, which is intolerable." That was only the beginning of the McCarthy era. It would get worse. But even before that *Time* admitted that education was "a profession that is already much harassed." "Why Johnny Can't Read and Write" was even then a standard article.[1]

The attack by so many conservative magazines raised an interesting paradox because students at normal schools, teachers colleges, and state colleges were overwhelmingly conservative in their own politics. The Ivy League colleges, with generally more liberal student bodies, were, until the McCarthy era, generally exempt from criticism. Now, even before McCarthy got into full swing, both private and public higher education were under attack.

Part of the explanation of the attack of the conservative magazines on their reliable political allies, the teachers colleges, undoubtedly lay in a lingering resentment over the influence of John Dewey. Another of Dewey's many sins, in their view, was his open espousal of New Deal politics. Flaws in teachers colleges could be shown actually to be flaws in John Dewey and in liberal Democratic politics.

There was also a hint that many critics came from private colleges and that they and their alma maters were nervous about the rapid growth of these new public institutions, which might preempt their traditional roles.

This interesting aspect needs further study.

Last, and very definitely last, there was some truth in the attacks. Teachers colleges, now supposedly colleges, all too often ran to the nearest high school when they needed a faculty member rather than search for a scholar. Too often Dewey was taught without an understanding of his philosophical base. Those making these charges, however painfully true, refused to consider the miserable salary scales at teachers colleges or the democratic pressures society forced on them to serve at people's colleges, or the pressures to handle social problems under the guise of educational problems.

Closing Keene Teachers College; or, Back to Keene Normal School

Students at Keene Teachers College were sensitive over the criticisms of teachers colleges and public education which were aired in the mass consumption magazines. One can only imagine the frustration when these students learned of movements in New Hampshire and in the General Court and by the governor himself either to reduce or to close their own alma mater.

By their very nature state colleges are answerable to the public, usually through the legislature. If the college is, or appears to be, taking on roles beyond the popular conception of it on the state level, it can then normally expect to be the subject of investigation.

As early as 1929, during Governor Tobey's administration, Keene and Plymouth were investigated. The four-year program prompted that investigation. As already noted, the English major at Keene and the history major at Plymouth came very close to making the normal schools de facto liberal arts colleges. Butterfield had blandly assured the public that no such thing would happen, but he did admit that the four-year programs were steps toward teachers college status.

The legislature was not sure about the actual status. It was sure that it could not afford two state colleges and a university. Tobey formed an investigation committee composed of three liberal arts people, the principals of Exeter and Andover academies, and Dean Gordon Bill of Dartmouth. They made a quick investigation and found little amiss and even had some nice things to say. Morrison, now in Chicago but still with a strong attachment to New Hampshire, was furious at the whole process. Tobey's actions, however, indicated support for the changing status of the normal school rather than criticism. He assigned a blue ribbon committee which removed the political heat, and nothing at all resulted from its innocuous report.[2]

The next investigations were the results of low enrollments and the desire to save money. The first of these investigations seems to have been triggered by the musings of some editor at the *Concord Monitor*. He or she, looking at the 1939 enrollments, figured out that if Keene had 628 students in 1931 and both Keene and Plymouth had only 531 students in 1939, then Plymouth could be closed and all the students could come to Keene. Governor Leverett Saltonstall, using the same logic, was trying to close four teachers colleges in Massachusetts.

As the idea of closing teachers colleges jelled, Senator Charles B. Knight of nearby Marlborough thought it so good that he incorporated it as Senate bill 87 in 1943. The key provisions of the Knight bill were to close Plymouth, transfer all Keene juniors and seniors to Durham, and return Keene to a two-year normal school for elementary teachers. Knight's bill had good support, particularly in the person of John D. Langmuir, executive director of the New Hampshire Taxpayers Association. He also claimed that United States Senator Styles Bridges supported at least part of the bill.

Speaking against the bill, besides Young himself, were Robert T. Kingsbury, longtime friend of the college; Laurence O. Thompson, the able superintendent of schools, Rev. and Mrs. Tremanye Copplestone; and Mrs. William Chapman, president of the Keene women's club. There was at the time a column in the *Sentinel* entitled "The Cheshire Cat." Its author, Henry Nadig, said that the Knight bill meant that "all we have fought for...will go up the spout....Without Teacher College status," he wrote, "we couldn't have gotten Young here. Don't make war an excuse or a reason for cramping New Hampshire's educational training and facilities any more than is necessary."[3]

The bill died in the 1943 legislature. When the idea came up again in 1945, it was submitted to a newly appointed state reorganization commission. When this commission made its final report in 1949, it had a particularly strong impact. It was in tune with the times. This time Langmuir was secretary of the reorganization commission, and Rae S. Laraba of Portsmouth headed the subcommittee that essentially reproduced the main provisions of the Knight bill of 1943. There was one important difference. Laraba's proposal did not specifically call for the closing of Plymouth, as did Knight's, but it did call for the closing of one teachers college *or the other.*

Laraba's proposal had particular strength because reorganization and efficiency were in the air. Herbert Hoover had made a number of sound recommendations to President Harry S. Truman for federal government efficiency. Essentially the same thing was now happening in New Hampshire. The new governor, Sherman Adams, was exceptionally able and progressive in his thinking. Adams also gave serious thought to closing either Keene or Plymouth. When asked about this in 1982, Adams said that his actions should not be taken as an attack on teachers colleges but as only one aspect of the total effort to reorganize state government. Certainly his actions bear him out on that. One reason that Adams wanted a broad-based tax was to properly support education. Many other states adopted broad-based taxes shortly after the war. Vermont had just done so. "Historically, it is very interesting to note," recalled Governor Dwinell, "that the New Hampshire Legislature came close to passing both a sales tax and an income tax in the 1949 session.... [when Adams was governor]. That was the turning point, the beginning of New Hampshire's dedication to frugality in state programs." Adams's reorganization ideas in total made good economic sense. The animus of the New Hampshire Taxpayers Association and the Knight and Laraba proposals, however, was to reduce funds for education. These antieducation proponents made good political capital out of Adams's efforts to modernize state government.

The National Commission of Teacher Education and Professional Standards of the National Education Association (NEA) tugged teachers colleges in just the opposite direction — and for good reason. "Now we face a world situation and a national emergency that threaten the very foundations of professional standards of teaching," the commission stated in 1951. "Manpower shortages can wipe out the gains of the past five years...the schools can soon be flooded with unqualified teachers."[4] The commission recommended that future teachers have absolutely no less than four years of college preparation.

Under all these pressures, both national and local, Young stayed remarkably calm. Regarding the state commission's report, Young replied: "I respect the committee's attempt to give some solutions to a very complicated problem within a short time and with no funds to make a professional study. I feel [however] that the committee has gathered very limited data, and some of it is not correct." Young went on to say that the report took no account of future growth or even correcting the current teacher shortage. Further, closing Plymouth or Keene and transferring part of the program to the University of New Hampshire might cost as much as $1.3 million. Young's deadpan matter-of-fact analysis and cool recitation of facts were devastatingly effective.

The citizens of Keene and nearby towns rallied to Young's support, turning out in large numbers at a meeting in Spaulding Gymnasium on November 1, 1949, to hear him speak. The meeting was conducted by Larry Pickett, a skillful Democratic politician from the college's own ward and a lifelong supporter of the college. The *Sentinel* commented that Young's was "a balanced presentation blaming no one." The meeting itself showed that "the people of Keene will turn out to support something in which they believe...and it proved beyond a shadow of a doubt that the report...is a document too hastily thrown together and full of serious inconsistencies with fact."

Young also went to Concord where he debated Langmuir in a face-to-face confrontation. Again, Young's dispassionate control of facts was effective. Soon the report was pigeonholed. Governor Adams said he did not have enough hard data to take the steps proposed by the commission.

Adams still wanted informed independent judgment. He hired Alfred Simpson, a professor of education from Harvard, and the Bigelow, Kent and Willard business management company of Boston to study the viability of Keene Teachers College. Instead of calling for a closing of the college, both reports called for expansion. The Bigelow, Kent and Willard report said that the closing of Plymouth (or Keene) would cost an additional $2 million. Instead of closing the college, the report recommended an addition to Butterfield Building and developing the campus on the west side of Main Street. Simpson's report also called for an addition to Butterfield, a classroom building on Appian Way near Spaulding Gymnasium, a men's dormitory, and lowering of tuition.[5] Thus, what started out in an effort to close the college or return it to normal school status in the end became a recommendation for substantially expanding the college.

Salaries

Meagre stipends during the 1940s and 1950s again became the stigma of the teaching profession in New Hampshire as it had been before Morrison's time. Salaries, which ranged from an annual $600 to $1,200 for beginning teachers in the 1920s, 1930s, and early 1940s gradually rose after World War II to $1,800 to $2,600 per year. For the 1950s the NEA recommended $3,200 to $8,000 "as a reasonable goal in professional salary schedules for qualified [high school and elementary] teachers." Keene faculty, in contrast, received barely more and sometimes less than the average high school teacher, who was always below NEA recommendations. On campus the problem was aggravated by the fact that, while enrollments had increased, the number of faculty had not, and faculty salary increases were pitifully small. The faculty had no private offices. Any faculty member living on or near campus was expected to use his or her home or living quarters as an office and reception area for helping students. The faculty member with only a fifteen-hour load was considered lucky; often it was eighteen or twenty-one, and to that would be added all sorts of campus duties — chaperoning, club advising, and so on. One report listed a faculty member as having thirty-one classroom hours a week.

Faculty salaries had not increased appreciably since the end of World War I. As prices increased in World War II, and particularly in the postwar era, some faculty began to push for better pay. One of the first efforts in this direction in 1944 was dramatic. No one can tell the story better than Ruth Kirk, longtime member of the state board of education:

I went to the door [of my house] and who stood there, I almost think it was Merton Goodrich. He handed me this letter as if it were something that was going to burn his fingers. He said to me, "Will you give this to the state board of education?" And I, being the type I am, said, "Certainly, I'd be glad to." The next Monday morning I went over to Concord to attend the board meeting; and it was Orton Brown who was chairman for the board...I don't remember what we talked about. It didn't impress me, because I was so conscious of the fact that I had this letter that I had to bring forth, and there never seemed an opportune time for me to do it. So Mr. Brown said, "If there's no further business to come before the meeting, then the meeting stands adjourned." I said, "Now, wait just a minute, Mr. Brown, I have something." And Joseph Epply, who was right over here, said, "You have no right to say that." I paid no attention to him. I said to Mr. Brown, "Here is something that was given to me by a member of the faculty of the normal school and I want you to have it." He took it and read it. He was no taller than I and three times as thick. And he said to the board, "All of you are to be back here." And there weren't many days when we were to be back there. In the meantime, he got hold of Dr. Young by phone, and he talked to Mr. Pringle [James N. Pringle, commissioner of education]. So we went back....Orton Brown was so infuriated at the contents of the letter that he went over here on the table and he was going like this in Mr. Pringle's face: "Did you, did you get notices? And what did you do with them?" That was the way he talked. Mr. Pringle didn't say a word. And then he went after Dr. Young, saying, "Did you try to do something for that faculty? Did you?" And Dr. Young never said a word, but his lips were trembling. I can see him now. His lips were trembling as if he were going to burst into tears. Neither of them opened his mouth. And it was the wildest thing I ever went to in my life because there was so much bellowing on the part of Orton Brown. That was the beginning of the salary schedule change. And the people at the college began to get a little more money.

Brown, the president of Brown Paper Company in Berlin, was actually devoted to education in New Hampshire and served as chairman of the board of education for a number of years. He rarely missed a meeting, although his business demands were heavy. He regularly boarded a Pullman from New York City, slept all night on the train, and spent the monthly meeting day in Concord with the board of education. In the evening he took the Pullman back to New York.

What probably brought on Brown's outburst was the fact that the board members had just established a pay scale with some increases in it and no doubt thought they had done the best they could. The official minutes recorded a faculty petition and also "a statement by Dr. Young voicing dissatisfaction with the proposed salary schedule already adopted by the State Board." The petitions brought on, say the official minutes, "considerable discussion." The board then directed Young to take the matter back to the faculty.

The faculty then replied directly to the board. It said it appreciated the board's efforts in establishing the new schedules. The faculty still wanted, however, an increase in the highest ranks, and it wanted these increases retroactive to the previous September. The board acceded to both requests.[6] Through the remainder of her term Kirk kept pushing for salary increases for faculty. It was hard going in the 1940s and 1950s, and the results did not measure up to all the effort and goodwill exerted.

Revolt of the Student Intellectuals

Students had made a significant gain with the social room, and they had achieved it through the democratic process. When one realizes the attacks on education in the popular journals (the professional journals are always full of self-examination and self-criticism), the debates among state politicians on whether or not to close the college, and the miserable pay scale that teachers faced, one can understand why student intellectuals could not be pacified with a social room and a few other minor reforms.

At the turn of the 1950s decade William Lafferrandre, Francis Sorger, Joseph Oakey, Donald Johnson, Donald Averill, Dean Corrigan, and Charles Eaton were the core of a group that questioned everything and found room for improvement everywhere. They were sure that Keene

Teachers College was behind the times, and they were determined to modernize it. Oakey identified the cause when he wrote, "Our popular and professional magazines have been flooded with articles which all asked, or tried to answer, one basic question, 'What is wrong with education?' "

One of the permanent contributions of this group of students, was the establishment of a school newspaper, the *Monadnock*, on a permanent basis. Student newspapers had a rough time in the 1940s. After the *Kronicle* newspaper died in 1939, it was replaced successively by the *News Bulletin*, *The Owl's Reporter*, *The Arborbynite*, and *The Hooter*, each one lasting only a year or so and seldom getting out more than three editions in any one year. Most students in the 1940s did not even know they had a school newspaper.

Averill seems to have been the mainspring behind the establishment of the *Monadnock*. In his first editorial he mentioned some of the recent failures. "In an attempt to remedy this situation," he wrote, "a survey was made by the editor of THE MONADNOCK of the campus newspapers of other colleges in New England. The results of this survey have led the editor to believe that KTC can have a printed campus newspaper every two weeks — if they will vote to support it."[7]

Vincent Russell was the managing editor. Fred Simmons, who was about to retire, and Ann Peters, who had just arrived in 1947, gave good support as faculty advisors.

This young intellectual group used the student council, assemblies, the newly founded *Monadnock*, and even the yearbook to state their aims and their concerns. The college newspaper had not had so much vigor since the early 1930s, nor would it have so much again until the late 1960s and some years in the 1970s. The force of some editorials has never been matched.

Oakey's question — "What is wrong with education?" — was answered by an editorial probably written by Bill Lafferrandre, editor 1950-51, whose first few editorials were unsigned. The editorial replied:

We choose to ignore the intrinsic value of knowledge; external pressure has become the single stimulus to modern learning. Course standards have taken the place of intellectual curiosity. Students regard knowledge with distaste, pursue knowledge only because it is the means to a materialistic end — the college degree. The scholar is a man with no place in modern society. Intellectual curiosity has almost vanished among American undergraduates, and worse, its passing is noted without mourning, without sorrow.

In frankness and in criticism, in breadth of view and in astute commentary, Lafferrandre's editorials have on occasion been equalled or nearly equalled, but never surpassed. Young was not allowed much time to fill gaps in the life of the intellectual community. When no philosopher was hired when Frederick Simmons retired, Lafferrandre thundered: "How can basic enrichment be so brutally ignored?" "How can values be so misinterpreted that [these practical courses are] put before man's study of himself?"

Striking out at the larger community two years later, Lafferrandre wrote that the teacher must "be something of a walking textbook," yet "he may not have opinions on controversial issues. . . . It is time," he said, "for the educator to rise and assert himself in New Hampshire communities."

The college bookstore was to be a "non-profit organization. . . . students were definitely promised this consideration," claimed one article. A guest editorial called for a mental hygiene clinic because one national study "found that about 20% of college students had emotional difficulties of so serious a nature as to handicap them in their life work."

The new seriousness was brought about, "whether we wanted it or not," Oakey said, because of "a growth from national adolescence to a national maturity." The same thing was happening on the college campus, he wrote. "Gone from our campus are the raccoon-coated, goldfish-swallowing rah-rah students of yesterday."[8]

In their efforts to modernize, the reformers attacked one of the college's oldest traditions—Rose Night. It is true that Rose Night was a throwback to the "female seminary," but it was a beautiful ceremony, so much so that townspeople drifted down to the college to witness it. Abolishing it divided even the reformers themselves. One editorial said, "Reform it if need be but don't abolish it." Nonetheless, the radicals had the day and it was abolished.

Another area of concern was school spirit. More editorials since 1914 have been written about school spirit than about any other issue. But in this era the automobile made its impact felt on the campus community life. One editorial noted:

Week-end social life. . . is dying. . . . Every Friday afternoon witnesses a mass evacuation of the campus as students pick up their suitcases and head home. The traditional Saturday night record hops now pass virtually unnoticed by the vast majority of students; only a few die-hard couples bother to attend—fewer still last the evening.

Most of the reformers' efforts were constructive. The student council became still more active. The Student Government Clinic of 1950 provided momentum for the early 1950s.

*Timoleon "Lindy" Chakalos, class of '53, comes off the floor
in one of his famous "Flying Dutchman" lay-up shots.*

In this atmosphere there were genuine campaigns for class officers —
for the first time in the college's history. Copying the University of New
Hampshire, a student mayor was established. The mayor was to be a go-
between for students, administration, and town in areas not generally
handled by the student council. However, the race for mayor soon took
on a carnival atmosphere rivaled only by the fraternities' Hell Week itself.
After much hoopla the first mayor was elected in 1949. He was no more
exempt from criticism than anybody else. "The newly elected mayor announced his council and promptly went into hiding." "His official con-
tenance has not since been glimpsed on campus," stated the *Monadnock.*
"We need a mayor; let's find him."

Francis L. Sorger was nearly as hard-hitting as Lafferrandre, and so
was Don Johnson who followed Sorger. After reviewing New Hampshire
pay scales in one editorial Sorger asked, "Just how much are you worth?"
He suggested, "This estimation can be arrived at collectively as well as
individually. The seniors as individuals can decide or not decide as a group
upon the minimum salary for which a graduate should go out." And what

if the whole thing backfires? — Well, "There are still forty-seven other states that have schools," he said.[9]

The tension spilled over even into boy-girl situations. "Repulsed Romeo" wrote to the *Monadnock:* "Do women wonder why they don't get dates?...I don't....When the women start wearing sneakers and jeans to Saturday night dances, where's the limit? What's coming next?" Romeo got his reply in the next issue from a female student who said, "If the spirit is within, the clothes are irrelevant without....On the other hand, what incentive do the girls have to dress up?" "Why don't you face it, boys — you're not irresistible as you like to think."

Despite all the tension, there was still plenty of what is considered normal 1950s atmosphere about the college. Presidents were always "prexies"; fraternities were "frats"; coffee was "java"; and "blow" meant "get lost." A gossip column was reintroduced to the school newspaper; and the great formals were taken with the utmost seriousness. "Dates were made well in advance," recalled Alice Hurd. "I went to the dance with another man who had asked me before the engagement. To make matters really bad, they were in the same fraternity." A Queen of the Ball was usually chosen at such events. In 1954 Mae Allen became Miss New Hampshire, as Peggy Wass did in 1962.

Bill Beane and Rolly Stoodley, editors of the mid-1950s, commented on everything under the name Rolling Beans and worked hard for school development. They once claimed that topics of concern for most male students were "the perilous situation of Formosa, the phenomenal basketball playing of one Bobby Hall," and Rush Week.[10] The tension had not disappeared altogether, and it would not, but by the mid-1950s it was wearing off.

21

Student Demonstrations
of 1957 and 1963

ASTUDENT of the 1980s once expressed surprise when she learned that Keene College students had become so involved with issues in the late 1960s that they demonstrated in behalf of them. As a matter of fact, even before those great demonstrations, Keene Teachers College students were involved between 1957 and 1963 in two significant demonstrations and two "riots." These undoubtedly indicated a growing restlessness during that period and were a harbinger of things to come. They were certainly much more significant than the national panty raid craze. Unlike the late 1960s, however, they were not nearly so much influenced by national and international events. They sprang much more from the local situation, on the campus and in the state.

By the mid-1950s the atmosphere on campus appeared to be more in tune with the traditional view of that decade. Sputnik I had not yet been launched. Most students were concerned about dates, proms, curfews, and sports rivalry with Plymouth or Fitchburg. The great majority, as always, were concerned solely about their jobs, meeting class demands, and conducting some sort of love life. In this typically 1950s atmosphere occurred the riot of 1957.

The main incident occurred on the unseasonably warm Friday evening of March 8, 1957. Two girls invited some boys to visit them in their room on the third floor of Huntress. It was the weekend before fraternity Hell-Week, and such a daring invitation for such a bold venture was not to

Sandra Greenleaf displays KTC spirit in 1957.

be refused! This was a good chance to get in a girls' dorm. The fraternities were game, and a few other boys decided to join in. Pretty soon there were nearly fifty who decided to make the raid. So, after curfew time, as prearranged, two girls let between thirty and sixty boys through the north door of Huntress. They then ran through the halls scaring other girls and bringing on all kinds of squeals and shrieks. After a quick visit to the room of the girls who offered the invitation, the boys descended, causing still more shrieks and squeals. Everyone knew what was happening, and there was no question that they would be nabbed by the housemother as they made their exit — and as they made their exit they were indeed nabbed. Some preliminary hearings were held, and the findings were sent to Young. On the recommendation of the hearings, Young decided to suspend three men for a semester and give the two women a month's suspension. As more and more students heard the sentences on Tuesday, March 12, the less they liked them. Too many people had been involved, both boys and girls. Singling out only a few for very severe punishments was basically unfair.

Students began milling around on the lawns in front of Huntress and Fiske on the evening of March 12. Some made some speeches against the sentences. Then others did so until the subject was exhausted. Some students began airing gripes about other situations on campus and the ways things were run. Soon some old clothes stuffed with burnables appeared, and one was clearly marked as Dorothy Randall, dean of personnel and housemother at Fiske. Students chanted "Down with Randall," demanded her appearance, and burned her in effigy. Randall was the dean of women who replaced Esten when she died in 1950. Randall was generally a popular dean, but she was still regarded as being too strict. None of these students knew, of course, about Esten.

In the meantime, Fred Barry undoubtedly had second thoughts about being dean of men, a position he had just recently assumed. This was the first demonstration since 1925, and no one in the administration remembered that far back or even went that far back. Barry always assumed that he would have the protection of the dean and the president should anything untoward happen. Young had some meeting to attend in Boston, and while there he also decided to attend the annual flower show. There was yet Dean Carle, but on that Tuesday evening Carle and some of his students were out on a science expedition. As Barry put it, "Now, wouldn't you know, as soon as I was dean of men, a riot broke out. Young was down in Boston to some damn flower show and Carle was out on the mountain collecting rattlesnakes. I was officially in charge of the campus and all hell broke loose." Barry gave permission for a campuswide meeting to take place immediately in Spaulding Gymnasium. Before Barry gave permission curfew was technically on. Two girls, fearing they could not get out the front door but wanting to join in, "leaped," according to the newspaper account, "from the dormitory's second-story window into the arms of men student demonstrators."

At the gym Nils Peterson acted as moderator. John Loughlin, Robert Halloran, and John Salo spoke to the issues. The main complaints at this meeting were about "spy tactics," old-fashioned rules, and which student groups best represented the students. Barry and Randall each made statements. Barry said that he did "not feel the college was yet ready to cope with a type of liberation which apparently was being demanded by some students." Nonetheless, he quieted the crowd by his soothing manner and by a promise to get in touch with Austin McAffrey, state commissioner of education.

That, essentially, was the riot. But things did not die down for the next week. There was meeting after meeting. News of the riot spread throughout the state. William Loeb, editor for the *Manchester Union-Leader,* said that the riot was the result of a "gimmie, gimmie" spirit on the part of the students and the "irresponsible behavior of our national leaders." By this time, however, the riot was clearly over, and student activities settled down to organized, well-planned demonstrations.

The students met again the next night to draw up a list of complaints to present to McAffrey, who was coming to campus the next day. When they finished, the list was surprisingly long — twenty-eight complaints! What is amazing about the list was that almost no one (except Loeb) disagreed with it. Young said, "I could go down the line and agree with almost every one of your grievances . . . there's not one that's not desirable." McAffrey himself did not disagree. He grouped the complaints under five headings and rearranged the groups so as to blunt the demands a bit, but he did not dismiss any. For instance, the first two students demands were: "1. We want certain incompetent faculty members investigated and removed. 2. More new and better faculty members." McAffrey put this under "Faculty and Adminstrators," which was his *third* large category. Nonetheless, he had dealt with all the complaints, and more important, both he and Young had done so sympathetically. But the students had told them very clearly: "We don't want to see this matter blow over. . . . We feel that we are being overlooked. The students generally anticipate some form of improvement, whether it be in parking lots, locks on rooms in girls' dormitories, or other areas . . . we'd like to see some improvement."

What became apparent from the hearing was that many complaints were budget items. McAffrey said that since salaries in New Hampshire were from $600 to $2,000 lower than in every other state in the Northeast, except Vermont, it was very difficult to attract talented faculty and not to overload the devoted ones already on campus. McAffrey also assured the students that "Dr. Young has been anything but derelict in his duties" working for budget improvements. The sentences were modified. The boys' sentences were reduced to four weeks, and the girls' were rescinded immediately.

There appear to be two reasons why the girls got off easier. One was a rumor that many thought had substance, that one of the girls was a daughter of a friend of the commissioner. The second was that many boys not involved, thought the girls were innocent and really went "out on a limb for them." One girl "was a small, young sweet innocent thing," recalls Harold Nugent. "At the time they told us they had nothing to do with it. We believed them," but after the girls were reinstated one of them sweetly and innocently said, "I let them in."

That McAffrey and Young handled the riot well is attested to by Lane Dwinell, who was governor at the time and who could not remember the incident at all in 1982.[1]

The Grand March, 1963

There was a spirit of improvement after 1957. The demonstration itself had shown what students knew all along, that Young was essentially on their side. With him everything boiled down to reason and practicality, and students accepted that well enough. Many of the gripes of 1957 were still not taken care of because there simply were not the funds to take care of them. By the early 1960s even Vermont had pulled ahead of New Hampshire in pay for its faculty. Faculty left not only Keene and Plymouth but also the University of New Hampshire for the West if possible, or for the South, traditionally a low-pay area but which now offered better salary scales than New Hampshire. That was immediately prior to a new statewide commitment to higher education.

The Grand March of 1963 was triggered by Governor John King's budget. King, the first Democrat to win the governorship in forty years, was elected on a "no-tax" platform. His budget called for a merciless hacking away at Keene Teachers College — one third of the total state appropriation! Particularly galling in these meagre budgets was the fact that the sum of $4.3 million was allotted for the university, which taught only 4,500 students, and only $600,000 for Keene *and* Plymouth, which taught 2,000 students. It is to the everlasting credit to a number of Keene students that they decided to make the whole state their classroom and give a state-wide lesson in innovative practice teaching.

Loeb in the *Union-Leader* had charged the students with the "gimmie, gimmie" spirit and with having no solutions to offer. They soon came up with many solutions. Richard Newel recommended a restaurant tax of 10 percent of bills over a dollar and, in jest, moving the state library to Keene, where it could be used; nearly each student had his own recommendation. In this atmosphere John Tate and John McNair, both freshmen and ex-servicemen, planned with the guided assistance of Harold Goder, who had recently joined the faculty, a grand march of students to the state capital to dramatize a four-point program: (1) restoration of the original budget Young had submitted in 1962, (2) a new gymnasium and a new science classroom building, (3) better salaries for faculty, and (4) changing the college to a multipurpose institution.

But soon after the announcement of the "Intelligence Fitness March," as it was called, important people began to have second thoughts. James O'Neil of Chesterfield thought a letter-writing campaign would be better strategy and would not stir up more antieducation votes. Young said, "I personally hope they won't have to do it." Professor Cornelius R. Lyle, Jr., said, "There's a better way." Representatives Hackler of Swanzey and Abare of Troy opposed it and also decided there was a better way. Then the Plymouth students declined an invitation to join the Grand March. In spite of these setbacks, Tate and McNair went ahead with their plans. Thomas Clow responded with a "We Must March" editorial.

Before the march, students conducted tours of the campus showing overcrowded conditions and the paltry holdings of the library, explaining why they were going to march and that they were reasonable citizens making reasonable demands. At one mass meeting in the gym, Representative Mary Brown, chairman of the House Education Committee, tried to tell why Durham was getting a new field house — the old one was "never finished" and was way below standards. Her words fell on a hostile and silent audience. Then all of a sudden someone yelled out, "We'll take it!" and the audience roared with laughter and applause. Another student, Leonard Pratt, said that he hoped the march would "turn a national eye on New Hampshire and turn pressure on the legislators [and] governor

A weary Peter Bixby and William Case were the first of 72 students to reach Concord from Keene in the great Intelligence Fitness March of April, 1963.

to correct the pitiful state of education" in the state. His comments were met with thunderous applause.

Meanwhile, groups of students walked to Marlboro and other towns shaping up for the Grand March. Tom Clow even did a fitness march from Concord to Keene; and the *Sentinel* gave good publicity to it all.

Finally, at 1:00 P.M. on April 8, 1963, the marchers, 76 women and 104 men, assembled and heard speeches by McNair and Tate. Young was supposed to be neutral, but he walked through the town with the marchers and said he would meet them in Concord the next day. The whole demonstration was well organized. Relays of cars kept track of the students, a long, long column of two abreast. First-aid units were on hand to treat blisters or fatigue. There were plans for rest stops, breaks for food, and communication with the college via ham radio. There were six radio cars and fourteen patrol cars, and a pickup truck carried the food and supplies.

Generally the demonstrators were given plenty of attention and sympathy along the way. When they got to Henniker they were met by New England College students, who took them in and had refreshments for them. John Agrafiotis, proprietor of the Bear Hill Restaurant, and an old Keene Normal School alumnus, had free coffee for them — over 350 cups' worth! There were about fifty dropouts in Henniker — due to blisters and to the hospitality of the New England students.

Shirley Ann Johnson rubs the feet of Jon H. Tate, co-chairman of the march on Concord in 1963.

At 1:45 the next morning Peter Bixby and William Case first reached the Concord city line, and thereafter seventy (fifty-five boys and fifteen girls) more students made the full trek to Concord, where they were well received by everyone. "The smell of liniment pervaded the municipal court room here today," wrote Glen Hipple of the *Sentinel*, as the fitness marchers arrived. At times the marchers were spread seven to twenty miles apart, but they "remained orderly and drew favorable comment from a special police sargeant in Henniker and Concord police."

The marchers then went to the state house where they were received by Governor King, House leaders Stewart Lamprey and Walter Peterson. Tate and McNair presented King their petition, and the other demonstrators were welcomed on the floor of the General Court. Part of the petition read that the state require "qualified teachers, not merely warm bodies, to put behind teachers' desks." It was a reiteration of Morrison's famous reports at the turn of the century.

The march was a tremendous success. Originally Governor King did not plan to meet the students, but he unexpectedly showed up. It was no doubt politically wise to do so. In fact, after he received the petition, he invited to lunch all those who had completed the march. Hipple wrote for the *Sentinel,* "WE'RE PROUD OF YOU!" The editors of the *Sentinel* wrote that the students "deserve a standing ovation for ACTING." The new campus minister, Fay Gemmell, in his column, "Proxy Pulpit," commented:

> Nothing I write can add in any way to the credit already won for themselves by the students who so effectively carried out their Intelligence Fitness March. As I was saying goodbye to Ted I asked how his feet were. 'They hurt,' Ted admitted, 'but I would rather have blisters on my heels than calluses on my mind!'[2]

The 1963 "Riot"

This spectacular success was shortly followed by a "riot" that nearly undid all the advantages accrued from the march. This "riot" does provide, however, an interesting case of how differently two sets of people, students and community, view the same events. It is, in some ways, similar to other town-gown "incidents."

The average citizen was shocked to read the *Sentinel's* five-columned banner headlines of May 27, 1963, "23 STUDENTS SUSPENDED AT KTC AFTER ARRESTS: Weekend Rowdyism Quelled." The arrests took place, according to the paper,

> in the aftermath of weekend rowdyism that brought Police Dept. Officers to the campus on two nights to quell complaints of student noise. Twenty-one students were jailed last night and two Saturday night following a ruckus of undetermined origin. . . . Sgt. Paul J. Fontaine said this morning that he believed that a complaint was made to the Police Dept. last night "by one of the ladies down at KTC". . . [police] reported that about 50 students were yelling, throwing firecrackers and beer bottles. The arrest of the students set off a stream of abusive and obscene language, and as the student group became larger, the two police officers called for assistance.
>
> The students reportedly took the court session quite lightly which led Eric J. Kromphold, City Solicitor and Prosecutor, to admonish the students. He said the students made the court "a circus."

Kromphold's comment was particularly serious. Loeb thundered away. Jon McLaughlin of the *Sentinel* ran a blistering editorial saying that the students "created a carnival atmosphere in the courtroom."

Many friends of the college were concerned about the incident because by the best political counting the new after-the-march-on-Concord-budget hung on a mere six to seven votes, and something like this could blow away everything. Media coverage continued to be generally unfavorable.

Then one student, Kenneth Morris, wrote a long letter to the *Sentinel* entitled, "Was It a Riot?" He gave the students' point of view.

Morris said he had been working on a term paper that Sunday night, May 26, and he learned that something was burning on Fiske lawn, which turned out to be something in the shape of a K

standing for a dormitory House Mother in Fiske. The students were standing around, talking to the girls in the windows, and then I was approached concerning three small cherry bombs I had in my room. Not thinking about our state law . . . I volunteered them. Perhaps the reason — and I am still not sure that was it — was that I felt like having a little fun, not knowing that it would disturb nearby citizens. After exploding the fireworks, the students started back to their dorm. For several minutes we stood on Winchester Street sidewalk talking.

The activities at this point were over. Then "within five minutes a Keene police car came around the corner." The police then began picking up students as fast as they could, and students began running as fast as they could. "Because of his weight, one student lost out in his race for the second floor." It was the random picking up of students that got the students angry and started the name-calling. Worst of all, wrote Morris, "a student opened his door in the late evening and saw a policeman chasing a dormitory student through the corridor with a drawn gun!"

"What happened in court the next day was a typical example of nervousness and anticipation. . . . Everyone could sense the tension in the air. Who was going to get the blame for the previous evening? The students; the police, or the administration?" And what would happen to those crucial votes in the legislature? Before the students were arraigned, one of the town drunks was brought before the judge. When the judge told him to raise his right hand and he raised his left hand instead, the students broke out in laughter. He provided the comic relief that was needed to end the tension and their nervousness. The judge understood the situation. If, said Morris, students "were treating courtroom justice with a 'circus air' or irresponsibility, then why didn't Judge Arthur Olson clear the courtroom, or even bang the gavel for order and warn the students?"

Six students admitted to Young their role in the K burning. For today's readers it should be noted that open fires were at that time not in violation of city ordinances. City residents often burned their leaves and house trash near their homes, and freshmen were traditionally welcomed to college with a giant bonfire. At any rate, of those involved in the burning K, one was suspended, four were put on probation until the end of school, and one was exonerated. None of these six had been arraigned, and charges had to be dropped against all those arrested. Young explained publicly: "to believe in democracy, one must participate and one must accept responsibility, we must expect some errors as well as gains. So [now] I must back up and not give the students as much freedom . . . as they had until this incident."[3]

Morris's letter undoubtedly helped the situation. An increased budget for Keene Teachers College, soon to be Keene State College, passed the legislature without the political backfire that was feared because of the "riot." The good results of the 1963 Grand March were saved. During this period, when many other campuses nationally were involved only in panty raids (a phase that Keene got over in the early 1940s), Keene students acted with extraordinary responsibility. They converted the 1957 riot into a meaningful, positive demonstration; they demonstrated again positively in 1963; and possible damage from the 1963 "riot" was salvaged by the courageous act of an individual student.

22

Becoming Keene State College

"**A** HUNDRED PERSONS or more have played an active part in the thinking behind it," said Senator Robert English. He was referring to Senate Bill 68 by which Keene Teachers College became Keene State College. Selecting only a few persons who played key roles is bound to work injustice: nevertheless, we can focus on only a few.

In the contest with Representative Rae Laraba who wanted to close

In 1952, (from left) College Business Administrator Gray Pearson and Governor Wesley Powell listen as Lloyd Young expounds on plans for a state college.

Keene Teachers College or Plymouth in 1949, the college came off well. That conflict produced Governor Adams's two studies, both of which recommended expansion of the college rather than contraction. The board of education eventually approved funds for the building of the college's first male dormitory — Monadnock Hall. "School spirit seems to have all of a sudden shot upward," wrote campus Mayor John Loughlin. "KTC is on the move!" wrote the *Monadnock* editors and, with a burst of enthusiasm, added, "one can see visions of Keene Teachers College in the future — the greatest in the U.S.A.!"

There were many obstacles to overcome even in reaching equality. Economics Professor Lloyd Hayn made a study of faculty salaries and found Keene to be "at a distinct disadvantage in its ability to attract and hold good teachers," a euphemistic phrasing of the situation. He could well have reported that Keene, Plymouth, and even the University of New Hampshire were operating with one of the worst salary scales in the nation.

When in 1957 the state board approved building a new classroom building and a bookstore/snack bar, Young realized that it was time to begin pushing, hinting, suggesting. He well knew that teachers colleges were rapidly becoming state colleges. Nationally, there were only twenty-five left, and all but three were in New England, and before 1963 all the

New England states would have changed to state colleges. The trend, started so long ago, of normal schools serving as people's colleges was coming to full fruition.

In January 1958 Young presided over the first public meeting at which a number of local citizens requested more varied courses from the college. Young reported that a number of people had approached him privately, "including members of the Keene Regional Industrial Foundation," with a request that the college teach courses "comparable to those offered at the State University. Following up on this opening, Young spoke to the Rotary Club, the chamber of commerce, and other groups, always posing the question: "Should the college program be broadened so as to offer courses for students who do not plan to become teachers?"[1]

Young's questions were then raised by many others. Alumni President Clair Wyman conducted a large meeting of Keene Teachers College alumni over the same question. Student Roy Brodsky, in a strong letter to the *Monadnok* editor, asked, "Does the State Department in Concord oppose the liberal or expansionistic viewpoint?" John Ballantine, editor of the *Somersworth Free Press*, suggested that Keene and Plymouth come under the university board of trustees.

Such calls soon found their way to the legislature. State Representative James O'Neil offered bills in 1959 and 1961 providing for more liberal arts courses in the teachers colleges. Representative Roland Batchleder of Deerfield wanted to combine Keene, Plymouth, and Durham in one unit. About a dozen bills in each legislature called for some kind of educational reform. Representative David Bradley of Hanover was the first to call for a thorough study of higher education in New Hampshire, and Young was most in sympathy with his bill.

In the meantime, Charles Eaton, one of the "Young Turks" of the early 1950s, had gotten himself elected to the New Hampshire Senate and sponsored a significant joint resolution along Bradley's lines—the creation of a commission to study the state's education's needs. (In the same session Eaton introduced a bill which authorized the college to employ a full-time alumni secretary.)[2]

There were still many twists and turns in the legislative process. One important figure to become involved was Nelle Holmes, senator from the twelfth district. She was chairperson of the education committee, but her prime interest had been for cooperative regional education for the public schools. She recalled:

Wesley Powell called me in. He said, "Nell, I'd like to put an amendment into this bill and include higher education. I promised David Bradley in Hanover that the next time we had a look into education we'd include higher [education]. I couldn't keep my promise before, and I would like to keep this promise. Would you add it?" I said, "I will if the commissioner is agreeable.... I talked to the commissioner [Charles Ritch], and he said, "No, that's all right with me." Then Wesley Powell offered me the chairmanship of the committee.

Holmes already chaired the committee on state libraries and so turned this offer down. "But," she added, "I did get on the higher education [sub]-committee, and that's where Mildred [Horton] and I worked together. She and I did most of it, except that Mr. [Kenneth] Purcell over in Keene did a lot of the vocational education planning."

Governor Wesley Powell, a colorful maverick-type politician, alternately supported and condemned higher education, especially at the University of New Hampshire. Nonetheless, he appointed an able interim commission, headed by Raimond Bowles of Portsmouth. The commission published a preliminary report in 1962 and the final report in 1963. Both are important works. They constitute the first thorough study of education from primary through university level since Morrison's reports of 1904-17.

"One reason I got on the higher education [sub]committee," recalled Holmes, was "that I wanted to improve the status of the teachers colleges. They were really stepchildren in higher education at that time.... Mildred got this Conant, remember Dr. [James] Conant [of Harvard] to her home in Randolph to talk to our committee.... He was a personal friend of hers."

After their conversations with President Conant and their investigative studies, Holmes and Horton ran into the university lobby in Concord. "UNH didn't want them [Keene and Plymouth] to step up unless they controlled them—I think—that was my feeling." "And Mildred got so discouraged. She just didn't think we were getting anywhere." "And I'll tell you where the turnaround came. It was in the ladies room, and I said, 'Mildred, we've just got to help these teachers' colleges,' and she said, 'Well, all right, we'll keep trying!' "

Horton was indeed a valuable ally. She had been a commander in the WACS during World War II and later president of Wellesley College. After her work on the interim commission, she became a valuable member and then chairperson of the board of trustees. Their statement in the preliminary report was strong. The programs of the state colleges, their report stated, "shall be upgraded to the extent that requirements for admission and for a degree, and for performance while in college, shall be comparable to those of the state university, *i.e.*, there shall be only one standard." This was modified in the final report.

Bowles's committee had barely started when Young submitted an unheard-of $3.6 million building plan to the state board. To the surprise of many, the board approved it. That was enough to make the expansion of Keene (and Plymouth) a political issue in 1962.

John Pillsbury, the leading Republican candidate for governor, claimed that the full potential of the teachers college was not being used. "New Hampshire needs now," he said, "a new leadership that is sympathetic toward education programs in general and will appreciate, in particular, the unrealized potential of the Keene and Plymouth Colleges." Governor Powell then announced a dramatic "multimillion-dollar bond issue for expansion programs" at the university, Plymouth, and Keene. Democratic candidate John King, in his "Fact Sheet," compiled by the League of Women Voters, stated clearly, that he favored the incorporation of the teachers colleges with the board of the University of New Hampshire and also a "master plan for the future of our technical schools, our teachers colleges and our State University."[3]

The state had done fairly well in student performance, but it was on the precipice. Ranking twenty-third among the states in per capita income, it ranked twenty-ninth in total financial support, state and local, of its public schools. Its eighth-grade graduates performed better than the national average, but not by much. Almost 50 percent of elementary teachers still had no college degree of any kind, despite all the graduates Keene had produced. Prevailing factors were the same as they were in Morrison's time. Too many good, qualified teachers were leaving for states (and other professions) where pay was better. "I believe," wrote Bowles, "we are running the supreme risk of standing still or sliding backwards in relation to the more recent achievements of the other 49 states for their children."

"Equal opportunity for higher education does not exist for youth throughout the state," Bowles's commission stated. It therefore recommended that the teachers colleges become state colleges, whose tuition would be less than that of the university, and whose admission standards might not necessarily be as high. Concerning the training of teachers, however, the report stated:

It is unwise for a state to permit the professional training of teachers to be — or even to be considered to be — inferior to that of other professions. Teachers colleges at present admit students who are not qualified academically for admission to the University. This is not good for the professional standing of teachers. Students with low academic records should not be admitted to teacher training programs. Scholastic excellence is no guarantee of good teaching, but neither is scholastic weakness.

The subcommittee [on higher education] believes there should be some women in the highest echelons of administration to demonstrate [especially] to women students that they need not be limited in their professional service and careers by the mere fact that they are women.

Was this the work of Holmes and Horton? "You can count on that,"[4] Holmes replied.

After the primaries in September 1962, New Hampshire had one of the wildest elections ever. The Republican party broke up after the death of Senator Styles Bridges, who had dominated state (and sometimes national) politics for a generation. A hot four-way race for the senatorship soon developed. Pillsbury dramatically defeated the volatile Powell in the September primary. Powell, once the bedfellow of William Loeb, jumped out of that bed and lined up his forces behind Democrat John King. King continued a furious campaign as if nothing had happened, but did say that he would take help from anyone and hammered away on increased aid to education as his number one issue. He linked it to the defense issue, saying, "We're at war right now, practically, with Russia," and the outcome "will be decided, not by who has the most guns, but whose people have the best trained minds. . . . Every penny that could be saved should be dumped into education." His main plan, lifted from Powell's primary campaign, was to float a $10 million bond issue.

King's opponent, Pillsbury, agreed on the need to beef up New Hampshire's educational system. Pillsbury favored a grant of $3 million and a "pay-as-you-go basis" thereafter — fiscally sounder than King's but politically less spectacular. King's landslide election in November meant that education expansion would take place but with flimsy financing.

King, nonetheless, proved to be a most imaginative thinker for educational expansion. At one point he suggested that Keene and Plymouth be kept at their present size, about 1,000 and that a third college be established in some rural area. Like Powell himself, however, after a brilliant insight or an imaginative statement, King often plunged as deeply into an antieducational foray. It was this maverick aspect of his administration that brought on the Keene student Grand March to Concord, recounted in the previous chapter. Once committed, however, King gave the faculty their biggest pay raises in history. He got money for this by keeping the headtax money in Concord. (It had normally been returned to the towns.) Then, in his message of April 12, 1963, King proposed a $20 million education bond issue; and, following the recommendation of the interim commission, he proposed a single board of trustees for Keene, Plymouth, and Durham.[5]

Political and educational leaders were not of one accord with King's proposals. Senator Robert English, Representative Walter Peterson, Trustee Jere Chase, and Dean David Sarner supported them. Young was lukewarm about them, since he had presented different ideas himself.

King's proposals and the interim commission's report spawned another half-dozen bills redefining the future of Keene, Plymouth, and Durham. The commission's report stressed that "advanced education is basically sound for the state's economy." It mentioned also a significant social reason: "Yesterday the state was called upon to provide secondary education for young people qualified to profit from it. Today, high school graduates and their parents expect the state to supply higher educational facilities as freely as secondary." The expectations were indeed more broadly based in 1962, but as pointed out, and is, indeed, the theme of this book, Keene (and other normal schools/teachers colleges) had been serving the purpose of providing nearly free higher education since their founding.

Eventually support rallied around Senate bill 68, which when passed and signed became officially "An Act Relative to the Reorganization of Public Higher Education in New Hampshire." The act states:

Keene Teachers College and Plymouth Teachers College are hereby designated [as of July 1, 1963] as Keene State College and Plymouth State College, respectively, and each shall be a division of the University of New Hampshire and shall be governed by the board of trustees of said University. Each said state college shall become a multipurpose college by expanding the current programs to provide instruction in the liberal arts and sciences and in selected applied fields to better serve the needs in its respective area of location.

Both Keene and Plymouth could grant also associate in arts degrees. The vocational technical schools remained under the jurisdiction of the state department of education.

The trustees, now broadened and newly constituted, had wide-ranging powers over finance, tuition, research — and even over plumbing — one might say especially over plumbing! The act states that among the duties of the new trustees were to "erect pumping machinery, lay water mains and pipes, install gates, valves and hydrants"; further, "to construct and maintain sewers, culverts, conduits and pipes, with all necessary inlets and appliances," "above ground and underground." Within a month after

*Teachers from parochial as well as public schools made good use
of the expanded liberal arts courses.*

creation, the new board, setting aside its plumbing duties for the time being, authorized another faculty pay raise for Keene and Plymouth. After
his first year in office Governor King said his greatest satisfaction came
from the merger of Keene and Plymouth with the University of New
Hampshire.[6]

When Keene Teachers College became Keene State College, it signaled
the end of an era. There were, practically speaking, no more teachers colleges in the United States. The teachers college era was a short interval
of twenty or thirty years between normal school and state college. In fact,
they were being hooted out of existence by the conservative journals, which
were astute at zeroing in on the excesses. *Life* magazine ridiculed the
"oompty-oomp credits in pedagogical methodology" needed for teaching.
Better Homes and Gardens ridiculed the "deep research" "in places like Fairly Normal." "One thesis, barely atypical, was entitled, 'Your Present
Classroom Pencil Sharpener, Its Care, Location, and Use.' " The headline
for the article was "How Well Are Our Teachers Being Taught? Never
Worse!" It was another crest in the ocean of "Johnny Can't Read" articles.

Keene itself did not escape the attack. In an article in the *Saturday*

Review James Koerner questioned the validity of NCATE decisions. NCATE was the National Crediting Association for Teacher Education. This was brought about because NCATE approved Keene Teachers College, "Crossroads State Teachers College," in the article but not Carleton College in Minnesota as having a qualified teacher education program. Koerner's real complaint was against NCATE, not Keene. Nonetheless, Keene did not fare well. "Two members of the faculty had earned the Ph.D. degree and five more held the Ed.D. degree," Koerner noted. "Most of the faculty degrees at all levels were from second-rank institutions, or lower.... Although 80 percent of the regular faculty had taken their highest degree in education and often their undergraduate degree as well, many were teaching the academic courses." It was obvious, even in Koerner's article, that "Crossroads" was poorly supported financially. Effective answers could have been offered. It is too bad that nobody responded. If the article had any local force at all, it was only added to many other voices clamoring for change.[7]

With the ending of the teachers college era, the perceived influence of John Dewey also diminished. William DeVane, author and educator, has written, "at its best, the effect of his thought was to revitalize collegiate education; at its worst — and there were bad effects — it diluted the intellectual content and standards of the educational enterprise."

Dewey, whose ideas were buried with such haste in the 1960s, would certainly be missed in the 1970s. He hated permissiveness and what he described as "deplorable egotism, cockiness, impertinence and disregard for others." Education was for him a social process, and it was to benefit society as a whole. He had no sympathy for acquisitive or pleasure-seeking individuals who had little or no regard for their neighbors' rights.

Keene Teachers College had not only trained teachers; it also gave them and many others dignity and self-respect by giving them a recognized college education. It carried on a tradition begun by Keene Normal School. Alumnus John Tucker, speaker of the General Court in 1983, said

First of all, [the college] got me into a specific career — education. It gave me a place in life, a place to throw my anchor, somewhere to play a role....It gave me a sense of purpose, a sense of direction, my role in education, to work with young people and move them along the continuum. It gave me a better understanding of history, literature, and my role in the scheme of things; and most important of all, it unlocked a door for me to take advantage of several opportunities in the legislature, in radio, in working with the NHEA [New Hampshire Education Association]. Without that education, I would not have been able to gain entry into any of these things.[8]

Keene Teachers College formed a homogeneous community socially. Intellectually, the climate was indeed sometimes sluggish; at other times, it was unusually vibrant — something that Koerner could not see during his three-day visit here. Admission standards remained reasonably high. In 1962 only 250 were accepted of 600 who took the test for admission, another factor which Koerner ignored. With Young's own full commitment to democracy and intellectual freedom, the college often imparted an unusually meaningful experience to its students.

Keene Teachers College produced about 40 percent of all the teachers for the state — more than any other institution. By the time of the college's demise, residents in the state "in percentage of population 25 years or older with at least 4 years of high school education" ranked "19th from the top in the list of 50 states." Further, "the state had only about 12.5 percent failing the selective service basic mental test — half the national average — ranking 15th among the states — an excellent showing," stated the interim report.[9] Despite the losses of good teachers to other states, teaching and teacher preparation were obviously effective forces in the state. As already pointed out, however, attrition of good teachers by the early 1960s was so severe, especially in the elementary schools, that the state was in real danger of losing the slight advantage it still held.

The teachers college era was nearly coterminous with the presidency of Lloyd Young. Many appropriate dinners, banquets, and speeches featured the retirement celebrations in honor of him. One could say that in certain circumstances Young should have been more demanding, especially in his relationship to the state board and the state legislature. On the other hand, the written record shows him to be much stronger in such matters than the faculty often perceived him to be. One cannot leave a discussion of his presidency without having great sympathy with him for all the problems that beset his years and his own commitment to moving ahead in an orderly and democratic fashion and admiration for him for handling all this with such equanimity and reasonableness. His program, his college, stifled as it was for funds for twenty-five years, must share in large degree for the slightly superior statewide performance of its public school system. How much more could have been done with adequate support! As it was, his students realized the value of his work and the difficulty of his role and have always honored him.

KEENE
STATE COLLEGE

1963 / 1984

A portion of the Science Center

23

Keene State College and
Roman ("Jay") Zorn

LLOYD YOUNG'S leaving in 1964 marked not only the end of the era of teachers colleges but also the end of a whole way of student life and administrative life. Governor Dwinell's recollection of teachers colleges being nice, quiet, no-trouble-type institutions, although it does some injustice to the efforts of concerned people at Keene Teachers College, was not wide of the mark.

The day that Dwinell talked about was surely over. Herman Wells of Indiana University said that the new college president needs to be born "with the physical stamina of a Greek athlete, the cunning of a Machiavelli, the wisdom of a Solomon, the courage of a lion, and if possible — but above all, the stomach of a goat."

The new president, Roman Joseph Zorn, had many of the qualities Wells described and a few besides. Born in 1916 to Henry Vincent and Elizabeth Zorn in River Falls, Wisconsin, Zorn graduated with a B.Ed. from River Falls State College, taught high school for a couple of years, then served with the U.S. Navy during World War II. After the war he attended the University of Wisconsin where he earned a master's degree in philosophy and a doctorate in American history. He studied under William Hesseltine, a national figure and the Dean of American Historians. Zorn was considered one of Hesseltine's best students. A long list of famous historians read Zorn's doctoral thesis on the birth of the Republican party in Illinois.

After holding several college teaching positions and doing some administrative work, Zorn became dean of arts and sciences at the University of Rhode Island, where in a short period of time he added new blood and vigor to its programs. Rapid growth in itself, wrote Dunham in his study on the colleges of forgotten Americans, "produces all sorts of strain in the network of relationships involved in the running of a college or university." He cited cases of "blood baths" in certain departments and claimed that "it was easier to start a new institution than to change an old one."

Zorn was familiar with the strains of growth. He even anticipated them in his opening remarks to the college community when he said, "Significant growth is not likely to come without accompanying stresses and strains, and there will be problems of adjustment in the years ahead."[1]

Zorn was overwhelmingly impressive. Sitting with him at the first interview, one caught a glimpse of his vision, his breadth of knowledge, his fine judgment. Clark Kerr wrote about the "identity crises" of state colleges. This was not the case with Keene State College under Zorn. Zorn knew where he and the college were going, and he let the faculty members know. He would build up five liberal arts majors—English, history, mathematics, psychology, and biology—with good supporting faculty in other areas such as philosophy, political science, economics, geography, chemistry, and physics. All these would complement, not compete with, the traditional programs. Further, he would attract the best possible faculty. Why not have a "Little Ivy" in a state system? That was his vision. That is what attracted so much talent and so many Ph.D.'s to Keene in the 1960s when Ph.D.'s were hard to find for state colleges.

To attract this talent, Zorn put on a good "sell." After the interview with him there was a tour around campus with one of the older faculty members, Ella Keene or Ann Peters, or a tour of the city with Bob Mallat, who was also mayor of the town (1961-65) and seemed to know everyone and everything. Then came dinner with Dean David Sarner, who promised everything he could (and a little more) and further convinced the candidate that his talents were needed here. Then came another friendly chat with Zorn, who said, in effect, "You're under no obligation to us, but think the matter over." Many excellent scholars and teachers decided to join in such an exciting enterprise. When new faculty arrived on campus, they confided to a colleague, "Zorn was the main reason for my coming here." Often the reply was, "He's the *only* reason I'm here!" Publicly Zorn stated: "Keene State College is now on the threshold of a new era—a period to be characterized by physical expansion, diversification in programs and activities, and broadening academic horizons."

The first faculty hired by Zorn were headliners. First was Albert Schatz,

Representative Saul Feldman speaking on behalf of his bill to ban subversive speakers from the campus to which Zorn effectively and eloquently responded. The bill never became law.

the codiscoverer of treptomycin. Then came Lloyd Hayn, William Felton, Benjamin Lucow, all with Ph.D.s from good to first-class universities. Frank Evans did not have his doctorate yet, but behind his name went "Fulbright Scholar, Ph.D. Candidate, University of Chicago." In the first two years, as the faculty grew from forty-eight to sixty-eight, the number of doctorates grew from six to twenty-three. Nearly all taught in their disciplines and came from good to outstanding institutions. Zorn spent day after day going through piles of dossiers tying to get the right person to come to Keene. In some years he attracted more earned doctorates than the University of New Hampshire, always more than Plymouth.[2]

Under Young a number of outstanding speakers came to Keene. Under Zorn the array was startling: writer William F. White, British author Stephen Spender, philosopher Paul Weiss, poet John Ciardi all came within a very short time of each other. Then came Max Freedman, aide to Lyndon Johnson, John Sloan Dickey and Wentworth Eldredge of Dartmouth and William Coffin of Yale. J. Seelye Bixler of Colby College came and told the freshman class, "the liberal arts college ought to be the beginning of wisdom." Richard Merrifield of Keene commented, "A very exciting, wonderful thing is going [on] in Keene. Our onetime normal school, onetime teachers college, is metamorphosing into what it now formally is — a liberal arts college. . . . We, too, of the nonacademic world are sharers of this birth." Merrifield regarded a recent concert by pianist Arments Adams in Zorn's new Concert and Lecture Series as the symbol "of the springtime flowering that is happening at Keene State College."

The plan was definite and was working. Each knew his role. The faculty, said Zorn, "must provide experience and knowledge derived from the scholarly pursuit of wisdom." To students he said, "You have a right to expect that the faculty will stimulate your learning by demonstrating that scholarship is not isolated from the exciting times in which we live." The student, on the other hand, must accept the task of becoming an educated and responsible human being — and be a good judge. "Let's not assume," Zorn said, "that every person that holds a college degree is an educated person — or that every adult is wholly civilized."

As the growth strains began to have their effect on the student body, Zorn took pains to explain the situation. He wrote Ralph Granger that he was aware of the hardship that contemplated Saturday classes would have on working students. Zorn then dropped consideration of Saturday classes because of well-presented opposition to them. One student complained that no two clocks on campus told the same time. Zorn had that problem corrected within twenty-four hours. Zorn once wrote the editor of the school newspaper, "I think the last issue of the *Monadnock* was probably the best of the year, and I want to extend commendations for your efforts." To student Norm Tardiff, he wrote, "The Dave Brubeck concert was an outstanding event, and I congratulate your committee for making this selection." "Never before," wrote the editor of the *Monadnock*, "had KSC made available such diverse and fascinating cultural avenues for students."[3]

Zorn starred also in his first public debate. Saul Feldman, a Republican member of the General Court from Manchester, sponsored a bill that would bar any "representatives or members of a subversive organization" from using the "facilities or premises" of state-supported schools. Republican House Speaker Walter Peterson, a man of wider and generally more liberal views, opposed the bill. What gave it real force was the governor, John King, who supported it. Zorn appeared at a hearing in Concord and made a beautiful statement.

I urge that the scope of academic freedom be maintained at all divisions of the University. The essential environment for higher education requires freedom of thought and speech, including the unhampered opportunity to evaluate new ideas and contemporary issues. . . . There should be no differentiation in the locale of discussion of contemporary ideologies or issues. The Bill of Rights . . . should apply throughout the nation, and its principles and control are entirely appropriate for the college campus. Since the Feldman bill represents the entering wedge of restriction, it would be unwise and undesireable legislation.

As a college president, Zorn had spoken effectively, even eloquently, and at the right time. The crisis was soon over, but Feldman's bill remained an issue for another two years.

No one worked harder than Zorn. He was usually in his office in Hale by 7:00 A.M. and stayed there without a break until 7:00 P.M., at which time he went to the Crystal Restaurant (now Henry David's), or sometimes home, for a big supper. He then joined his family for a few hours in the evening. After that, he took a tour of the campus to see how the new construction was coming along or to see what students were up to. Stories were told of his roaming campus until 2:00 and 3:00 A.M. He seemed to be working all the time. He expected his chief aides to work equally hard. "I never worked so hard in my life as when Zorn was here," recalled Robert L. Mallat.[4]

When reviewing these facts, and many more could be added, it is hard to believe that Zorn left as the most unpopular president in the college's history. That such was the case few would deny. What went wrong? Part of the problem lay in the times, and no one at Keene could change that. Part lay in the inherent difficulty in changing an existing institution, as Dunham noted. Part also lay in Zorn's character, another factor that could not be changed.

What on the surface appeared to be so enigmatic about Zorn's unpopularity was that his primary adversaries (although not all) were the very faculty that he himself had worked so diligently to recruit. So let us take a little closer look at Zorn's character and the general situation to see if a reasonable explanation can be found for this phenomenon.

At historical conventions one could readily find Wisconsin graduates who either knew Zorn or knew about him. Although this cannot be described as thorough research, it can be pieced together to provide a plausible interpretation. Zorn's father was a talented blacksmith who provided well for his family. There is a possibility, however, that smithing was not as highly regarded in River Falls, Wisconsin, as it was in Germany and that Father Zorn did not feel as appreciated for his talents as he had a right to be. As young "Jay" grew up in the 1920s and 1930s, he (and his family) may also have felt the pressure of the 100 percent Americanism that got to be in vogue. There are many German-Americans, of course, in Wisconsin; but River Falls was predominantly English/Scotch-Irish. One story told was of the Zorns walking to mass on Sunday morning, better dressed and very likely more prosperous, in fact, than their more numerous and socially more prestigious Protestant neighbors. The Zorns were in the town but not of the town.

This background story, which certainly rings true, explains a lot about Zorn. He was more of an "outsider" to society, even to his own college community, than an "insider." He was too ready to work against forces,

*Fay L. Gemmell became chaplain
for Protestant students in 1963.*

powers, people. He needed to take more time and patience in working with them. If one proposed an idea to Zorn, he grasped the full impact of it immediately. Here another character trait of his came into play. Zorn became so occupied with the idea that he never let the proposer know how it struck. Thus, there was no immediate satisfaction in knowing how the idea went over. Sometime later one would be gratified to learn that the idea was welcomed and had been fully implemented and to a much better degree than one ever expected — or shocked to learn that it had been completely rejected and that the exact opposite course of action had been taken.

Further, Zorn was an intellectual, and he expected ideas and suggestions to come to him, particularly from the faculty, in the manner of intellectuals — that is, by an assessment of the problem followed by suggestions for solution. To the students to whom he chose to reply in the school newspaper, he was always complimentary for the manner in which they made their suggestions. Faculty who demanded their rights had an immediate fight on their hands. Zorn's toleration for this kind of behavior was extremely low, and this was his weakness. The tragedy was that too many faculty chose the demand rather than the suggestion approach.

Still another factor in the growing discontent was that those assisting Zorn in hiring stressed the fact that new good talent was needed for the ideas they could contribute. Once the new faculty arrived, however, they found that Zorn and his staff were so busy that they never had, or took, the time to consult with the new faculty. Thus, the new faculty, who should have been the natural allies with Zorn, often felt left out, became disillusioned, and eventually became the most vocal critics of all that Zorn did.

The first serious overt clash between Zorn and faculty was the Hapgood-Cunliffe case. Charles Hapgood was one of the most colorful members of the faculty. He was also one of the most published. His *Earth's Shifting Crust* was published in 1964 and his *Maps of the Ancient Sea Kings* had been accepted for publication when the controversy erupted.

Apparently Zorn did not approve of Hapgood's research techniques or his teaching methods. Citing a dizzying array of evidence, none of which made much sense, Hapgood concluded not only that there had been an Atlantis but that it was the seat of an advanced civilization with an excellent technology long before the Egyptians developed their culture. As time went on, Hapgood got involved in psychic research, and could thus talk to Moses, Jesus, Lincoln, and other departed authorities for confirmation of his discoveries. Since Zorn had done most of his research in the major libraries of the Northeast, and had done it by going through page after page of difficult-to-read manuscripts, he did not take Charlie's unorthodox, and much quicker methods seriously. Nonetheless, research methods aside, Hapgood was an effective classroom teacher. He got the students interested and involved in his "research." The big difference between the two, wrote Ernest Hebert, was that Hapgood communicated well with the students and Zorn did not. At the time, Zorn was more interested in how valuable such knowledge was. Further, as one faculty member said, "no matter what the title of the course, Charlie always taught the 'earth's shifting crust.' "

Zorn made changes, and he made them rapidly. They were the result of his careful consideration and hard work. Some changes were made without sufficient consultation with the faculty who remembered Young's democratic governance. As a result, by the fall of 1965 Eric Cunliffe, professor of education, and Mary Haskins, the college dietician, joined Hapgood in circulating an eight-point letter criticizing some of Zorn's changes. Some of the points appeared to be serious, such as "arbitrarily phrased orders to the faculty and interferences with their liberties and functions should cease," and "the Dean should never change textbook orders by professors." Other points appeared odd, even petty, but indicated that something deeper was wrong. Two were "Privileges granted for life by Dr. Young should be observed. [1] in particular the telephone exchange should be located in a better place."[5] Point 2 was the fact that Zorn had messed with the sacred cow of faculty parking rights. Unilaterally he im-

*Father Richard Connors assumed duties
at the Newman Center in 1976.*

posed a five-dollar per year fee for all faculty using the lots. This was an irritation that brewed unnecessarily for years.

Dean Sarner explained the textbook case. He said that one professor had ordered a text which cost forty-five dollars. In 1965 he thought that too much of a financial hardship. He was unable to contact the faculty member duirng that summer, and so he changed the order. The deeper problem was the arbitrarily phrased orders. Once one had alienated himself or herself with Zorn, the communications from him, and sometimes from his aides, were arbitrarily phrased. Often the faculty member was not opposed to Zorn personally (although some were) but merely to a particular point. The arbitrarily phrased communication alienated faculty who should never have been alienated. As soon as one faculty member saw such a communication received by one of his colleagues, he was not sure where he stood. The tendency was to stand with one's colleagues.

Soon other faculty members became dissatisfied. One, Harold Goder, had come to Keene in 1962. He was the main faculty spirit behind the March to Concord in 1963, and as a result he became the students' choice for "Professor of the Year" for that year. He had a strong influence on the younger Ph.D.s coming on campus.

Soon a whole group of the dissatisfied hired a lawyer to take care of their complaints. Zorn then fired Hapgood and Cunliffe, who immediately insisted on "show cause" hearings. Finally, at a special meeting of the board of trustees in Concord on the last Saturday of January 1966, the board decided to uphold the dismissals and to end the controversy by allotting severance compensation to the aggrieved parties.

The editor of the *Monadnock*, in his February 11, 1966, issue, gave a good assessment, entitled "LET'S MOVE ON": It deserves to be quoted:

According to a news release from UNH President, John McConnell, the controversy at KSC is over. An amiable solution, a compromise, has been reached. The eventual consequences of the controversy are not yet clear. But this much is: the school as an entity has been hurt. Its central authority has been questioned, and the repercussions are bound to weaken its academic and financial bargaining power in Durham and Concord.

And both sides must share the responsibility for this.

The nature of controversy is dynamic. It can clarify or confuse, advance or retard; but always it creates tension and energy, and things are never quite the same after it has past.

The recent controversy of KSC, in the view of the *Monadnock*, has been a failure. Little thought has come from it, and much tension created.

But it is over — hopefully.

And it is time to pick up the pieces.

Time to look to the future.

Perhaps in the future, lines of faculty-administration communication may be better understood; valid grievances given a fair hearing; and petty, selfish ones properly ignored, without fear of backlash.

Perhaps in the future, students won't have to be interviewed by lawyers and asked to sign affidavits about internal college matters which only concern them obliquely, and which strain their loyalties.

KSC is a school on the move, possessing a competent administration, a dedicated faculty, and an inquisitive student body. A coordinated effort will make it go.

Controversy is needed, but only if it is rationally conceived, justly heard, and kept in perspective.

The controversies, however, were never kept in perspective. They always appeared to be larger than they were. As a result, many faculty left, and often the best faculty. In a still earlier editorial the *Monadnock* stated, "KSC must attract and RETAIN competent professors. Retaining is important — we have had a steady exodus of professors leaving here each year."[6]

If ever there was a time for an update of Cicero's work, *In Defense of Old Age*, the Zorn years were it. The update itself actually was not so necessary as old people themselves. By an unusual set of circumstances nearly all the old respected faculty members such as Drenan, Keene, Blackington, Waltz, and Christine Lancaster (of the Wheelock School) reached retirement as Zorn took control, or soon thereafter. There was no significant group of "old professors" who commanded the respect of both the administration and the new faculty, who could occupy the middle ground, who could not be intimidated, and who could communicate the wisdom of their years. Had there been, the questions of faculty leadership and faculty policy powers would not have been as uncertain and as chaotic as they were.

In retrospect, one sees more clearly the priorities Zorn set. He came to build, to build quickly and to build well. To build well, he hired a faculty with extraordinarily good qualifications for that time period and for the money that he had. To build quickly, he hired a pliant administration. That meant, however, that the "new Ph.D. faculty" had neither "old professors" nor an administration (and scarcely a departmental chair) to whom to turn, to take up issues, to voice concerns except Zorn himself. Zorn did not have that kind of time. The result was that the new faculty, recruited by Zorn himself, either stuck with him through thick and thin or, more generally, opposed him through thick and thin.

Most of the new faculty shared Zorn's intellectual background. They both saw the liberal arts college (or the university) as the heritage of the medieval university or of Plato's Academy, where pursuit of knowledge, by professors and students, was the first order and all else was secondary, including practical curricula and even teaching itself.

It was commonly believed that when Zorn first came he wanted to completely detach the Wheelock School from the college. Plymouth had done so in its steps to liberal arts status. But as the new faculty, after it arrived, found itself out of touch with the president, and siding more and more with Hapgood, Cunliffe, and other dissidents, the president relied more and more on the old teachers college faculty and the Wheelock School faculty for his support.

In 1964 a fifteen-member college senate had been created, one of Young's last official acts. It was so new that it had little tradition or respect. It always met in camera. There was also an all-encompassing Faculty Association which inlcuded almost everyone except the grounds crew and the secretaries. It elected the senators but otherwise had no policy functions. Many regarded it as worthless, although it served well for social functions and as a "free speech" arena. It was in the association that the idea of a yearly convocation be established as an avenue of communication between the administration and faculty and students. Zorn picked up on it right away and held the first convocation in the fall of 1967.

Most faculty, however, sought more tangible power. Like the Pilgrims, they wanted their compact written on paper. Unlike the Pilgrims, they were not willing to endure many hardships. One faculty member was distressed that so many liberal arts faculty took positions hostile to the president. He was sure that, if president and dissident faculty were forced to work together, a satisfactory meeting of the minds would take place. With that in mind he proposed in the spring of 1967 a slate of candidates composed of representative new liberal arts faculty members, some of whom had particular grievances, as members for the next year's senate. There grievances and issues could come out in the open instead of forever being talked about in the corridors. Soon, however, the "other side" heard about his slate. "They" got up one of their own kind and outvoted the "dissidents" in the election.

This was the first of many faculty slates. Now they are done openly and are seen as beneficial rather than as subversive. The idea then was to get those vocal, idealistic, high-powered faculty members together with Zorn in the same forum, where the difficulties could be hammered out honorably. Nonetheless, the overriding fact was that Zorn controlled more votes and did, in fact, want his own people on the senate. The key factor in his control was the solid bloc of twenty votes from Wheelock School.

It is only fair to note here that the Wheelock faculty were pawns in the game. Except for Christine Lancaster, they did not know what was going on at the college or what the issues were. The new faculty generally did not understand the importance and historical significance of Wheelock to the college. Thus, the Wheelock School issue was controversial until Redfern's administration.

At any rate, because of the situation just described, a faculty constitution committee was formed with faculty member David Harvey as chairman. Harvey's committee worked long, hard, and carefully and presented on March 8, 1968, a complicated but well-thought-out constitution in which the academic faculty had primary voice. An associate faculty, those teaching less than 50 percent of normal college load, also had a voice, but prime policy decisions rested with the academic faculty. When ratification came up in April, the atmosphere was electric. The Wiseman case (discussed in Chapter 25) was under way; students demanded more liberalization of dorm rules and curriculum changes. The McCarthy and Robert Kennedy campaigns were under way; there were student demonstrations at other campuses. There were then ninety-eight members of the Faculty Association; ninety-six voted. Of those who did not vote, one, Cornelius Lyle, was in Michigan, and the other was supervising student teachers. The constitution was defeated 54-42.

Zorn knew, of course, how he had won and where real faculty sentiment lay. He soon had another constitution committee at work. It drafted the present senate constitution, which gave the faculty broader representation and provided for three students. John Carey, Marilyn Treat, and Roger Goldsmith were soon elected the first student senators. The next year student representation was broadened to fifteen.[7] That constitution remained basically unchanged until 1983.

Zorn had made an exceptionally good beginning, but the honeymoon was short. An exceptionally rough storm in the Hapgood-Cunliffe case developed in his second year. The debate about the new constitution tried to resolve general faculty-administrative differences as well as to define the faculty's role during the third and fourth years, and in the meantime the Wiseman case was brewing.

Thus far nothing has been said about the construction of buildings since the old Spaulding Gymnasium and the old Mason Library were built in the late 1920s. For convenience' sake, included in the next chapter are the physical building accomplishments of Young and Leo Redfern. It is now time to turn to an overly brief account of the "new construction." Zorn loved it. It was highly visible, and unlike the faculty kept its place.

24

The New Construction, 1955-1978

FACTUAL INFORMATION about major campus buildings is listed in the appendices, but each major building deserves some mention here. By and large, the new construction, if we may date the period 1955-78 as the era of new construction, is marked by the principle of functionalism in architecture and for the first part of the period, at least, by penny pinching in financial appropriations. It was also the era of the cement block and drywall construction. For people who do not like it, it is often called "American Rectangle" or "American Bland." Nonetheless, each building is marked by some distinctive features and occasionally even by aesthetics.

Monadnock Hall, 1955, was the first of the modern structures. It is, of course, rectangular. Successful art student Roy Brodsky called it a "monstrosity." Still, it has unique characteristics and a lot of thought went into it. Young, Plymouth President Harold Hyde, Keene architect John Holbrook, and others toured colleges and universities in New England looking for new building ideas. One idea, which all accepted, was to plan the new dormitory so that fraternities or other organizations could continue as units within a large building. This was the case in 1955 when Kappa and Alpha fraternities moved in. The arrangement continued until it became a women's dormitory. The dorm was nearly named for Henry C. Morrison, but those arguing for naming it after the local geological wonder, Mount Monadnock, won the day.

Another unusual feature of Monadnock Hall was that it was built by the "lift slab" or "pancake" method of construction. Four large slabs of reinforced concrete were poured on top of each other, as in a stack of

Morrison Hall

pancakes. When each floor dried, it was hoisted up to the roof, third, or second floor, respectively. Each pancake weighed about 270 tons and contained all the necessary building materials on it needed for that floor. It was the first time this type of construction had been used in New Hampshire.[1]

The old bookstore, built in 1959, subsequently the Computer Center and in 1984 the Management Center, appears to be the campus's best example of limited vision. It has often been called the campus "wart," but given enough age it may even be considered "cute," despite the "U.S. Route No. 1" flavor of its style. "It was built," explained Clair Wyman, "with limited funds accumulated within the Keene Endowment Association. No state appropriation was forthcoming, and it was built where it is [on Appian Way] because that was the only open piece of land on campus at that time. It was built when it was because of student pressure on Young for a suitable campus bookstore." It is too small to be of much use, yet so solidly built (with the idea that a second floor might be added) that it would be very expensive to remove it.

In the same year, 1959, and costing ten times as much, the Butterfield addition was built. Unlike the bookstore, the legislature had to do something positive for the Industrial Arts program. Recommendations had been made since Governor Adams's first administration ten years prior. The "T&I boys" had, since the end of World War II, learned their auto mechanics in the backyard of the Butterfield Building.[2] The Butterfield addition had been long overdue.

No building caused more controversy than Morrison Hall, a large twenty-room-classroom building erected in 1961. Coming shortly after Monadnock, the bookstore, and the Butterfield addition, people in town became alarmed and wanted a master plan. The decision to put it on the tennis courts in front of Huntress was, said Mayor Alfred Dennis, "an offense and abomination: against the city and the school." Indeed it was. Dennis obviously had some aesthetic sense for the campus as a whole, even if educational authorities did not. Possibly he became impatient with the niggardly appropriations the legislature made to the teachers college. At any rate, Dennis wanted the new building located where the library now is. Soon faculty and students got involved in the controversy. It then went to the attorney general's office for a decision. The attorney general ruled in the spirit of the legislature, that is, that the $600,000 appropriated was for the building only and not the site. "To wait two years for another legislative decision," wrote Wyman, "was out of the question, since the original appropriation could . . . [have been] lost." In other words, insufficient as the funds were, one had best use them or even that little might be lost.

The desirable site, south of Appian Way, could not, therefore, be purchased. There was nothing left to do but to put it on college property; hence its present location attached to Parker and behind the President's House. That meant that the unique and lovely sunken garden, where so many romantic trysts had taken place, despite Dean Esten's careful eye, would be sacrificed for the expediency of the moment. While the building is obviously functional, Kohler Issac, the architect, did what he could with limited funds. The lines are modestly classical, in keeping with Huntress, Fiske, Parker, Butterfield, and old Spaulding. Inside the harshness of cement block was thoughtfully covered by tile and wood paneling. It is in many ways an architect's triumph over parsimony, and was thus a fitting, but unplanned, tribute to its namesake.

At the dedication in May 1961 were Governor Wesley Powell, Mayor Charles Coolidge, Samuel Green (president of the state Senate), Education Commissioner Charles Fitch, Young, and many others. Also speaking briefly at the ceremonies was Hugh S. Morrison, professor of art and architecture at Dartmouth, and son of Henry Morrison.[3] The college and the state had at long last given proper recognition to its founder by means of a building, if not to his ideas.

In the same year the legislature provided for new family housing

Artist and former art professor Etta Merrill creates a painting of Elliot Hall in oil.

quarters on Hyde Street and for a new library. Getting rid of the old family quarters, Bushnell Barracks, caused quite a stir in that the first proposal was to burn them. A great boon when they first arrived, they were in time considered unseemly, vermin-infested, and diaper-drenched. Without insulation, they were too hot in the summer and too cold in the winter. The main purpose they served was the incorporation of family life into campus life. Eventually they were sold to Mr. Robert Lynch, who agreed to take them down without burning them. The new family apartment complex, which kept the Bushnell name, went up quickly and was ready for occupancy in the fall of 1963.[4] The complex was of excellent design, but paucity of funds precluded sound-resistant walls between the apartments. The Tisdale family units constructed in 1973 were much better in this respect and gave a greater sense of privacy and individuality to each apartment.

The 1961 legislature also approved funds for a new library. Architectural plans for it raised debate because its modern, flat-roof design did not fit in with the architecture of the old quadrangle. Governor King named a committee "to study the situation"; as Francis Parker would have known, the result was a foregone conclusion. University of New Hampshire President John McConnell, chairman of the committee, said that although the "flat-roof design is not in congruence with the colonial-type architecture, the overwhelming majority of libraries being built today are made with flat roofs." Therefore, a library with a pitched roof could not be built in Keene, New Hampshire. The design of the library "happened" to be identical with the Lamson Library at Plymouth, begun several months earlier. As far as the librarians are concerned, there was, however, one great difference. The Lamson Library has a nice large basement, for storage. Both libraries were unique in that they were built, not all at once, but in stages over a ten-year period with a long-range need in mind. Thus, after the library was "finished" and dedicated in 1965, three other additions were planned for and made as the college grew. The last addition, in 1976, was nearly as large as the first three sections combined.

The Mason Library was unique also in that attached to it is the Monadnock region's only art gallery. The gallery was the gift of Beatrice Thorne Sagendorph. Her generous gift was originally conceived when she was an art student on the third floor of Hale Building. The room was hot and cluttered with art materials, and there was no place for students or faculty to show their works. Those poor conditions, plus the dedication of Professor Lloyd, made such a lasting impression that, when she was able, she made a gift of $30,000, her first of several, for an art center. Friends of the Thorne Sagendorph Art Gallery have made substantial additional

The special staircase and Barry Faulkner murals of Elliot Hall.

gifts from time to time.[5]

Two more buildings were completed in 1966. One of them, the Dining Commons, won the 1966 architectural design award of the New Hampshire Chapter of American Institute of Architects. The harsh rectangle design was abandoned, thus creating a softer, more pleasing building, one that residents can more easily "see around" on their way to the gymnasium or from Carle Hall and the Owl's Nests to Appian Way. The building is topped with a cement fascia band which is noteworthy, and the fascia supports are particularly pleasing to the eye. The second building, Randall Dormitory, has similarities to Morrison Hall, that is, the design is functional overall but takes into account the campus's older architecture. One account described it as being of " 'Contemporary colonial' design . . . to blend in with the other buildings." Randall pointed up a difficulty in town-gown relationships that expansion often brings because an eminent domain proceeding had to be invoked to acquire property belonging to Horatio Colony. The college had a similar situation in the 1950s with John Duffy when it needed land for the Butterfield addition to Duffy Court. Colony's scholarly nature and his disposition to will his property and his house with its educational artifacts to the college made the college's steps

*In February of 1980 Joan Mondale,
wife of the Vice President,
paid a visit to Elliot Hall.*

look untoward. The college had to acquire and build soon; and other alternatives augured for even more complications. Good relations were eventually reestablished to some extent. In his last will and testament Colony made the college's president (or designee) an ex officio member of the Horatio Colony Trust.[6]

On November 17, 1968, there was a grand celebration and dedication of three major new buildings: the Science Center, Adams Technology Building, and the new Spaulding Gymnasium. Ernest Hebert said that the new Science Center looked like a fortress. In a way it does, but the University of New Hampshire featured the building on its 1969-70 catalogue cover. The very sharp pitch of the roof over its entranceways, the planetarium, and the top-deck greenhouse break up the flatness and fit in with the surrounding hills. Both Adams and the new Spaulding Gymnasium are flat-roof specials. The design of each, however, called for a judicious interrelation of brick and poured concrete so that neither material is overwhelming to the viewer. With the completion of these three buildings, Zorn proclaimed that Keene State had "come of age." "We now have," he said, "the basic resources of a quality institution. . . .We ought not overstress the factors of bricks and mortar. Building and equipment can facilitate learning, but in themselves they do not teach."

South facade of the Fine Arts Center.

Before Zorn left he also got under way the college's largest dormitory, Carle Hall, which was ready for students in 1969. The same design was used for Belknap Hall in Plymouth. Belknap has been Plymouth's most trouble-free dorm. Carle Hall was Keene State College's most trouble-free building in its construction. Everything, said Robert Mallat, went like clockwork. In the 1970s it was one of the most troublesome residences, whereas Plymouth's most troublesome buildings were its tower dorms.[7]

Four buildings are associated with Leo Redfern's tenure. The most innovative were the Owl's Nests and the Tisdale apartments. One commentator in *Architectural Record* stated that one of the "most persistent student complaints dating even from the pre-hip, pre-beat, pre-Acid/Rock Pleistocenes was that educational institutions had become too large and depersonalized." Carle Hall and the 1970s students brought this point home with unexpected force.

Students began to talk of the need for privacy and quiet. Psychologists talked about the need for space, both mental and physical. Studies were made showing that students spend one third of their waking hours in their rooms and that their total room experience was equal in value to their total classroom and library experience. Because of this, architects came up with the suite design for dormitories in which large buildings were divided up into groups of three of four rooms of various sizes. It proved to be successful and required no more space than the traditional corridor dormitory.

Redfern, in his democratic fashion, set up a committee to study student desires for dormitory life. The result was the Owl's Nests, a combination, wrote Leslie Van Alstyne, class of 1984, of both the old and the new concepts. "The middle floor is similar to the corridor design, having mostly double-occupancy rooms and a common lounge and bathroom. The first and third floors, however, were designed in the suite fashion."

Although built somewhat close to each other, the Owl's Nests have been successful in taking care of students' psychological and sociological needs. While they have been highly successful in this regard, they were designed in total disregard of previous campus architecture. The Tisdale apartments, built to augment family living quarters, took into account some Owl's Nests principles and rectified the obvious deficiencies in the Bushnell apartments.

A significant acquisition in 1974 was Elliot Hall, which was purchased from the hospital before it moved to its new Court Street location. With it the college gained three full floors for office space and also another historic house of major significance. The house was built between 1811 and 1813 for Capt. William Wyman, son of Col. Isaac Wyman of Revolutionary War fame. The house was then owned by James Wilson and then by James and John Henry Elliot, who deeded it to the city as a hospital in 1892, and for whom it is named.

Originally a two-story house, the third floor was added after the Elliot occupancy. It remains, nonetheless, the best example of Federal architecture in Keene. Inside the grand entrance hall are mural paintings of Barry Faulkner, which pictorially describe the history of Keene in the nineteenth century. The companion building, south of Elliot Hall, Joslin House, came with the hospital purchase. It was built in 1902 as the Edward Joslin Home for Nurses and was made possible by a $12,000 gift from his heirs.[8]

The building that took much of Redfern's time as well as that of Trustee and State Representative Margaret Ramsay was the Fine Arts Center. They developed and were given support and assistance by many active alumni, Senators Clesson ("Junie") Blaisdell and D. Allan Rock, Keene State College's Robert Mallat, Representative Augustus Marshala, and indeed all the area representatives to the General Court, the fine arts faculty, and many others. The main controversy surrounding it was its location. Some trustees wanted it behind Elliot Hall. Art Professor Jack Marshall claims to this day that the overpass on the west side of the building was intended as a crossover of Hyde Street, and when Redfern and Ramsay finally convinced the board to locate the building at Brickyard Pond, it was placed there as designed overpass and all. Actually, the architects capitalized on the beautiful Brickyard Pond setting. They wanted to "lift" the building up as much as possible so that on approach to it one could view the pond and (hopefully also someday) a large fountain in the center of the pond.[9] The viewer quickly detects a few (but minor) defects in the building's design, but performers pronounce that it is one of the best such facilities north of New York City. The outside lights on the grand north side entrance hark back to the old triad lights of the first construction. Certainly the building is highly attractive without and highly functional within. It continues to employ the basic rectangle, but it is also a successful effort to maintain a tradition of campus aesthetics. It is a good conclusion for "the new construction."

25

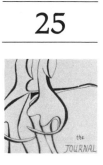

From Poetry to Demonstrations

T HE INTELLECTUAL ABILITY of students in the 1960s was good. Zorn hoped that SAT scores would never go below 500, and he was able to stick pretty well to that. He and Young before him had about three applicants for every opening. The male-female ratio evened out at nearly 50-50. After World War II it was never as bad as the women claimed. Rumor usually had it at 4-1, but that was a prewar ratio. In the postwar years the campus was usually 40 to 45 percent male. Of these, however, the T&I men often lived off campus or were married, whereas most of the women lived on campus and were unmarried. Looking out from a large female dormitory onto a quad of few all-male campus residences, many women no doubt perceived a sparsity of men; those enrolled in the elementary education curriculum classes saw further support for the rumor.

College life was exciting in the 1960s. Because of the selectivity, students were less concerned about *what* college they attended. "We were," said Ernest Hebert, "just glad we were in college." The 1960s was a decade of MERPs and MENCs, the end of the mayoralty and the beginning of Greek Week, a decade of twist, and twists of the twist, of continuing whist, of the Kappa Kapers and the Alpha Operas, of snow sculptures of poetry and poetry reading, of college bowls and Miss Keene State College pageants. There was intense interest in campus politics and international affairs, especially Vietnam, and finally a student strike and boycott.

The 1960s acquired such a reputation one is apt to forget how much traditional student life continued. The Miss Keene State College pageant, an authorized Miss America preliminary, continued throughout the decade. Greek Weekend (now Greek Week) got started in 1965 with chariot races, relay races, tugs of war, parties and election of Greek God. Thater (later TKE) joined Kapper and Alpher as the third social order on campus. Greek Week replaced the old mayoralty campaign which was always attended with a lot of hoopla, but not as much student participation. The first Greek Weekend even had an open whist tournament.

The Alpha Opera continued through the 1960s. Most plays still used the old theme of faculty weaknesses and foibles and were of considerable ability with the brothers doing the writing, music, staging, and the like. The Kappa Kapers also continued but declined rapidly in quality. Both of these annual events faded out in the early 1970s, killed as much by extremely short semesters as by anything else.

Chaperons were still required at college dances. The dances themselves continued to "progress" in faster body movement and in decibels as more and more electronic equipment was added to the orchestras. Orchestras? They would soon, and more fittingly, be known as "groups." The decade started off with a shocking new dance called the twist, which was replaced by others, such as the Monkey, the Potato, the Frugg. The *Kronicle* of 1965 headlined "THE TWIST IS OUT – THE MONKEY'S IN!" It wasn't very complicated: "you don't really have to know how to dance, just make like you're climbin' a tree and you're in!" If that did not help, there was more explanation: "Arms moving, eyes concentrate on nothing, let yourself go! You put your left arm in, you put your left arm out," and so on.

February was the month for mammoth snow sculpting contests during the 1950s and 1960s.

With the male-female ratio becoming ever more equal, the MERP Weekend became exceedingly popular. Coming from the home economics department, it provided an opportunity for girls to invite boys out for the weekend and stood for Men's Economic Recovery program. Restaurateur Michael Blastos was quick to pick up on it and ran ads in the school paper: "Merp him at Mr. Pizza!" or "Remember, girls, only at Mr. Pizza do you get your Beau's drink Free during MERP Weekend!" Boys enjoyed the free weekend and talked about getting "merped."

They did not talk, however, about getting "Mencked"! MENC was the Music Educators' National Conference. In the late 1960s the conference put on "Mencospectrums," in which student performers such as Tom Powers, Dave Colby, Wendy Fiske, and others led large sing-in crowds in traditional and contemporary songs.

There was the average number of editorials against apathy. In 1967 Phil Cournoyer ran an editorial, "♀ Equals Low Pay," and complained the next week that "not a word was said about it." He then endorsed Marxism in his next editorial, which brought a response only from William Loeb, but this pleased Cournoyer because, as Larry Colby said, "until that time, he thought he was the only one who read his editorials."[1]

Beginning in 1967 faculty member Peter Jenkins organized freshmen orientation and registration on a much more modern scale. This development continued through the 1970s, so that today the college clearly has one of the finest orientation programs in the Northeast. "It is unfortunate," stated the *Monadnock*, "that incoming freshmen will not be aware of all the major improvements instituted by Dr. Jenkins, but it should be noted that hazing will be at a minimum, there is more opportunity for incoming students to meet one another, and 'meet' the college."

Significant new clubs in the 1960s were the biology club, which sponsored a good reliable series of Audubon lectures; the international club, which offered several good programs but died out in the 1970s; and the nonresidents club, which did not survive the 1960s. It established, however, a "nonresident" lounge where nonresidents continue to congregate for coffee breaks and brown-bag lunches on the second floor of the Student Union.

In a mock election in 1964 students overwhelmingly favored Lyndon Johnson over Barry Goldwater, but by 1967 they preferred Richard Nixon in a primary sponsored by the Young Republicans.[2] In all these ways students and student life developed along expected or traditional lines.

In other ways the 1960s students were much different or, more accurately, there was a highly vocal, intellectual, dedicated, or idealistic minority of students who, like many of their national counterparts, gave the 1960s its special flavor. In tone and temperament they were similar to the "Young Turks" of the early 1950s.

Poetry

Students at Keene from the time of their first publication in 1914 have used poetry more frequently as an art expression than any other form. The number and quality of poems far exceed those of short stories, essays, cartoons, paintings, and sculptures. It has been a more or less constant output, but from about 1964 to 1970 the normal output nearly quadrupled. English Professor Malcolm Keddy was faculty advisor for *Insight*, 2 forty-paged booklets of poetry published in 1964 and 1965. Soon Sigma Pi Epsilon, a poetry society formed in the 1930s, had David Battenfeld as faculty advisor to the *Journal*, which came out from two and four times a year between 1966 and 1972. It featured, besides poetry, photo essays and short stories. Student poets not only wrote for the *Journal*; they also often collected and published their own works.

Sigma sponsored a number of poetry readings in which students read their own works or favorites from the masters. In February 1968 the group brought May Sarton to campus who stressed, no doubt to their dismay, "that it is considerably more difficult to write a book of poetry than it is to write a novel."

The poets had their own hangout, The Knothole, a coffeehouse on Roxbury Street where they met with like-minded souls from Nathaniel

Christopher Papazoglou conducting the "slave" (later changed to "service") auction in 1967, a fund-raising effort for Kappa Delta Phi.

Hawthorn, Franklin Pierce, and New England colleges, read poetry, sang, and played guitars.

No poem caused more comment than John Carton's "Prayer Before Prostitution." Very likely all the publicity and attention this one poem brought gave other poets hope that they too would receive attention. They could be sure that the next few issues of the *Journal* would be scanned rigorously by everyone. To be sure, many of them wrote much better poetry. Unfortunately, none received so much attention.

The poem as it appeared in the *Journal* in October 1966 is as follows:

Prayer Before Prostitution
John M. Carton

(written in the back seat
of a '59 Olds convert [*sic*] on
Saturday, October 12, '64)

Hail Mary—full of ale
The Lord is with thee.
Bested art thou by other women
And blessed is the fruit of thy womb
Jesus—if you get pregnant I'll strangle you.

afterthought

Holy Mary, Mother of God

Pray for us sinners
Now and at the hour
Of our death. Amen.

Letters poured into the administration, the *Sentinel,* the *Manchester Union-Leader,* and a few even to the *Monadnock.* Faculty advisor Battenfeld had to explain publicly how it was that such a thing could be printed. Father Valle, the Newman chaplain, did not like the poem. Loeb gave it a full editorial entitled "Garbage on a Pedestal." Fay Gemmell, the campus Protestant minister, wrote, "Be affronted, yes, my friends, but not at the poem or at Mr. Carton, [but] . . . at the picture he so boldly paints in words salty with his tears." The *Monadnock* rather sensibly said, "Read the poem for yourself and then decide."[3]

Activist students were also concerned about the college's size and its growth. Soon, we see, said the *Kronicle,* a "breakdown of communication. . . professors in little boxes, announcements on bulletin boards, paint splashed on canvas, purchase of all kinds of printed material. Fighting against numbers, we try to save the friendliness of Keene State amidst the mass of expansion."

Students became more politically active in the 1960s. The *Kronicle* in 1965 boasted: "We set up Robert Mallat, our Placement Director, for his win over Fred Fletcher for Governor's Council." William Joyce, an industrial education student, filed a petition in superior court to have his name added to the checklist. His petition raised the whole issue of residence requirements and the right to vote. Eventually through court decisions students were granted the right to vote in their college town. As the antiwar movement grew larger at the college, usually a student ran each biennium from Ward Five for the General Court. Usually he or she ran with an antiwar Democrat from the ward — and invariably lost. The possibility was always great, however. If ever 200 or 300 students would bloc-vote in Ward Five, they could put "their" people in. It was an intriguing idea but was always thwarted by early filing deadlines, the early September primary, and lack of time for organizing such a campaign. Nonetheless, in the late 1960s and early 1970s students ran regularly for at least one of the Ward Five seats. Often they also ran in Wards One and Three.

The most spectacular student campaign was in 1974 with David Gagne and Peter Ramsey as candidates. *The Wall Street Journal* later featured them in 1981 in a special article about the New Hampshire General Court: "it costs little to run for election, a boon for students," the *Journal* stated. "At age 20, Mr. Ramsey borrowed $37 from fraternity brothers at Keene

"So I Said To Those Wise-Guy Kids, 'Do You Know Of Anyone Who Is Living In Abject Poverty ...?'"

Keene State students got the better of presidential candidate Barry Goldwater in a debate over national wealth distribution on March 5, 1964. This satirization of Goldwater's views of the event by political cartoonist Herb Block received wide attention. Reproduced from Straight Herblock, *(Simon & Schuster, 1964) with permission of Herblock Cartoons, Inc.*

State College to finance his first campaign. 'My parents told me not to run. They said I wasn't qualified.' Now 28 and in his third term, he sits on the appropriations committee."[4] Behind this cute story was a political decision to oust Sumner Raymond from his seat in Ward One.

The campaign really began with an offhand comment after a dinner Leo Redfern was having with Thomas Bonner, president of the University of New Hampshire, Trustee Margaret Ramsay, and History Professor Michael D. Keller. Bonner had already announced his decision to leave the university and take a college presidency in New York State. Taking a look at the future, he said, "Well, if you do anything, get rid of Sumner Raymond." Raymond had served five terms in the House; he was on the Appropriations Committee and in line for the chairmanship. Raymond not only wanted to cut the higher education budget but had moved to cut the New Hope Center appropriations as well.

Keller became the campaign manager for David Gagne, Democrat and recent graduate, and for Peter Ramsey, a Republican (now a Democrat), who was in his senior year. Keller got Frank Easton, a student, to organize the students. The focus of the campaign, however, was not students and higher education, but the county courthouse, an issue that had been brewing for years. Some of the county delegation, like Raymond, wanted to build a new county courthouse in or near Fuller Park. Other delegates were more concerned about urban sprawl and preserving the vitality and the historic buildings of downtown. This, then, was the issue, and Keller made it unmistakably clear. The appeal, however, was to the pocketbook: "no new courthouse; no new taxes. Campaign 'buttons' consisted of 3 × 5 cards pinned on lapels which read simply, 'No Court House, No Taxes: Vote for David Gagne and Peter Ramsey.'"

After that, Keller recalled,

we ran a traditional campaign. We card filed every voter in the ward. We updated the checklist. We put Gagne and Ramsey out on the street every weekend, knocking on doors. We followed up with phone calls. The only money we spent was for some beer and one flyer at the end of the campaign, saying again, 'No Courthouse, No Taxes.'

Keller recalled that some people at the University of New Hampshire were upset with him and Redfern because of the campaign. If Raymond won, and the chances seemed likely (all student efforts up to this point had failed), he might slash the higher education budgets even more severely, and that was the fear. Both students had to win in order to knock Raymond out. Running a campaign for a ticket consisting of one Democrat

So many people in the doghouse around here, no room for the dog !

This cartoon accurately represented the feelings of many faculty during the Zorn years.

and one Republican also presented unusual problems. But then in the last week of the campaign came unexpected aid from the mayor, James Masiello. He endorsed both Gagne and Ramsey because of the courthouse issue. The real fireworks of the campaign then took place between Masiello and Raymond. Gagne and Ramsey continued to knock on doors; Masiello and Raymond continued to thrash it out verbally; and Keller and Easton continued to organize. Before election day there was really nothing left to organize — a rare circumstance in political history! The result was an overwhelming victory for Gagne and Ramsey. Katie Hanna, a Smith College student and a Keene native resident, had run a similar campaign in Ward Five with like results. "Two things stand out" in these upsets, commented the *Sentinel*, "the Court House controversey, and hard stumping, which the youngsters parlayed into victories."[5]

In a way, the Gagne/Ramsey victory was the culmination of student efforts in politics in the 1960s. The 1960s students, however, did not organize in the traditional ways. They were, in fact, against the traditional ways. They preached and hoped to convert people by their preaching. It was dramatic but not successful.

In the late 1960s, even with Zorn as president students gained more rights and clearer definitions of rights. This began with a dramatic issue of the *Monadnock* February 29, 1968. Banner headlines read: "COLLEGE SUSPENDS FIVE: Girls Given No Hearing." The case involved purchase and partial consumption of two four-packs of beer by five girls in Randall Hall.

218

Beyond that there was much else—national students' rights, Vietnam, Wiseman, Zorn, and so on. Other incidents in the case of the five girls made it still more confusing. A student counselor observed one of the students, who was of age, buy the beer, but she was in company with other students who were not of age. The girls thought that if the counselor did not like it she should have said something then. The young women were all good students and had been at Keene for two to three years. The counselor witnessed no wrongdoing and did not act until she suspected drinking was going on in the dormitory room. There were also the unclear issues of entering the room, the search, and the nature of the preliminary hearing. From this James Hicks, editor of the *Monadnock*, Marilyn Treat, Jack Brouse, and Lawton Bourne put together a blistering editorial attack:

> This past week five women were suspended from Keene State College. The facts concerning their suspension are on the front page of this issue. The facts alone should speak for themselves, but for the great flock of passive Keene State sheep who seem to care little about themselves and less about their fellows, THE MONAD-NOCK will point out the obvious and shameful inconsistencies surrounding the administration's handling of this case.

The editors found six inconsistencies. The first listed, and the most obvious, was the difference in treatment between girls and boys for such an infraction. The second dealt with the severity of the punishment, since the girls' records were generally very good. The remaining four dealt with procedure.

Zorn called the editors and the faculty advisor in and pointed out that the counselor was doing her duty, that the girls were guilty, and that normal procedure had been followed. Nevertheless, out of it all came that very spring a new policy allowing alcoholic beverages in women's dorms if the individuals were of legal age. The case also gave incentive to a faculty senate-student body group in drafting a new Student Handbook in which students rights were more clearly spelled out. In fact, the *Monadnock* headlined its appearance with "STUDENTS' RIGHTS ACHIEVED."[6]

Vietnam

Nothing in recent years had a greater effect on higher education than the war in Vietnam. One has only to visit the campuses of colleges and universities of Western Europe and Japan to catch a glimpse of what college life and attitudes were like in the United States in the 1950s. Vietnam erased the leisurely pace, the aura of calm reflectiveness of college life, the teacher and administrator as authority figures, and put in its place a hustle-bustle, a demand for relevance and practicality, more freedom of choice, a virtual end to the general education requirements, competence from teachers, but not necessarily from students.

Tony DiMichele wrote shortly after Johnson sent the first combat troops to Southeast Asia:

> Vietnam has become one of the most popular and most controversial topics of discussion. Not a day goes by without hearing it on the radio, reading about it in the newspapers, and most important of all [discussing it] among students. . . . The majority of students, I can safely say, are in favor of U.S. participation and justify it, but a small percentage of students are opposed to it.

DiMichele's assessment was correct. The minority of Keene never became a majority, but it did grow in size, and it usually controlled the *Monadnock*, the *Journal* and sometimes even the *Kronicle* (which was usually controlled by the Kappa brothers). Generally this minority were the activists on campus. They were Jeff Parsons, Ernest Hebert, Marilyn Treat, Jack Brouse, and Robert Higgins. The real spark plug for the movement, however, was James ("Jim") McDonald. Hebert later said, "We knew nothing about Vietnam, but Jim had been over there, and he said, 'it's nothing like what the government is saying.' He got us all the information on Vietnam."

Parsons in his first issue said editorially: "The *Monadnock* does not like war, the *Monadnock* does not like the situation in Vietnam. A solution to Vietnam must be found — quickly." In subsequent issues, Higgins and McDonald hammered away at United States policy. The next year an organization called People Concerned for Peace sponsored a day-long Vietnam seminar moderated by Robert Mallat in the gymnasium. Most of the speakers were critical. Jonathan Mirsky of Dartmouth said his Vietnam friends advised, "You must leave. You are so much worse than anything the Communists could bring to this country."

Eventually citizens, Constance Wood, Mary Gregory, and Joan Foldeak set up the Center for Human Concerns, which shifted around from various vacant offices in town as they became available. It counseled prospective draftees on procedures for claiming conscientious objection to the war. The center took on other projects, such as aid to the starving Biafrans. The center worked closely with activists on campus and, in December 1969, sponsored a "rap session" between student Domi O'Brien, Professor Thomas Stauffer, and Constance Wood on why the United States should get out of Vietnam.[7] Demonstrations continued as long as the war continued. The last sizable one occurred in the early 1970s when about 150 students from Franklin Pierce College joined an equal number of Keene State students for a grand march up Main Street around Central Square and back to the college. The leaders of the march carried a large sign which read simply "OUT NOW!" Antiwar sentiments were easily translated into local antiadministration sentiments.

The Wiseman Case

The acme of faculty/student versus administration tensions was the Wiseman case, which came to a head in the winter of 1968-69. Many people chose sides in this case because they actually had other axes to grind. Siding with Wiseman or with Zorn seemed to them to be the best way to express their views. By comparison, those issues were much smaller than the case itself.

Like all such cases, this one, too, had its tragic aspects. Both John Wiseman and Roman Zorn were men of ability and goodwill; both were bright; both held degrees in American history. Intellectually they were related in that Zorn was a Hesseltine student, as already mentioned, and Wiseman was a student of Horace S. Merrill, also a Hesseltine student and, as a graduate student, a colleague of Zorn's. All that, however, did not help in the personal relationship between the two men.

There was, in fact, a natural personality antagonism between Wiseman and Zorn. It started from their very first meeting in Silver Spring, Maryland, when Zorn was out recruiting new faculty. From that very first meeting Wiseman, who was busy concluding his graduate studies, believed that Zorn had taken advantage of him on the salary contract. When Wiseman completed all Ph.D. degree requirements before December of his first year at Keene State College, he expected a raise but did not get one. Zorn always maintained that he had hired Wiseman at the Ph.D. level and that Wiseman was merely fulfilling a part of the original agreement.

Before December, however, one or more students had complained to Zorn about Wiseman's classroom performance. When Wiseman persisted in the salary matter, Zorn maintained his original position, noting Wiseman's alleged teaching deficiency and lack of cooperation. Although to a degree true, Wiseman was incensed at what he felt was an unfair allegation considering his studies, his move to Keene with his young family, and his three class preparations. He felt that under such circumstances it was unrealistic to expect a winning daily lecture for every class. He had

LET'S KEEP A WISE MAN ON CAMPUS
"SING IN"

AT THE STUDENT UNION T.V. LOUNGE

WEDNESDAY, NOVEMBER 13, — 8:00 P.M.

*One of the many efforts during 1968 and 1969 made on behalf
of history Professor John B. Wiseman*

refused to teach a Western civilization course on professional grounds because his training was in American history.

Matters worsened in his second year when Wiseman became deeply involved in Eugene McCarthy's antiwar campaign. He and David Gregory of the biology department managed the McCarthy primary campaign for southwestern New Hampshire. They coordinated their campaign with like-minded people in the Nashua, Durham, and Hanover areas. The whole campaign was a stunning success, a major factor in the unseating of Lyndon Johnson. Part of it entailed gaining control of the state Democratic party, and in this effort Wiseman collided with Robert Mallat, who was with the Johnson forces and well, if only recently, established in the party. The struggle for Democratic city chairmanship in 1968 was particularly bitter, but contrary to some claims, this political infighting had nothing to do with Wiseman's contract not being renewed in 1968. As on other campuses, the political activists of the 1960s, whether logical or not, aligned the local college administration with the national political administration and its support of the Vietnam War. In some cases this was undoubtedly true, but it was an oversimplification.

The antiadministration sentiment was well phrased by Mario Savio, leader of the Free Speech movement, a student group in California, when he said,

> There is a time when the operation of the machine becomes so odious, makes you so sick at heart that you can't take part, you can't even tacitly take part, and you've got to put your bodies upon the levers, upon all the apparatus, and you've got to make it stop. And you've got to indicate to the people who run it, that unless you're free, the machine will be prevented from working at all.

Zorn was as independent in his thinking as Morrison, but in the late 1960s all administrators were linked as somehow being agents for, and as cooperators with, the presidential administration in Washington.

The Wiseman case then took a new turn when Pete Selkowe of the *Sentinel* interviewed Dean Edward Pierce over the phone and got the two reasons for the nonrenewal of Wiseman's contract: the complaint about teaching and "uncooperativeness." The write-up the following day in the *Sentinel,* later copied by the *Union-Leader,* made the affair public.[8] Many issues resulted from this, but the main one taken up by the student and faculty was a grand effort to keep Wiseman.

In the fall semester of 1968-69 one demonstration followed another on Wiseman's behalf. Students sent petitions to Zorn and to the board. The Faculty Association sent petitions. The American Association of University Professors sent petitions. Dozens of articles were written; there was a "Keep Wiseman Sing-In"; and "Keep Wiseman" buttons were issued.

Besides student activists already mentioned, Kenneth and Cheryl Paradis, Gary Jonah, Steven Skibnowski, Kathleen Doody, Anthony Rosinski, Martha Nitzchelm, and Dana Sullivan became active in the "Keep Wiseman campaign."

At the students' request, Zorn held a convocation on the Wiseman case on December 16, 1968. About 300 students assembled at the new Spaulding Gymnasium. Zorn – flanked by Dean Clarence Davis, Director of Administration Edward Pierce, and Howard Wheelock, history department chairman – reviewed the Wiseman case for about forty minutes. Zorn then allowed, as in a normal class, about ten minutes for questions. However, the situation was not normal, and after ten minutes there were still many questions from the floor. At least four students and one faculty member sought to be recognized when Zorn decided that "class was over" and left the gym. "The convocation was a complete farce... an insult to the students and faculty members present," said Marilyn Treat. Other students were upset. The student senate held an emergency meeting that night and announced a student boycott of classes, effective immediately, until: (1) the president apologized to the students, and (2) a new convocation date be set. Don Nelson, student senate president, was the one who had to deliver the "ultimatum" to Zorn. That night, when Nelson knocked on Zorn's door, he was received coolly, but graciously, into the house, and he told the president of the action. "You known," said Zorn, "this hurts me personally." He did not respond immediately to the demands, as was his custom, but that caused the student senate to call a boycott of classes. Tom Kearney took a picture for the *Sentinel* the next day of Professor Thomas ("Tim") Antrim in front of a nearly empty classroom. Overall, the boycott was about 50 percent effective. Finally, Nelson and Frank L'Hommedieu worked out with Zorn an acceptable statement, and a new convocation was set for January 9, 1969. Then a three-hour-long, inconclusive convocation took place, at which there was ample time for everyone to speak. In the meantime, Zorn had accepted a post in Nevada. After he left at the end of February 1969, there seemed to be another opportunity to retain Wiseman.

On April 22 another campuswide convocation was called with University of New Hampshire President John McConnell in attendance. This was the most dramatic of all the Wiseman demonstrations, with over 1,000 students in Spaulding Gymnasium. After several student leaders spoke, Jim McDonald got up and said that the students could force the retention of Wiseman. "WE CAN HOLD SCHOOL WITHOUT THE ADMINISTRATION," McDonald yelled into the microphone, "BUT THERE'S ONE THING THEY CAN'T DO. THEY CAN'T HOLD SCHOOL WITHOUT STUDENTS! THERE WOULDN'T BE ANYTHING FOR 'EM TO DO!" And the crowd went wild with cheering and yelling and stomping. A student strike of major proportions was obviously in the making. McConnell, a labor specialist, quickly recognized it.

McDonald's first resolution demanding the retention of Wiseman passed overwhelmingly. When McDonald offered his second resolution calling for "A peaceful strike to impress the trustees with our sincerity," McConnell quickly summoned a number of key faculty members for a brief meeting in Waltz Lecture Hall and promised them that the board of trustees would hear complaints from the entire campus that very Saturday. The young faculty thought they had something and agreed. On the other hand, McConnell did not know that, as he was promising a new hearing, the strike motion failed by a 514-380 vote. (Numerous abstentions were not counted.)

That Saturday there was still hope that the board would retain Wiseman. Nearly all those who spoke, spoke for him. The board's 12-2 vote to sustain the administration was a great disappointment. It represented the final victory for "the system" and another defeat for "the people." David Battenfeld of the English department more accurately assessed the situation when he said, "The issue is not really Dr. Wiseman's performance but the judgment by the administrators on that performance... I confess I can see no way out of this impasse without questioning the competence of the administrators themselves who made the judgment."[9] A number of students under the leadership of Marilyn Treat produced several talent shows to establish a Wiseman scholastic scholarship fund. One show, *Give a Damn,* was particularly successful. They earned about $1,000, which has now been merged into Keene Endowment Association funds.

The main consequences of the Wiseman case were (1) the establishment of FEAC (Faculty Evaluation Advisory Committee) to advise the dean on personnel decisions before they went to the president and (2) in the 1970s, at least, too much reliance on FEAC and abandonment by the administration of its old-time role. At one meeting in the 1970s the question came up about faculty teaching performance between Keene and Durham. Bruce Poulton, the chancellor, answered, "Oh, I wouldn't touch that with a ten-foot pole." Other colleges in the 1960s underwent similar experiences. The effect of all these cases on administrators of the 1970s is well summed up by Poulton's comment. The 1960s activist students carried their reforms and their momentum for a year or two more, and then their influence quickly faded. Their greatest achievements were — whether one agrees with them or not — student representation on the college senate, the practical abolition of the general education requirements, and dorm visitation rights (discussed in the next chapter). Their most dramatic expression was their efforts on behalf of John Wiseman and particularly the dramatic April 22 convocation.

26

Leo Redfern and the Redfern Administration

WHEN IN THE SUMMER of 1969 Leo Redfern became president of Keene State College, nearly everyone thought the golden age had arrived. When Redfern left ten years later, the majority were happy to see him go. It will be necessary to discuss the major features of this development in several chapters. In dealing with his administation, first, however, one sees two important aspects: (1) his own humaneness and his own laudable principles often did not serve him well as an administrator; (2) he had, despite many troubles, over the course of the decade laid the basis of a solid administration.

Leo F. Redfern, the son of Mr. and Mrs. Frank C. Redfern, was born on June 3, 1923, in Berlin, New Hampshire. He attended local public schools and the University of New Hampshire, where he was editor of *The New Hampshire*, the university newspaper. During World War II he served as an enlisted man with a fighter intercept squadron in the Pacific with its main base on Okinawa. After the war he worked for Arthur Adams, president of the American Council on Education. Undoubtedly it was this experience and his natural brightness that enabled him to win a base tuition scholarship for Harvard Graduate School, from which he earned his doctorate in 1957. There was intellectual excitement in Cambridge in the mid-1950s but without the tenseness of subsequent years. Course and performance standards, however, were often lax. The title of Redfern's dissertation was "State Budget Control over State Universities in New England," a problem he had run into both as editor of *The New Hampshire* and as assistant to Adams. Redfern commented:

> I came to the conclusion that government in general tries to control its institutions, including higher education, in a preaction mode, that is, through such devices as budget allocations and preaudits and central purchasing, rather than doing a thorough postaudit or management review, to see how well management accomplished its objectives as stated during the budget hearings. . . . My research indicated that legislators very rarely referred to the past biennium or year when they were considering a budget request.

Redfern taught two years at the University of New Hampshire and two at the University of Wisconsin before joining the administration at the University of Massachusetts, where he became dean of administration. His work there was liaison to the legislature. He was easy to approach, ready to listen and to learn, and extremely democratic. His qualities were highly desired in Keene in 1969.

Redfern had a basic trust in democracy and the democratic system. Actually, he trusted it too much. Redfern's weakness was the methods by which he handled problems. His two most often used methods were based on political science models, both involving exchange of ideas, compromise, solution, and goodwill because the democratic process had worked. The first method was to get people of opposing views together over a drink or in a congenial atmosphere in which each would get to know and appreciate better what the other was doing. The second method was to refer the problem to a broad-based committee and then follow the committee's recommendations. Had Zorn used these methods, he would have been an unquestioned success. These methods actually did Redfern good service, but they could not be used to solve everything.

Some problems required insight, good judgment, courage — problems that Zorn handled so well and that Redfern faced so reluctantly, sometimes not at all. Redfern deeply believed in the team spirit and the team effort.

Everyone was to try his best, and if everyone did so, we would "win."
"He was the best friend the faculty ever had," said James Hobart; but
Hobart significantly added, "in general, but not in particular." Indeed, that
was it. Redfern did not know how to deal with the rebellious spirits on
his team. Those spirits should have been on the other team, conservative
Governor Meldrim Thomson's team, and they should have been located
in the "enemy" camp, with the "tax-slashers" in Concord, not here in Keene
and on the faculty! Redfern could not reprimand or say no kindly, firmly, and effectively to one of his own "teammates."

A trustee once commented about Redfern: "He's a wonderful guy, but
what's going to happen when he has to say no?" Not only could Redfern
not say no (or at least not say no well), but neither, by and large, could
his deans. Had Redfern had strong, firm, nay-saying deans of the college,
he, as "court of last resort," could have modified some of their decisions
and thus remained popular and democratic. Neither of his two major
deans, however, took strong positions. That meant that some of the tough,
unpopular decisions were left up to Redfern himself. He hoped that the
problems would just go away. Of course, they did not. They smoldered
and smoldered until it was the accumulation of particular grievances that
was the undoing of his administration.

Quality judgments on individual performance were avoided if at all
possible. Programs, enrollments, votes, dollars, buildings — those things
involving quantity were the type of judgments that Redfern liked. Of
course, more was always better, and going with the majority was fun —
and it was popular.

When Redfern had difficult decisions to make, or when committee decisions went against what he wanted, he did not perform well. Hobart gave
an excellent description:

I think he personalized the job [too] much. He suffered great successes and
great defeats and had trouble coping.... When he felt good, and was having a
good day, and everything was going well for him, there was no more charming
person. He was a great raconteur and had a wonderful sense of humor. He was
a source of *Punch* magazines for me. He kept me happy for hours. But, many
days he did not feel good, you knew his stomach was churning. He had suffered
a defeat here... or some psychologicl muscle was being strained, and then he was
miserable; and he knew he was miserable. He would never direct that kind of
frustration against an individual, but the frustration was still there. It permeated,
and that put the organization in a very difficult position.... When the head of
the institution is unhappy for one reason or another — it's a real inhibitor.

Nor was Redfern a bookish man. He, of course, hoped that the library had a lot of books, and the right kinds, but he himself did not peruse them. His doctoral dissertation, while informative, was not of the rigorous kind that appealed to intellectuals. Yet one would do Redfern a great disservice if he stopped here in the description of him.

Even without the assistance of books, Redfern had a feel for the value of intellectual exploration. He made a number of important decisions that were not quantity-based judgments. He was more willing to commit time and money to experimentation and innovation than any previous president had been. One of his great achievements, as far as he was concerned, was the Fine Arts Building and its location at Brickyard Pond. In a way that, too, was quantifiable, but what mattered most to him was the fact that it enhanced the cultural atmosphere on campus and in the region. He supported classroom innovation, the Alternative Education (A-1) program, faculty internships in administration, the information retrieval system for the Library, the Owl's Nest concept for dormitory living, and the development of many new curricula, none of which was quantifiable.

"He had a fine mind," recalls Richard Gustafson. "He always enjoyed much more talking about the future than about the present. He was always talking with some group or another, 'Where are we going to be five years from now?' "

Redfern's method of changing personnel also did him credit, and was not much appreciated. If a certain person was not efficient or suitable to his or her position, Redfern always tried to get that person to take another position without any loss of face to the person involved and to the betterment of all concerned. When that method worked well, as it often did within his own immediate circle and with the departmental chairs, no one noticed anything unusual; and so Redfern got no credit. He was, however, so unwilling to embarrass anyone publicly that he tolerated not fully competent people in certain positions for too long.

Gustafson recalled:

> I know some of us who worked with him would say, "How can you allow that to continue?"... He would say, "Well, I'll talk to him,'... but you knew he had a heart of gold. So some people did get away with things that perhaps they shouldn't have.
>
> From my point of view, he provided a structure for people to be successful.... He gave assignments and expected them to be done. He was not checking your work every morning or every week. I liked that. He also had a good balance [of what was needed for the office staff]. He'd get people together who had been working hard, jump in a van go to Boston to see the Red Sox play. People appreciated that. He was also after people to make sure they took their vacations.

He said, "I know you can't stand me if I don't take my vacation. I feel the same about you."

In order to appreciate Redfern's efforts in building up an administration several facts must be taken into consideration. First is the fact that he inherited a basically weak administration from Zorn. Second, he was committed to changing this inherited administration humanely, which meant slowly. In addition to that, Dean William Whybrew estimated that about three fourths of the time in the 1970s one key position or another was in the process of being filled. That meant that most of the time decisions in one area or another had to be delayed until the new person could assume his or her duties. With all these limitations, Redfern began to piece together a solid administration.

The one strong administrator that was already in place was Robert Lester Mallat, Jr., generally referred to simply as "Bob" Mallat. No history of the college would be complete without some attempt to take his role in its development into account. His role has been no less than equivalent to that of a president, and he has on occasion acted as such. Some would say that he acted as such on too many occasions. His title, Director of Resource Administration is certainly comprehensive. He is deeply involved in plans for the future of the college and in major administrative matters.

Mallat first came to the college under Lloyd Young, as director of placement in 1962. As he recalled: "In August, Vangie [Ruskowski] called and wanted me to talk with Dr. Young right then and there, and I said that I was in my painting clothes and had just knocked down a plaster ceiling. He said he didn't mind, so I went over on a Wednesday and went to work [at the college] on Thursday."

Not far into the Zorn administration, Mallat became director of physical plant development. He recalled:

> I was responsible for all the capital budget. I was still doing placement, but I built Randall Hall, all three aspects of the Mason Library, and then the dining commons and Science Center, the gym, Adams Tech, Carle Hall, renovations to the Lloyd Young Student Union, the first six Owl's Nests, renovations to Elliot Hall, Tisdale apartments, and then the second set of Owl's Nests.

Not only has Mallat handled millions of dollars in contract money, but he had often acted as public liaison officer, the person who dealt with town-gown and town-state relationships. This came by virtue of his own active role in politics. While a college student, Mallat worked at White's Dairy Bar, which was located at the corner of Winchester and Ralston streets where "Mike" Blastos's Pub now is. Mallat said:

As I recall, my interest in politics developed as a result of being at White's Dairy Bar one evening and complaining about what was going on in city hall... and having a fellow tell me that it would cost me two dollars to change it, the two bucks being the cost of the filing fee to run for city council. I said that I might just do that. Now, I had been involved in the teaching of social studies, so I was not unaware of the obligation.... Once I filed and got elected in 1959, my interest became a sincere interest. I got involved very deeply in the John Kennedy campaign. Then I ran for mayor in 1961 and took office in 1962. I served four years [as mayor].

Thus, Mallat knew the workings of city government quite well. Subsequent elections to the Governor's Council and to the New Hampshire General Court made him familiar with important aspects of state government.

Mallat's coming to the college, however, was accidental. He had been working with Davis Engineering in Boston. He lost out there on a promotion to someone who had just received a college degree. The president of the new company told him that

if ever the time presented itself that it would be in my best interests to get a degree, and it didn't really matter, he told me, what kind of a degree it was, as long as it was a degree.... So when I came out of the service... my career objective when I enrolled here was to enroll [at Keene Teachers College] for a year, and then transfer to Northeastern and go into industrial management.

But by that time he was married, had a child, so he stayed at the college, graduating in 1958.

Mallat has performed in almost every conceivable role at the college. He has issued memos on room assignments, bookstore orders, and the faculty line of march. He traditionally heads the alumni parade and supervises the seniors for the graduation exercises. He teaches the defensive driving course and has taught college-level political science courses. As director of physical plant development, he had taken significant part in discussion with major builders and architects in the area which has given him a familiarity with the business community. He is also a landlord of modest proportions on the east side of Keene.

Mallat is prodigious in his work efforts; takes his committee assignments seriously; and spends inordinate hours on the school board, of which he has been a member since 1968. He has learned to familiarize himself with basic documents and rarely speaks without knowledge of the documents relevant to a particular case.

Mallat is often described as controversial. One reason for this is that he can, and often does, say no. Another reason is that he takes a stand, sometimes very early in the process. One who does that is the focal point of attention and criticism. While he is quick to criticize, he himself is sensitive to criticism. In public meetings he can appear to be pompous, edgy, abrasive. In private he is considerate, polite, humorous, and a thoughtful administrator. He has served four college presidents, and three of them have relied heavily on his judgments.

In 1972 James C. Hobart became dean of administration after having been city manager of Keene. It will be best to let him reminisce. He recalled:

The community and I got along very well. Keene is an unusually diversified and progressive community. It is disguised as a Yankee town, but in reality Keene is very modern, and I'm pretty modern too. The town was interested in such things as trees and sign control, and health ordinances, and building codes and inspections. There was a strong commitment for housing of low income and the elderly. It was a community that cared a lot about how it was growing, and I walked right into a situation tailor-made for me. I felt the same way, and there were a lot of people who were willing to work. A lot got done as far as I can tell.

As manager, Hobart supervised the redevelopment of Main Street south of the tracks and also the renovation of Central Square. Keene, he says, has "the best-looking downtown in all New Hampshire. It's a beautiful spot and people come there just to walk. It's like Portsmouth in that regard, only it's more organized."

On coming to Keene State College, Hobart recalled:

there was a small committee of six of us who met together once a month for lunch. We didn't broadcast it about, but we liked to think we controlled the town. These six consisted of Leo Redfern... and myself and Bill McGowan, the director of the chamber of commerce; and Jack Jordon, the director of the industrial foundation; Bob Wood, who was the president of the hospital; and John Day, superintendent of schools. We got together and complained about our respective boards of directors.... When Ed Pierce left, Leo and I were having lunch at the Black Lantern Restaurant — and I think I paid, as a matter of fact — at least he liked to boast that that was the least costly search he ever conducted. He figured out what my price was, and I said, "Yes, I'll do it." Three days later Decatur, Illinois, called up and offered me the job of city manager, but I had made my commitment and there I was....

The institution itself was sort of nervous about its administration when I got there. My purpose for the first couple of years was to open things up — make people knowledgeable about the data of the institution, what the budgets were, lay it all out on the table so that they could deal with the same facts and figures and have confidence in the operation. I helped organize the budget process.... The budget process is setting of priorities, and you put dollar signs on it — and the sharing of that information among all those allocations is a very important kind of mechanism.

That Hobart could recognize there were problems at the college beyond his own particular job description, but yet use his office to attempt to remedy these problems, shows that he was an administrator of unusual caliber. Not only could he see such problems and address them; he always conducted his office efficiently, and he communicated well with the faculty. On several occasions he was "caught" in the library reading a book! — and faculty opinion of him soared. It was a great loss to the institution when he left in 1977.

Redfern hired Richard A. Gustafson in 1973 as an assistant dean and director of career studies. This was done on the basis of the LRAPC (Long Range Planning Committee) report of 1972. Gustafson began work with faculty and staff to help develop more grants for the institution and also to work with faculty in developing career-related programs as called for in the LRAPC report.

Gustafson was a straightforward, open administrator and generally held the confidence of the faculty. Before he became vice-president in 1982, his contacts with the faculty were on an individual basis concerning individual grants. He thus had no jurisdiction over some of the important personnel decisions that caused so much furor in the 1970s. As time went on, both his administrative colleagues and his faculty colleagues saw that Gustafson was efficient, that he listened well, had a real knack for discarding emotion, and made judgments on good evidence. He also had a sense of humor! For these reasons he was easily elected vice-president of the college in 1982.

Joseph V. Stewart, with a Ph.D. in physics from the University of Rochester, was an assistant dean of the college for five years during the 1970s. He was generally regarded as not being efficient in detail administration. He was so decent a person, so honest, so intellectual that faculty generally were glad to have his voice in administrative councils.

Redfern hired Ronald J. Herron as dean of student affairs in 1977. Herron has a degree in student personnel administration from Columbia. He has a good sense of the faculty role in college life. He was quick to know their concerns, and he saw the ramifications of problems into all other areas of college life. He has also been up to date on the legal status of students and has understood the importance of social and intellectual experience of campus life.[1]

Michael Durfor-Simpson was hired to take charge of vehicles and work scheduling from 1976 to 1984 and has employed his efficient methods in budget, energy, and security management. In the meantime the capable Wayne Wyman became director of physical plant and Glenn Hipple in charge of vehicles. Redfern put Norma White in charge of the switchboard and Patricia Lilly in charge of the mailroom, both demanding and sensitive positions. Good public relations and good service have always been part of their performance.

While Redfern put together his own administration bit by bit, he was involved in larger administrations outside the campus, which had an effect on his own administration.

The Systems: The Consortium and the University of New Hampshire

Redfern was not president long before he invited Dr. Henry Munroe to address the faculty. Munroe was the chief officer of the New Hampshire Consortium of Universities and Colleges, sometimes called "Newhook" (which was not meant to imply a new entanglement) after its acronym, NHCUC or, more often, simply "the consortium." It was obvious during Munroe's address that Redfern wanted to join this group and saw advantages in it. Munroe's long-winded description of the consortium was hardly exciting. His main point was that, if Professor X from College A talked with Professor Y from College B, a number of great things might develop. The idea was very much in the Redfern tradition. As far as the consortium was concerned, some things actually did develop when Professor X talked with Professor Y. In real life Professor Frank Haley of Keene got together with Arthur West from New England College and approached Robert Friedman of Suffolk University. These three were then joined by Galen Jones from the University of New Hampshire, Lawrence Spencer from Plymouth, and Clifford Coles from Franklin Pierce College. They put together a statewide Marine Science program with a key station on Cobs Hook Bay in Maine. The consortium was also successful in putting together some other unusual cooperative programs.

NHCUC served Keene State particularly well. Due to a lapse in reporting, the college learned too late that it would lose over $184,000 in financial aid from the federal government. A large portion of Keene's enrollment depended on the availability of that money. Munroe came through beautifully in this case. He encouraged Redfern to appeal to the consortium to make up the difference. Redfern made the appeal, and the consortium voted without opposition to turn over part of their collective financial aid funds to make up exactly what Keene State had lost. The federal government was so impressed with this type of local cooperation and the magnanimous posture on the part of the participating institutions that it scouted around and found some national funds still unused, which it transferred to Keene as emergency aid. The generous consortium members actually did not have to give up any of their own funds.

The consortium was a loose voluntary federation, and Redfern was always fond of it. When one spoke of "the system," however, he referred to the University of New Hampshire system. The System was really created by the 1963 legislature when Keene and Plymouth became state colleges and parts of the University System of New Hampshire. Like the consortium it, too, was amorphous and undefined or ill-defined, but it was stronger. It presented greater opportunities and greater difficulties. It certainly caused Redfern many more headaches than the consortium.

John W. McConnell was president of the University of New Hampshire from 1963 to 1971. It is best to let Redfern reminisce about McConnell's role in the System. McConnell, Redfern said, was

a kind of primus inter pares among the presidents, but he was more equal of the equal. Being a labor negotiator, by profession and training, he played it very well. He kept it loose because it was a fuzzy structure. McConnell tried several times to get the trustees to focus more sharply on what it was they perceived the System to be. On the other hand, I think he felt it needed a period of maturation before it became too formalized. He was very astute in that regard, but it meant that there was some uncertainty as to what the respective roles of the institutions were in this new System concept.

The next University of New Hampshire president, Thomas Bonner, more forcefully played the two roles of university president and president of the System, which Bonner enlarged even further by developing an extension college, the School of Continuing Studies. By 1974 the legislature added a new function to the role of the board of trustees. It empowered them simply "to appoint a chancellor of the university system." In an opinion the attorney general defined the "interrelationships" of the various institutions. In that opinion he stressed the independence of the component parts. In another opinion he elaborated on the "integration of functions" of Keene and Plymouth "into the university system as need for integration arises."[2] The latter opinion appeared to give the System a relatively strong hand.

After Bruce Poulton was hired as chancellor in 1974, Redfern had de facto a new system to deal with. "A definite framework of a system and

Margaret Ramsay, class of 1956, who served as Alumni Association President, member of the UNH Board of Trustees, and as Representative to the General Court at an alumni area meeting in Claremont in 1976 with Senators James A. Saggiotes (left) and Clesson J. Blaisdell.

its purpose and what the respective roles of the constituent units of the system were to be never really existed," said Redfern. For instance, Redfern claimed that in some states, such as Kansas, the role of the System was clearly spelled out to be service to the individual members. In other states the System was much more powerful and was an entity unto itself. Redfern preferred the first type but feared that the second type was developing in New Hampshire. Further, he claimed the System caused a "kind of schizophrenic role" for the presidents. "Were the presidents to work together as a team for the chancellor... or were they to be spokesmen and champions for the respective campuses?" Third, what "should be recognized is the removal of many policies and standards from the campus level to the system level and the trustees — such as many aspects of fiscal management, the use of reserve funds at the [individual] institutions, for example, is taken over by the finance committee."

One advantage of the System was its united front to the legislature. "Following the separation of functions," commented Richard Gustafson, the System "began to emerge as a powerful political force in the State.... Over the next several years the university and the state colleges did quite well in obtaining their share of the state's appropriation in support of public higher education. The chancellor also began to develop a staff in financial planning and resource allocation and [hired]...highly qualified professionals to help in this process."

That public higher education did so well during the Thomson years, 1972-78, was undoubtedly due in part to the political effectiveness of the System. "I fought the university to help the teachers colleges, you know," said Senator Nelle Holmes. "Now, of course, I'm fighting the whole bunch of you."

When a more favorably disposed governor, Hugh Gallen, entered the office in 1979, it appeared as if the University of New Hampshire System as a political force got overconfident. The 1981 System budget was subjected to many deletions, and the System itself was the object of a blistering attack by the conservative Senate President Robert Monier. Even Christopher Spirou, a liberal Democratic leader in the House, admitted that higher education had not properly done its homework and that he himself was that year reluctant to come to its aid.

Probably the greatest advantage of the System was having one agency in charge of coordinating public higher education in the state.[3] Having to clear new programs through SAPC (System Academic Planning Council) might at times be frustrating. By it, however, New Hampshire tried to avoid the duplication and planlessness that had plagued other states. Evaluation of the System, however, is much beyond the scope of this book. Suffice it here to say that it was a new type of administration of which Redfern and the whole college were a part. All benefited from it, but it caused Redfern many headaches, which the local campus never realized.

While Redfern dealt happily with the administration of the consortium and less happily with that of the System, he was, over the decade, putting together a strong, able administration in Keene.

27

Democracy at Work
in the College Senate

THE COLLEGE SENATE quickly became a focal point of democratic activity under Redfern's administration. Never before had the college senate undertaken so much. Some of the activity will no doubt astound later generations. In 1973, for example, 133 documents were debated and acted upon; 113 the next year; and 114 in 1976. That averages out to 15 issues per month! The 116th meeting of the senate, in April 1978, held five different sessions for a total over fifteen hours; and thus finally was the 116th meeting of the college senate concluded. By then, of course, it was time to begin the 117th meeting.

Even before Redfern came, in the spring of 1969, but after Zorn left, the Senate voted to expand student representation from three to fifteen members, making a total senate membership of about forty-five persons. After Redfern assumed duties, the students with their interests and ideas of reform and the faculty with theirs rushed to the senate to get their proposals enacted. Each senator could bring up whatever he liked and speak as long as he liked. It was glorious democracy. The trouble was that with so much business and so much talk the end of the year, particularly the months of April and May, became one big, long senate meeting as far as the senators were concerned. Senate meetings went past the supper hour. A bylaw to end meetings at 6:15 P.M. had to be passed so that student senators could get supper. That meant that at 6:15 the senate often recessed rather than adjourned, and two and three recesses were not uncommon

Groundskeeper Henry Oya shows Leo Redfern how democracy works on the college hedge.

before a session's full agenda was completed. Eventually a bylaw limiting debate to fifteen minutes was passed, so that debate had some reasonable limit.

The great changes that went through the senate between 1969 and 1972 were sponsored by 1960s students or by faculty with the 1960s students in mind. By the time it came to implement these changes, the whole nature of the student body changed, and therein lay a good bit of the problems of the 1970s.

During this era the semester was shortened from 16 weeks to 14 (sometimes 13½) weeks. Further, the college senate adopted a performance-only policy rather than an attendance policy. According to Senate document 69/70-24, "Attendance shall not be a criterion for evaluation." Students set up measures to evaluate faculty performance, and in 1973 they even published the results of their evaluations. Some faculty nearly died of mortification at their grades, now made public. Steve Skibnowski, chair of the Student Affairs Committee, persuaded the fraternities, for a while at least, to abolish hazing. All these provisions were debated extensively, but not nearly so much as the new policy known as parietals.

Parietals was a new word of the 1970s — almost as popular as "beootiful," and "soopa!" [super!] If one remembered Latin well enough, he remembered that *parietes* meant walls or rooms. Parietals thus came to mean the privilege to visit rooms previously forbidden. Hours and hours of debate, thoughts and second thoughts transpired before the policy was established for all dormitories. The policy began first in the spring of 1969 when parietals were approved for Huntress Hall, which was then a men's dormitory. For the first time in the college's history a young woman could legally visit a young man in his dormitory room. At first the visitors were limited to certain hours on the weekends. The next year other men's residences were included. Then the women's dormitories were included. Then the weekend restrictions were lifted. At first Dean Ernest Gendron reported carefully on the new procedure: such as giving a day-by-day account of the total number of visitors and problems which arose. A sample report ran:

Problems: Unkept Rooms, Solution: Guest will be asked to leave if room is not satisfactory to persons in charge of visiting hours. Problem: Nude posters on walls during visiting hours, Solution: Left up to person on duty to administer as he sees fit. Problem: Doors shut while entertaining guests (no other problems were evident), Solution: Official reprimand on the part of the Judiciary Board was given and suspension of visiting hours were recommended upon further infraction.

In the fall of 1970 Carle Hall, originally designated as a men's dorm, became coed, and Huntress again became a woman's dorm (and the resident ghost became even more active). On March 10, 1971, the senate abolished most of the remaining oldtime regulations. At that time abolished in very quick succession were: dress regulations, campusing as a punishment, sign-in, sign-out regulations, and all curfews. The senate with good majorities then proceeded to extend parietals to such an extent that overnights, while still not technically legal, were for all practical purposes in effect.[1]

The faculty, too, realized their ambitions. Redfern was adept at naming committees. Soon 34 faculty committees (of a total faculty of 110) were in operation, each planning and proposing resolutions for the senate and each solving problems that existed under Zorn's presidency. Further, each of these committees used college facilities and met to its heart's content. There was no longer a worry about coming up with an anti-administration proposal or a proadministration proposal. They were all simply proposals, and they would be voted up or down [usually up] on the floor of the senate.

The disciplines in particular had a hey day in the senate. Zorn had kept a close tab on what was taught and who taught what — and how well he or she taught it. Now disciplines began renumbering their courses without restriction but according to new senate-adopted numbering guidelines and proposing new courses by the dozens. Even new majors sailed through the senate. Academic disciplines had such success that Senator James Quirk reported that the Interim Curriculum Committee, "sometimes called the 'railroad committee,' was not called upon to function this year." Previously the senate debated new course descriptions word by word — only to find out each September that an ad hoc committee had "railroaded" through a dozen or so new courses because of some exigency or another. Often the faculty were upset by the surprises that related to their disciplines. Quirk's comment indicated that the faculty were at last in control of their own curricula.

Faculty were so involved with committee work, new student regulations, debate, and the discussion of the new athletic program that they paid little attention to one of the most important proposals passed by the 1970-71 senate. That was the new general education requirement, which allowed a student many options in choosing his "general education," that is, the courses normally required in the first two years of college. Under the new regulations, the student needed six semester courses in three disciplines of the humanities, four courses in three disciplines of the social sciences, and four courses in two disciplines of the sciences. The matter was taken up at the end of a Thursday, that is, at a recessed session. It passed with virtually no debate. One reads in the minutes only "motion carried" and "adjournment at 6:16 p.m."[2] Few faculty could imagine students wanting a degree with absolutely no history, literature, mathematics, economics, or foreign language. They soon learned that many people wanted a degree but not an education. By 1980 most faculty questioned whether they had acted wisely in 1971 or not. It must be added, however, that nationally other colleges and universities were going through the same thing. The administrations approved; the students approved; and the boards of trustees approved.

One reason there was not much time for debate on the new general education requirements was that most of that March 4 meeting was taken up with a discussion on the repeal of the "Smart Resolution," one of the most controversial senate enactments of the early Redfern years. Smart, an at-large faculty senator, was the author of two resolutions, which were passed at a special meeting of the senate on May 6, 1970. The first called for an expansion of sports to be in the direction of intramurals. That passed by a 30-4 vote and was never the basis of controversy. Actually, it was the more important resolution, but one of those statements about which everyone agrees but about which nobody does anything. The second

An active and competitive intramural sports program has been a college tradition.

resolution was controversial and came to be known as "*The* Smart Resolution." It "resolved that no amount of money from college funds of any kind be spent for recruiting athletes, and that the college receive no aid of any type from any organization or association for the purpose of recruiting athletes." That passed 18-16.

Redfern was very much disappointed that the second resolution passed because he wanted to have winning athletic teams. Basketball Coach Glenn Theulen had just organized a local boosters club, the Keene State College Athletics, Inc., for that purpose. Winning teams were seen as a way of building up good school spirit, community relations, and quick recognition. Smart, however, had evidence of irregularity in the admissions of athletes, in proportionately more damage of their section of Carle Hall where they were housed in 1969-70, and the arrest records for criminal break-ins at the Brentwood Golf Course and the Student Union by several members of the new winning basketball team. Further, he and a number of his colleagues believed that students should be recruited on the basis of intellectual ability and that all sports programs should be tailored to students recruited primarily for intellectual and/or professional goals.

An older student senator, Jack O'Brien, introduced a motion in the 1970-71 senate to have the "Smart Resolution" repealed, and that was the main emotional topic for the day. Academics feared that the sanctity of college life was being taken advantage of by athletic programs and events, the distracting sideshows, as Woodrow Wilson called them. Many coaches and their supporters felt that their role in college life was neither understood nor appreciated by those who had these concerns. It was after the failure of the O'Brien motion and all the catharsis that that entailed that the new general education requirements were taken up. They were postclimactic, and the senate treated them as such. The results, however, were far-reaching. The very purposes of higher education, which are to give one wisdom from studying a broad cultural background as well as a specialty in his own particular major, were queered. The problem was compounded when many local high schools, following the lead of the colleges, also adopted the elective system for their general education requirements.

Recruitment of athletes continued despite the "Smart Resolution," and the 1970s was a decade of many winning athletic teams. Soccer coach Ronald Butcher wrote:

The decade of the seventies were the glory years for the athletic teams. The men's basketball, cross-country, soccer and swimming teams represented the college, the state and the New England area at no less than 19 national championship events. Women's sports became an integral part of the program and the basket-

Five players leave the ground in a tough bout with New Hampshire College. In white jerseys are Ian Wilson (left, All American, 1981), Chris Morrill, and Bert Poirier (9).

ball and softball programs had regional success. Add the numerous all-conference, all-New England and All-America selections afforded some 30 student-athletes and it's quite an achievement!

Butcher's soccer team starred often between 1971 and 1981 by going to the national playoffs seven times during that period. Some teams were really outstanding, especially those of 1971, 1974, and 1978, when Keene came in second nationally. The basketball team went to the national NIAI playoffs in Kansas City three times, in 1972, 1973, and 1977.[3] Under Athletic Director Joanne Fortunato's impetus, the whole athletic program moved from NCAA Division III to Division II competition in 1983. It is posited that this move will produce better scholastic students as well as better athletes.

Student leaders, Patrick Coughlin, Duncan Berkeley and Nancy McNamee raised the whole issue in 1984 as it had been raised in 1970 of who should support athletics. The athletic budget became ever larger, and was dependent upon student enrollment. By 1984, $57 of the student activity fee was earmarked for athletics, and only $14 for recreational sports despite the fact that a larger portion of the students (as many as 1,300 in 1983-84) participated in intra-mural type activities, the necessary ingredient to a meaningful college life. In a referendum February 6-8, 1984, with 14% voting, students decided 3-2 to transfer $9 from the athletic

Women's soccer achieved distinction in 1983 through excellent performance and the naming of Coach David Lombardo as Coach of the Year by his peers on a national level. The women's field hockey team under Coach Edward C. (Chuck) Sweeney and the gymnastics team under Wallace and Jan Eyman have also performed extraordinarily well.

budget to the intra-mural budget.

Talk arose in 1970 of athletic scholarships; and questions developed about comparable academic scholarships. There were none, although there had been various forms of student aid since the creation of the Harriet Lane Huntress Fund in the mid-1920s. Redfern then did a remarkable thing. He established ten scholastic scholarships *a year.*[4] Scholastic ability alone was the determinant. Through these scholarships many students of excellent mental caliber have been added to the student body.

The high point of senate power undoubtedly occurred in 1974. In the spring of 1972, Peter Ch'en, controversial head of the history department, convinced the Academic Council and the dean to recommend that some money earmarked for faculty raises be used for new faculty positions. At this time there were also some personal faculty grievances not properly attended to. As a result of these factors, the Welfare Committee of the senate took the unprecedented step of legislating how faculty raises would be divided. The committee's proposal passed the senate on April 4, 1974. Never before had — and probably never again will — such a body dictate how the faculty would receive its raises.

Never had the faculty had freer reign. It determined what courses would be offered and when, prerogatives few institutions have. It debated freely anything and everything it saw fit to debate. When Hobart said that in general the faculty never had a better friend than Redfern, he was undoubtedly referring in large measure to Redfern's commitment to democracy at work in the college senate.

28

Experimentation

ONE OF REDFERN'S characteristics, Gustafson noted, was a penchant for thinking about the future. He was willing to test new ideas. "I felt," recalled Psychology Professor David Andrews, "Redfern was very eager to try new things at the college." "He told me once that his approach to the management of the curriculum and of other things was to allow or to encourage activities to burble up from below and take what ideas people had, to try to find ways to develop them further, rather than proposing a set of programs and structures and beating them down people's throats." Whether or not Redfern could distinguish the weeds from the good fruit in the faculty's garden of ideas caused unease. Nonetheless, he was more given to educational experimentation than any previous president.

Michael Franklin of the education department suggested some unusual classroom innovations for two rooms in the basement of Rhodes Hall and for Room No. 74 in Morrison Hall. Redfern adopted the suggestions. In Rhodes the rooms were carpeted, furnished with couches, easy chairs, and floor ash trays. The room in Morrison, soon to be known as "the arena," had tiers of colosseumlike benches, also carpeted, on which were scattered a few pillows here and there. Conducting class in "the arena," the professor could, if he were so disposed, could lie down on a bench or curl

As the college grew in the 1970s trips in college vans became common and close friendships were made through these experiences. Here a group of fifteen leaves the campus on the first leg of a trip to York, England, as part of a student-teacher exchange program.

up with a pillow. All these were efforts to make the classroom — and, hopefully, learning — more congenial, less formal, and less formidable. Soon, however, the pillows disappeared from "the arena," and the benches were uncomfortable without them. The ventilation and the heating in the basement of Rhodes Hall were poor. As a result, these innovations were at best only moderately successful. They were, however, modifications of the traditional desk, podium, and blackboard setting.

Another experiment was the 4-1-4 school calendar. By it the first semester ended before Christmas. After the New Year there was a month-long winter term. The second semester began in early February and ran to the end of May. Faculty traveled in January if they could afford it. If they could not, they either carried on their research projects or taught in the January term for extra pay.

The faculty always believed that the administration did not promote the 4-1-4 calendar sufficiently. The biggest factor in putting an end to this experiment, however, were the parents of traditional Keene State College students. For them the January term was an extra financial burden if they sent their sons or daughters to it. If they did not, the students lay around the house running up the food, heat, and light bills. Parents let the administration know that they preferred the old schedule. After two years of experimentation, this calendar, so beloved by the faculty, was discarded for one preferred by students and their parents.

The greatest, the most controversial, and the one that can be taken as the best example of experimentation of the 1970s, however, was the Alternative Education, or A-1, program. This program was proposed by Professor David Andrews, Music Professor James Bolle, and Don Land, professor of computer science. Each of these men was over six feet six inches in height. They made, indeed, an impressive presentation. Faculty were not fully impressed with their program, however. Their program had several models. One was the experimental Hampshire College, recently established in Amherst, Massachusetts. Another was the Summer Hill School, promoted by Carl Rogers, who taught that people are bound to do well if their environment is nurturing. He is often considered the father of the "free school" movement of the 1970s. Another model was Philadelphia's Parkway Program — the "school without walls" — that developed in the late 1960s.

The A-1 program was to appeal to "the 'creative' student rather than [to] the 'achieving student.' " The idea, Andrews recalled,

> was to try to create some sort of program which would enable people to (1) develop some skills rather than plunging them into things they were not quite ready for and getting them frustrated in the fact that they did not achieve well in them but also (2) to utilize the opportunity to select things to work on as a way of helping them find their own abilities and skills, to develop a clearer set of motivations, to have some academic experiences that were satisfying, that they could achieve something that they value, rather than always getting B minuses or C's in things we value. . . . The basic idea was to create something where students had more involvement in decisions about what they would be doing, as a way of helping them while in college. That was one of the reasons it was designed to be a two-year replacement of the general education program.

The senate debates on it were long. Senator Peter Jenkins thought that the proposal was not specific enough and that "it would be giving the [A-1] school a 'blank check.' "[1] The senate gave the proposal a two-year trial period.

The program had major problems all along. First was the A-1 house, 32 Emerald Street, which was to house most of the students. The old Fairmont Hotel was, wrote Clair Wyman, "a rambling, rickety building of uncertain vintage and unsavory reputation." Further, it was not properly prepared. The landlord lived out of state and was difficult to deal with, according to Andrews. It violated a number of city regulations. As a result, twenty-two of the first forty-six students assigned to it had to be reassigned at the last moment. Nonetheless, seventy-two students enrolled in the program with a great deal of enthusiasm in the fall of 1971. Some of the results were spectacularly successful. Students were working successfully with the New Hope Center, local forest rangers, and veterinarians. Others studied Oriental art, Indian history, various forms of writing, child psychology, photography, cancer research, nutrition, botany, and chemistry. Some were at MIT with the United Science Study Project. Most of these experiences were not available in the regular curriculum.

Don Land once described it as a system to beat the system. The real trouble with it was that this "nonsystem" had no administration. Bolle was the only salaried member — and that only for the first year. The program really needed its own paid administration. Those running it did not have the time to properly supervise so many individualized programs. Andrews once estimated that he often worked up to 110 hours a week on the program. Soon the volunteer help wore out.

Inevitably students took (and got) credit for the most unusual courses, given by people of very questionable credentials; but at least these people were giving their "expertise" freely. Some music faculty, to cite only one example, were upset to see students given credit for basic music courses, which in turn would qualify them as music majors. These regular faculty were convinced that such students could not pass the basic courses in the regular music curriculum. Andrews always insisted, probably correctly, that the unsuccessful cases got ten times the publicity the successful cases did.

In 1972 there was even talk about giving the A-1 students six credits for their communal experience. That was defeated in the senate. The following *Equinox* interview shows why many faculty were skeptical of the results of the program. "The purpose of the house was to incorporate the living and learning experience of college life," the *Equinox* stated as an introduction to an extensive multiple interview. "The house had no connection with the college other than the fact that its residents were students. The entire household was run by students who, besides cleaning, were responsible for cooking, purchasing food, and renovating the house."

Del: "The building itself was a physical wreck."
Sue: "Why did Alternative One house fail?"

April: "I think it didn't. It succeeded."

Ted: "Only, success in its failure."

Sue: "Why was that a success?"

Ted: "I learned that if I was ever in a situation like that again it would work, because I learned that there's no one to f— — — but themselves. Living together in the house, we had notices about doing dishes for other people, but somehow we didn't have the sense that the only people we were hurting was us — whatever the situation was, was because of us."

Sue: "Just things like keeping your room clean, little garbage ditty things that really added up once you had 40 slobs living together. . . . I was talking to some people who live on campus towards the end of last year and one of the things we came up with that was really funny was that people in the dorms are more into the whole "freedom trip" in a lot of ways than the people at the A-1 house were. Like parietal hours and the bullshit at Carle Hall that no one pays any attention to."

Ted: ". . . It makes sense that a lot of kids would feel better living in a dorm situation, because it's more what their used to . . ."

Sue: "What do you mean, it's more what we're used to?"

Ted: "What we were not used to was living on Emerald Street, in that situation. Chaos, no order at all."

Pat: "In the dormitory I felt stifled."

April: "Yeah, so did I, except we got away with murder."

Del: "I think that there was a lot more activity in the A-1 house with drugs than there was in the dorms."

Ted: "I don't think so."

Pat: "I think it was more open and obvious to all the people involved than in the dorms on campus."

Del: "OK then why was it more open and obvious?"

Pat: "Because we all lived in the house together in the situation that we were in."

Sue: "We weren't uptight about any dorm counselor coming in . . ."

Ted: "It was something to do together, getting wrecked."

April: "The thing I really liked about the house was that if you were depressed there was always someone there to listen to you, and if you really wanted to get it on there was somebody to get it on with. If you wanted to talk intellectual bullshit about something, there was someone to talk intellectual bullshit with."

Del: "It's sort of a unique thing now, to have been at the A-1 house, because there aren't many people left who were there. It's sort of become a myth, a legend in its time. . . ."

The incorporation of drugs into the A-1 house was a sad thing according to Normand Michaud, an A-1 student. One of the students was a Buddhist, very naive and very loving. In his efforts to convert someone he invited into the house a cynical drug hustler. Drugs were easily obtained on the public streets, but according to Michaud not only their presence in the house but the way they got there was particularly unfortunate. Andrews, who has kept track of the former A-1 students, and particularly the ones in this interview, noted that they have since then made adjustments and established themselves successfully.

Andrews admitted before the senate that "many mistakes and bad judgments were made in the early parts of the program."[2] Ten years later Leslie Thayer, who was in the program, thought that it was neither so bad as often believed nor so great as sometimes claimed.

The A-1 program attracted a number of students to the college who would not otherwise have come. In the first year the drop-out rate was about 50 percent. Eventually most of the A-1 students went back to college. In A-1, said Andrews, students had to confront their own lack of direction. Andrews commented:

What concerned me most [on the death of A-1] was that there would cease to be the kind of laboratory for experimentation, that one of the big advantages of the program was that a lot of moderately risky kinds of . . . things were tried. There were other things that were wise and overdue, which by virtue of its being separate did not really taint anybody else. If they looked OK, one could move them over. It was a testing ground of sorts, and that does not exist anymore — with the contract course and the individualized majors, a little, but there is no oversight to any of it. . . . The option for creating new courses, trying things out, just to see where the interest lies, is wholly in the Continuing Education office now. That's a funny operation — in that people view it as not really being related to us at all, but being a kind of entrepreneurial activity on the part of Howard Croteau [Director of Continuing Education]. His motive is mainly to keep his operation afloat and profitable and not somehow to catalyze anything at the college in general.

Stemming directly from the A-1 program were the experimental 199 and 399 courses which a faculty member may "float" once to determine student reaction. From it also came, as Andrews noted, the contract major and a number of individualized courses. Further, from all this experimentation, the college got a good idea of the types of courses students wanted, and new majors and curricula were developed on that basis. Students "voting with their feet" became sacred scripture for the 1970s.

Andrews also noted that there were all sorts of problems in translating for the registrar just what A-1 experiences satisfied what general education requirements. By the time the program ended, Andrews was just getting a good system for commuting A-1 experiences into the general educa-

The construction of the owls nests was an attempt to improve the quality of dormitory life.

tion requirements. By the end of the second year the program was a much different program than at the beginning. Undoubtedly so. But the college senate had heard so much adverse publicity about the program that it decided against extending its life.

Alternative 1 was probably the boldest such program in the state, but it was not the only one, not even in the Monadnock region. In 1972 a free high school organized and began operations at the old GAR Hall on Mechanic Street, but the students left that building a wreck at its closing a year later. At Franklin Pierce College, Taylor Morris's course, "Philosphy of Walking," evolved from a student walk to Nova Scotia. It was a combination alternative education and outward bound course, and Morris got a book out of it. The A-1 program was one of a couple of dozen college-level programs in the country at the time that sought to provide a different kind of educational experience.[3] It was a tribute to Redfern's openness of mind that he accepted Andrew's, Land's, and Bolle's ideas so easily.

An experimental program that Redfern himself instituted was the Faculty Internship in administration. He began the program in the early 1970s when Thomas Havill and later Thomas Stauffer were made assistants to the president. Their course load was reduced 50 percent, and they devoted half of their time to administration. Eleanore Vander Haegen, Charles Weed,

Stuart Goff, and Merle Larracey served faculty internships under the dean. The program was not as novel as the Alternative 1 program, but it was new, experimental, and on the whole, successful.

Program Development

In the 1950s and 1960s junior colleges had a spectacular growth in the United States. A number of states built so many junior colleges and built them so rapidly that they nearly ruined their own four-year institutions. New Hampshire tried to avoid waste of this sort by founding five vocational education institutions, which remained under the jurisdiction of the New Hampshire Department of Education. It also began a modest development of two-year programs at the newly created state colleges. These programs were, de facto, community colleges, but they augmented the existing institutions rather than devastating them. In the late 1960s several two-year programs in technology were developed at Keene State through the industrial education department.

Under Redfern the college senate in 1976 authorized a two-year associate in arts degree. This began as broad-based education, not dissimilar from the old general education requirement. Soon, however, career options were offered in traffic safety, drug and alcohol abuse, child development, and computer science. The two-year programs have never been strong, but they grow each year, and through them the state has been able to avoid duplication and to provide some type of junior college education.

As mentioned in the previous section, one of the most useful spin-offs from the A-1 program was the experimental course, number 199 for lower division and 399 for upper. These "trial-balloon" types of course were a good way of determining where student interest lay. Through this technique many new courses and programs developed. From English came public affairs and journalism, theater arts and film. Macroeconomics was not far from microeconomics; and microeconomics was not far from management. From this emphasis developed the management program, one of the most heavily subscribed programs in the college for the anniversary year. From biology came concentrations in life sciences and environmental studies. From chemistry came industrial chemistry, which many people, to whom general chemistry is an engima, thought could not survive; but in the job-hungry 1980s the program has done very well. Mathematics contributed heavily to the budding computer science program Redfern had started.

A number of new programs came from education — traffic safety and special education, which for a while in the 1970s was the largest major in the college. With the assistance of grant funding a Safety Center was developed which now offers specialties of safety in the areas of highway, industry, occupations, and hygiene. From home economics came a food preparation program and an early childhood development program, which was developed further, in 1976, into a Child Development Center, where children were cared for, studied, and taught.

"Virtually every discipline on campus now has an experiential part to its discipline offering," commented Richard Gustafson. So it was. Some respected old names fell by the wayside. "Phys. Ed." was no longer "P.E." It became "Kinesiology and Sport," a discipline which offered concentrations in recreation, sports management, sports medicine, as well as the old teaching option.

Not even such sacred preserves as history and philosophy remained free from the taint of practicality. Out of philosophy came a course on medical ethics; and the historians offered internships, workshops, a course in museum management, and moved a few steps closer to archaeology by sponsoring a dig at Pisgah State Park.

Much of this development, Gustafson noted, could be understood as a sign of the times. Undoubtedly, and most of it began through the experimental courses.

Change in the Student Population

Keene has always had as part of its student population a number of nontraditional students. As already noted, the first five graduates of the school could be said to come under that category. Enrollment of nontraditional students, however, took a dramatic increase in the mid- and late 1970s.

When Dean Joseph Stewart announced the merger of the day and evening programs, no one paid much attention to the announcement. By the end of the decade, it was clear that this policy had a direct effect on the life of the college. Part-time students, the majority of whom were older women, became a "traditional" part of campus life. By the end of the decade they had organized as the Association of Non-Traditional Students. They conducted their own survey. Defining a nontraditional student as anyone who did not enter college directly from high school, they learned that over 1,100 students could be classified as nontraditional.[4]

The part-time student caused a new way of reckoning enrollments. Now there were three sets of enrollment figures. There were the traditional full-time students, say for 1983-84 — 1446 resident and 1073 non-resident students. Walking around campus, taking a course here and there, credit and non-credit, were nearly 4,000 people. All the courses taken by all the people were then divided up into what used to be a normal full-time load, and one talked then about FTEs, full-time equivalents, which for 1984 there were 2774 excluding graduate students. Opening the college up to the community at large was very much in keeping with past tradition in general, and it was in keeping with Redfern's readiness to experiment at all levels of college life.

29

The Roaring Seventies

AS PREVIOUSLY NOTED, the quality of a "generation" of students usually does not get its characteristics from the majority, who are busy with their own lives, programs, schedules, and are inactive in campus affairs. It is the significant minority that give an age its characterizations. So, too, was it with the 1970s. Redfern never condoned excesses on the part of students or laxness on the part of some faculty and administrators, but unfortunately his manner often did not help him. In the fall of 1969 he donned a freshman beanie, became one of the class, and shared in many of their activities. In 1969 it was good, but after awhile it was almost too familiar. Redfern was so popular near the end of his first year as president that Thomas Havill, acting for the executive committee of the college senate, gave him a gift — a pair of red suspenders. Redfern obviously treasured them, for he wore them often. Redfern was, recalled City Councilman Michael Blastos, "a patter-on-the-backer, red suspenders, good-time Joe," as different from Zorn as night and day. "I always thought he was less than presidential," commented Trustee Horton. Unfortunately, Redfern's playing with these symbols of democracy gave the impression to students of lax discipline. When they found out that discipline was in fact lax, it is not surprising that they went to excess. Redfern, like many of the faculty, was still thinking of the 1960s students, when in fact a totally new group of students was upon him.

The makeup of the student body changed drastically in the 1970s. Colleges built rapidly in the 1960s, and under Johnson's "Great Society" programs more people than ever were able to attend. After the great physical plant buildup of the 1960s and the end of the Vietnam War in the early 1970s, available spaces were very nearly equal to the total number of applicants. College administrations felt compelled to maintain their momentum. Soon educators talked about the "lower third," that is, those students who up until the 1970s had normally been rejected for academic reasons but were now being accepted. Problems were further compounded because the 1960s generation had just established basic curricula and dorm policies geared for sophisticated adult students. The striving of this decade was clearly not as strenuous as it had been in the 1960s.

The 1970s at the college got off to a roaring start when a group of students took advantage of lax regulations and hired for November 10, 1970, a performance by the Jefferson Airplane. The *Monadnock* explained that the "Jefferson Airplane doesn't sing songs of protest, but rather of love and thus, has been described by Donovan as 'translove airlines.'" Grace Slick, one of the key performers, "is expecting a child in December (to be named God Slick regardless of its sex)." The Airplane was a sign for area pot smokers and dope users. The great number, 4,500 people, who turned out for it, indicated that the audience came from a wide area. "The temperature of the overcrowded gym rose higher and higher," reported the *Monadnock*.

The heat and the thick haze caused by the thousands of joints of grass flickering in the bleachers, almost made the conditions unbearable. The concert finally ended at 2 a.m. The Keene police present were not enforcing busts. Had they been, the evening would have turned into a giant free-for-all. Fifteen able student marshalls patrolled the area and led people experiencing bum trips to the "Crisis Center" downstairs.

The music was louder even than the 1960s, and some aspects more vulgar. The Shittons was the name of a rock group which played here. One fan wrote to the editor about another band: "Dear Mr Baloney, I think you are an ass-hole. If you describe the James Montgomery Band as playing 'jive mixed with jive.' That's a lot of shit, JMB plays the blues. If you can't even tell what kind of jusic [*sic.*] it is, then you shouldn't be reviewing their concerts."[1]

The use of drugs by students was extensive enough, even in the late 1960s, to bring forth several editorials. The Jefferson Airplane was a signal that there were many more like-minded souls at Keene in the 1970s. If most of the tickets were sold, as apparently they were, the receipts were $20,000; and if the airplane cost as much as $10,000, an informal group who had taken advantage of scheduling regulations had made itself a neat profit. If this were used for the purchase of more drugs for sale is impossible to say. One can say for certain that there were drug dealers on campus, and they were used to dealing in big money.

The significant minority of students immediately took advantage of the open structure just created by the 1960s students. The new structure allowed them to major in the well-known "gut" courses. One had only to sign up for two "Caseys" and two "Jonesies," make three or four appearances in each course each semester and, with little or no work, walk off with a 3.0 average at the end of the semester. The rest of the time could be devoted to having a bash.

Such a situation, alarming as it was, was not new to higher education or to the American scene. Previous generations had also entrusted adult decisions to younger generations with like results. Ralph Waldo Emerson commented on the same situation over one hundred years ago. "How sad a spectacle," the sage of Concord said, "to see a young man after . . . years of college education, come out ready for his voyage of life, and to see that the entire ship is made of rotten timber!"

The intellectual tenor of the campus declined rapidly in the 1970s. Since 1914 students had produced poetry, some of it excellent. But in 1974 the student senate abolished the *Journal*, mainly because no one had contributed to it for the last two years; no one "gave a damn." Writing dropped significantly from the yearbooks. Seniors, those who bothered to show up for their pictures, were not identified by name, or if so, by nothing else, not even their curriculum. Many of the photos, while technically well-done, had no explanation and often had nothing to do with college life. Even the word "college" declined in use. Faculty and administrators talked more about "post-secondary" education. It was a disheartening day for those committed to "higher" education.

The distinctive spirit of the 1970s "generation" was exhibited by the editor of the yearbook, who had hand-printed, free style, for the 1976 *Kronicle:*

THIS BOOK IS DEDICATED TO

Frisbee's, [*sic*]
Baloon's, [*sic*]
Halloween Parties at 440 Main St.
Our Thursday night treks (later changed to tuesday),
To Richard Nixon who made our college years interesting,
and Gerald Ford, who made them humorous,
Artificial Recreational Chemicals,
To Henry and Volvo's, [*sic*]
To KAWS in the barn,
Rainbows,
Student Senate earings, [*sic*]
To All the Pamela Brown's, [*sic*]
To Washington, D.C., Conway, N.H., Houlton, ME., Thatcher Cottage, the Attic,
To the C.I.O., P.P. M.F.I., R.B. S.F.C., B.L.F., (and Flesh Barges)
To Monty (and the Spanish Inquisition)
to Poppy with Love

To You, From us, and remember
There is no hiding from a dope sniffing rhino.

Martha McDonough commented interestingly and knowledgeably about part of the drug problem: "One of the reasons I didn't go into Hillsboro House [at first], I had heard stories about Hillsboro House in Boston. When I told people I was going to Keene — Oh my God, there's a wild house up there. This was before I came. You know it used to be a big bootleg drug center, so that people from Boston knew."

Q: "What people in Boston? High School?"

"Yes, one fellow's big brother went to Keene and lived in Hillsboro House and they made drugs, and sold them — they made them — a big difference — Acid, bootleg LSD.... When I moved to Hillsboro House they had just taken the bathtub out the semester before — and that's where they made it, in the bathtub.... [Drug] abuse is too tolerated here. In some classes, you can say, don't call on me, I'm loaded.... What's here and what's there [administration] seems so vast for the size school we have.... Keene has the power to get away from drugs. But drugs are still on the streets. Some of the most intellectual are the wildest."

A student of the early 1980s wrote,

I remember asking my father about Woodstock. He told me how frightened he was during that time. He said he was so scared because he was seeing tomorrow's generation and all the most intelligent minds going to waste. He was afraid for the future because he felt it would be deprived of all morals and values. He saw minds being destroyed by drugs, alcohol, and free love. He could see no rules or restrictions and it really affected the way he viewed the future. I can't say that I blame my father.

Teaching methods had to change drastically, and usually they did. One could not present concepts easily anymore. Class presentations had to be concrete, graphic, and dramatic. If the professor did not conform to such standards, he lost out either by small enrollments or by bad evaluations. Ironically, the 1970s student evaluated the professors. If the student attended class three or four times, the evaluation was still counted as valid. In 1973 the *Equinox* published the professors' grades on a 1-4 scale. Many students thought the evaluation carried no weight. Members of FEAC (Faculty Evaluation Advisory Committee) could testify otherwise. The student evaluations were quantifiable evidence of performance, and quantification was the byword of the decade.

In 1973 activist students still had enough gumption to rally around House bill 50, which lowered the age of majority from twenty-one to eighteen. Many faculty and administration supported it, figuring that legalized alcohol was not as bad as illegal drugs. The bill had wide support. Police Chief Ficke, Mayor Masiello, and City Attorney Morang all supported it.

The next move was to have a pub on campus. The *Equinox* opposed the idea of having a pub in the Union, but it seemed the most logical place. The pub first opened for business in 1973. The first year went fairly well, but the second year was a year of trouble. The *Equinox* charged that the pub was "a perpetrator of decadence on the college campus." "Things were getting out of hand," said student pub worker Karla Baldwin; "they were turning down the lights, turning up the music, giving out free beer, and encouraging people to get drunk." Baldwin quit in protest. Student Pat LaPree said, "I agree that you can't be too strict, but you can't be without order at all."

Charles Hildebrandt recalled:

I had a radio show late at night, Wednesday night, till one in the morning. I would come out of that and it just looked like a slum. Students were drunk lying in the snowdrifts. . . . Drinking was rampant and open. I remember I was down here one Sunday night and I called the police because there was just bacchanalia out there. People throwing things. Where was security? Where did they get the permit to have this keg? It was just wide open. Students lolligagging around drunk on the campus. I just thought, I don't see any visible control.

259

There was a direct relationship to drunkenness and at least some of the vandalism, which up until the 1970s had been practically nonexistent on the campus. Students reeling out of the pub went into the toilets, destroyed doors, mirrors, soap, and towel dispensers. One sensitive student, David Tranchida, wrote, "Vandalism is at an all-time high, and out of the realm of college pranks. The things going on in Carle Hall aren't only ugly, they're scarey."[2]

Another "fun" activity of the 1970s was turning in false fire alarms. This started in 1972 and continued for about five years. Occasionally there was a real fire, and a couple of times a spider actually did climb into the mechanism and set off the alarm, but most of the alarms were false. Sometimes false alarms were pulled when the fire truck was already at the college on a false alarm. "Maybe you don't know it," said City Councilman Peloquin, "but there is a lot of resentment in the community against KSC. People are disgusted with the situation. . . . I say pass an ordinance. In some cases, the maximum fine is $1,000. If that doesn't work, 'then pull the plug.' " Eventually the city did pass an ordinance signed by Mayor George Rossiter, charging the college $100 for each false alarm. The ordinance had effect. The next year, before Thanksgiving, fire trucks responded to twenty-one alarms, but Fire Chief Robert Guyette was not particularly upset. The number was down from previous years.

Bomb scares were another "joke" of the 1970s. On one occasion, at least, the perpetrator did call a second time to say that it was an April Fool's joke. Others did not bother to call the second time. One student thought it was just a tactic by the administration "to search the rooms for drugs."

One student who was caught in having given a false alarm complained of his "misfortune of getting 'screwed' by the administration" and gave a bit of advice to fellow students — "act tough, and lie and deny, and you will always beat them."[3]

By the late 1970s thefts became common on campus. In March 1979 the *Equinox* reported $1,700 worth of thefts from different minihouses on one weekend. That November it reported losses of five clocks and eight toolboxes from Butterfield, a videotape monitor from Parker, plus $800 worth of damage to Carle Hall. One student who was changing her clothes in the bathroom at the Student Union had some of them stolen in the process of the change. "I was so angry," she wrote, "that after stomping around in the bathroom in a state of utter confusion for a few seconds, I stormed into the pub half-dressed to ask anybody and everybody if they had seen a suspicious-looking person carrying an ungainly wad of clothing towards the nearest exit. I . . . tried to think coherently. It was a very hard thing

With the return of the bicycle on campus came the return of maintenance problems.

to accomplish at that moment." She was working her way through college and had to buy her own clothes.

How many of these thefts were by students and how many by "walk-ons" is hard to say. Thievery is similar to drugs and may be related. If a student does not buy drugs on campus, he can step onto Main Street and buy them. Street people have long used the college facilities, especially the showers. Over sixty taped interviews of the Keene State College Oral History Project were taken from the library. The boys, who were from town, were caught red-handed, but one was freed and the other given a light sentence to be served on weekends, and weekend duty at the county farm with TV sets and served meals was not known to be heavy duty. Thievery was, on the whole, more of a town problem than sending false alarms. It was also a problem of other dimensions, not drug related, but psychological. The campus community not only had valuable things stolen but small things like a packed lunch, a cup of coffee, a carton of milk. One faculty member had to plead nolo contendere to an unauthorized taking charge. Another was "indicted [charges were dropped] for stealing tires and wheels from a car in a used car lot on Marlboro Street."[4] It was generally assumed, probably correctly, that much of the petty crime was due to the street people. The last two instances indicated, of course, that there was a problem much nearer home.

How can one explain all these activities? Lax administration was one, but certainly not the only cause. Nearly every campus in the country had similar experiences. Mircea Eliade in his book, *The Sacred and the Profane*, claimed that, when nothing is held sacred anymore, there is nothing left but profanity. This, of course, applies to society as a whole. Since Plymouth actually closed its pub on certain nights of the week in an effort to curb similar problems, it was always assumed that the situation was worse there. The possibility that Plymouth took stronger corrective measures was not given consideration. Vandalism seems so senseless, but Dean Gendron noted a not unusual case: "Suppose you are a young man or woman of 20, and you just receive news that your parents are getting a divorce. You go the pub, you get drunk, and in your anger and frustration you destroy school property. That still does not excuse the action, but it does make it somewhat more understandable."

Clay Foster of the *Equinox* wrote, in 1975, "Students five years ago didn't realize how powerless they were and now they realize it so they don't run around with a lot of causes anymore."[5] They had power but certainly no causes. They had torn down but not rebuilt. Lack of idealism, and especially the lack of inspiration for idealism, led to pessimism and self-indulgence.

Nationally the oldtime Protestant optimism was dying out. The Puritan ethic had been attacked viciously and vigorously by Catholic, Jewish, and minority-group writers, even by old-line Yankee intellectuals themselves. WASP no longer stood for the effort to build a better world but was a newly coined pejorative expressing self-interest and prejudice. A moral cause was unthinkable. Anyone espousing the Puritan ethic would have been regarded as a witch.

The effects of taking in the lower third, of overcrowding in the dorms, of the drug culture, and of lack of a meaningful sports program for the less athletically able became visible in a few years. Students began to see life as meaningless and dropped out at alarming rates, so much so that student attrition became a cause of concern and study. Keene State's self-study, which put the best possible light on the situation, was nonetheless revealing. In the fall of 1977 almost 200 students preregistered for the spring semester but never showed up. That was nearly 10 percent of the student body! Only one out of four cited the traditional (and expected) excuse — economics. "The report indicates," noted the *Equinox*, "that one of the main problems . . . is the lack of involvement or communication with the college." The report itself stated that "retention can be enhanced by making changes in the campus environment."[6]

Private colleges, which were now significantly more expensive than state colleges and not that much better academically, made their pitch to

Vigorous editorials and cartoons were part of a long-term effort, finally achieved in 1982, to close Appian Way to vehicular traffic.

students on the better quality of life they offered. Alexander W. Astin's book, *Four Critical Years*, emphasized that point. Their pitch was successful, not because of their good propaganda techniques, but because they had, in fact, a better quality of life to offer.

The 1970s held for Keene State College, of course, lighter and more positive efforts. It will be a more joyous task now to refer to those.

The beginning of a return to healthful activities was one positive aspect. One drug user complained that he was no longer able to enjoy such simple things as picnics and days at the ocean. Soon others began to realize that healthful living was actually more fun. The student senate first began the campaign by banning cigarette smoking in classrooms and other communal areas of the college. The Student Affairs Committee of the college senate took a hard line against pot and hard drugs. The general message was clear, and programs were set up to help those in trouble.

Bicycles returned to campus in the early 1970s. Professor Keith King started in 1970 the LIVE program, which emphasized out-of-doors living and experiences as a teaching mechanism. In 1979 Paul Keenen was hired to give the intramural program a much-needed umph, and he and now Hazel Varner have worked hard to make students participators rather than spectators. They were doing the necessary work of getting the (majority) less athletically talented students involved in college life — the necessary ingredient, as the attrition report pointed out.

In the 1960s the bad words were in loco parentis. In the 1970s the

Students have their favorite stations along "The Way." Here, a group enjoys the sunshine section at the corner of Morrison Hall.

students had the opportunity to live without the college acting as parent, but they learned the hard way that some sort of authority, some mature person was needed. A pseudo or advisory in loco parentis situation developed. The parent was no longer the taskmaster. Instead it was the advisor, the support group, the hot line, the substance abuse program and other such programs; and people such as James Wolterbeck, the college psychiatrist, Fay Gemmell, the campus minister, or Father Richard Connors, the Newman chaplain. None of these existed before 1963. By the mid-1970s they were all vital parts of college life.

The closing of Appian Way was a significant achievement of the students of the 1970s. The New Hampshire Board of Education talked about it as early as 1928 but had done nothing. It was closed temporarily in 1959 when Barbara Critchett, who was on crutches, was knocked down by a car. The *Monadnock* suggested closing it in 1967, but the campaign really got under way in the 1970s. Two students were struck by vehicles in the 1970s, and the Way was soon called "Death Zone," and over 1,000 students petitioned to have it closed. "We guess," wrote Robert Owen, Thomas Paidan, Stephanie Hamaty, and Benjamin Tilton, all student leaders, "the road will never close until someone dies on it." Owen himself had been struck down by a vehicle on the Way. On October 25, 1979, Sean Bailey organized a giant rally, on Appian Way, of course, with music, speeches, and collected hundreds of signatures for a petition to ban motor traffic on the Way. Elizabeth Medici wrote, "Closing the great military road of ancient Rome may have been easier than Keene State College's present-day Appian Way."

But their voices and petitions were heard both in Hale Building and in city hall. In March 1980 the Way was closed on a temporary basis. In April 1981, after fifteen months of debate, the city council, by a 13-2 vote, transferred Appian Way, Hyde Street, and Duffy Court to the college.[7] Finally, between June 15 and June 21, 1982, the permanent curbstones were extended from Main Street, and the Way became closed to all but emergency traffic.

The Way had become the central part of the college. There on a sunny day the sun soakers are all lined up against Morrison sitting on the pavement. Across the Way in the Library Triangle is the old "hippie" crowd, the poets, the guitarists, the flutists, the singers; on down is the TKE station, then a sorority group, each one with its own station. What is amazing is that it doesn't change much from year to year even though the students do. The same type of students gather at almost exactly the same places year after year.

Another center of social life is the Student Union. Built in 1969, it was from the start a success. It had its antecedents in the old social room of 1949, and had proved a success also when it was in Rhodes Hall in the 1960s. Commuters gather there for their morning coffee, breakfast, or lunch. There they often meet dorm students and faculty in a social setting and usually Lindy, Kicki, or Mert behind the counter and John Chaklos, at the door side table holding his own *petit salon*. For many commuting students, often single parents struggling with family, job, and education, the visits to the Student Union comprise their primary social life. For some it is the highlight of their week. There they can meet other students, young and old, resident and nonresident, faculty and administrators. There they see society in motion. There they see the possibilities for their own self-betterment. If they stick to their grueling schedules, their striving may at length be rewarded.

Another positive achievement to come from the 1970s student was the Owl's Nest concept. As early as 1971 the *Monadnock* ran an editorial entitled "NOT ANOTHER CARLE HALL" and strongly supported a student idea of "apartment type living" in clusters of smaller-sized residences. Redfern immediately accepted the idea. The minidorms, soon to be called Owl's Nests, were an immediate and, thus far, a lasting success. If they are given enough air and lawn space between them, they, undoubtedly, will continue to be desirable.

There were in the 1970s another group of innovations and reform ef-

*"Streaking" became a short-lived fad in 1974
as participants were soon reminded of city
ordinances against nudity.*

WELCOME TO THE FIVE O'CLOCK NUDES!.

forts. In October 1970 college headlines noted the start of STOP — Stop
Today's Over-Population. It was a genuine concern over preservation of
the environment and prevention of the explosion of "the population
bomb" — too many children for mother earth to support. ROCKS was a
group committed to the recycling of used paper on campus. The English
exchange began in 1971, continued throughout the decade, and proved
to be successful both to English and American students involved in it. Finally, one must add that the evaluation of faculty by students, a student-
engineered reform, with all its drawbacks, had, nonetheless, the net effect of improving classroom teaching methods.

The biggest event on the lighter side of the 1970s was streaking. One
warm night in March 1974 all of a sudden the evening classes heard a
massive scream as if everyone on campus had yelled at once. Several
students in the classes explained to their professors with one word —
"Streaking." There were at least three or four streaking experiences on campus. The greatest one was on March 7, 1974, and planned, apparently
by one of the fraternities, from 8:30 on, with "special events" at 9:00, 9:15,
9:30, and the highlight of the evening at 9:45. Appian Way, of course,
was the thoroughfare for naked runners, bicyclists, motorcyclists, riding
on top of a car, riding on a pickup truck. The "highlight" of the evening
occurred on the tennis courts where two male streakers, one with soda,
one with beer, toasted each other. "Bernie," a coed from Carle Hall who
had made her debut on Wednesday night, rode in the pickup on Thurs-

day night.[8] The administration and the town were quick to remind students that there were ordinances against nudity in public places, and the streaking episodes quickly died down.

Three restaurants with which college people identified closely, which were part of the cultural milieu, and which were a positive aspect of the decade, went out of business at the close of the 1970s. Two of these were nearly coterminous with the decade. The first of these was Foodstuffs, managed by Woody Dorsey, Joe, and others (usually). Foodstuffs specialized in tasty health foods and desserts. It was part grocery store and part snack bar. The service was not fast but it was kind and pleasant. Servings were never exact, but always generous. If errors were to be made, Woody and his group believed in erring on the side of the customer. The store was more of a cause, to restore healthful habits, than it was a business.

Similar in philosophy, but with more exact measurements, was The Square Meal, 51 St. James Street owned, and managed by Devik Rich. It was a restaurant only, although Ms. Rich did some catering. At The Square Meal one was served by tall wispy young ladies who glided around braless but in full length dresses. In the evening one could listen to poetry readings, folk singers, guitarists and other instrumentalists. Local artists displayed their work in the dining area. The bulletin board was tacked full of reformist notices and causes.

Ending also with the decade of the 1970s was the Crystal Restaurant, 81 Main Street, which had been owned and managed by the Houpis family since the 1920s and most recently by Constantine (Dino) Houpis. It had a formal dining area. More noteworthy, however, were the lounge and especially the coffee shop. They were noteworthy because the "high," the "middle," and the "low" of society met there on more equal terms than anyplace else in town, more often and more intimately. A real and unusual crossing of paths took place there.

These establishments were as much cultural aspects of the town and town/gown relationships as they were businesses. Many were sorry to see the old owners retire or change occupations. The businesses that succeeded them reflected the new time period, more conservative in taste, more businesslike, higher prices — and were greater economic successes. In many people's minds pleasant aspects of college life in the 1970s will also be associated with rewarding experiences at these three establishments.

Student Michael Dodge, concerned at the moment not about the restaurants of Keene but about the troublesome minority of 1970s students reminded the editor of the *Equinox* that he "should see the vast majority of the students at Keene State College as they truly are, hardworking and conscientious people who believe in the virtues of an openminded, total college experience."⁹ Undoubtedly so, but often it is the unusual minority that flavors the age. In United States history texts one often reads about the Roaring Twenties. It will not be inappropriate when referring to the history of Keene State College to talk about the Roaring Seventies.

30

The Faculty Unionizes

REDFERN was so committed to democracy, so wanted to be liked, was so kind — even indulgent, particularly with students, one would not suspect that the faculty would vote to use the police power of the state to force him and his administration to the collective-bargaining table; but so it was. Unionization was, according to Hobart, "a terrible indictment." What went wrong?

It was basically simple. Redfern's greatest strength, as already alluded to, was also his greatest weakness. He did not want to say no; he did not want to hurt. Often on personnel decisions, the key issue, thinking he would not hurt someone, he would tell that person a different reason for his or her not getting a promotion or a raise or whatever. Such people easily saw through the fake reasons, felt like they were getting the "run around," became embittered, and often could make a good case for themselves. Redfern was further hampered during this period, as also noted before, by not having forceful deans. A few cases will illustrate the general problem.

One year a faculty member nominated himself for promotion — according to proper procedure. FEAC wrote the dean and advised against promotion and cited the particular reasons. The faculty member was so angered that he insisted on seeing members of the committee. Meeting with two members of the committee and the dean, it became obvious that the dean had merely given as the reason "because the committee advises against it," rather than going into the substantive, but more unpleasant, reasons. The dean also wished to be a "good guy," by appearing sympathetic to the faculty member's desire for promotion. The FEAC members had to state the real reasons. This particular case ended happily because the faculty member learned at length the real reasons for his denial of promotion. Other cases, however, did not end so happily.

There was a "famous" case in which a faculty member was given only half a pay raise because he had spent half the year on sabbatical and, therefore, had technically served the college only half-time. It is plausible that in this case also the administration had its own sound reasons but was unwilling to undergo a difficult but honest personal encounter. It, therefore, made one that was more measurable, if not real.

The most famous of all these cases was the Christine Sweeney case, which was appealed all the way to the Supreme Court of the United States, where professor Sweeney won her case. Sweeney started her case and won it on the basis of sexism. One member of FAC (Faculty Appeals Committee) commented, "We did nothing with sexism, but our committee was convinced she had been mistreated through incompetence, not getting explanations... We thought she was treated shoddily... We felt she had a grievance."

"We did a poll," recalled Charles Hildebrandt, "on what the faculty considered the most important issue for negotiations and number one, ahead of money, ahead of everything else was grievance."

In 1972 Paul Blacketor, who had been chairman of the education department, 1966-72, got recognition from the AFL-CIO for a chapter of the AFT (American Federation of Teachers) on campus. The trustees refused recognition of the unit, but even at that early date Blacketor had attracted a large following among faculty.

The AFT conducted an evaluation poll of principal administrators in December 1974. There were, to be sure, some flaws in the evaluation instrument, and many faculty were smarting under similar instruments from the hands of students. These factors compounded with the grievance cases did not produce a favorable atmosphere. Nonetheless, the results of the AFT poll were nothing less than devastating. It was clear that some change in administrative personnel would have to take place soon.[1]

The second thing that "went wrong" was Redfern's democratic diffusion of power. In the Young and Zorn years, the faculty had been used to having the president decide tenure, promotion, merit, and termination. With centralized control a fairly uniform standard was applied throughout the college. In 1968-69 FEAC was created to advise the dean on personnel decisions. The committee was to prevent the repetition of another Wiseman case. It was assumed that tough negotiations would take place between the committee and the dean. No one ever dreamed in the late 1960s that FEAC would have the power that it assumed in the 1970s. Redfern and his deans felt that they were being democratic as well as good administrators when they followed FEAC's recommendation a high percentage of the time. The trouble was that FEAC changed in its composition from year to year. Each committee set up different standards, different procedures. FAC underwent similar changes.

Another aspect of Redfern's diffusion of power that was new in the 1970s was the increase in responsibilities of the departmental chairs. Personnel decisions hinged in large measure on the actions of the department and the department heads. With the diffusion of power, however, there was no standard from one department to another. One department might require publication of original research for promotion to full professor; another might think that if one had spent time in grade, met classes regularly, and had over twenty advisees he or she deserved promotion. Redfern was unwilling to meet head on these qualitative differences.

Under Redfern individual departments were also given the power to hire new members, but their collective performance was not impressive when compared with Zorn's of the previous decade. One year in the early 1970s thirty-one new faculty and staff were hired. Of them only one held the doctorate, and he was in administration. If Keene outshone Plymouth and even Durham in this regard under Zorn, it did not fare as well when the individual departments first exercised control over hiring.

Redfern commented later:

> In all honesty, I should say another source of frustration was the fact that constituent units of the college seemed uncomfortable and unhappy with the democratic structure that I had always thought would be the most creative and most open.... When I first came, I understood that ... hiring was done by the president, period. In opening this up to departmental involvement and collegewide committees, I thought that would be in large measure remedial, and yet I found ... there was unhappiness, and people would come to me to override the peer group.[2]

Redfern's diffusion of power was extended also to a number of broad-based committees. A number of these committees were hand-picked so that the "right" people were on them, but an unusually high number were truly representative. Whatever the composition of the committee, Redfern tended to follow its recommendations. In many instances the results were happy, but often, as he commented, they were not.

The dean's Search Committee in 1975 will serve as a good example in this regard. Redfern wanted to pick one candidate out of three nominees when the deanship came open. A number of highly desirable and qualified candidates came down to the final screenings. The committee, however, recommended only one name and said that, all things considered, they were unwilling to recommend other names.

One could say in retrospect that Redfern should have insisted on the original understanding — three nominees. Nonetheless, at the time, faced with a unanimous decision of a broad-based committee for only one person, Redfern was not disposed to upset a procedure with which he was in basic agreement.

The choice of William Whybrew as dean was a broad-based, democratic choice. Whybrew himself was a man of impeccable character. He served Barbara Seelye well in the first year of her administration. The particular situation at Keene State College in the mid-1970s was such, however, that it placed extraordinarily heavy problems on a man of Whybrew's talents and temperament.

Although conjectural, it seemed likely that a number of committee members felt threatened by a strong academic dean. "I felt," recalled Redfern, "that probably part of the motivation of the committee could have been that they did not want too strong a dean because they did not want to disrupt the democratic process and procedures that they had built. They didn't want an authoritarian dictatorial-type person. Whybrew certainly was not that."

Redfern himself believed that a powerful academic dean "would have facilitated an important segment of my responsibilities." Redfern's statement was by no means a criticism of Whybrew himself, whom both he and the general community always highly regarded. This whole incident, however, underscored the fact that democracy and democratic procedures could not be relied upon to provide exact remedies. Redfern himself, however, was so committed to the democratic process that he generally abided by it.

In 1975 the administration had again gotten control of money for faculty raises out of hands of the senate, where it had been the year before. Raises were now to be divided into three levels of merit beyond a normal increment. The idea was basically sound. The real failure lay with the various departments in determining guidelines as to what constituted the bases for various levels of merit. At any rate, many faculty were dissatisfied with the wide discrepancies, and that gave AFT's voice added force.

Forced recognition of a faculty union was now a distinct possibility. Some hastened to beef up the AAUP, believing that if unionization must come the AAUP was the best representative for an institution of higher learning. Others wanted the NEA because of their familiarity with it in the teaching program.

Enough faculty (30 percent is the minimum) petitioned the state labor relations board to have an election on a collective-bargaining agent, which was held April 26-27, 1977. The results of this election were: no agent — 55, NEA — 34, AAUP — 18, AFT — 15. Those who were opposed to unionization were pleased with these results. They believed that many were voting for collective bargaining only as a device to scare the administration and that when the runoff election came some AAUP people and some "vote-to-scare" people would vote no agent, and the issue would be settled.

In the meantime, other factors developed. The faculty had not been well organized for bloc voting since the late 1960s. In 1976 Jo Beth Wolf, a political science teacher, who had worked with Senator Vance Hartke of Indiana, joined the faculty. She was able to concentrate her abilities on the doubtful votes, and she was ably assisted in this process by Sherry Bovinet and Charles Weed. Another significant addition to the proagent forces was William Sullivan. He was able politically and widely respected. Soon he and most of his colleagues in the English department were committed to collective bargaining. Nonetheless, the "no-agent" forces were still confident. Wolf, herself, did not believe there were enough votes to win the runoff election. David Costin of the education department went so far as to place a $75 bet on the "no-agent" side. Thus, many on both sides of the issue were stunned to hear on the evening of May 12, 1977, that the KSCEA had won by a 62-60 vote.

James Smart (previously introduced) was prepared to accept the election results until he heard the following story, which he believed to be true. Three "no-agent" teachers went to vote. One was particularly naive politically, who may be called "George." George was a great admirer of James Hobart, the dean of administration. When the three got to the polls, they were handed campaign literature, and on one of these pieces George noted that Hobart advocated a vote for the KSCEA, and George so voted.

Returning to the Science Center, the other two learned in dismay what had happened. Steve Hobart from the geography department had endorsed the KSCEA, and George had thought he was James Hobart. Had that mistake not occurred, the vote would have been 61-61, and the KSCEA, failing to get a majority, would have lost the election.

There was no difficulty in getting over 70 percent of the faculty to petition for a new election. Many of the signatures were prounion voters who wanted a clearer decision. There was not only George's vote, but there were "Chris" and several others who still professed that they only wanted to scare the administration but did not really want to become part of a labor union. Given George's votes plus a number of "scare" votes, Wilfred Bisson, Michael D. Keller, James Smart, Klaus Bayr, Ernest Lohman, Cornelius R. Lyle, Jr., and a number of other faculty believed that, if another election were held, the union that had just been established could be decertified. Had an election been held immediately, that was entirely possible.

The decertification election, however, was not held until late January 1979, nearly twenty months later. In the meantime, more happened to convert more faculty to the KSCEA point of view. The most significant of these events was "Black Friday," February 24, 1978, the date of an extended senate meeting. The industrial education department had on campus a candidate for department chair. After showing him around campus, his hosts said, "Let's stop in here, you can a KSC senate meeting." Much to their and everyone's surprise, the faculty were receiving word from the board of trustees that all department chairs were abolished, that there would instead be three full-time divisional deans, and that everyone else would be faculty, which would be more in accord, the trustees felt, with normal labor-management situations. Many faculty believed this to be punitive action. This and other events caused a fairly 66-57 decisive prounion vote on January 25, 1979.

In the meantime, the issue had gone to the board of trustees. "I remember," said Trustee Horton, "we used to have all kinds of meetings of the board to straighten out this 'terrible chaos' on the Keene campus because of the faculty union. . . . There were people on the board whose idea of a union was that of a militant employee union."

Conservative Governor Meldrim Thomson had been in office, by 1978, six years, the first Republican ever to serve three terms. He commented:

How professional are you, if you go union? . . . I tried to appoint board members so that we had a good cross-section of community life. Some people were appalled that I appointed Joe Moriarity to the board. Yet Joe brought . . . a balanced view with respect to labor. He was a workingman. In fact, he came to me . . . with tears in his eyes and a catch in his voice thanking me for appointing him. He said, "if my old mother were alive now, she couldn't believe it!" Joe . . . had a lot of good common sense, which is part of which is necessary on a public board in my judgment. So I tried to create a balance there.

Some people thought that it would soon be a "Thomson board." "There was no way for it ever to be a Thomson board," the governor commented. "There are twenty-five members, I could appoint only twelve. The board would be afflicted with the Thomson influence. And they knew that good and well!"

Horton said:

I could never understand why people were horrified at the thought of a union. I never felt that it was the last straw in academic deficiency. If the faculty wanted to do it that way, probably there was something in the administration that made them want to do it — that was my theory . . . I was always in the minority on this.

Unionization was a fact, whether the board liked it or not. Howard Croteau, Jean Blacketor, and Sherman Lovering, who made a study of the development of collective bargaining at Keene, saw unionization as the beginning of a bright new day. The KSCEA was fortunate in having Professor William Sullivan as its first president. His role in conducting negotiations for his colleagues for the first contract was long and arduous. It was not until March 20, 1980, that a contract was signed and approved by both the KSCEA and the board of trustees. Jean Blacketor, Croteau, and Lovering found that, besides eventual concessions on both sides, much credit was due to the mediating influence of the governor, Hugh Gallen, who had replaced Thomson in 1978. "There is no doubt it helped." "We can say," concludes this study, "that a new era had been born at Keene State College."[3]

Richard Gustafson admitted that collective bargaining did force the administration to pay more attention to certain areas that they had thought had not needed so much attention. Charles Weed saw the problem of continued high-quality leadership of the KSCEA as one of the union's chief internal problems. In the late 1970s, however, many faculty were ready to commit themselves to long hours of negotiations on faculty rights and prerogatives.

In January 1979 Redfern announced his resignation, citing "Frustration with inadequate budgets and an unimaginative bureaucracy as the major factors in his decision." One poll as early as 1974 showed that 46 percent believed that Redfern ought to resign, and in 1976 he admitted, "There are problems on almost every operation we have."

If ever a man wanted to be popular, Redfern did. Certainly he always remained so with the students and alumni. It is ironic that there was so much disaffection between him and the faculty (and eventually between him and the trustees). Never had the faculty had freer reign. Faculty activity of the 1970s will no doubt astound later generations, as it did previous generations.

Redfern's weakness, again, was his inability to say no openly, diplomatically or firmly. Further, he could not appeal well to the better instincts of the faculty — or of the students. He made too much of a casual link between good pay and good teaching. Personnel problems he hoped would either simmer down or disappear. While he always liked to think toward the future, as Gustafson noted, he could not well define goals or roles. Everything, he hoped, even the mission of the college, would be solved by democratically composed committees. Much could be; but not everything. "The one intolerable thing in education," wrote Mark Van Doren, "is the absence of intellectual design. Nothing so big can long remain meaningless."[4] Thus, without purposes clearly stated, faculty did not know how far he might go with his experiments such as A-1 or how far student freedoms would extend. This caused unease. Some faculty fell to nursing individual grievances, some legitimate, some not; some sought more meaningful solutions in the KSCEA than in direct negotiations with the president or the dean.

Nonetheless, Redfern's term stands as a monument to intellectual freedom, and he will certainly always be "the student's president." He will also be remembered as the alumni's president. Marion Wood, class of 1926, discusses that in special chapters on the alumni association in Part 4.

31

The Seelye Administration:
Beginnings

Interim ("Acting")

THE TIME BETWEEN the second union vote on January 25, 1979 (or perhaps even from "Black Friday," February 24, 1978), and the coming of Barbara Seelye in July 1980 was a depressing period. Within a few months after the unionization vote Hobart resigned. Redfern took a sabbatical in 1978 and resigned in 1979. Ed McKay resigned, as did Dennis Hayzlett, director of personnel; so also did Suanne Yglesias, coordinator of student activities, and Philip Grosnick, director of residential life, the third director to do so in three years. So many administrators were resigning, and their places being filled by "acting" functionaries, that the 1980 yearbook picked "On Stage" as its theme, with everybody "acting" at something or another. "It was so odd," recalled Martha McDonough. "Every time you went to some office, they would say, 'I can't help you with that, I'm only acting.'"

William E. Whybrew, who had been dean since 1975, was acting president for the 1979-80 school year. He was a very gentle person who was particularly insistent on correct and authorized procedure for whatever event took place. He did not want to be president, although his looks and demeanor fitted him for the job. He continued to do most of his work in the dean's office on the first floor of Hale Building, going to the president's office on the second floor only when he had to act as president.

The year was trying for him. Faculty salaries had been frozen until a satisfactory contract could be arranged with the KSCEA. In a year of unusually high inflation even the most optimistic became discouraged. Soon the KSCEA mounted a three-week picketing demonstration around Hale Building in protest of the negotiations impasse.[1]

Added to that, town-gown relations took another step for the worse. The college modified several parking lots and began construction of new Owl's Nests on Butler Court without going through the city's site plan review process, an unnecessary offense to the city planning board and the city council. Neighbors from Winchester, Blake, and Madison streets complained about student loudness, parties, indecencies. The TKE brothers were forced to vacate their house on Marlboro Street because of health code violations. "The city is out for blood," noted one of the brothers. The *Sentinel* fell into sensationalism on a few of the stories, but there was enough truth in them to be concerned about Keene State being a poor neighbor. In the meantime, college students began to air some of their complaints, which focused on slum landlords, on unevenness (and injustice) in enforcing building safety regulations, and on drivers who failed to stop for pedestrians. In 1979 and 1980 police had to be called at least twice to eject "outsiders" from the Owl's Nests and from Carle Hall. The Daisey Day fund drive for Cedar Crest, contributions to the Red Cross blood drive, and many other normal friendly relations continued, but nonetheless poor town-gown relations was often the topic of talk in street, shop and tavern.

No one ever worked a quicker, more dramatic turnaround in town-gown relations than the new president, Barbara Jane Seelye.

Seelye was born of John Arvil and Mayme Dwyer Seelye on November 29, 1930, in Manito, Illinois (population, 840), a farming community south of Peoria. John Seelye was an automobile dealer in the town. Seelye recalled that "he believed that one started out in the business on the ground floor — and I did, literally — servicing cars." There was nothing like crawling under a car for an oil change to remind her of the literal truth of her father's words. She attended the local public schools, after which she attended Eureka, a small denominational college where she majored in biology and English. Her goal was medicine. Only a few fellowships existed for women in the best of times, but after World War II even those dried up. One of the few fields open to women at the time was teaching, so Seelye entered it. Once she started to teach, she loved it.

The road to her doctorate was a long one. It started with summer schools at the University of Denver. Due to personal circumstances and financial necessity, she had to piece together her graduate education. She

Above (from left) are Mary Misavage, Annette LaPointe, Gayle Patrea, and Rebeccah Ogg of the 1983 pledge class of Tau Phi Xi. Since the 1970s, two new fraternities (Phi Mu Delta and Zeta Beta Tau) and six sororities (Kappa Gamma, Sigma Rho Upsilon, Eta Gamma Chi, Delta Phi Epsilon, and Zeta Omega Psi) have been organized.

realizes fully the advantages and disadvantages of such a method. "I am one of those," she recalled, "who wrote the dissertation at night." She earned her doctorate from the University of Denver in 1967. The title of her dissertation was "An Investigation of Language Development in Non-Institutionalized Mentally Retarded Children."

Her first college position was in speech pathology at Washington University, St. Louis, where she taught two and a half years. She then went to St. Louis University where for fifteen years she was department head. She was in line for the dean of arts and sciences position, but many among the faculty questioned the appropriateness of having both a woman and a Protestant in such a position in a Jesuit University.

Seelye relieved their discomfiture by seeking another post and obtained a good one as dean of the College of Professional Studies at Northern Illinois University. There she had more faculty, more budget, more buildings and grounds, and more students under her jurisdiction than she would have at Keene State.

Why did she go into administration? She responded:

All my life, whenever I've worked, I've ended up with some kind of administrative job, because there was something that needed to be done. Nobody else did it, and so I did it. The first year I taught high school, I said, you people do not have a public relations program, and boom! I'm in charge of public relations. I found that I could be as happy and as satisfied doing administrative work as I could be teaching and doing scholarly work. I like there to be a job that needs to be done. I felt, as in the case at Northern Illinois, I was going into a situation [here] where there was a job and a challenge.

Indeed there was. The first thing Seelye did was to look at her living quarters, the President's House. She decided that it had been long overdue for restoration and renovation. Some students complained about the cost, but not much had been done to the old mansion since 1940, shortly after Lloyd Young moved in, and modifications then were limited to some new electrical wiring and plumbing.

In the meantime, at her request, Campus Housing fitted Seelye up with an apartment on 24 Madison Street, at the sorest point of town-gown relations. No gesture could have been more effective than her move to the trouble area site. Further, she recalled, "I promised the neighbors that we would meet together and talk issues, and that there would be some kind of community action committee setup — and there now is." Through her own commitment and a series of meetings and socials between rooming students, fraternities, and neighbors, town-gown relations improved rapidly and dramatically.

Because of her avocational interest in the past, Seelye made a mutually beneficial arrangement with the Cheshire County Historical Society, whereby the society placed several attractive and authentic period pieces in her house. This not only helped her to furnish the mansion properly, it also provided proper and caring display for some of the society's prime possessions.

Also stemming from Seelye's avocation was the establishment on December 8, 1983, of the Historical Society of Cheshire County Archive Center in Rhodes Hall. Marion Wood, David Putnam, Muriel Robbins, David Leinster, David Proper and other members of the Cheshire County Historical Society all helped make this possible. Managing the Center is Alan Rumrill, a Keene State College history major and a trained archivist. The Center houses documents relating to the area which belong to the society. Adjacent to the archives room is the Monadnock Center, a small art gallery featuring Monadnock area artwork with an emphasis on the nineteenth century. Maureen A'Hearn, the director of the Thorne Sagendorff Gallery, was the impetus behind this.

In 1982 Edith Notman produced the spectacularly successful Long Day's Journey Into Night, *followed in 1983 by Anton Chekhov's* Three Sisters *(above) which qualified for the Region I finals of the American Theatre Festival. Shown here are Sandra Rowe, Dominique Plaisant, and Kathryn Nelligan.*

Seelye made some quick changes in personnel. Some of the opportunities were fortuitous, some not. With all the "acting" positions, there were a lot of vacancies to fill. With the appointment in 1980 of Carole Henry and Ellen Lowe, she had two good, strict, yet sensible people in charge of student life. She was able to appoint the efficient Ms. Gail Bys as manager of the book store. Not all positions were vacant — "and I fired some people!" Seelye said. Several headlines supported that statement.

Seelye demanded responsible action from the students as well as from her own administration. She found that, while she no longer had the force of law to coerce students to act with propriety, she could still get much done by moral suasion and some plain old-fashioned "jawboning." The word got out quickly. Florence Wheeler in Wilton, class of 1917, said of the events of the late 1970s, "The morale of the school went down like the dickens, but it's starting to come back, and Dr. Seelye's doing something about that. I guess she's whipping them into line because she's got it." "Word's out now," said Martha McDonough, class of 1981. "You're caught with drugs, and you're out!" A visitor to the campus in the evenings found a much greater degree of quiet, order, and study. Very good students were seeking a room in Carle Hall, which had been a trouble dorm throughout most of the 1970s.

By 1981 Seelye was made a trustee of both the Cheshire County Savings Bank and the Horatio Colony House Museum. By 1982 she assumed similar positions for the Greater Keene Chamber of Commerce, the Keene Cooperative Bank, Cheshire Hospital, and the Greater Monadnock Arts Council. Such rapid elections to these positions were a measure of the public esteem by which she was held by the community at large. The fact that the presidential inauguration fund was started by a number of people in the community was another measure of approbation and renewed goodwill toward the college community.

"I hope the integrity, system of consultation, humaneness, and efficacy of my total administration will have an impact on the students and faculty," Seelye said in an early interview. Once on campus she announced "Commitment to Care" as her theme.

The most serious challenge to her commitment was the dismissal of four janitors in 1982. The grounds crew and the janitors had generally had a significant place in the life of the college. James Beers, the first janitor/grounds crewman, usually had his picture in the catalogues. He suffered his last fatal stroke on campus, and it was a sad day for everyone when he died. James Whitcomb of the maintenance department and Henry Oya of the grounds crew were both beloved and properly remembered. In the

1970s an unusual crew of janitors joined the college: Roger LaMothe, Herbert Twombley, and Anthony Perowlski. But in 1982 the situation became more complicated than in the old days. Because of financial stringency the janitorial operation was leased out, and it was assumed that the janitors would keep their jobs. However, they were all very independent and had qualities of mind and character that everyone loved. They soon ran afoul of their management, and all were fired on one weekend. The college offered them jobs in other areas, but feelings at that time ran too high for them to accept these jobs. It was one clear evidence that the college had gotten so big in one area, at least, that it could not care when it wanted to.

The case of the janitors represented on a small, understandable scale the problems that Seelye faced on a much larger and more complicated one. She had given a commitment to caring. She herself felt that the "9 percent rollback" was the greatest disappointment she had in her commitment-to-care policy.

Because negotiations with the KSCEA were unsuccessful in 1982, the trustees not only decided not to give the faculty a pay raise for the coming year but also took away (or "rolled back") the 9 percent raise the faculty had achieved the previous year. Seelye said:

> That was the most threatening to me in terms of my trying to show a steady kind of commitment to the campus and to its people. It looked as if I did not care. I did not want to do it, and it was clear that I did not want to do it. We had some difficult words about it at the trustee level. There were some legal aspects involved and I couldn't not do it. It set us back in our campus relationships. I think everyone knows that. I told the board it would, and it did. They are very much aware of that.

"Right now," said Seelye, "one of the things I am happiest about is that the campus runs smoothly. We have good administrators, good discipline coordinators. A good team is intact. I can go on vacation, and everything is fine."[2] Indeed, a good administration is the most important aspect of college governance.

Problems continued, sometimes with negotiating the KSCEA contracts, generally with the stringency of the legislative appropriations. Despite these problems, some definite forward steps, modernization in particular, have been made. Most notable in this regard was the complete updating of the library and the Computer Center. A user at the library now has access to information in over 8 million books in over 2,000 libraries worldwide through the DIALOG computer system and to about 200 indexes to

Excerpt from
An Evening of Mime and Gown
March, 1982

periodical literature through the OCLC (On-line Computer Location Center) System. In 1983 the whole library was rearranged with a greater emphasis on accessibility for all, including the handicapped.

Under the direction of Charles Thompson the Computer Center by 1984 had two major VAX systems with almost 90 terminals and 21 Apple computers devoted to campuswide use. Students, faculty, and staff soon learned how helpful Thompson, Karen Runcy, Kenneth Whittaker, Richard Stauder, and their staff were in helping them to adjust their lives to the new machine gods (our own *dei ex machina*). "The computing environment," commented Richard Gustafson, "has been improved to the level that there are few colleges in the Northeast which can boast the computer studies opportunities which we provide for our students."[3]

While all this and much other development has taken place, Keene State College strives to do what it has always striven to do — to provide good to excellent education for those who have been adequately prepared and to serve as an avenue of opportunity, that is, as a "people's college," for those striving to begin a new life. A wind-blown diary leaf, letter, or English assignment, accidentally dropped and accidentally picked up in 1983 reinforces the latter point. "Today," began the author of this unsigned piece,

I went to... [college] for the first time... All last week I was scared to death, but now, that fear has been replaced by excitment [sic]. I guess the reason I was so fearful of attempting this is that I dropped out of high school... My boss won't allow me to work part time which means I have classes at 9:15 to 10:45 and 1:00 to 2:35, then turn around [sic] and work from 3:00 to 11:30 at night, which doesn't leave much time for studies or sleep. My wife and everyone tells me I am crazy but it's the only chance I have to do anything about my education so I intend to do my damnedest. Hopefully it will all work out OK.

The fear, the replacing of it by hope and intellectual excitement, the determination and the effort of this student hark back to the same themes written by the early editors of the *Kronicle* and the very first student historians of the college.

Most students, better prepared than the one quoted above, but not so heavily compelled to effort, continue under faculty direction to learn skills both new and old and to think for themselves and about themselves and about their culture in a way which is not new, but very old, but which must be taught generation after generation if mankind is to retain the gains of the past and continue to have hope for his life and that of his successors. This kind of teaching and learning is the essence of the college as it has been from its beginning. Despite all the vicissitudes of the past, many of which have now been recounted, this type of learning between serious student and committed teacher continues after seventy-five years. Often it does not get the attention it deserves — even in history books. The reward of this kind of experience not only brought students to Keene but was also the source of selfless dedication of faculty and administration for three quarters of a century.

Conclusions

One often hears the question: "What lessons does history have to offer?" One might well, then, ask the same question, after all this investigation, about this history. The history of Keene State College furnishes a few "awareness points" which may be called "lessons," some of which reinforce those found in a careful reading of good general history.

First is a greater awareness of the very difficult role a small state college must play for its continued success. The demands on a small state institution are many, often conflicting, and generally more complicated than those of private institutions or a large university. The small state college is answerable to the legislature, its local community, its students, parents, and alumni, and to the intellectual world at large. If its faculty is not of proper academic stature, it will be chastised by the larger intellectual community in the universities and quality private colleges. If it seeks through increased pay to upgrade its faculty, it may be chastised by the legislature or the state at large. The small state institution must produce a quality graduate, yet it is expected to accept students at the freshman year more on the basis of equality than quality and to a greater degree than any other institution. It must satisfy parents, alumni, and friends that it is doing all these things and doing them well, that it is open at all times yet in control at all times.

Second, there is a pattern in Keene State College's past of lenient/democratic presidents followed by authoritarian/strict accountability presidents. What little evidence there is suggests that Rhodes was lenient and democratic. Mason was clearly authoritarian, Young democratic, Zorn authoritarian, Redfern democratic. The Seelye administration is marked thus far by an emphasis on accountability. It is only natural that, after the experience of one kind of administration, all constituents see the weaknesses at hand most clearly and seek in the subsequent administration the opposite type of leadership. Some may see this seesawing back and forth of styles as a curse. Being aware of this process (and natural tendency), one can see how, over the long time span, the institution takes a step with the foot of one style and then takes the next step with the foot of the other style. If enough history is remembered and capitalized on, the striving made by each kind of step can be maintained for the betterment of the whole.

The third lesson, that of equality versus quality, has been noted, but it is of such importance that it needs special attention. It is a particularly American problem. It yields both extraordinary greatness and disaster. One hopes that in his institution (as in his country) he can have both quality and equality. In practice, however, large grants of equality such as with a number of the male students of the 1920s and a number of the students of the 1970s or the faculty's filling out self-evaluation forms (it could be argued) meant a lessening of quality and led to frustrating even frightful experiences. Participatory democracy is time-consuming, takes advantage of the conscientious worker, and often yields poor results. On the other hand, the sense of the people at the college, to an even greater degree than to the country at large, demands participation, consultation, and equality. At the same time, they strive for quality. Further, the state expects its colleges to be democratic to its constituents, and the college itself has for seventy-five years been a vehicle of opportunity for many who could barely pay their first bills and get together their transportation money to Keene.

It seems unfortunate in this regard that the college did not remain in the 1920s with Morrison's ideas maintaining strict, high performance levels. Possibly the "equality" pressures on Mason were at the time too great to withstand. Perhaps he was so busy he had not time enough to sort out Morrison's philosophy from John Dewey's and conscientiously adopt or reject one or the other. There was time only "to keep up with the latest" and then plunge again into activity. Lack of records, plus the challenge, and the possibility, of having a "Morrison school of education" rather than a "Dewey school of education" make this the college's most puzzling and unanswered turning point in the past.

The fourth lesson is also well established historically: the problem of liberty versus order. Again, everyone wants both. At extremes, liberty and order are antagonistic to each other. With different large segments of the college community insistent on their liberty to achieve their will, the orderly advance of the institution can be hampered or even halted. At the other extreme, if individuals and communities are denied their rights for the sake of order, the intellectual advance of the institution can be hampered or halted. The administration of an institution has the difficult task of seeing to it that liberty is maintained without sliding into chaos on one hand and, on the other hand, of seeing to it that order is maintained without sliding into authoritarianism.

Last, in reviewing the history of an educational institution one is made more aware of the spiritual nature of the whole enterprise. President Hopkins of Dartmouth likened it directly to the religious experience. "Like objects," he said, "pertain to both; namely to know the truth and to live in accordance with it."[4] It was this aspect of the teaching/learning experience that made the normal school more than a normal school, made it a college from the beginning and, under the circumstances, a people's college.

For the past seventy-five years this college in its efforts to impart the spiritual nature of education has experienced phases which at one time emphasized democracy, equality, liberty, experimentation. In other phases it experienced order, quality, accountability, and reliability. The institution entered each phase, whatever it was, in good faith. It experienced much. It accomplished much. It has provided so much opportunity for so many "forgotten Americans" that its lessons, its steps, its striving are causes for rejoicing on its seventy-fifth anniversary.

IV

THE ALUMNI ASSOCIATION

1910 / 1984

Alumni Gate

32

*History of the Alumni Association**

Early Beginnings and Triennial Meetings

NEARLY seventy-five years ago, a group of five women who had just graduated from the new Keene Normal School sat down to the first alumnae luncheon. With their guests and members of the faculty, their number swelled to twenty people. The luncheon was held in the library of the school building, Hale Hall.

Principal Rhodes, newly arrived from Kansas, had a strong conviction that this new college must lay a "foundation securely and broadly" that it might become a great educational bulwark of the community and the state.

Little is recorded of this event. The program consisted of speeches, one of the longer ones given by Principal Rhodes, in which he told the recent graduates that the offer of a college was to make "a host of friends among others of your own age who are to be leaders in all walks of life." He urged the graduates to lose themselves in generous enthusiasm and to cooperate with others for the common good of all. It is doubtful that those attending had any idea that they were the beginning of an organization that would have a profound influence on the strength and growth of this newly created college. That began an association which was later to be known as the Keene State College Alumni Association.

Wallace Mason also felt the need of an alumni association. Thus, after assuming the role of chief administrator in 1911, he called together, in January 1912, a number of local people to discuss what they could do

*Text for Part IV was contributed by Marion Tebbetts Wood.

for their alma mater. This was probably the first midterm meeting ever held by the alumnae.

Dinner was served by the division of the senior cooking class.

The members of the reunion gathering decided that there should be an alumnae group and that they should have triennial meetings. A president would be chosen every three years.

Triennial meetings consisted of long speeches called toasts. These toasts were usually written around a favorite literary theme such as: "Kindle bright the fires upon her altar — to burn while time shall last!" This was the motto for the sixth triennial gathering. The theme as well as the topic was carefully printed in the program. To vary the program, musical selections were given by the college orchestra or glee club.

Decorations for these occasions were elaborate. In one instance, the normal school's colors, red and white, were used with floral decorations of red and white peonies. Red candles in silver candelabra were on the guest table, and bouquets of red and white carnations were on the other tables.

The banquet of June 1933 was the first to be served in the new Spaulding Gymnasium, the building now called the Lloyd Young Student Union Building. The students of the home economics department, under the supervision of Marion MacDonald, did an excellent job. The meal was similar to today's meals — fruit cup, cold meat, a potato, vegetable, salad, rolls, coffee, and ice cream. The state commissioner, Mr. Pringle, was so delighted with the entire affair that he said in his talk that he "wished students could sit around tables like this and listen to educational talks rather than have them in the formal spirit of a classroom lecture."

The dinner was well attended. Two members from the first graduating class and 200 other alumni were present. The entire affair was considered a huge success. In describing this banquet, the *Keene Kronicle* said: "Much of the success was due to the efficient work of Ruth Seaver Kirk, who cooperated with the school administration in arranging the meeting. Ruth was both President of the Alumni Association and Toastmistress of this occasion."

At this meeting, "Daddy" Mason introduced the idea of a three-year curriculum for elementary teachers. Up to this time, the three-year course had been for those who were preparing to teach either in junior or senior high school. In his announcement, Mason said that this forward step was a growing trend and that similar programs had already been adopted by several state boards. Another advantage, Mason said, was that "it would greatly help in reducing the number of surplus teachers." The alumni gave their enthusiastic support of this announcement. It was as though they were hearing the words of Dr. Rhodes when he said, "We must lay a secure and broad foundation."

As part of her job as toastmistress, Ruth Seaver Kirk commented: "It is a splendid thing for any school to have an alumni association; there is a feeling of loyalty that is manifested in a significant way when graduates of a school return to renew friendships with former faculty and classmates."

It is interesting to note that the former New Hampshire commissioner, Mr. Ernest Butterfield, expressed the hope that at the next legislative session one of the first acts would be to change the name of the normal school to Keene Teachers College. He felt that we should do away with the misnomer of calling our college a normal school.

Sprague Drenan Day

No history of the Keene State College Alumni Association would be complete without mentioning the role that our beloved Sprague Drenan played. In essence, he was the first director of the Alumni Association, although his title was executive secretary. In writing about his association with the Alumni Council, he made this comment: "Your editor of the *Bulletin*, Sprague Drenan, of no class, but an instructor in English at the College and a member of the Alumni Council for sixteen years, thus fell from this position into the delightful editorship of the *Bulletin* without intent."

Falling into that editorship happened when Doctor Young asked Drenan to supervise the building up of the permanent alumni files.

Etta Merrill, class of 1925, spent many hours supporting Drenan in his efforts to find the addresses of former graduates. College students aided also. They would know that there was a Mrs. John Doe of Henniker who attended Keene. They would not know the first or maiden name and seldom knew the addresses of the same person. Finally, one would learn that the person had been married four times and had taken back her maiden name.

Patience and perseverance resulted in the assembling of 800 names and addresses. Merrill asked to have 800 letters duplicated, to receive only 75. When she inquired why her list of 800 had shrunk to 75, she was told that not more than 75 letters were ever sent out; in addition, there were no funds to cover the cost of mailing 800 pieces. An appeal was made to Dr. Young, and Merrill got her letters duplicated and mailed. Here began the organization of the alumni files.

Sheldon Barker (left) of the class of 1921 gets a hearty greeting from John E. Wright, class of 1932, at the alumni reunion weekend Friday night mixer at the Crystal Restaurant in the late 1960s.

Asking Sprague Drenan to take charge of these files was a wise decision. Drenan was ideal for the job. He had a wider acquaintance of students than any other person on campus. One Alumnus, in writing of this man, said: "For thirty-three years, Keene State College and the alumni were richer for this man who honored the arts and brightened the lives of those who came to learn."

It was most fitting when the alumni held a Sprague Drenan Day, May 21, 1962. A total of 500 alumni returned to honor him. When James McKeon stood up at the beginning of the program and said, "I proclaim this Sprague W. Drenan Day," Sprague Drenan could only say, "I'm stunned."

Drenan continued his duties with the alumni even after he retired from teaching. He felt that with his secretary, Jean Kells, he could continue the work with the alumni. The Alumni Council breathed a sigh of relief, for they knew their *Bulletin* and their files were still in capable hands.

Etta Merrill did not stop with mailing those 800 letters. She began to encourage the older graduates to return to celebrate their twenty-fifth anniversary.

In November 1961 Sprague Drenan wrote of these reunions: "The most heartening picture was the fine attendance and obvious happiness of 1916 and 1926. These classes should have reunions every year because they show good examples to all others!"

This led to honoring the fifty-year class. In 1962 only five class members returned to campus for the fiftieth reunion; but in the 1970s several classes had over sixty members present. Often they came in on Friday for a banquet held at a local restaurant, stayed in Fiske Hall where they once lived, and on Saturday received a copy of their commencement program and a booklet containing the life history of each member of the class. It is a tradition now to honor the fiftieth class on Reunion Day.

One fifty-year class, the class of 1926, revived the traditional Rose Night ceremonies as part of its celebration. Rose Night, as all remember, was a memorable event, which Professor Smart has described in Chapter 13.

33

Alumni Activities and Special Events

USUALLY THE ALUMNI manned a hospitality room during the October convention of the New Hampshire Educational Association. Here alumni had an opportunity to catch up on the latest campus news. It was a place where the old gangs, groups, and cliques of undergraduates met. President Redfern was there to greet these groups. The alumni also held a coffee hour before the general session. Exhibits of Keene's courses were available. When the convention moved from Manchester, the book exhibitors ceased their exhibits, and as a result there was nobody in town the night before the general session to attend Keene State College's Hospitality Night. Consequently, this event became history.

In 1971 the board of directors voted to initiate a travel program for the alumni. Arthur's Travel Agency in Philadelphia was contacted, and the first trip was to London. Six alumni spent one week in London and were so enthusiastic on their return that in February 1973 another trip was planned, a one-week trip to Spain. This time, the alumni caught the travel bug, and twenty-four alumni participated. Other trips included Rome, Hawaii, and the Virgin Islands. Though interest continued to grow, the enrollment became insufficient to continue the travel program.

Doctor Redfern, always supportive of alumni activities, seldom missed a board meeting and faithfully attended the screening committee meetings. He solicited alumni support by giving them many presentations on the growth and problems of creating a multipurpose college. He believed that the alumni should serve on such college committees as the physical plant committee, the health and physical education committee, the academic planning committee, and the parents' day committee. From 1969 to 1971 he initiated the custom of having the alumni represent him and the college at inaugurations and other ceremonies. The following people were asked to perform this service: Bruce W. Crowder, Carlton E. Brett, James Pendleton, '59; Frank Kelland, '52; Harold Hapgood, '54; David Staples, '55 M, '60; A. F. Gigliotti, '51 M, '66; Dorothy Bolton Colpitts, '52; Ralph Duso, '35; Edward Brown, '67; Edward T. Greene, Jr., '56; Tinker Trow, '70; and Maitlon C. Rexford, '52.

Homecoming, a fall event, although not as big an event as the traditional Alumni Day, was a move to involve present students with the alumni programs. A soccer game, open houses, a special luncheon (sometimes called the tailgate lunch), and a dance sponsored by the students made a full day for those attending. The 1982 Homecoming included a float parade, an athletic event, a reception at the President's House, and the usual Saturday night dance. Fourteen student organizations enthusiastically built and entered floats for the Homecoming parade.

Another innovation of the 1970s was the auctioning of the Hale Building painting given by Naomi Sylvester, class of 1926. Each year at the Hawaiian Luau, the picture was raffled off. But instead of giving the winner the painting, the winner would be presented with a small picture of it and have his or her name embossed on the brass plate which hung under the painting in Hale Building. During the 1970s this picture accummulated many dollars for the Alumni Fund.

A Keene State College Alumni Camperama was held in June 1971. Nineteen families participated, which meant that sixty-one people camped at Gunstock for the weekend. Ninety-three attended the barbecue on Saturday evening.

The university relations office at Durham suggested that the University of New Hampshire, Keene State College, and Plymouth State College support an information office in Concord to be under the direction of Lila Chase Marshall. Support was to be on the basis of 70 percent, 15 percent, and 15 percent, respectively, and the purpose of this office was to better communicate the needs of the campuses to the legislators. Keene State College alumni have shared in supporting this office since its inception.

The college camp at Wilson Pond was in danger of being closed and sold. Many alumni remembered when the camp played an important role in their college life and urged saving at least the fireplace. This beautiful fireplace, made of rocks from all over the world, was constructed in the 1920s. Three decades of students had shared a common experience, the school camp. If the camp couldn't be saved, save the fireplace! Doctor Redfern assured the alumni that, if the camp were demolished, there would be an effort to preserve the fireplace. That raised the question of what to do with a badly run down camp. Major repairs were needed. Margaret Ramsay encouraged alumni, faculty wives, and faculty to get together for Saturday work bees. They scraped, scrubbed, tore down partitions, put in insulation, and did the paneling. Then came the campus plumbers, electricians, and maintenance men to fix the utilities and refinish the floor. When the work was completed, the camp consisted of a four-room apartment and a small conference room upstairs and a modern kitchen and a large social room downstairs. The rock fireplace was intact, with a special diagram hanging on the social room wall describing the rocks. Today faculty, staff, alumni, and many campus groups enjoy the cozy, friendly atmosphere of the college camp because the alumni cared enough to contribute over $5,000 for this renovation.

The Alumni Association played an important part in the college's bicentennial celebration. Marion Wood was appointed to research the history of Keene State College's historical buildings. Aided by the records of the state's department of resources and economic development, and with assistance from David Proper and Marjorie Smith, both of Keene, three houses were approved by the National Parks Commission for listing in the National Register of Historic Places: Hale Building, the President's House, and Elliot Mansion.

In the 1980s the Alumni Association furnished the music lounge in the Fine Arts Building. Money was given to the history club so that it might provide a gallery of portraits of Keene State College's presidents. They are now attractively displayed in the Mason Library. Many athletic programs benefited from alumni generosity. Thus, the Keene State College Alumni Association continues to work with the administration, the faculty, the staff, and the students so that all may have a quality educational experience.

Special Events

The alumni under the leadership of Stan Johnson made the 1959 reunion a special occasion celebrating the fiftieth anniversary of the founding of Keene State College. Programs were printed with gold covers. Former Professor Merton Goodrich's committee assembled a remarkable group of pictures and other memorabilia in the library. In the evening participants viewed movies of college days and listened to the Westfield Teachers College and the Keene Chapter Chorus.

Children's prize books were displayed in the library. These books, purchased with income from the Marion Frost Hudson Memorial Fund, had been selected by Pauline Lorandeau Croteau. Pauline and her students in children's literature planned this exhibit for many years after Mrs. Hudson's death. Each book carried a bookplate designed by the well-known illustrator, Nora Unwin. Marion Frost Hudson was a teacher in the English department from 1923 until her death in 1958. The fund in her memory had been established by students, alumni, and friends.

The Alumni Association takes pride in honoring special people. Concerning the Sprague W. Drenan Day, mentioned earlier, Drenan himself said: "I can never be grateful enough to the sneaky Alumni Council who did this so cleverly that I never suspected. I wish that I could go on being your secretary for the next fifty years!"

The alumni honored Dr. Lloyd P. Young in 1964 on the occasion of his retirement as the third president of the college. The spring issue of the *Bulletin* carried this caption: "Retiring President Lloyd P. Young, Ph.D., to whom the 1964 Alumni Day is dedicated and in whose honor Alumni and undergraduates planned the Lloyd P. Young Memorial Union. Many will bid him and Mrs. Young Godspeed on his educational mission to Peru." And they did; many attended the banquet to give Dr. and Mrs. Young a memorable spine-tingling reception.

In 1977 the Alumni Association honored Dr. Fred Barry, its director for the past twelve years. About 500 friends and alumni attended this special reunion and the testimonial reception held in the Mabel Brown

Room. Fred received a chair, a book of letters, and a money tree signifying twenty-nine years of service to the college. In the morning President Emeritus Young had officially dedicated the Alumni Center as the Fred Barry Alumni Center. Alumni from far and near acclaimed Fred as being an outstanding example of a person who "enters to learn, goes forth to serve." This man had endeared himself to many.

The 1970s, Dr. Fred Barry Years

The 1970s will go down in the history of the Alumni Association as one of the outstanding decades of progress. In 1964 Dr. Zorn, then president, felt the need for a strong Keene State College alumni group and interviewed candidates for the first executive director of the Keene State College Alumni Association. Fred was an excellent choice for this position, as he had served the college in many positions: bookstore coordinator; director of veterans affairs; grounds crew coordinator; professor of history, English, and sociology; dean of men; and financial aid officer. Besides, Fred was a past president of the Alumni Association and had served on many of its committees. When announcing Dr. Barry's appointment, Dr. Zorn said: "His years of service to the college will be a strong asset in developing a strong alumni."

In accepting the assignment, Fred said, "It is my objective to serve the college and the alumni as I have in the past and to guide this association in its transition from the respected image so well established by Sprague Drenan to a model Alumni Association."

In working toward his objective, Fred was assisted by two Judys. Judy Trow was secretary in the alumni office for four years and still continues her interest. She and her husband, Tinker, often arranged a Keene State College Alumni meeting in Washington, D.C., entertaining the visitors from campus as part of the program.

Judy Moody served as secretary during much of the 1970s, leaving the position in 1979. Judy's service to the association was such that the alumni board of directors made her an honorary member of the Keene State College Alumni Association in 1976.

Both women did much to support the alumni in their interest in becoming the "strong arm of the college," and both women were made honorary members of the association.

Dr. Barry and the two Judys handled the fund drive and the publications and planned and organized the reunions and the area meetings. They kept records of all alumni and maintained the alumni archives and the

Robert L. Mallat, Jr. leads the traditional alumni march to Saturday luncheon on an Alumni Weekend in the 1970s. Fred L. Barry (left) and John Moody follow with the banner.

alumni quarters. They participated in Parents Day, the various athletic events, and commencement and Homecoming. There was the constant need to encourage and recruit volunteers — volunteers for committees to help with the programs and volunteers for class secretaries and agents. The hours were long, and many a weekend was devoted to some social function with the alumni.

Judy Moody wrote of her work in one week: "This week we have addressed 5,000 envelopes for the Fine Arts Project; 8,000 Alumni magazines are to be addressed; ballots need to be composed and sent to the printer; the announcement of the area meetings will be run off on the addressograph; 524 pieces for the Seacoast Area meeting were mailed out." There were letters to the legislators inviting them to the Seacoast meeting that had to be prepared. And, of that particular day Judy was describing, she said: "This evening we hosted an alumni coffee and chat after the basketball game between Keene State College and Plymouth State College. Over 100 alumni attended."

These activities were positive proof that the alumni were actively supporting Keene State College students and staff and could take part of the credit for their achievement. Many aspects of the college now viewed as traditional were helped into being through the funding and support of the Alumni Association.

A New Director

In July 1977 Donald Carle assumed the position of director of the Alumni Association. As Carle said in his 1978 report to the alumni, it was a year of change as he became acquainted with the well-developed programs of the 1970s. The first major event of the new administration was Homecoming. Recent graduates joined the undergraduates for the Rock Dance on Friday night. On Saturday there were tours of the campus and an exciting soccer game between Keene State College and Southern Connecticut State College. Almost 1,000 people danced to Ted Hebert's Band in the gymnasium.

Although the Keene State College exhibit at the Teachers Convention seemed to be fading away, over 200 alumni visited the Keene State College booth in Peterborough, the location of the NHEA Teachers Convention in 1977.

Recognition Day for secretaries and agents continued, as did the area meetings. The renovations at Elliot Hall were completed, and the alumni were loyally supporting the annual fund drive.

New President Barbara Seelye challenged the association to share in the excitement of building a unique college. She stressed the need for telling prospective students about the quality of the college and experience at Keene State College. She urged the alumni to give recommendations for change, improvement, and aspiration.

Clubs and Area Meetings

During the 1920s and 1930s when the alumni were holding triennial meetings on campus, clubs were encouraged. There were local clubs and clubs in some of the state's leading cities. During one March the Boston club had Miss Vaughn as its speaker. Little was said about her message, but she did encourage all to attend the triennial meeting to be held on campus in June.

In 1958 Malcolm Keddy, Keene Teachers College English instructor and president of the college's Monadnock Region Alumni Association, organized a panel discussion on the college's future. They prepared for an attendance of 200 alumni. Registration was at 3:00 on a Saturday afternoon, and the two-hour panel discussion began at 3:30 P.M. Dr. Young moderated the panel. Participants were: Dean Carle, Dr. Barry, Lloyd Hayn, Dr. Ann Peters, Clair Wyman, and Gray Pearson. A buffet supper was held in the gymnasium after this discussion.

A more recent successful club is the Florida Alumni Association. This club, organized by Norm Hartfiel and Ray Harwood, held its first meeting in 1977. In 1978, with assistance from the alumni office, a second meeting was planned. Seventy-four people attended this meeting. The club continues to grow and is now one of the largest affiliated with the Alumni Association.

Another recent club, the $100 Club, was organized by those alumni giving $100 annually to their alma mater. For several years in succession these members were invited back to campus for dinner and a reception with Dr. and Mrs. Redfern as hosts. Usually the evening ended with musical entertainment. From the success of the $100 Club grew to Golden Carillon for $50 donors and the $500 and $1,000 Club members!

Rather than clubs, area meetings became popular in the 1970s. Regardless of the number of area meetings, Dr. Redfern seldom missed one. His presence was appreciated by the alumni, who enjoyed hearing directly about the college, its plans, the programs, and the problems. Trustee Margaret Ramsay also made an effort to be in attendance; from her, the alumni learned about the University System as the trustees moved ahead with the appointment of the first chancellor.

As many as eight area meetings were held during some years, but the pressures of planning entertainment and supplying personnel seemed to dictate that five or six meetings might be better. Don Nelson was appointed to chair a committee to study area meetings. The committee suggested five regional meetings to be held in the five different sections of the state: the North Country, the Lakes region, the Seacoast region, the Dartmouth-Lake Sunapee region, and the Merrimack Valley region. Area meetings could then be rotated between the cities and towns in these five sections. The committee felt that area meetings should be continued because they were a valuable tool in bringing alumni together for an evening of social activity as well as informing them about what was happening on campus.

The year 1975 was probably the most active year for area meetings. Two purposes were achieved by these meetings. First, the college was proud that five New Hampshire vocational-technical colleges were under the directorship of former graduates: Roland Stoodley, '56, Claremont; Robert H. Turner, '50, Laconia; George Know, '34, Manchester; and Edward Oleson, '44, Berlin. Second, it was timely that the alumni meet in these respective colleges to learn at first hand what these colleges were doing for the education of New Hampshire's youth.

This was also the year that the popular Celebrant Cabaret was organized by the college drama department. With their dinner-theater motif, they provided an excellent program. Everywhere they went they were proof that Keene State College was rapidly turning into a small multipurpose college with a strong liberal arts program. They and the Jazz Ensemble were excellent demonstrations that the Fine Arts program was now moving ahead at the college. These student groups stimulated alumni interest in supporting the Fine Arts Building, which was so much needed if the college was to continue building its image as a multipurpose institution.

As an outgrowth of these meetings, the board of directors of the Alumni Association voted to present the trustees of the University System with a resolution stating its support for locating the Fine Arts Building at or near Brickyard Pond. Its president presented this resolution in person to the properties committee of the board of trustees.

The Seacoast meeting under Joanne Grasso was one of the most successful during this period. Ninety alumni attended the meeting along with ninety area legislators, who responded to the committee's invitation to see the Keene State College fine arts group in a lively performance. It was an evening of sociability and provided an opportunity for Keene State College alumni to meet their legislators and discuss the value of their college.

Out-of-state meetings were held in Connecticut and Rhode Island. The Connecticut, a biennial meeting, was generally held in Willie's Steak House in Manchester, Connecticut. At one such meeting a group of students described the freshman camp project which was held in the summer of 1975. The alumni had voted to support this activity, and students selected for their leadership potential went to a camp located on Wentworth Lake near Wolfeboro. Here they learned about the traditions at Keene State College and developed into a nucleus group to welcome entering freshmen. Although an extremely effective program, it declined as changes were made in the college administrative staff. However, many of the ideas developed at this freshman camp are used in the present-day college orientation program which welcomes freshmen and their parents to the campus.

One activity that showed the leadership of Keene State College alumni was a System meeting of the alumni boards. Dr. Redfern was instrumental in getting together a meeting of the Keene, Plymouth, and University of New Hampshire board members held in Manchester. Keene State College and the alumni were hosts for this excellent meeting. Information sharing with fellow board members in the System with respect to budgetary needs, legislative strategy, publication, and social activities was particularly valuable to those attending.

Stories of early clubs reinforced the fact that even in its early history the Alumni Association was alive and very active. During Dr. Young's presidency the Alumni Association voted to have annual meetings. The programs generally followed this format: registration in the morning, a coffee hour, athletic contests, class meetings, lunch around 12:30 P.M., baseball and tennis in the afternoon, and the garden party at 3:30 P.M. Dr. and Mrs. Young and the faculty would be in the receiving line. Sometimes there would be a concert by a choral group.

34

From Then to Now

THE KEENE STATE COLLEGE Alumni Association is nearly sixty-five years old. For the first nine years of the life of the college, no attempt was made to have a formal association. Graduates of the college got together in triennial meetings to enjoy a luncheon and to renew former friendships. In 1920 a group of alumni living in the area decided that there should be an association and elected Mildred B. Murphy as its president. Little is recorded of these years. In 1925 there was a meeting of the southern New England alumni in Boston; Mildred attended this meeting and was still president. Mabel Fisher was president from 1927 to 1930, when she relinquished the presidency to Ruth Seaver Kirk. Ruth served a three-year term, and then Cleon Heald took over. Heald's presidency ended in 1939 when the association decided to have annual meetings.

The association was called the Keene Alumni, and the governing board was the council. In 1967, the trustees of the University System voted to change the name to the Keene State College Alumni Association, and the governing body became the board of directors. Each year the association increases its membership by about 500 members as the graduating seniors associate themselves with this voluntary group.

Through the years the organization has changed its structure, but its purpose has remained constant — promoting the welfare of the college and its alumni so that a mutually profitable relationship may be established between the two. Just as a healthy institution needs an endowment, it also needs an active alumni association. The record of the Keene State College Alumni Association is a record of a vigorous and vital alumni!

The Alumni Awards Program

An alumni brochure carries this line — "They have served." These are the people that our Alumni Association has chosen to honor through their awards program.

The first award given was the Dorothy Elizabeth Potter Award for proficiency in English; it was established in 1958 by a generous gift from Professor Emeritus Ella Keene. Dorothy Elizabeth Potter, a cousin of Miss Keene, taught in New Hampshire until her death in 1957. She was a successful teacher and a sympathetic and outgoing person. She participated in many campus activities; she was a member of Sigmi Pi Epsilon and Kappa Delta Pi.

Each year, a senior is chosen by the English department to represent the qualities of scholarship, leadership, and personal growth that make him or her worthy of the Dorothy Elizabeth Potter Award. Each time the award is granted, an official record is placed on file with the alumni director. The record contains a brief biographical sketch of the recipient.

The student receives a certificate and a check for $200. It is interesting to note that through additional contributions and the original capital fund being invested, this award, which was once $50, has now become $200.

The second award was established by the Keene State College Alumni Association in honor of Professor Frank H. Blackington, Jr. Professor of French and metal crafts and director of the placement bureau at Keene State College. Professor Blackington is often referred to as the complete

Keene State College personage, not only because of himself, but also because of his family. Dora Haywood, his wife, was a Keene State College art teacher at the time of their marriage. Their children, called the Blackington twins, Frank III, and Priscilla, graduated from Keene Teachers College in 1950.

Members of the class of 1933 were largely responsible for initiating this award, which is given to a senior who must demonstrate proficiency in a foreign language and in the rest of his or her academic pursuits. The recipient must be a member of the Keene State College foreign languages department. This award has grown to $300.

The Sprague W. Drenan Award was first presented to Etta Merrill, class of 1925. The award is given for outstanding participation in alumni activities. Drenan served the college for thirty-three years. He was known for his love of drama and was the first director of the *Old Homestead* upon its revival in the Potash Bowl in Swanzey Center. He was head of the English department, an ardent philatelist, and served as executive secretary of the Alumni Association. For years, he was editor of the Alumni Association's *Bulletin.* He was a trustee and treasurer of the Keene Endowment Association.

It is most appropriate that an award in his memory should honor outstanding service to the Alumni Association because Sprague Drenan not only encouraged his students to do their best but also challenged them to *want* to do their best. His dedication to Keene State College remains unchallenged.

Prior to 1971, the Alumni Achievement Award was given with the Sprague Drenan Award. Since that time, the Alumni Achievement Award has been a separate award honoring those who achieve in their chosen field. Honoring such people reflects the strengths of Keene State College and its students. At the present time, Marion Wood is the proud recipient of both the Sprague Drenan Award and the Achievement Award. Plaques identifying the recipients of those who have received awards are kept as a permanent record in the Barry Alumni Center.

In 1971 Margaret Ramsay recommended to the alumni board that it establish the Distinguished Teacher Award. A committee composed of three past recipients, the vice-president of the college, the president of student government, the senior class president, one alumnus, the alumni trustee, and the director of the Alumni Association meets to screen the applicants. Nominations for the teacher award may be made by students, alumni, or faculty. Dr. Ann Peters, who had been head of the mathematics department for ten years, was chosen as the first recipient. Through this

May 1957 photo of the founders of the Keene Endowment Association who served as its first Board of Trustees. From left: John Goodnow, Clair Wyman, Lloyd Young, Alfred Dennis, and Sprague Drenan

award, the alumni honor and promote outstanding teaching and service to the college.

The retiring faculty is another group honored by the Alumni Association. This award is given at the luncheon on Alumni Day in May. It is based on distinguished service and dedication to the Alumni Association.

Gifts and the Keene Endowment Association

The first scholarship by the alumni was given at the 1933 meeting. The alumni had raised a fund of $60 to be called the Henry C. Morrison Scholarship Fund. This scholarship was to be lent to upperclassmen who were considered worthy of assistance by the president and the faculty.

Gifts had been given before, but this was the first financial assistance donated by the alumni. Other gifts had usually been pictures, a frieze, gates to Parker Hall, bird bath, water fountain, and the pergola through which alumni marched on the annual Alumni Day. Some of the pictures hang in the Barry Alumni Center.

In 1966 Keene State College alumni donated $5,000 to match a 1965 grant. It was then that the Alumni Council decided to make fundraising an annual event. Until that year the only regular call upon the alumni was the $2 support dues for the Alumni Association. These dues generally covered the cost of mailing the *Bulletin*. The idea to give financial assistance to students began to grow.

In 1969 Mrs. Alma Matson Hodgkins of the class of 1921 and her husband, Russell C. Hodgkins, gave $18,000 to establish a loan fund at Keene

State. In establishing this fund, Mr. and Mrs. Hodgkins said that it was their "investment in youth."

Prior to this, and in memory of Dr. Young's son, Maxwell, who had been killed in an automobile accident, the faculty and friends contributed funds to establish the Maxwell Young Scholarship Fund.

In the mid-1950s all monies at the end of the fiscal year had to be returned to the state treasury. Feeling that the funds of the Maxwell Young Scholarship were not state funds, Dr. Young approached the attorney general of the state and asked what action should be taken to maintain these funds as a scholarship.

The attorney general suggested that Dr. Young form an association separate from the college and incorporate it so that it might be custodian of any funds donated for the benefit of Keene State students.

On May 9, 1957, Alfred Dennis, Sprague Drenan, Lloyd P. Young, John Goodnow and Clair Wyman signed the articles of incorporation bringing the Keene Endowment Association into being. Of this original group two members still serve as trustees: Dr. Young and Clair Wyman.

From time to time, new trustees have been appointed until today there are eighteen members. These members manage and supervise all property acquired by devise, legacy, or purchase and hold the same in trust for aiding and promoting the education and welfare of the students at Keene State College.

An investment committee meets quarterly to monitor the investments. Since 1957 the original funds have grown to nearly $500,000. The Keene Endowment Association serves the important function of highlighting and insuring that donor's wishes are achieved. Through the work of the trustees, the memorialization of people is protected and preserved. The accumulation of these endowment funds furnished a base for a solid endowment so essential to a quality institution.

In 1983 the funds from the Keene Endowment served 281 borrowers. Scholarships were granted to 29 students.

Funds managed by the Keene Endowment Association are of two types: (1) those in which the principal may be invested but must remain intact, with only the interest being used annually; (2) revolving funds in which the principal and any income it earns may be used. A record of each fund and how it is administered is kept on permanent file by the Keene Endowment Association.

Since 1979 four new scholarships have been added to those already established. They are the Leo Redfern Scholarship, the Leona Day Henderson Scholarship, the Keene State College Family Assistance Scholarship, and a new Keene State College Alumni Association Scholarship. It is apparent that, as the need became greater for student assistance, the alumni turned from picture giving to donating dollars for the benefit of scholars.

The trustees serve willingly and without recompense so that these funds donated by loyal alumni and friends of Keene State College may be successfully managed. These trustees are doing their part to make Dr. Rhodes's vision of Keene State College a "bulwark of education."

Thorne-Sagendorph Art Gallery

Keene State College and the community were greatly enriched by Mrs. Beatrice Sagendorph's gift of the Thorne-Sagendorph Art Gallery. The gallery opened in 1965 and quickly attracted the support and interest of many alumni. Alumni donated generously to the gallery in 1977, 1978, and 1979, when Mrs. Sagendorph agreed to match their gifts.

The original gift by Mrs. Sagendorph was in memory of her mother, Mrs. Thorne. She later added the beautiful wing to honor her husband. Many important pieces of art have been accumulated by the gallery due to Mrs. Sagendorph's interest and work. This gift was the second major capital gift by a philanthropist and came some thirty-five years after the Huntley Spaulding Gymnasium.

A New Office

Upon Fred Barry's appointment in 1965 as the new alumni executive secretary, it was obvious that the alumni needed a new office with new furnishings. The generosity of the alumni enabled the committee in charge to redecorate the second-floor suite of rooms in Rhodes Hall with a golden decor of rugs, draperies, and furniture fabrics. In this second-floor suite Fred Barry and Judy Trow conceived and conducted the alumni programs, the aim of which was to promote the welfare of the college and the alumni. Through this office and back to campus flowed the dedicated efforts of the alumni.

In 1975 the Alumni Association office was given the opportunity to move to the second floor of the Elliot Mansion, the college having taken over this building and constructed many administrative offices there.

Ruth Young Kimball, class of 1970, and her committee worked for three years to restore the Alumni Center to its original decor. As Ruth stated in her report, "The Keene State College Alumni Association is proud to be, in a sense, the curator of the mansion section of Elliot Hall." The second-floor section, now named Barry Alumni Center, is the home of the offices, the workroom, the social room, the conference room, and the archives room of the association.

In 1978 the decorating committee concentrated its efforts on completing the third-floor guest section. The alumni board had voted to provide overnight lodging on the third floor for visiting alumni and campus guests. Eight classes made furnishing these bedrooms their class gift: 1916, 1918, 1926, 1927, 1928, 1936, 1938, and 1942. The first overnight guest on the third floor was Dr. Lloyd Young, president emeritus.

Other gifts to the Barry Center were the history and archives room given by the class of 1925 to celebrate its fiftieth anniversary; a beautiful crystal chandelier that hangs above the curved stairway, a gift of the class of 1917; and a graceful grandfather clock made by Spencer Eaton that stands in the corner of the conference room.

Other Gifts

When Barbara Seelye accepted the presidency, she began an extensive renovation of the President's House. Again, the alumni gave chandeliers and beautiful oriental rugs for the reception room and for the hall. These gifts may be viewed at the annual reception held by President Seelye as a featured activity of the Alumni Day program.

Gifts that appear at every graduation are the medallion and the mace. The medallion, worn by the president, was designed by the inaugural committee for the fifth inauguration. The mace, designed by Frank Tisdale, professor emeritus, symbolizes civilization and human understanding. The ball at the top of the mace represents wholeness of persons and things.

Every noon, the campus hears beautiful tunes from the carillon, a constant reminder that Keene State College has alumni who care. When the Fine Arts Building was under construction and money was needed for chairs in the recital hall, the alumni purchased chairs. Each chair now carries the name of its donor.

Through the years, the alumni have supported the Keene Summer Theater at the college. This is one of the oldest summer theaters in the region and one of the few remaining in the area. It has grown and prospered, and some of this growth has been greatly aided by alumni support.

The list of gifts is long; only a few are mentioned here — enough to show that Keene State College graduates have built and continue to build on the first president's dream that Keene become an educational "bulwark in the state." It would be difficult to find a more dedicated and generous group than the Keene State College alumni. Annually they demonstrate the motto that hung for so many years in Parker Hall: "Enter to learn, go forth to serve."

APPENDICES

PRESIDENTS AND MAJOR DEANS OF THE COLLEGE

Presidents

Jeremiah M. Rhodes Jr.	1909-11	Roman J. Zorn	1964-69
Wallace E. Mason	1911-39	Leo F. Redfern	1969-79
Lloyd P. Young	1939-64	William F. Whybrew (acting)	1979-80
	Barbara J. Seelye	1980-	

Major Academic Deans

Isabelle U. Esten	Dean	1919-32
H. Dwight Carle	Dean	1932-60
Lloyd Hayn	Dean of Instruction	1961-62
David Sarner	Dean of Instruction	1962-66
Edward L. Pierce	Dean of Instruction (acting)	1966-67
Clarence Davis	Dean of Instruction	1967-69
	Dean of the College	1969-75
William E. Whybrew	Dean of the College	1975-81
Richard A. Gustafson	Vice President: Academic Affairs	1981-

Major Personnel Deans

Isabelle U. Esten	Dean of Women	1919-50
H. Dwight Carle	Dean of Men	1925-55
Dorothy A. Randall	Dean of Personnel	1950-66
Fred L. Barry	Dean of Men	1955-65
Ernest O. Gendron	Dean of Men/Student Affairs	1965-
Margaret Smith	Dean of Women	1966-67
Ruth W. Keddy	Dean of Women	1966-76
Thomas Aceto	Dean of Student Affairs	1970-75
Ronald J. Herron	Dean of Student Affairs	1977-

PRESIDENTS OF THE PARENTS ASSOCIATION

A resource and continuing help to the college that Leo Redfern officially recognized were the interested parents of students. He did this by the formation of the KSC Parents Association. The association is headed by an executive board, which has varied between seven and thirteen in number. The following is a list of the association presidents.

Joseph Spallone	1973-1975	Roger Moore	1978-1980
Joseph Dimaria	1975-1976	Andrew Kinne	1980-1981
Richard Clason	1976-1978	Maryann Wallace	1981-1983
	Allan Taylor	1983-1984	

BUILDINGS OF THE COLLEGE

Building*	Architect	Style
Hale Building		Italianate
Presidents House		Federal
Parker	Brainerd & Leeds	
Fiske	Mr. Brainerd of Brainerd & Leeds, Boston	
Fiske (east end)	"	Classical
Heating Plant	"	Classical
Penelope House		
College Camp		
Blake (original)		
Blake Addition		
Huntress	C. R. Whitcher	Classical
Butterfield		Classical
Butterfield addition		
Spaulding	C. R. Whitcher	Classical
Monadnock	John Holbrook	Functional
Old Bookstore		
Butterfield addition	John Holbrook	Classical
Morrison	Kohler Isaak	Modified classical
Bushnell Apt.		Modern
Newman Center (Old Stearns Property)		
Whitcomb Building		
Dining Commons	John Carter (Nashua)	Modern
Library		Modern
Randall	Holbrook Assoc. & Guy Wilson of Concord	Contemporary Colonial
Science Building	Frank Grad & Sons Newark, NJ	Modern
Spaulding	Perry, Dean, Hepburn and Stewart, Boston	Modern
Student Union		
Carle Hall	Griswald, Boyden, Wylde & Ames (Boston)	Modern
Tisdale Apts.	Fleck & Lewis (Hanover)	
Owls Nests (1st 6)		Shed Roof
Elliot Hall		Federal
Last Library Addition		
Fine Arts Bldg.	Jean-Paul Carlhion Shelpey, Bullfinch, Richardson & Abbott (Boston)	Modern

In order of acquisition by the College

Date Built	Builder	Date Opened	Capacity	Cost
1860	Daniel Buss & Cyrus Woodward (Keene)			
1805	James Bond			
1914	Nashua Bldg. Co.		200	
1914	Nashua Bldg. Co.			
1915				
1914				
bought 1912				
bought 1929				
1836	Capt. Abel Blake			
1927-28				
	H.P. Cummins (Ware, MA)	6/18/26	157 5 classrooms	$ 25,000
1958				
1927-28	Glenroy Scott	9/14/28		
1954-55	MacMillan	5/19/56	150	$ 350,000
12/38	MacMillan			$ 30,000
1957-59	MacMillan	11/1/59		$ 350,000
1959-60	MacMillan	5/20/61		$ 600,000
1963	MacMillan	Mar. 12	32 families	
bought 1965		open 1966		$ 354,857
				$ 581,000
1966	R. E. Bean	5/1/66		
	MacMillan	5/23/65		$ 428,957
	MacMillan			$1,367,250
1966				
1967	MacMillan	11/17/68		$1,679,710
1968-69	Joseph E. Bennett Co. (Needham, MA)		1600 main gym	$1,499,700
		10/26/69		
1968-69	MacMillan	5/17/70	304	$1,777,109
	M. W. Goodell	8/13/73	26 families	$ 398,000
1973-74	Emile Leger			
1811	Cpt. Wm. Wyman			$1,400,000
				$1,001,857
1979-80	MacMillan			($4,514,000 tot.)

ALUMNI

Alumni Association Presidents

1983-84	Jacqueline Abbot '58	1965-66	Sherman A. Lovering '49
1981-83	Clair E. Wyman '39	1964-65	Fred L. Barry '36
1980-81	Richard A. Neilsen '60, M. Ed. '70	1963-64	Harold E. Nugent '58
		1961-63	Arline V. Lund '37
1979-80	Phyllis Hall Curtiss '49	1960-61	Paul C. Perkins '39
1978-79	Donald Nelson '69	1958-60	Stanley Johnson '38
1977-78	John H. Moody '71, M. Ed. '76	1957-58	Malcolm H. Keddy '41
		1955-57	Clair Wyman '39
1976-77	Philip R. Hammond '57	1954-55	William Wolffer '40
1975-76	Marion Tebbetts Wood '26	1952-54	Fred L. Barry '36
1974-75	Donald P. Carle '52, M. Ed. '56	1951-52	Albert Mosley '46
		1950-51	Harold Bridge '32
1973-74	David Costin '56, M. Ed. '59	1949-50	Etta Merrill '25
1972-73	Harold A. Hapgood '54, M. Ed. '64	1946-49	Vacant
		1945-46	Vera Bertler '29
1971-72	David B. Staples '55, M. Ed. '60	1941-45	Vacant
		1939-41	William Steele '31
1969-71	Margaret Russell Ramsay '56, M. Ed. '64	1936-39	Leonard B. Dewyea '28
		1933-36	Cleon Heald '21
1968-69	Gordon Bean '59	1930-33	Ruth Seaver Kirk '17
1967-68	Marion S. Ball '59, M. Ed. '60	1927-30	Mabel Fisher '15
1966-67	Sydney W. Lorandeau '58	1920-27	Mildred Murphy* '15

*The records in the Archive Room of the Keene State College Alumni Association give little information on association activities in the early 1920s except to say that a group of graduates in the area decided to form an association. From the few records available, it is apparent that Mildred Murphy served as president from 1920-1927.

Sprague Drenan Award Recipients

Etta Merrill '25	1968
Stanley A. Johnson '38	1969
Newell J. Paire '36, M. Ed. '55, Hon. '71	1970
Arthur Giovangeli '37	1971
F. Marion Tebbetts Wood '26	1972
Sherman A. Lovering '49	1973
Herbert J. J. Spichter '55	1974
Paul H. Nordman '38	1975
Joanne C. Stroshine '65	1976
David B. Staples '55	1977
Constance C. Tremblay '57	1978
Bertha Stearns Davis '18	1979
Ruth Y. Kimball '43	1980
John H. Moody '71	1981
Phyllis Hall Curtiss '49	1982
Margaret Russell Ramsay '56	1983

Alumni Distribution

By State as of 1980			
Alabama	5	Missouri	10
Alaska	8	Montana	7
Arizona	40	Nebraska	
Arkansas	5	Nevada	3
American Samoa		New Hampshire	5965
California	124	New Jersey	177
Canal Zone		New Mexico	9
Colorado	25	New York	370
Connecticut	644	North Carolina	27
Delaware	11	North Dakota	1
District of Columbia	8	Ohio	34
Florida	265	Oklahoma	3
Georgia	15	Oregon	12
Guam		Pennsylvania	65
Hawaii	4	Puerto Rico	2
Idaho	2	Rhode Island	81
Illinois	28	South Carolina	8
Indiana	10	South Dakota	2
Iowa	8	Tennessee	6
Kansas	6	Texas	33
Kentucky	2	Utah	4
Louisiana		Vermont	587
Maine	232	Virginia	67
Maryland	43	Virgin Islands	3
Massachusetts	1114	Washington	20
Michigan	16	West Virginia	7
Minnesota	7	Wisconsin	15
Mississippi	1	Wyoming	3

Ranking by State

NH - 5965	CT - 644	NY - 370	ME - 232	CA - 124
MA - 1114	VT - 537	FL - 265	NJ - 177	RI - 81

Total Active Alumni
10,183, as of 1980 with 12,800 estimated for 1984.

IN MEMORIAM

Occasionally the exuberance of college life is interrupted by untimely death which deeply affects the whole community. The following list honors those students who were unable to complete their careers because of fatal illness or accident. Since records are so incomplete this list cannot be regarded as definitive. It is, however, a beginning; perhaps alumni will subsequently supply further information.

Student	Year of Death	Student	Year of Death
Helen Adams	1915	Lisa Trent	1977
Mildred McDowell	1922	Cherylee Van Rossum	1978
Hazel Barden	1925	Bissell Alderman Jr.	1979
Myrtle Straw	1938	Sandra Bedell	1979
Kenneth E. Bailey	1949	Dawn Gauthier	1979
Edward L. Reynolds	1949	Broderick Lee	1981
Jeanne Pearson	1965	Kenneth Smiarowski Jr.	1982
Karl L. Koski	1970	Mary Frances Flemming	1982
Christopher Bunce	1970	Leonard Martin	1982
Tracey Thomas	1974	William Scott	1983
Irene Calhoun	1976	Suzanne Callis	1983
Valerie Shank	1976	Nils David Larson	1984
Arlene Boland	1976		
Niles Blunt	1976		

The following alumni and students are known to have died during World War II.

	Class		Class
Thomas D. Dillant	'41	Lloyd Marin	'43
Frederick Clayton	'42	Lewis Montrone	'36
Francis Discoll	'33	Bruce Sullivan	'34
Thomas Essie	'46	Edwin Hill	'34
Hollis Furbush	'43		

A p p e n d i c e s

BIBLIOGRAPHIC NOTES AND COMMENTS

The Nature of the Sources and the Nature of the Book

Nearly all of the presidents of the United States arranged for the preservation of their papers so that subsequent generations could know their thoughts and deeds. With the exception of Lloyd Young, the presidents of KSC appear to have packed up their correspondence, both official and unofficial, and to have taken it with them on their departure. Young donated some material to the college and his chief aide, Dean Carle also donated a large collection of memorabilia. Some of Young's collection found its way to the library and is now in the Preston Room. Part of it, however and nearly all of Carle's collection were thrown out, it is believed, in a general clean-up campaign in the 1960s. Boxes of materials were supposed to be stashed away in this place or that, but no leads were fruitful. Leo Redfern, Stacy Milbouer and James Smart made a thorough search for the campus in 1976 and found only a few boxes of miscellaneous receipts and cancelled checks.

The absence of an official archives has meant that this history, by necessity, relied much more on personal interviews and student publications than is normal with institutional histories. This is not necessarily a negative, in fact it may be a positive aspect of institutional history. It means, however, that the locus of the view is more often from that of the student or the faculty member, rather than the more centralized view of the chief administrator.

In looking at other college/university histories one learns that anywhere from eight to thirty-five oral interviews are considered a significant source of information. Well over a hundred interviews were used for this work. Interviews were conducted with ex-governors of the state, members of the board of trustees, townspeople, faculty members, students and alumni. These interviews are now stored on tape in the IRS (Information Retrieval System) section of the library.

Precious little manuscript material relating to the history of the college is available. There is some in the Robert Bass Papers at Dartmouth; special permission is needed to view them. There is more information in the papers collected by Dr. Richard A. Martin of New England College on Henry Morrison. Hopefully these, or copies of these, will soon be in the Preston Room. Recently alumni have contributed scrapbooks, letters and other memorabilia to the alumni archives in Elliot Hall. Some of this material is valuable.

Of the official and/or printed matter available, the most important are the State Board of Education Reports; the college "Circulars and Catalogs," the yearbooks, and the college newspapers; and in the Preston Room an extensive scrapbook collection begun in 1914, and maintained until about 1970. This was largely a labor of love on the parts of former librarians Vryling Buffum, Alice Stone and Marion Goodwin. These scrapbooks were most useful, but they were, indeed, a labor of love. Articles critical of the college rarely found a place in the scrapbook collection.

The following, more traditional bibliography was also duly consulted.

General Works

The number of excellent general works on higher education and the history of higher education is staggering. Those used in preparation for this particular study were
Barzun, Jacques. *The American University: How It Runs, Where It Is Going.* New York, 1968.
_____. *Teacher In America.* Boston, 1945.
Berg, Ivar. *Education and Jobs: The Great Training Robbery.* Boston, 1971.
Brickman, William W. and Lehrer, Stanley. *A Century of Higher Education.* New York, 1962.

Brubacher, John S. and Rudy, Willis. *Higher Education in Transition: A History of American Colleges and Universities, 1636-1968*. New York, 1968.

Carnegie Commission on Higher Education. *The Purpose and the Performance of Higher Education in the United States Approaching the Year 2000*. Hightstown, N.J., 1973.

DeVane, William C. *Higher Education in Twentieth-Century America*. Dehli, India, 1967.

Dunham, E. Alden. *Colleges of Forgotten Americans*, Berkely, 1969.

Harvard Committee. *General Education in a Free Society*. Cambridge, Mass., 1945.

Kerber, August, and Smith Wilfred (eds.). *Educational Issues in a Changing Society*, Detroit, 1964.

Meyer, Adolphe E. *Grandmasters of Educational Thought*. New York, 1975.

Messerli, Jonathan. *Horace Mann: A Biography*. New York, 1972.

Moore, William, Jr. *Against the Odds*. San Francisco, 1970.

Nystrom, Dennis C. *Occupation and Career Education Legislation*, New York, 1973.

Partridge, Lelia E. *Parker's Talks on Teaching*, (Memorial Edition), New York, 1883.

Thompson, John F. *Foundations of Vocational Education*. Englewood Cliffs, 1973.

Van Doren, Mark. *Liberal Education*. New York, 1943.

Wolff, Robert Paul. *The Ideal of the University*. Boston, 1969.

Specialized Book-Length Works

Babcock, Donald C., *et al. History of the University of New Hampshire 1866-1941*, Durham, N.H., 1941.

Bagley, Norton R. *One Hundred Years of Service: A History of Plymouth State College, Plymouth New Hampshire, 1871-1971*. Plymouth, ca. 1971.

Bishop, Eugene. *The Development of a State School System: New Hampshire*. New York, Columbia UTC, 1930.

Brown, Harry Alvin. *Certain Basic Teacher-Education Policies and their Development and Significance in a Selected State [N.H.]*. New York, Columbia UTC, 1937.

Keene History Committee. *"Upper Ashuelot": A History of Keene, New Hampshire*. Keene, N.H., 1968.

Latham, Edward Connery (ed.). *John Sloan Dickey: The Dartmouth Experience*. Hanover, N.H., 1977.

New Hampshire. Interim Commission on Education. *Preliminary Report of the Interim Commission on Education*. Raimond Bowles, Chairman. Concord, 1962.

_____. *Report of the Interim Commission on Education*. Raimond Bowles, Chairman. Concord, 1963.

New Hampshire. *State Education Reports*, 1900-1940. These twenty volumes, particularly the reports by Folsom, Morrison and Butterfield, constitute the fundamental reading for educational conditions in New Hampshire.

New Hampshire. Normal Schools, Trustees of. *Reports 1909-12*. Concord, N.H.

New Hampshire Retired Teachers Association. *Our Yesterdays: An Anthology of Memories and History: A Bicentennial Project, 1975-76*. Keene, 1976.

Sackett, Everett B. *New Hampshire's University*. Somersworth, N.H., 1974.

Smith, Majorie Whalen. *Historic Homes of Cheshire County*. Vol. III. Brattleboro, VT, 1979.

Widmayer, Charles E. *Hopkins of Dartmouth*. Hanover, N.H., 1977.

Articles, Pamphlets, and Booklets

Agan, Thomas, "The New Hampshire Progressives: Who and What Were They?" *Historical New Hampshire*, 34:32-53 (1979).

Beichman, Arnold. "Is Higher Education in the Dark Ages?" *New York Times Magazine*, November 6, 1983.

Clark, A. Chester. "The Legislature of 1907," *The Granite Monthly*, 39:No. 4 (1907).

Hale, Sarah Josepha. "Fiske, Catharine" [*sic.*] in *Women's Record; or, Sketches of All Distinguished Women* . . ., republished, New York, 1970.

Heath, Irving S. "History of Keene State College Campus," NYA study 1940, Preston Room, Keene State College.

Herbst, Jurgen, "Nineteenth-Century Normal Schools in the United States: A Fresh Look," *History of Education*, 9:3 (1980), 219-227.

Hill, Gardiner C. "A Famous Institution: Miss Catherine Fiske's Boarding School of the Early Days," *The Granite Monthly*, 39:335-338 (1907).

_____. "Old Academies of Cheshire County," *The Granite Monthly*, 40:No. 1 (1908).

Hurt, Mary Lee, and Alexander, Margaret. "New Challenges for Home Economics Education," *Journal of Home Economics*, 61:No. 10 (1969)

Ingraham, Mary Elizabeth. "Keene Normal School, 1909-1916." B.A. history thesis, 1978, Keene State College.

Keene School District. *Report of the Board of Education in the Union District of the City of Keene, N.H.* 1901-1950. John Day Education Center, Keene, N.H.

Keene, N.H. "Keene, Souvenir, 1908: An Industrial and Trade Center of the Granite State," (1908). Keene Public Library.

Letourneau, John. "Alpha Pi Tau: History and Handbook," n.d., n.p., New Hampshire State Library, Concord, N.H.

Merriam, Gertrude. "New Hampshire, Our Home State," New Hampshire Historical Society. Concord, N.H.

Metcalf, Henry H. "A Successful Educator: Henry C. Morrison, Superintendent of Public Instruction," *The Granite Monthly*, 42:35-38 (1910).

National Commission on Excellence in Education. David P. Gardner, Chairman. *A Nation At Risk: The Imperative for Educational Reform*, Washington, D.C., 1983.

Pearson, H. C. "Leaders of New Hampshire: Henry B. Quinby," *The Granite Monthly*, 44:No. 12, (1912).

Rockwood, Vivian V. "History of the Home Economics Department at Keene State College, Keene, New Hampshire," 1981. Preston Room, Keene State College.

Scudder, H. H. "New Hampshire College: The New Department of Home Economics," *The Granite Monthly*, 45:No. 10, (1913).

Tufts, Arthur (Chairman). "Report of the State University Study Committee," mimeo (Dec. 1980), New Hampshire State Library, Concord, N.H.

U.S. Congress, 63rd 2nd Session (1913-14). "Vocational Education Commission Report, House Document 1004:1-89.

_____. *Congressional Record*, July 22, 1968. [Debate on Vocational Amendments Act]

Wyman, Helen L. "Keene — On the Ashuelot," *The Granite Monthly*, 41:Nos. 11 & 12, (1909).

Recent Histories of State Colleges - Superior Quality

Brush, Carey W. *In Honor and Good Faith: A History of the State University College at Oneonta, New York*. Oneonta, 1965.

Gamble, Richard D. *From Academy to University, 1866-1966: A History of Wisconsin State University, Platteville, Wisconsin*. Platteville, 1966.

King, James T. and Wyman, Walker D. *Centennial History: the University of Wisconsin — River Falls*. River Falls, 1975.

Lahey, W. Charles. *The Potsdam Tradition: A History and a Challenge*. Appleton-Century-Crofts, N.Y., 1966.

Lee, Arthur O. *College in the Pines: A History of Bemidji State College*. Minneapolis, Minn., 1970.

Serinko, Regis J. *California State College: The People's College in the Monongahela Valley*. Kendall/Hunt Publishing Co., Dubuque, Iowa, 1975.

Vance, Russell. *A Portrait of Edinboro [Pa.]*. Rochester, N.Y., 1977.

STRIVING

Recent Histories of State Colleges with Substantial Information

Fisher, Rosalind R. *The Stone Strength of the Past: Centennial History of the State University College of Arts and Science at Geneseo, New York.* Geneseo, 1971.

Forsythe, James L. *The First 75 Years: A History of Fort Hays State University, 1902-1977.* Fort Hays, 1977.

Sturzebecker, Russell L. *Centennial History of West Chester State College.* West Chester, Pa., 1971.

Watson, Robert J. *Slippery Rock State College: the Legend Behind the Name.* Slippery Rock, Pa., 1982.

White, Kenneth B. *Paterson State College: A History, 1855-1966.* Paterson, 1967.

NOTES

Introduction

1. John Brubacker and Willia Rudy, *Higher Education in Transition: A History of American Colleges and Universities, 1636-1968,* 389; William W. Brickman and Stanley Lehrer, *A Century of Higher Education* (1962), 19; I. L. Kandle, "The Humanities in Search of Students," *American Scholar,* 14:323,325 cited in Brickman and Lehrer, 24-25.

2. See "Historical Introductions" of *Catalogs,* 1980-83 for Alabama A&M, founded by William Councill, the ex-slave; Longwood College, Va., "This was the first State institution of higher learning for women in Virginia," p. 3; University of North Alabama by a carpet-bagger; U. Maine, Presque Isle by dedicated white citizens; Bowie State College, Md., by dedicated black citizens; *re* John Mercer Langston, Virginia State College at Ettick and Langston U., Okla. In some cases other colleges could be cited.

3. Ruth E. Finley, *The Lady of Godey's: Sarah Josepha Hale* (Philadelphia, 1931), 230-33; *Catalog,* Western Montana State College.

4. See "Historical Introductions" of *Catalogs,* 1980-83 for Western Montana College (act of Congress); New Mexico Highland U. (as a territory); Valley City State U. (Texas, by Constitutional Convention).

5. Albany State College, Ga., was originally the Albany Bible and Manual Training Institute (for blacks); Valdosta State College, Ga., for young ladies and also Lexington founded by Horace Mann, which remained a single sex institution up until the 1964; Northeastern State University, Okla., grew out of seminaries for Cherokee men and women; Wilbeforce University remained private while being united with a state supported normal school. See "Historical Introductions" of *Catalogs* 1980-83 for the above colleges. Peru State College, Neb., and Southern Oregon State College from Methodist Episcopal Church; Central State U., Ohio, from the African Methodist Episcopal Church; Chadron State College from the Congregational Church; Western Oregon State College from the Disciples of Christ; both California State College and Clarion State College of Pa. for private white academies.

6. Harris-Stowe College, Mo., was attached to a high school as were the three normal schools created in Oklahoma in 1909; South Carolina State College was created in 1896 as "a normal, industrial, arrgricultural and mechanical college." See *Catalogs;* Alabama A&M was the state normal and industrial school. Many others could be cited.

7. This manuscript sketch, entitled, "Morrison, Henry Clinton . . . Submitted for publication in J. F. Ohles, ed., *Directory of Eminent American Educators,* A Bicentennial project of Phi Delta Kappa; to appear in 1976 or 1977," was given to the author by John A. Morrison. Szoke did not make the same claim in John F. Ohles, ed., *Biographical Dictionary of American Educators,* Greenwood Press, 1978, II, 920. I believe, however, the claim is valid.

8. Cited in Jurgen Herbst, "Nineteenth Century Normal Schools in the United States: A Fresh Look," *History of Education* (English) (1980), Vol. 9, No. 3, 219-22/.

9. *Ibid.*

10. E. Alden Dunham, *Colleges of Forgotten Americans: A Profile of State Colleges and Regional Universities* 1969, front matter; *Monudnock,* 11/22/54.

11. Leo F. Redfern, "Commencement Address," 5/13/79.

Chapter 1

1. Eugene Alfred Bishop, *The Development of a State School System: New Hampshire* (Columbia U.P., 1930), 54 ff.; *New Hampshire State Board of Education Reports, 1907-08* (Morrison), 327-28. Hereinafter cited as *N.H. State Education Reports* with author's name in parenthesis. For the choice of Keene see also Chapter 3.

2. Isabelle Webb Entrikin, "Sarah Josepha Hale and *Godey's Lady's Book*" (Ph.D. dissertation, U. Penn., 1946), 50; "Fiske, Catharine," (*Sic*) in Sarah Josepha Hale, *Women's Record* (New York, 1855, 1970), 866-68. See also Gardner C. Hill, "Old Academies of Cheshire County" and "A Famous Institution: Miss Catherine Fiske's Boarding School of the Early Days," in *The Granite Monthly*, Jan. 1908 and Oct. 1907, respectively.

3. See references to Hale and Fiske in *Upper Ashuelot* (Keene, 1968); *Sentinel*, 5/7/1845.

4. Eliza White, *William Orne White* [Keene Unitarian minister] (New York, 1917), 112; Jonathan Messerli, *Horace Mann: A Biography* (New York, 1972), 438.

5. *Sentinel*, 3/19, 26/45; 5/7/45.

6. *Sentinel*, 10/13, 20/70; Norton R. Bagley, *One Hundred Years of Service: A History of Plymouth State College, 1871-1891* (Plymouth, N.H., n.d.; ca. 1972), 8-9.

7. *N.H. State Education Reports, 1899-1900* (Folsom), 5.

Chapter 2

1. Bagley, *Plymouth State College*, 13.

2. A. B. Rotch to Richard A. Martin, 5/6/49; Ernest L. Silver to Martin, 3/22/46, Richard Martin Papers.

3. John Morrison to J. Smart, 8/16/81; William Foster Rice to Martin, 4/27/46; Edward Watson to Martin, 4/8/46; Joseph Ford to Martin, 3/28/46, Martin Papers.

4. Joseph Ford to Martin, 3/28/46; Ernest Hopkins to Martin, 5/17/46; W. B. Fellows to William H. Crobin, 11/15/17, Martin Papers.

5. Edward Watson to Martin, 4/8/46; A. B. Rotch to Martin, 5/6/49, Martin Papers; John Morrison to J. Smart, 8/16/81.

6. On Herbart from Adolphe E. Meyer, *Grandmasters of Educational Thought* (1975), 236-43; Hopkins to Martin, 5/17/46, Martin Papers.

7. H. C. Morrison, "New Hampshire" (Address on Plymouth's 60th anniversary), Martin Papers; *N.H. State Education Reports, 1905-06* (Morrison), 236-37.

8. *N.H. State Education Reports, 1909-10* (Morrison), 249; Morrison, "New Hampshire," *op. cit.*

9. *N.H. State Education Reports, 1905-06* (Morrison), 267.

10. *N.H. State Education Reports, 1915-16* (Morrison), 172; Hugo Beck to Martin, 4/4/63; Martin Papers; John Morrison to J. Smart, 11/30/81.

11. John Morrison to Smart, *ibid.*; Morrison to Churchill, 10/2/12, Bass Papers, Dartmouth.

12. Richard A. Martin, "Footnotes on a Distinguished Educator and Alumnus," unpublished article, Martin Papers; John Morrison to Smart, 6/16/81.

13. Morrison to Butterfield, 6/16/27, Martin Papers.

14. Martin, "Footnotes," *op.cit.*; John Morrison to Smart, 11/30/18; Harry A. Brown, "Henry C. Morrison and His Contribution to American Education," *School and Society*, 6/9/45, 380-82; Charles Judd to Martin, n.d. but ca. 1947, Butterfield to Morrison, 7/7/26, Martin Papers.

Chapter 3

1. Dunham, 27; The story originated from Peru Normal, Neb., now Peru State. Considerable horse trading had taken place in the 1866-67 legislature over the location of the capital and university. Peru got the normal school as a "consolation" prize. Col. T. J. Ma-

jors, representing Peru, was supposed to have said, "He didn't know what a normal school was, but anything for higher education would help his people." Ernest Longfellow, *The Normal on the Hill* (Grand Island, Neb., 1967), 12. *N.H. State Education Reports, 1905-1906* (Morrison), 184-85; N.H., *Journals of the Senate and the House, 1905*, 492.

2. *Sentinel*, 3/2/05; *N.H. State Education Reports, 1905-06* (Morrison), 198; New Hampshire, Annual Reports, 1905-06, Vol. IV; *N.H. State Education Reports, 1907-08* (Morrison), 627-31.

3. N.H., *Journals of the Senate and the House, 1907*, 74, 91, 144, 172; Chester A. Clark, "The Legislature of 1907," *Granite Monthly*, 4/07, 111-12.

4. *Sentinel*, 2/8, 11/07.

5. *Sentinel*, 2/21/07; N.H., *Journals of the Senate and the House, 1907*, 4/5/07, 805.

6. Thomas Agan, "The New Hampshire Progressives: Who and What Were They?" *Historical New Hampshire*, 34:1, 32-53; *Cheshire Republican*, 1/8/09; *Nashua Telegraph*, 4/1, 10/09; *Concord Monitor*, 4/9, 10/09.

7. KNS Clippings, 1/23/14, Preston Room, KSC Library, hereinafter cited as PR; *N.H. State Education Reports, 1907-08* (Morrison), 325-29.

8. *Cheshire Republican*, 3/19/09; 4/9/09; *Sentinel*, 3/31/09; *Concord Monitor*, 3/25/09; 4/1, 6/09; *Nashua Telegraph*, 3/25, 31/09; 4/1/09.

9. "Bertram Ellis" in *Granite Monthly*, July, 1910; KNS Clippings, 4/14/39, PR; *Cheshire Republican*, 4/2/09.

10. N.H., *Journals of the Senate and the House*, 4/1/09, 285-86, and 4/8/09, 379; *Cheshire Republican*, 4/9/09.

Chapter 4

1. From Newman's essay, "The Idea of a University," which can be found in many editions; William T. Seller to Robert Bass, 8/26/10, Bass Papers, Dartmouth.

2. *Sentinel*, 3/22/09. See also "Minutes," of "Meetings of City Councils," 3/18, 20/09, Keene City Hall.

3. *Sentinel*, 5/4, 5/09.

4. Resolution is from *Sentinel*, 5/25/09; see also issue of 5/28/09 and "Minutes" of City Council, 6/17, 24/09, Keene City Hall.

5. *Sentinel*, 6/25, 30/09; 7/3, 9, 23/09. See also Executive Council Records, 1904-09, 8/4/09, p. 404, N.H. State Archives, Concord. On Plymouth see "Report of the Special Committee Appointed by the Governor and Council . . . to the Legislature, June Session, 1877," Preston Room, KSC.

Chapter 5

1. Dunham, *Colleges of Forgotten Americans*, 27-28; National Education Association, *Proceedings* (Philadelphia, 1926), 833.

2. KNS, *Circular and Catalog*, 1910, 1911; Donald C. Babcock, *History of the University of New Hampshire, 1866-1941* (Durham, N.H., 1941), 19 ff.; Bagley, *Plymouth State College, 1871-1971*, 10; *Cheshire Republican*, 12/29/10.

3. *Cheshire Republican*, 8/27/09; *Sentinel*, 7/7/09; flyer from Special Collections, PR, KSC.

4. *Sentinel*, 9/28/09.

5. KNS, *Circular and Catalog*, 1910, 22-23.

6. Interviews with Millicent Washburn and Margaret Gallagher; Alice May Lord, "Class History, 1910-11," PR; Babcock, *History of UNH*, 171-72.

Chapter 6

1. "KNS Class History, 1909-10," PR.

2. *Sentinel*, 10/30/09; "KNS Class History, 1910-11," PR.

3. KNS Class Histories of 1909-10 and 1910-11, PR; *Kronicle*, 5/30/19.

4. "KNS Class History, 1909-10," PR; interviews with Margaret Gallagher and Alice Lord.

5. *Cheshire Republican*, 7/1/10; "Announcements," PR: "KNS Class History 1909-10," PR.

6. KNS Class Histories of 1909-10 and 1910-11, PR; *Cheshire Republican*, 8/11/11; interviews with Alice Lord.

Chapter 7

1. *N.H. State Education Reports, 1911-12* (Morrison), 153-54; KSC *Bulletin* (Alumni), 9/69, 13.

2. *Daily Mirror and American*, Manchester, N.H., 8/23/11 in Bass Papers, hereinafter cited as BP; *Cheshire Republican*, 4/21/11.

3. Lawrence N. Barrett to Bass, 4/16/11; Dorothy D. Groves to Bass, 4/18/11, BP; KNS Clippings, 1/23/14, PR; N.H., *Report of the Trustees of Normal Schools, 1912*, 29.

4. KNS Clippings, 1/23/14, PR.

5. Rhodes on Kent, KNS Clippings, 9/19/32; KNS, *Circular and Catalog*, 1911; *The Alpha*, 6/16/26; KNS Clippings, 9/9/32, PR.

Chapter 8

1. N.H., *Report of Trustees of State Normal Schools, 1911-12*; "Plymouth Normal Affairs," Feb., Mar., 1911, BP; *Sentinel*, 8/11/11.

2. N.H., *Report of Trustees of State Normal Schools, 1911-12*, 20-21.

3. *Kronicle Monthly*, 12/3/29, 10/19/31.

4. *N.H. State Education Reports, 1913-14* (Morrison), 172-173; on Sanger and the motto, memory of Ella O. Keene; KNS Clippings, 3/30/39, PR.

5. Letter of 3/22/37, Box #1 of Miscellaneous Materials, PR; Cannonball story from Patricia Cunningham; Irving S. Heath, "History of Keene State College Campus" (1941), 16, PR; *Kronicle*, 1921, 2; Evelyn Fuller Scrapbook, Alumni Archives, hereinafter cited as AA.

6. "Minutes, Board of Normal School Trustees," Special Meeting, 12/30/12, "Normal School," BP; *Sentinel*, 1/23/14; Leila E. Patridge, *Parker's Talks on Teaching* (1883, Memorial Edition); Meyer, *Grandmasters*, 272.

7. *Sentinel*, 10/20/14.

8. Harry Alvin Brown, *Certain Basic Teacher-Education Policies and Their Development . . . in a Selected State [N.H.]* (1937), 54.

9. Memory of Eleanor Gibney Paine, '16; Messerli, *Mann*, 437; *N.H. State Education Reports, 1913-14* (Morrison), 175-76; *Kronicle*, Jan., 1920.

10. *Kronicle*, Jan., 1920; emphasis added.

11. *Kronicle*, June, Nov., 1914, June 1918, May 1919; *Kronicle Monthly*, 1/20/33.

12. *Kronicle*, Apr., June, Nov., 1914.

13. Interviews with Elinor Gibney Paine, Carry Burr Paine, Bertha Davis, and Florence Wheeler.

Chapter 9

1. "Tomato Club," KNS Materials, PR; KNS, *Catalogue and Circular, 1912*, 38, *1915-16*, 44.

2. KNS, *Catalogue and Circular, 1913*, 12; *N.H. State Education Reports, 1913-14* (Morrison), 172-73.

3. *N.H. State Education Reports, 1913-14* (Morrison), 144-48, 152-53.

4. *Ibid., 1915-16*, 200, 203; *1919-20* (Butterfield), 127.

5. *Ibid., 1915-16* (Morrison), 203; KNS, *Catalogue and Circular, 1916-17*, 18-21.

6. *N.H. State Education Reports, 1915-16* (Morrison), 203-06; KNS, *Catalogue and Circular, 1916-17*, 21-22; Brown, *Certain Basic Teacher Education Policies*, 63-68.

7. Jacques Barzun, *The American University: How It Runs, Where It Is Going* (New York, 1968), 54-56; N.H. Retired Teachers Association, *Our Yesterdays* (Keene, N.H., 1976), 27-28; interviews with Ruth Seaver Kirk, Elinor Gibney Paine, and Florence Wheeler. I have substituted fictitious family names in Wheeler's interesting account.

8. *N.H. State Education Reports, 1915-16* (Morrison), 200; "Minutes," Board of Normal School Trustees, 8/28/12, BP; "Keene School Report, 1915-16," John Day Center, Keene, N.H.; Bagley, *Plymouth*, 61.

9. KNS, *Catalogue and Circular, 1918-19*, 16.

Chapter 10

1. "Miscellaneous Collection, KNS," PR; *N.H. State Education Reports, 1919-20* (Butterfield), 110; *Congressional Record, Senate*, 7/31/16, 11873.

2. "Miscellaneous Collection, KNS," PR; *N.H. State Education Reports, 1917-18* (Butterfield), 190-92; Babcock, *History of UNH*, 238; *Sentinel*, 2/9/18.

3. *Kronicle*, Mar., June, 1918; Gertrude Merriam interview.

Chapter 11

1. *Sentinel*, 5/4/20, 3/17/21.

2. *Sentinel*, 2/8/21.

3. *Sentinel*, 3/16/21; 3/16, 17, 19, 23, 24, 25/21; City of Keene, "School Report, 1920-21," 10, John Day Center, Keene, N.H.

4. City of Keene, "School Report, 1920-21," 4-5, John Day Center; interviews with Ruth S. Kirk and Gertrude Merriam.

Chapter 12

1. C. W. Bickford to F. B. Preston, 2/19/15, Martin Papers; N.H., *Journal of the Senate and the House, 1915*, 468.

2. *Sentinel*, 1/2, 15/19, 2/12/19.

3. *N.H. State Education Reports, 1917-18* (Butterfield), 8; see also subsequent issues under "Americanization"; *Sentinel*, 1/14, 20, 26/19; N.H., *Journal of the Senate and House*, 2/3/19; 3/13, 27/19.

4. Bishop, *Development of a State School System* (N.H.), 1; *Sentinel*, 2/10/21.

5. *N.H. State Education Reports, 1919-20* (Butterfield), 75-77.

6. U.S. 63rd Cong., 2nd sess. (1914), "The Need for Vocational Education," 12.

Chapter 13

1. Robert A. Caro, *Years of Lyndon Johnson* (1982), 142 ff.; *N.H. State Education Reports, 1921-22* (Butterfield), 149; interview with Carpenter.

2. *N.H. State Education Reports, 1915-16* (Morrison), 176, and *1928-30* (Butterfield), 51-52.

3. *N.H. State Education Reports, 1925-26*, 131, and *1923-24*, 29 (both Butterfield's).

4. *Alpha*, 2/1/27, KNS Clippings, 1929.

5. Isabel Esten transcript from Middlebury College; interviews with Harwood, Wood, and Lovering.

6. Quoted in *Kronicle*, 5/25/36.

7. Information on personnel and departments is taken from KNS *Catalogues and Circulars* of the 1920s.

8. KNS, *Catalogue and Circular, 1915-16*, 31; *1916-17*, 33; *1917-18*, 33-34; *1922-23*, 41.

9. Meyer, *Grandmasters*, 291; *Kronicle*, 5/20/31; *N.H. State Education Reports, 1927-28* (Butterfield), 142.

Chapter 14

1. Interviews with Dorothy LaPointe, Elinor G. Paine, Florence Wheeler; *Kronicles*, 1923, 1925, p. 26.

2. Interviews with Marion Wood and Sheldon Barker; Scovell, Wellington, & Co., *State of New Hampshire: Normal Schools at Plymouth and Keene* (1925), PR; Bagley, *History of Plymouth State College*, 89; *Alma Mater*, 3/76; KNS, *Catalogue and Circulars*, 1921, 1923-24, pp. 28-29; *Kronicle*, 1921, 23, 25; clippings from Evelyn Fuller (Lamond) Scrapbook, AA.

3. *Sentinel*, 1/12/31; KNS Miscellany Box, PR; *Alpha*, 4/7/26; *Kronicle Monthly*, 2/11/35; *Kronicle*, 1935, 68.

4. Interviews with people mentioned in the text; on Rose Night, notes from Ruth Wilson Keddy and Clair Wyman to author; Evelyn Fuller (Lamond) Scrapbook, AA; Jasper Grigas to J. Smart, 12/7/83.

Chapter 15

1. KNS Clippings Scrapbook, 6/14/28; Irving Heath, '40, "History of Keene State College Campus" (1941), PR, is a poorly written but generally accurate work on campus buildings; *Sentinel*, 6/17/26; *N.H. State Education Reports, 1925-26* (Butterfield), 135.

2. *Alpha*, 6/11/27; KNS Clipping Scrapbook, 6/14/28, PR; interview with Louise Barnum; Leo Redfern on the swimming pool story; *N.H. State Education Reports, 1927-28* (Butterfield), 34-36.

Chapter 16

1. On job placement see *Kronicle*, 11/16/31, 11/14/32, 12/12/32, 8/9/33, 8/31/35, 11/15/37; interviews with Mariam R. Carpenter, Harwood, and LaPointe; Barbara Rowe Freese, '41, in *Alumni Reunion Bulletin*, 1981; Clair Wyman Ms., PR.

2. *Kronicle*, 10/3/29; *Kronicle* (yearbook), 1940; *Alumni Reunion Bulletin*, 1981; feminism and humor in *Kronicle*, 4/9/30, 1/26/31, 6/17/31, 5/25/36; also, *Alpha*, 5/15/26; *News Bulletin*, 4/5/40, 6/13/40; memory of Chester Brach, '41, in *Alumni Reunion Bulletin*, 1981.

3. Paul Nordman to author; interviews with B. J. Stimson, Bertha Gauthier Ericson, Frank Knox, Ruth Keddy, Dorothy LaPointe, Annette Collins Larson; *Kronicle*, 1/30/33; Wyman Ms., PR.

4. Wyman Ms., PR; *Kronicle*, 3/25/, 11/16/31, 2/5/38.

5. *Alma Mater*, 10/80; *Kronicle* yearbooks of the decade; interviews with Ruth Keddy, Laverne Bushnell, Arthur Giovannangeli; Clair Wyman Ms., PR.

Chapter 17

1. *Sentinel* 3/19, 20/36; *Upper Ashuelot*, 194-96; KNS Scrapbooks, PR, AA; KNS Clippings, 4/14/39; *Alumni Reunion Bulletin*, 1981; Wyman Ms., PR.

2. *Sentinel*, 6/4/24; Wyman Ms., PR; *Kronicle*, 1923, 1936, 1937; *Alpha*, 5/5/26; *Kronicle*, 3/30/36, 5/25/36.

3. *Kronicle*, 12/17/30; *N.H. State Education Reports, 1921-22* (Butterfield), 152; Wyman Ms., PR.

Chapter 18

1. *News Bulletin*, 6/13/40; KTC, *Catalogue and Circular*, 1940-41, 13-14; KNS Clippings, 4/14/39, PR.

2. *Monadnock*, 11/22/49.

3. *Kronicle*, 1938, 1939, 1941, p. 58; *News Bulletin*, 4/5/40; Jessie D. Lombard, Charlotte F. McClary, and Elese Wright Tarris in *Alumni Reunion Bulletin*, 1981.

4. *News Bulletin*, 11/22/41; interviews with Lloyd Young, Pat Shedd, and Ruth Keddy.

5. KTC Clippings, 1942-43, PR; Lloyd Young interview; *Kronicle*, 1944, p. 63.

6. Interviews; *Sentinel* Clippings, PR, 8/5/43, 11/2/43, 12/13/43.

7. *Equinox*, 8/27/76.

8. *Sentinel* Clippings, PR, 1/27, 29/42; 3/17/43; 4/24/43.

9. *Sentinel* Clippings, 11/9/44, 10/10/45; *News Bulletin*, 11/22/43; Dexter interview.

10. *Kronicle*, 1944, p. 63; *News Bulletin*, 11/22/43, 11/26/45; Wyman Ms., PR.

Chapter 19

1. Interview with Dwinell; *News Bulletin*, 11/26/45; *Kronicle*, 1946, 73, 76.

2. *Kronicle*, 1944, 15; 1946, 18; KTC *Sentinel* Clippings, 3/29/47; Don Carle interview; Wyman Ms.

3. *The Owl's Reporter*, n.d., ca. 4/30/47.

4. *The Owl's Reporter*, n.d., ca. 4/30/47 and ca. 5/20/47.

5. *Monadnock*, 6/7/50; 3/11/52; 10/17, 31/50.

Chapter 20

1. Interview with Dwinell, talk with Benaquist; on Bell, *Time*, 4/25/49; on Berlin, *Time*, 12/12/49; the others in order are H. Guthrie, *Vital Speeches*, 15:476-8, 5/15/49; *19th Century*, 145:332-37, 6/49; *Science*, 111:399-403, 4/21/50; *School and Society*, 70:331, 11/19/49; *Reader's Digest*, 55:110-12, 7/49; *Rotarian*, 77:11-13, 8/50; *Time*, 2/23/53.

2. KTC, *Sentinel* Clippings, n.d., 1927, and 1/12/29, PR; Morrison to Butterfield, 5/8/29, Martin Papers.

3. KTC, *Sentinel* Clippings, 4/4/39, 4/13/43, PR.

4. KTC, *Sentinel* Clippings, 1949, PR; interviews with Adams and Dwinell; NEA, *Proceedings and Addresses*, 1951, 307.

5. KTC, *Sentinel* Clippings, 8/30/49; 11/1, 16, 22, 23/49; 6/5/52; *Monadnock*, 11/22/49, 5/5/51.

6. NEA, *Proceedings and Addresses*, 1951, 307; Ruth Kirk interview; "Minutes," 11/22/44, 1/26/45; N.H. State Board of Education, Concord, N.H.

7. Oakey's Message in *Kronicle*, 1950; *Monadnock*, 11/22/49.

8. *Monadnock*, in order, 1/30/51, 2/13/51, 3/25/52, 3/22/50; *Kronicle*, 1950.

9. *Monadnock*, in order, 8/17/50, 2/15/50, 11/14/50, 2/8/52.

10. *Monadnock*, 1/18/50, 2/1/50, 2/10/55; *Equinox*, 4/9/75.

Chapter 21

1. *Sentinel*, 3/13-19/57; *Monadnock*, 3/15/57; *Manchester* (N.H.) *Union-Leader*, 3/22/57; talk with Fred Barry and Harold Nugent; Dwinell interview.

2. KTC Clippings, Mar., Apr., 1963, PR.

3. KTC Clippings, 5/29-6/8/63, PR.

Chapter 22

1. *Monadnock*, 11/22/54; KTC Clippings, 1/14/58, 4/6-7/58, 12/9/58, PR.

2. KTC Clippings, 1/13/58, 1/31/59, 5/1/59, PR; *Monadnock*, 10/14/59, 5/17/62, 4/17/61.

3. Interviews with Holmes and Horton; N.H., *Preliminary Report of Interim Commission on Education* (Raimond Bowles, Chm.), p. E-10; KTC Clippings 5/1/61, PR; *Monadnock*, 3/16/61; *Sentinel*, 9/5/62.

4. N.H., *Report of the Interim Commission on Education*, 24-25; Holmes interview.

5. *Monadnock*, 10/11/62; KTC Clippings, 12/12/62, 3/14/63, 12/12/63; on the political campaign, *Sentinel*, 9/18, 26/62; 10/25, 31/62; 11/1-3, 7/62.

6. N.H., *Report of the Interim Commission on Education*, 24; N.H., *Revised Statutes Annotated*, 1963, 617-20; KTC Clippings, 12/13/63, PR.

7. Summation of the conservative journals in August Kerber and Wilfred Smith, eds., *Educational Issues in a Changing Society*, 444-45, 452-53; *Saturday Review*, 10/20/62.

8. William DeVane, *Higher Education in Twentieth-Century America*, 71-72; Meyer, *Grandmasters of Educational Thought*, 283; *Alma Mater*, 4/83.

9. KTC Clippings, 10/30/62, PR; N.H., *Report of the Interim Commission on Education*, 7.

Chapter 23

1. Wells quote in *Alma Mater*, 3/76; Dunham, *Colleges of Forgotten Americans*, 47, 98-99; *Monadnock*, 9/17/64.

2. Zorn in *Directory of American Scholars*; author's memories; quotes and information from *Monadnock*, 9/17/64; KSC Clippings, 8/27/64, 11/8/66, PR.

3. KSC Clippings, 9/15/64, PR; *Monadnock*, 3/25/65, 10/7/65, 4/29/65, 3/4/66, 2/8/67.

4. *Monadnock*, 3/4/65; author's memories; interview with Robert L. Mallat, Jr.

5. Author's memories and experiences; talk with Frank Haley, communication from Ernest Hebert, 7/83; KSC Clippings, 10/14/65.

6. *Monadnock*, 2/5/65; author's memories.

7. *Monadnock*, 10/2/68; author's memories.

Chapter 24

1. *Monadnock*, 5/16/56; KTC Clippings, 8/28/53, 1/13/54, 5/20/55, 7/28/55, PR; N.H. State Board of Education, "Minutes," 2/27/57.

2. KTC Clippings, 12/8/58, 10/31/58; Wyman Ms., PR.

3. *Monadnock*, 12/2/59; KTC Clippings, 11/26/57, 5/18/60, 5/19/61.

4. *Monadnock*, 10/18/61; *Kronicle*, 1963, 1964; KTC Clippings, 1/6/64, PR.

5. KTC Clippings, 8/2/63, 9/19/63, 5/24/65; *Kronicle*, 1965.

6. KTC Clippings, 3/10/65, 4/5/66, 5/2/66; on Randall, 5/14/66, 8/10/66; Randall Gates, '83, study, "Town-Gown Relationships," PR, contains copies of the Colony will setting up the Colony Trust and also a copy of the eminent domain proceedings. On Duffy see N.H. State Board of Education "Minutes."

7. KTC Clippings, 11/6, 22/67; 11/18/68, PR; *Monadnock*, 10/9/68; on Carle Hall, *Sentinel*, 7/5/68; interviews with Mallat and Hobart.

8. *Architectural Record*, 10/73, 145, cited in "Campus Design" by L. Van Alstyne, '84; *Equinox*, 1/18/73; 10/10/73; 9/11/74; 9/10, 17/75; Wyman Ms., PR.

9. Redfern's report in "Reunion, 1976"; *Equinox*, 5/24/79; talks with Ramsay, Redfern, and Marshall.

Chapter 25

1. *Kronicle*, 1965, 38-39; *Monadnock*, 11/19/64; 3/21, 28/67; 4/8/67; 8/2/68.

2. *Monadnock*, 9/4/68; *Kronicle*, 1965; KSC Clippings, 12/8/67, PR.

3. *Kronicle*, 1968; *Journal*, 10/68; *Monadnock*, 11/4/66, 12/9/66, 2/28/67.

4. *Kronicle*, 1965; *Monadnock*, 4/9/69; *Wall Street Journal*, 11/24/81.

5. *Sentinel*, 11/1, 6/74; interview with Keller.

6. *Monadnock*, 2/29/68, 5/9/68, 9/18/68; author's memories.

7. *Monadnock*, 4/29/66; 9/23/66; 12/7, 14/67; 12/3, 10/69; KSC Clippings, 12/11/67, PR.

8. Conversations with Wiseman; Savio quoted in *Kronicle*, 1967; *Sentinel*, 5/28, 29, 30/68; 6/1/68.

9. *Monadnock*, 11/6, 13, 27/68; 12/11/68; 1/8, 15/69; 3/12/69, 4/30/69; 5/7, 14/69; *Sentinel*, 12/17, 18, 19/68; 4/23/69; interview with Nelson.

Chapter 26

1. Interviews with Redfern, Whybrew, Mallat, Hobart, Gustafson, and Herron.

2. Interview with Redfern; N.H., *Revised Statutes Annotated*, 187:8:VII, and "Annotations."

3. Interviews with Redfern, Gustafson, Holmes; talk with Spirou.

Chapter 27

1. KSC College Senate document 69/70-4; KSC College Senate "Minutes," 3/10/71.
2. KSC College Senate "Minutes," 9/30/70, 4/4/71.
3. *Equinox,* 4/5/83; conversations with Butcher and Theulen.
4. *Monadnock,* 11/30/70.

Chapter 28

1. Interview with Andrews; *Monadnock,* 4/21/71; KSC College Senate "Minutes," 4/21/71.
2. *Equinox,* 12/6/72, 3/20/74; talk with Michaud. Names have been changed from those given in the *Equinox* interview of 3/20/74.
3. *Monadnock,* 11/17/71; interview with Andrews.
4. Memo from Gustafson, 8/25/83.

Chapter 29

1. *Monadnock,* 11/4, 18/70; *Equinox,* 2/13/74.
2. Interviews; also *Equinox,* 2/5/75, 12/11/79, comments on Woodstock from English paper found in Morrison hallway.
3. In order, *Equinox,* 2/11/76; 11/16/77; 3/7, 28/73; 5/11/77.
4. *Equinox,* 9/19/78, 3/13/79, 11/20/79; Wyman Ms., PR; author's memories.
5. *Equinox,* 3/5/75.
6. *Equinox,* 4/19/78; KSC Senate document 77/78-50.
7. KTC Clippings, 4/15/59, PR; *Equinox,* 5/12/76; 1/18/78; 2/6/79; 10/30/79; 12/4/79; 4/7, 15/81.
8. *Equinox,* 3/13, 20/74; *Kronicle,* 1974.
9. *Equinox,* 2/5/75.

Chapter 30

1. Author's memories; interviews with Gustafson, Hildebrandt, and Paul Blacketor; *Equinox,* 1/24/73, 2/21/73; Croteau, Jean Blacketor, Lovering, "Negotiations: The Keene State College Story," 29-30, PR.
2. Interview with Redfern.
3. Interviews with Trustee Horton, Governor Thomson, Paul Blacketor; Croteau et al., *op. cit.,* 59.
4. Interview with Gustafson; *Equinox,* 1/16/79, 4/3/74, 12/1/76; Van Doren, *Liberal Education* (New York, 1943), 11.

Chapter 31

1. Croteau, Blacketor, Lovering, "Negotiations: The Keene State College Story," 58, PR.
2. Interviews with Seelye, Wheeler, McDonough.
3. Interviews with Seelye and Gustafson.
4. Charles E. Widmayer, *Hopkins of Dartmouth* (1977), 104.

A p p e n d i c e s

ILLUSTRATIONS AND CREDITS

The illustrations which appear in *Striving* came from a number of sources. The author is particularly indebted to the Alumni Association for use of the extensive collections of the Alumni Center and the Alumni Archives, to the Office of College Information for its unstinting help and cooperation, and to the numerous individuals who supplied material for consideration from their own collections. Special thanks are also due Medora Hebert for the caliber of the photographs taken specifically for this volume.

In the following, illustrations are listed in the order in which they appear. The small, uncaptioned illustrations which embellish the chapter titles are listed only if they are not repeated later in the chapter on a larger scale.

3 3 1

STRIVING

INDEX